WRITING THE STORY OF TEXAS

Charles N. Prothro Texana Series

WRITING THE STORY OF TEXAS

EDITED BY PATRICK L. COX
AND
KENNETH E. HENDRICKSON JR.

UNIVERSITY OF TEXAS PRESS
Austin

Portions of the essay on Carlos E. Castañeda were published, in a different form, by Félix D. Almaráz Jr. in *Red River Valley Historical Review* 1, 4 (1974): 329–350.

Printed in the United States of America
First edition, 2013

Requests for permission to reproduce material from this work should be sent to:
Permissions
University of Texas Press
P.O. Box 7819
Austin, TX 78713-7819
http://utpress.utexas.edu/about/book-permissions

♾ The paper used in this book meets the minimum requirements of ANSI/NISO Z39.48-1992 (R1997) (Permanence of Paper).

LIBRARY OF CONGRESS CATALOGING-IN-PUBLICATION DATA

Writing the story of Texas / edited by Patrick L. Cox and Kenneth E. Hendrickson Jr. — First edition.
pages cm. — (Charles N. Prothro Texana series)
Includes bibliographical references and index.
ISBN 978-0-292-74537-7 (cloth : alkaline paper)
1. Historians—Texas—Biography. 2. Historians—United States—Biography. 3. Texas—Historiography. 4. Historiography—Texas—History. I. Cox, Patrick L., 1952– II. Hendrickson, Kenneth E.
E175.45.T45 2013
976.4—dc23
2012031468
doi:10.7560/745377

CONTENTS

ACKNOWLEDGMENTS

Patrick Cox and I believe that we are lucky enough to have one of the best teams ever assembled to produce a book such as this. It is difficult to put into words how grateful we are to our colleagues for their splendid work and their remarkable patience. For several reasons, none of which can be laid upon their shoulders, eight years passed between the day we launched the project and the day the book appeared on the market. At times we feared the latter day would never come, our dream would die, and a major work of Texas historiography would never exist. But our colleagues stayed with us because, like us, they believed in the importance of the project. And so our dream has become reality.

Thank you, Félix D. Almaráz Jr., Carolina Castillo Crimm, Michael L. Collins, Light T. Cummins, Don Graham, Nancy Baker Jones, David G. McComb, Archie P. McDonald, B. Byron Price, Mary L. Scheer, Jesús F. de la Teja, and Dan Utley. And from all of us a special thank you to Patrick Cox, the captain of our ship. He kept it afloat and steered it in the right direction until it docked in the harbor of the University of Texas Press. We also appreciate the staff at the Dolph Briscoe Center for American History, especially Amy Bowman and Aryn Glazier, who assisted us in getting the excellent photos that accompany this work.

All of us are professional writers. All of us are aware of the potential pitfalls that can be encountered in the publishing business, and all of us agree that we have never worked with a better, more professional, more helpful, more accommodating, more encouraging team then our friends at the University of Texas Press. Thanks, Allison Faust; thanks, Nancy Bryan; and thanks, Lynne Chapman. We will never forget.

Kenneth E. Hendrickson Jr.

PATRICK L. COX

INTRODUCTION

Nearly a decade ago, several of my fellow Texas historians—Ken Hendrickson Jr., Light Cummins, Mike Collins, and Dan Utley—and I met for a cold drink and a discussion on a recurring topic among historians who reside in Texas. As we surveyed the landscape of historical literature and the significant contributors to the field, we came to the conclusion that someone should furnish a collection of essays on those who had provided outstanding contributions to the interpretation and writing of our history and how this has changed over time. Since we happened to have our discussion during the 2003 annual meeting of the Texas State Historical Association in El Paso, we dutifully concluded we should also base our survey on those who had roots in Texas—or who had at least spent a great deal of their professional careers between the Rio Grande and the Red River.

In keeping with many other cultural and historic traditions, we toasted the idea and christened Ken Hendrickson and myself as the editors of this august undertaking. Whether this was the hot afternoon sun or the intoxicating idea of acknowledging some of our predecessors, we set about to make a selection of the dearly departed historians and to secure the services of some of our esteemed colleagues in this very worthwhile enterprise.

As a result of this afternoon discussion in El Paso a number of years ago, Ken Hendrickson and I are pleased to announce that we have assembled a very distinguished list of Texas historians for this book. History and its interpretation is not a new profession. Recording and writing history dates to the ancient works by the great Greek and Roman historians Herodotus, Thucydides, Plutarch, and Tacitus. Oral tradition preceded written history and has been passed down and subsequently recorded. As centuries progressed and history became a more demanding study of people, events, culture, and analysis, those who chose to study and write about history reflected the times and eras in which they also lived. Even the most admired ancient historians had faults and biases that are reflected in their writings. Modern historians often studied and contemplated the writings of early historians as they began their own studies. A classical education was often a critical component of the education curriculum in the modern age. Just as with the earliest historians, contemporary ideas and prejudices penetrate the work of even the most scholarly authors of history to this day.

A large gap, both chronological and theoretical, exists between the classical approach to history and the modern era of historical research, writing, and interpretation. For most people today, historians serve as the mediators between current generations and the past. Historians strive to present our past based on factual evidence collected from our history. In order to offer an understanding of past events, they devise explanations that include interpretation and analysis. Without interpretation, history becomes nothing more than a long uninterrupted litany of unrelated stories — not unlike many family holiday gatherings. Along with this perspective (which some may appropriately call bias) and interpretation, historians also provide a narrative and sometimes a visual context for relating the past. They bring a sense of order and understanding to events and people that may on the surface appear to be unimportant or disconnected.

Historical studies and perspectives also change over time. Each generation is influenced by a number of factors that are reflected in our histories. For example, American "exceptionalism," how we and those in other nations and cultures view our history, is one of the constant themes throughout our history. Over the past century American historians have been influenced by the culture in which they lived, the education they obtained, and the influence of their peers who study history. Furthermore, more materials for research continue to become available. For example, newly discovered correspondence, government archives that are unsealed, oral histories, and many other primary sources allow historians to refine their perspectives and subsequent generations of historians to depart from established viewpoints and beliefs. This is what brings meaning to history. It is also a reflection of how historians are just as fallible as politicians, doctors, military and business leaders, and other social icons who succumb to poor judgment and suspect conclusions.

In keeping with these themes, we selected a group of historians from the nineteenth through the twentieth centuries who were connected with Texas and provided substantive contributions to the profession and our history. Texas and the greater borderlands region is the focus of their histories. They each offered new historical perspectives and interpretations, not just from a regional standpoint but also from the broader perspective of our national and cultural history. As stated earlier, source materials, perspectives, critical studies, ideology, and interpretation evolve over time. We believe that each of the historians selected for this volume illustrates how professional historians approach their selected topics. In addition, each selected historian provided his or her own unique influence in a broader context through teaching, civic involvement, and sometimes involvement in controversial events. In doing so, they also became part of the historical record.

In each of the essays on the chosen historians, we asked our contributors to develop a biographical sketch of the individual and the environment in which he or she lived, and to recognize the subject's significant research and publications, noteworthy achievements, and contributions to the profession and to general knowledge about history. The authors also cover major public controversies or other disputes in which these historians were involved during their professional careers. They examine how their theories and impact have fared over time and how contemporary historians view them; in some cases, they place their subjects in the context of ongoing or emerging debates. Each article is written by acknowledged experts and extensively documented.

In making our selection, we cast a broad net to include both professional historians and others who contributed to the historical literature of the borderlands region. Thus we include folklorists, oral historians, and others who chose to look beyond the traditional borders of history. Anglo Texans of the late nineteenth and early twentieth centuries had their roots and education in southern, not western, culture. Later historians of the twentieth century moved beyond the traditional male, southern culture to relate a more inclusive story of gender, ethnicity, and the cultural environment. Historians of later generations realized that not only the deeds of a few great men influenced our past; many others who did not possess fame and fortune provided notable contributions with significant results.

All of the selected men and women historians on this list provided noteworthy publications and ideas for their generation and for those who followed. Their understanding of history along with human attributes and foibles provided great drama and tension. They also understood that progress, whether in the realm of democratic ideas, economic gain, or social justice, is never a predetermined or foreordained outcome. Some were more cynical than others. Yet all were taken with the idea of historical change and significance. In addition, these men and women were, and still are, considered accomplished writers who share a narrative that will still engage the modern reader in the Internet age. In many ways, we historians are a metaphor for the Texas weather—constantly changing, often turbulent, frequently unpredictable, yet often beautiful and inspiring.

Our readers will note that the majority of historians in this volume were associated with the University of Texas. Many of the early professional historians of the late nineteenth and early twentieth centuries maintained ties to the university in Austin for several reasons, including financial support and the existence of research archives and professional historical associations. The Texas State Historical Association (TSHA), founded in 1897 at the University of Texas, received much of its early support from that institution. For more than a century, members of the University of Texas history department worked closely with this association and other organizations throughout the state to further the study of Texas, the American South, and the borderlands region.

As the profession expanded along with a growing population during the twentieth century, new generations of historians not directly connected to the University of Texas began to make their mark. This study reflects that change both in the locus of interest of historical study and the broader perspectives and interpretations that newer generations of historians offered. Nationally recognized regional and borderlands history programs and publishing outlets exist today at universities and colleges throughout the state, such as Texas Tech University, Texas State University, Texas Christian University, the University of Houston, North Texas University, Southern Methodist University, Angelo State University, Midwestern University, Stephen F. Austin State University, Sam Houston State University, Austin College, Trinity University, Southwestern University, and several others. Notably, the TSHA relocated to North Texas University on the main campus in Denton in 2008. Many other regional and local historical associations are located throughout the state and affiliated with local colleges and universities.

In choosing the deceased historians and folklorists for this list, we had to make difficult decisions, and we should note that many others who provided significant contributions could have been included. In addition, many current historians who are very much alive and producing outstanding research and publications will also one day merit a place on the roll of honor. For the purposes of this publication, we chose to begin with a select group of individuals who provided groundbreaking research along with a unique approach to relating the history of the region and its people. We also wanted to select individuals who could provide a compelling story for the reader, both at the academic level and at the level of reading history for personal insight. Not everyone can contribute solid research, coherent interpretation, and an appealing story; we believe that the historians we have selected meet these high standards. Thankfully, we also have an outstanding group of contemporary historians who furnished these insightful, engaging essays and, as an added bonus, lists of recommended readings, which will allow readers to engage with some of the seminal works by the historians chosen for this book.

Sadly, as we entered the final stages of publishing this book, in 2012, two very notable Texas historians passed away. Dr. Archie P. McDonald, who provided the essay on Robert Maxwell in this volume, was Regents Professor of History at Stephen F. Austin State University. He served as the director of the East Texas Historical Association, president of the Texas State Historical Association, and a Texas Historical Commission board member. Dr. Ben H. Procter was Cecil and Ida Green Emeritus Chair in the History Department at Texas Christian University and a president of the Texas State Historical Association. Before Dr. Procter became a history professor he played football with the Los Angeles Rams. Both of these historians influenced an entire generation of historians, many of whom are contributors to this volume. Both of these scholars certainly will be missed and will earn a place in future publications on historians who have provided significant works, interpretations, and voices to our history.

We offer these essays to the reader in chronological order. The early professional historians — Charles Ramsdell, Eugene C. Barker, Walter Prescott Webb, and Earnest W. Winkler — represent the professional historians who set the first modern standard for historical works. The second generation, in the mid-twentieth century — Llerena Friend, J. Frank Dobie, J. Evetts Haley, Robert Maxwell, Carlos E. Castañeda, and Robert Cotner — provided new interpretations, sources, and methods. The generation of historians in the modern, post–World War II era reflect expanded research, cultural diversity, and challenges to the histories provided by earlier generations. The final essays on Américo Paredes, Joe Frantz, Ruthe Winegarten, and David Weber illustrate the changing interpretation and telling of our history.

We hope you enjoy this presentation of insights into these unique and impressive historians.

WRITING THE STORY OF TEXAS

LIGHT TOWNSEND CUMMINS

CHARLES W. RAMSDELL

CHARLES W. RAMSDELL

Charles W. Ramsdell, who was a member of the history department at the University of Texas from 1906 until his death in 1942, was acknowledged as "the Dean" of southern historians during his lifetime. Ramsdell was a southern regionalist who believed that Texan uniqueness and exceptionalism rested on its historical development as part of the Old South.[1] For him, Texas was historically southern, and understanding the South was essential to understanding the Lone Star State. Ramsdell himself was a proud southerner and a native Texan by personal background, descended from sturdy frontier folk who had made the westward-moving trek across the Sabine from the older regions of the South during the nineteenth century. His forebears settled at Salado in Central Texas, a place that appealed to them because it was developing as a commercial and educational center along the banks of a picturesque stream of the same name. His father, Augustus Ramsdell, married into the Halley family, one of the first families to settle there. Charles would eventually be one of four brothers and two sisters. He attended Thomas Arnold High School in Salado, a rigorous private institution established by a local educator and named for the great master of the Rugby School in England. As Thomas Arnold's founder, Dr. Samuel J. Jones, proclaimed, the school sought "to rigidly maintain the high school standard, to supply the gap that exists between the grammar schools of the State and the University, and to prepare for active work." In young Ramsdell's case, this process proved successful. After graduation, he worked for several years as a teacher in rural schools at Alvin and McGregor, entering an occupation that was then open to high school graduates because relatively unsophisticated, one-room schools could not attract instructors with collegiate training.[2]

Charles enrolled at the University of Texas in the fall term of 1900, where he embarked on the study of a "classical curriculum." The distance between Salado and Austin, although not great in miles, proved to be a span of great proportions for Charles Ramsdell as he entered an expansive world of ideas and intellectual accomplishment. The university that Ramsdell first encountered at the dawn of the new century was almost as raw and unsophisticated as many of the young people who were arriving from across Texas to study there.[3] Ramsdell was acknowledged as a popular and well-liked student. This, in part, flowed from the fact that he played football at the university and enjoyed status on campus as a gridiron hero. As historian Joe B. Frantz has noted, many football players of those early days were rough characters who "openly smoked their cigars and drank their whiskey and beer and played all night as if they were the privileged king's guard." Ramsdell rejected such activities. He instead had the good fortune to join the team at the same time that a new coach, Samuel H. Thompson, sternly put an end to such rollicking behaviors. One of Ramsdell's first road trips with the team occurred in the fall of 1900 when the squad went to Dallas, where they played Vanderbilt to a 22–0 victory for Texas. Following the game, Coach

Thompson and several players who shared his views, including Ramsdell, stayed up all night, posting themselves in the hallways and lobby of the hotel in order to ensure that the more ribald players remained in their rooms and behaved. Ramsdell's leadership skills earned him the honor of being named captain of the football team during his senior year, during which time he also served as president of the senior class. He helped to establish a family football dynasty at the university as well, since his three brothers also eventually played on the team. These positive athletic experiences caused Charles Ramsdell to develop a lifelong commitment to fair play and proper decorum for all varsity athletes, values that he sternly upheld in later years when he served as a faculty member on the university's athletic council.[4]

If young Ramsdell's heart was on the gridiron, his head was clearly focused on academics and scholarly accomplishment. He proved to have a facile, quick, and ready mind that was well adapted for success in the classroom. He was articulate, hardworking, industrious, and well spoken—just the sort of young man who would capture a professor's attention. This occurred very soon in Ramsdell's case, and the professors whose attention he garnered came from the history department, a subject for which the young scholar had a natural affinity. He entered the history program at a propitious time. The University of Texas history department was just beginning its development in 1900, on its way to eventually becoming one of the strongest in American higher education. Much of the credit for building this department rested on the labors of George Pierce Garrison, a stalwart historian who had served on the faculty since 1884. Garrison was among the first historians in the United States to write about Texas as a legitimate part of the nation's mainstream academic history. His major book, *Texas and Texans: A Contest of Civilizations*, was published in 1903 during Ramsdell's senior year in the department. The young undergraduate also knew another of the talented historians in the department, Lester G. Bugbee, a gentle soul whom students considered one of the most inspiring professors on the campus. Unfortunately, Professor Bugbee developed tuberculosis during Ramsdell's second year and took a medical leave of absence from which he never returned, passing away in 1902. Bugbee was nonetheless an inspiring figure who influenced a love of history in the younger man. Two other historians also shaped Ramsdell's historical vision during his years as a student in the department: Herbert Eugene Bolton and Eugene C. Barker.[5]

Since, as department chair, Garrison administered all of the financial aid and assistantships, Ramsdell approached him the summer before his senior year requesting some sort of employment that could help meet student expenses. This seemed a logical course of action since he had been making high grades in all of his courses and had recently been elected to Phi Beta Kappa. Garrison offered him an assistantship on the journal of the Texas State Historical Association and

Charles queried: "Would the work that I might get on the *Quarterly* amount to very much?" Ramsdell received his assistantship and the answer to his question proved to be yes. Thus began an association between Ramsdell, the historical association, and the *Southwestern Historical Quarterly* that would last until his death almost forty years later. Upon receiving his B.A. degree in 1903, Charles decided to remain at the university in order to work towards a master's degree in history. It was at this time that he developed an interest in the area of U.S. history that would eventually become his acknowledged specialty: the South. He worked with Professor Garrison in developing this interest, writing a thesis on presidential reconstruction in Texas and receiving his M.A. in 1904. The graduate program at the University of Texas was only a few years old that year, and any serious student who aspired to be a professional historian, as Ramsdell now did, received fulsome encouragement from Garrison to attend one of the major doctorate-granting universities, in his case Columbia University. Ramsdell received a fellowship there for the 1904–1905 academic year that made his attending a realistic financial possibility. Ramsdell found New York City an exciting place to study, and although he took full advantage of his academic possibilities through regular hard work, Charles also partook of the urban pleasures available in one of the nation's largest cities. He enjoyed what he called "this noisy quarter of the world," attending operas and plays and visiting the museums of the city when he could tear himself away from his studies.[6]

Above all else, however, Ramsdell remained consistently committed to academic endeavors during his time in New York City. Graduate work at Columbia took center stage for him. He relished the accomplished group of professors who composed the Columbia University history department, then one of the strongest in the nation. Ramsdell might have developed a primary love for European history had it not been for the Columbia professor who, above all others, captured his imagination. William Archibald Dunning taught graduate courses on the history of the South with particular emphasis on Reconstruction after the Civil War. A native of New Jersey, Dunning himself was a product of Columbia University, having graduated in 1881. He joined the faculty of the history department several years later after postgraduate study in Germany and continued to teach at Columbia until his death in 1922. In spite of his northern background, Professor Dunning developed in his own writing an historiographical interpretation of Reconstruction that was decidedly pro-southern in its sentiments. He believed, for example, that the newly freed slaves of the South were inherently incapable of self-government, and hence had to be appropriately controlled by whites under the banner of segregation. Dunning also stressed the punitive nature of congressional Reconstruction, a process that he felt had a devastating impact on the region. He viewed the former Confederate states as having undeservedly existed as a conquered province during the decade after the Civil War. His analysis of the congressionally reconstructed governments of the South therefore highlighted Unionist corruption and graft, exploitation of the Freedmen for political purposes, and the unreasonably punitive manner in which the Republican-controlled state governments dealt with the white ex-Confederates.[7]

Ramsdell eagerly gravitated to Dunning as his major professor, especially since the young Texan had already worked on the Reconstruction era for his master's thesis under Garrison. Indeed, Dunning had already been attracting a series of southern students who wrote doctoral dissertations dealing with a state-by-state analysis of southern Reconstruction. Ramsdell soon chose Reconstruction in Texas as his dissertation topic. This project brought him into close and mutually agreeable contact with Dunning, who would remain his champion for the remainder of their respective careers. Charles A. Beard, who was a stalwart fixture of the faculty at Columbia during those years, later observed that Dunning was the historical "godfather" to Ramsdell.

At the end of two years at Columbia, Ramsdell had amassed enough doctoral-level coursework to enable him to secure a teaching position while he completed his dissertation. This proved especially fortuitous since an entry-level position had opened in Austin at the University of Texas, a department where Ramsdell as an alumnus had strong ties and for which he felt a great emotional attachment. In September of 1906 he joined the history department as instructor, which meant that he taught lower-level sections of European and American history courses. The following year, 1907–1908, his teaching load increased when departmental colleague Eugene C. Barker received an Austin fellowship for study at Harvard University. Ramsdell proved to be a hard worker, although he privately felt that Garrison somewhat unfairly exercised his prerogative as department chair to teach all of the desirable courses in U.S. history. Nonetheless, Ramsdell kept his counsel and diligently worked on his dissertation while he carried a full teaching load. His residence in Austin enabled him to mine the state archives and manuscript collections in order to research the story of Reconstruction in Texas. By 1910, the dissertation had been completed and Ramsdell received his Ph.D. in history from Columbia University. In those days, doctoral dissertations often received speedy publication with minimal expansion or significant editing.[8] This proved to be the case for Ramsdell, who was now also a young husband. On his return to Texas in 1906, he had married Susanna Griffin, who was notable as a descendent of Susannah Dickinson, the woman who had survived the siege of the Alamo. In steady succession the Ramsdells had two children, and by the time *Reconstruction in Texas* was published, they constituted a young family happily putting down roots in Austin.[9]

Ramsdell's study of Texas Reconstruction would prove to be the only book-length monograph based on primary document research that he would publish during his entire career. It was, nonetheless, a work of scope and analysis that would stand the test of time, earning a place, where it remains to the present day, in most bibliographies of Texas and southern U.S. history. "Primarily political and constitutional history," as one scholar has noted of the book, "it provided only incidental consideration of social and economic aspects of the period."[10] The study proved to be shorter and less analytically exhaustive than some of the other state-based studies written during that era by Dunning's students, especially the Alabama study authored by Ramsdell's graduate school friend Walter Linwood Fleming, who would remain a lifelong associate in the field of southern history. Fleming, who was establishing himself on the faculty at Louisiana State University in Baton Rouge, liked *Reconstruction in Texas* and gave it a solid professional review. "The work is well done," he noted, stressing its solid writing style.[11] In its pages, Ramsdell unabashedly highlighted his orientation as a southerner, writing in the opening passages that he was "naturally drawn into a sympathetic attitude toward the people whose social and political system was being 'reconstructed.'" Accordingly, Ramsdell manifested a very stern and critical opinion of Republican leaders in Texas during the era, calling Edmund J. Davis "self-willed, obstinate, pigheaded almost beyond belief, a most intense and narrow partisan." The book further portrayed the group around Davis as "the most unprincipled adventurers that ever graced a government," while the governor's state police force contained as members "the worst desperadoes in the state."[12] These viewpoints reflected Ramsdell's opinions about the treatment afforded the South during Reconstruction, a region that he felt had been unfairly characterized in the general historical literature of the early twentieth century. "I believe that most of our histories are free from conscious sectional bias," he would observe several years after the book's publication, "but some fail for natural reasons to treat the South sympathetically, not only with regard to the period of a half century ago, but also that of the more recent past or the present." Ramsdell clearly envisioned his own historical opinions as correctives to that situation.[13]

The appearance of his book on Texas Reconstruction presented the young scholar with the necessity of making choices regarding his future academic career. His teaching position at the University of Texas had been tenuous at best, since he had been carried on the rolls only as an adjunct professor. In that capacity, he did not have full faculty rank and could not participate as a voting member of his department. Moreover, he chafed at the fact that since the fall of 1906 he had been teaching mostly European history; Professor Garrison, as department chair, had steadfastly reserved for himself most of the courses in U.S. history. Indeed, Ramsdell's senior colleague Eugene C. Barker was also discomfited by Garrison's reserving for himself all of the desirable courses in American history. "It is very unfortunate," a friend told Barker, "that Professor Garrison is not willing to welcome others in the same field with him, as it would seem plenty large enough for co-workers."[14] That situation had already in part caused the defection of historian Herbert Eugene Bolton to Stanford University, and eventually to the University of California.

The teaching situation in the department changed unexpectedly during the summer of 1910 when Garrison died of a heart attack. University president Sidney Mezes promptly appointed Barker as the new chair. Barker quickly redistributed the teaching assignments and, for the first time, Ramsdell found himself teaching U.S. history.[15] Ramsdell and Barker each taught sections of a course known as History 5, a sophomore introduction to American history. In addition, Ramsdell developed an upper-level offering on the Civil War and Reconstruction, to be followed later by one dealing with the antebellum South.[16]

Nonetheless, Ramsdell had previously been complaining to his mentor Dunning that he would like to find a position more to his liking. He was particularly concerned since the publication of his book had not resulted in a promotion or an increase in salary. This news incensed Dunning, who wrote to a mutual friend about Ramsdell's situation in Austin, "I think this is one of the greatest outrages, and worse than that, the greatest blunder ever made by an educational institution."[17] Dunning concluded that he would make it his special task to find a better faculty position for Ramsdell. Such an opportunity presented itself during the spring of 1911 when U. B. Phillips, another Dunning student, resigned a position at Tulane University to join the faculty at the University of Michigan. Dunning excitedly wrote Ramsdell about this development and told him to apply, which the young historian did.[18] Ramsdell contemplated the possible move to Tulane as a most agreeable development and, valuing honesty, told Barker of this development. "I should greatly regret to see him leave Texas," Barker noted, "but circumstances are such that he cannot expect as much as he deserves."[19] Securing Barker's support proved to be a wise strategy, since complications soon developed regarding Ramsdell's application at the New Orleans school. The president of Tulane somehow formed the impression that Ramsdell was a troublemaker and a malcontent on the faculty at the University of Texas. This, of course, was not the case. Once Dunning learned of this development, Ramsdell mobilized Barker in his defense. "It would be hard to imagine a man further removed from the character of a factionalist than is Ramsdell," Barker wrote Tulane, further noting that his colleague was "a good teacher" who was "plain, straightforward, and likable." Barker also noted that he hoped Ramsdell would not leave Texas, where his services were very much appreciated.[20]

In the end, nothing came of the position at Tulane and it remained unfilled. From his vantage point in New York, however, Professor Dunning still had aspirations that Ramsdell could find a teaching position that appeared—at least from an eastern academic perspective—more prestigious than serving on the faculty at the University of Texas. Such an opportunity presented itself the following year when the administration of Columbia University authorized a new faculty line in the history department, an expansion occasioned by the needs of a growing student body. Dunning hurriedly wrote to his star pupil in Austin, unofficially (yet in reality) offering the position. He reported to Ramsdell that the entire department enthusiastically supported his application and hoped that he would consider the position, which would pay $2,000, an amount larger than his University of Texas salary. The only negative consideration for Ramsdell, Dunning reported, was that the new position demanded primary teaching duties in European history. Ramsdell speedily replied that he would give the matter his serious consideration, reporting nonetheless that "my situation here is not bad, in fact it seems pretty favorable." He also noted that he had no great desire to teach European history, a subject he had only recently escaped in his duties at Texas.[21] When the history department chair was informed of this development, Barker saw an opportunity to use this offer as the excuse to gain for Ramsdell the promotion and salary increase he desired. Baker met with Sidney Mezes, the university president, in an effort to convince him to match Columbia's salary offer. Mezes could not agree to this because there was then in process a university-wide abeyance in salary increases and, consequently, the funds were simply not in the school's budget. Nonetheless, the president did his best to convince Ramsdell to stay in Austin by telling him that a promotion and salary increase would be forthcoming at the first opportunity. Ramsdell candidly told Mezes that "for many reasons I would like to stay in Texas, but that an opportunity to go to a place like Columbia was a rare one and that I would have more time to do research work there than I have here because of the enormous amount of committee work that I have had loaded on me here."[22] Nonetheless, after much consideration, Ramsdell decided to stay in Austin. "I was sorry," Charles A. Beard wrote Ramsdell, "that you did not see your way to coming back to Columbia when they were stirring around to find a place for you."[23] In 1916, Ramsdell received his promised promotion from the University of Texas and became a full professor the following year. He later confided to his colleague Walter P. Webb, "I knew all the time that I didn't want to go and I am glad that I don't have to go. I suppose that I shall never leave."[24]

Ramsdell's decision to remain at the University of Texas placed him foursquare in the position of becoming a founding member of what would eventually become known as the "Old Department," a group of historians who remained together as colleagues for almost forty years. This group included Eugene C. Barker, Milton R. Gutsch, Thad W. Riker, Frederick Duncalf, Charles W. Hackett, Walter P. Webb, Frank B. Marsh, and Ramsdell.[25] From the first decade of the twentieth century until the era of World War II, these individuals built a cohesive department that made the study of history one of the strongest disciplines in the university and brought a national reputation in professional historical circles to Garrison Hall, an office and classroom facility that was built especially for them and that became their departmental home when it opened in 1926. Ramsdell played a major role in this elevation of history at the university, but interestingly he never became well known for publishing books. Instead, his reputation came to rest on the publication of book reviews and journal articles, his historical editing, and his active participation as both a member and an officer in a number of historical associations, including the Texas State Historical Association, the Southern Historical Association, the Mississippi Valley Historical Association, and the American Historical Association. In addition, he consistently carried a heavy load of committee responsibilities throughout his career at the university, especially representing the faculty in athletic matters.[26]

It was in this latter capacity that he had a significant impact outside the discipline of history, not only at the university but throughout the state of Texas. Ramsdell had been placed as a faculty representative on the University Athletic Council as early as 1910 and took this responsibility very seriously, no doubt because of his own career as a varsity athlete. Ramsdell insisted upon good sportsmanship and clean athletic competition. For several years as a young faculty member he coached the track team and, in the absence of a director of athletics position at the school, he also personally booked the football games for the university. Moreover, in the years before World War I, he wrote a series of rules and regulations for athletic competitions, both at the university and for high schools in Texas. In that regard, Ramsdell was the person who envisioned and proposed creation of the modern University Interscholastic League, the agency that became the arbiter of high school athletic competition in the state. In fact, he was the author of the 1912 plan that created the league. As Ramsdell suggested that year to a group of high school administrators, "Don't you think it would be possible to bring it within the scope of our present Interscholastic Association" and create an oversight organization that "could have a general supervision over all high school athletics?" He further explained, "It seems to me at first thought it would be necessary to district the State and have local officers carry out within the district the rules and regulations which apply all over the State." Ramsdell accordingly wrote the proposal that, in effect, became the Athletic Division of the University Interscholastic League.[27] And, in addition to his interest in regulating high school competition, he worked diligently to promote University of Texas athletics. In the fall of 1913, President Mezes excused Ramsdell from his teaching duties so that the newly promoted professor could travel to a selection of universities to determine the structure of their athletic programs, evaluate their coaching practices, and examine their football facilities, the last because the University of Texas had begun to contemplate the construction of what would later become Memorial Stadium. Ramsdell dutifully traveled throughout the Midwest making various site visits, writing a long report upon his return to Austin that resulted in the reorganization of university athletic programs and the creation of a new position he suggested be known as Director of Physical Training; soon thereafter it was filled by L. Theo Bellmont.[28] During World War I, Ramsdell assumed the chair of the University Athletic Council, a position that greatly expanded the level of his daily workload as he routinely dealt with eligibility issues regarding individual athletes, the policies of the Southwestern Conference, and the functioning of the Intercollegiate Athletic Association.[29]

Ramsdell's most enduring contributions as a historian and a faculty member naturally came in the area of pedagogy, research, and publishing. He undertook all of these activities using a frame of reference of the American South and his self-concept as a southerner. Academically, in the emerging historical profession of the early twentieth century, subspecialties in U.S. history such as "Texas" and "Southern" history had not yet taken shape. Indeed, it would be historians such as Ramsdell, Barker, and their colleagues in the "Old Department" at the University of Texas who would help validate these historical orientations as legitimate fields of professional study. During the early decades of his career, it is clear that Ramsdell saw little difference between Texas and the American South as distinct historical entities. To him, they were simply one and the same. This viewpoint coincided absolutely with the accepted norms of life in the Anglo-dominated Texas of that era and specifically at the University of Texas. From its founding, the university had explicitly manifested a strong support for Southern traditions and institutions. In 1897, for example, the Texas Legislature passed a resolution containing this statement: "As representatives of the people, we request the regents of the university to exercise great care hereafter in selecting as faculty members only those who are known to be in sympathy with Southern political institutions."[30] Ramsdell completely fitted this description, which flies in the face of present-day social values. In particular, Ramsdell often articulated Anglo viewpoints about racial minorities that reflected the prevailing assumptions of his time and that he voiced without question. This can be seen in some of his scholarly articles, which overwhelmingly ignore the role of African Americans in the South. He was consistently attracted to topics that reflected the world of the white Southerner almost exclusively. "The Negro is thousands of years behind the white man," he once wrote a correspondent, "and the mass of Negroes will never catch up."[31] These viewpoints even permeated his private life. For many years, the Ramsdell family employed an illiterate African American cook named Malvina, who earned a reputation among their friends in Austin as a consummate expert in the kitchen. Ramsdell and his wife often entertained guests who eagerly enjoyed Malvina's cooking. Most everyone in the faculty community knew about the cook's unusual background: early in her service to the family, she had returned to her own home one evening where she found her husband engaged in compromising activity with another woman. Malvina killed him in a fit of passion, speedily returned to the Ramsdell home, confessed her crime to them, and asked her employers what she should do. They secured an attorney for her, and as an esteemed member of the university faculty, Ramsdell later appeared in court on her behalf to argue that "being a Negro, she was rather like a child who should not be held fully responsible for her actions." The court found Malvina guilty but, in considering the professor's testimony, did not order her incarceration; instead, she was paroled to work out her sentence for the Ramsdell family as their domestic servant.[32]

As harsh as these views may seem today, they went unremarked in Ramsdell's circle since they reflected the prevailing social norms in the white community. On the other hand, Ramsdell was considered for his time to have been a progressive and enlightened person regarding the role of women, especially in his teaching activities outside the traditional classroom. Unlike other professional historians on the East Coast, Ramsdell and his colleagues at the University of Texas paid particular attention to the needs of classroom teachers at the elementary and secondary levels. This arose from necessity since public school teachers in all subjects were required to take university coursework in order to maintain their certifications. In addition, the university's Bureau of Extension regularly monitored public school teaching throughout Texas and offered teachers correspondence courses, while it sent professors to various locations to observe teachers in the classroom. Ramsdell engaged in these activities for many years, especially encouraging women to take advanced history courses at the university during the summer and to seek graduate degrees.[33]

This interest in secondary education also helped motivate the publication in 1912 of a textbook on Texas history on which Barker, Ramsdell, and Charles S. Potts of the political science department collaborated as joint authors. This book represented the first textbook of Texas history written by professionally trained, academic scholars to assess the state within the context of an analytical and historiographical perspective. It provided a balanced political, economic, constitutional, and institutional examination of Texas history that was based on a solid array of sources. Naturally, given the temper of the times and Ramsdell's viewpoints, it stressed the southern roots of Texas culture as part of the expanding southwestern frontier of the United States. Beyond that, however, the appearance of this volume served in itself as an additional legitimization of Texas history as an increasingly valid subject of professional historical research and mainstream pedagogy.[34]

Ramsdell, in particular, was very proud of the book and had high hopes that it would be adopted by the State Textbook Committee, thereby insuring its financial and pedagogical success. To that end, Ramsdell embarked personally on a letter-writing campaign in the spring of 1912, encouraging school superintendents all across Texas to push for its adoption. "We believe we have improved upon the scholarship as well as upon the arrangement of other books," he wrote, "and that the teachers of Texas will heartily welcome it if it should be adopted."[35] To his chagrin, Ramsdell soon learned that he and his two coauthors had a battle on their hands with their adversary being Anna (Mrs. Percy V.) Pennybacker, a prominent Texas clubwoman and Democratic Party leader whose textbook *A New History of Texas* had been the statewide classroom standard since its first appearance in 1888. In many ways, although an influential book, the Pennybacker text represented the sort of nonacademic and antiquarian view of Texas history that the University of Texas authors were attempting to correct with their new volume. Pennybacker, who apparently took the appearance of the new textbook as a personal affront to her volume, launched a campaign among the women's clubs of Texas encouraging prominent members from throughout the state to lobby the state selection committee to continue use of her book and to reject the Barker, Potts, and Ramsdell volume. Many members of these clubs were women who had significant local and statewide influence on school boards and also had influence with the legislature regarding educational matters in the public schools.

To counter this development, Ramsdell sought the assistance of a wealthy and powerful university regent, H. J. Lutcher Stark, who was also a prominent booster with whom he had worked on the university athletic reforms. He complained to Stark about Pennybacker's lobbying of the women's clubs in the state. "Knowing that your mother and grandmother are prominently concerned in the work of the clubs," he explained, "I wanted to see if you could not help us by checking any pressure that could be brought to bear on the clubs in your part of the state."[36] Ramsdell's counterattack proved successful when the textbook selection committee adopted the volume, which subsequently enjoyed a long and distinguished life for decades as thousands of schoolchildren across several generations received their introduction to Texas history within its pages.

Beyond the recognition that the textbook brought Ramsdell in Texas school circles, he also established a reputation for himself in the scholarly associations of professional history, an activity to which he devoted much time during his entire career at the university. He became an active member of the Texas State Historical Association at the time he joined the university faculty, continuing this affiliation until his death. He served the organization in a variety of important positions and in various capacities for almost four decades. He was the associate editor of the *Southwestern Historical Quarterly* from 1910 until 1938. Importantly, he also performed yeoman work for the organization by serving as its secretary-treasurer from 1907 until his passing in 1942, a record that will probably never be surpassed. Ramsdell kept meticulous financial records for the association, recruiting and enlisting members and handling most of the routine office work of the organization in a small space allotted to the association in Garrison Hall, assisted only by occasional support from a student. Concurrently, Ramsdell also served for many years as membership representative in Texas for the American Historical Association, keeping the dues records and monies of that scholarly association for the southwestern United States.[37]

It was these membership funds that involved Ramsdell in one of the more colorful episodes to occur in Texas during the mid-1920s, a saga widely reported in the press as the escapades of the "flapper bandit." During the fall term of 1926, Ramsdell employed a young female graduate student, Rebecca Bradley, as the person to assist him with keeping his association records. Unknown to him, Bradley stealthily embezzled the membership funds he kept in his office to support her social life. Shortly before Christmas she panicked, fearing that Ramsdell would discover her transgressions as he prepared the end-of-the-year deposits. It was at that point that she decided on an absolutely unorthodox scheme to repay the missing funds, money that she had already spent. She would rob a bank and thereby secure the cash to replace the embezzled funds, with the professor none the wiser. One morning toward the end of the semester, she attempted to rob the Farmers State Bank in Round Rock, located north of Austin on the highway to Dallas. In comic opera fashion, she set fire to a vacant structure located next to the bank, after which she ran into the lobby yelling, "Fire, fire!" It was her plan that surprised bank employees would be distracted in the excitement, and that she could scoop money from the teller's drawers. Instead, they remained in place because several of them had seen her setting the fire through the bank windows and had already called the police, who arrived shortly after Rebecca fled the scene—but not before bystanders had taken the license number of her automobile. Now distraught and unaware that the Round Rock authorities had issued a regional bulletin about her car, she drove the main highway south through Austin to the nearby small town of Buda, where the very collegiate-looking, demure young woman boldly entered the town's only bank, the Farmer's National Bank of Buda, and, in more traditional robbery fashion, brandished a pistol. She forced startled employees to hand over $1,000 in cash. That was all she wanted. Making her getaway, she returned to Austin, where police recognized her car and arrested her, the ill-gotten gains from Buda still on the front seat next to her handgun. Somewhat improbably, it was Ramsdell whom she telephoned from the jail. He arrived to assist her and posted her bail after she gave him a full explanation of her activities. Thereafter, he worked diligently over a several-year period to have her acquitted, testifying on her behalf in a series of widely publicized trials and circuit court appeals that eventually found her innocent of bank robbery.[38]

Ramsdell's other activities with professional historical associations and organizations proved much more traditional and scholarly. He began in the years before World War I, for example, to attend regularly the meeting of the Mississippi Valley Historical Association, predecessor of the present-day Organization of American Historians, and also the annual gathering of the American Historical Association. Here he made the acquaintance of leading historians at the better colleges and universities in the nation, who readily accepted him into their circle. He formed strong friendships with many of these individuals over the years and engaged in an extensive correspondence with them. Following the fashion of the time, Ramsdell used these connections to secure a variety of summer appointments as a visiting professor. During the 1920s and 1930s he taught during the summer term at the state universities of Illinois, California, North Carolina, West Virginia, and Missouri, as well as at Columbia, Western Reserve, Northwestern, and Duke.[39] In turn, he arranged for his association colleagues to secure reciprocal appointments in Austin, sometimes renting them his home near the campus. Ramsdell's growing activities in the Mississippi Valley Historical Association and the American Historical Association resulted in his appearing on the program as a presenter and session commentator on many occasions. He also reviewed an increasing number of books for scholarly journals, concentrating on volumes on the antebellum South and the Confederacy. He had been increasingly attracted to the idea of a study of the Confederate government in the years after publication of his book on Reconstruction. By the early 1920s, he openly told colleagues that he was working on a comprehensive survey history of the Confederacy. And, in that regard, he began presenting a series of scholarly papers dealing with economic matters behind the lines in the Confederacy. The first of these came in 1917 when he presented a paper on the Confederate government and railroads, styling it a study of wartime administration. This resulted in the speedy publication of the paper as an article in the *American Historical Review*.[40] He followed this essay four years later with an equally significant paper dealing with the Confederate government's attempts to control manufacturing and the private economy during the Civil War.[41] These articles established Ramsdell in the profession as the historian who would be writing a general history of the Confederacy. Over the next two decades, Ramsdell spoke regularly about the project and assiduously collected information for it. However, at the time of his death, no draft manuscript of the project could be found in his personal papers.[42]

Ramsdell's inability to produce a second significant historical study after his book on Reconstruction in Texas, however, did not diminish the esteem and respect that the profession afforded him. In 1928–1929, he served as president of the Mississippi Valley Historical Association. He followed this assignment with a term on the Executive Council of the American Historical Association. By the early 1930s, he also found himself a leader in a group of historians across the South who were working hard to organize a regional professional association for themselves. This culminated in 1935 in the creation of the Southern Historical Association, whose founding members elected Ramsdell as their first president. The crowning accolade for Ramsdell as a southern historian came in 1937 when he received an invitation to deliver the inaugural group of lectures in the Walter Linwood Fleming Lecture Series at Louisiana State University. This lecture series, named for his late friend and graduate school associate, was designed to highlight the work of distinguished southern historians. Ramsdell labored assiduously on these lectures, to which he gave the encompassing title *Behind the Lines in the Southern Confederacy*. These essays constitute a sophisticated analysis of the Confederate economy and the resultant inability of the southern government to provide economically for the waging of war. Ramsdell offered a cogent thesis for the failure of the South in the Civil War. "If I were asked what was the greatest single weakness of the Confederacy," he told his audience at the Fleming Lectures, "I should say, without much hesitation, that it was in this matter of finances." The Confederate government's inability to manage a stable currency and its failure to maintain a functioning private economy destroyed any chances it had of winning the conflict. This interpretation eventually became known in southern history circles as the "Ramsdell Thesis," and it contributed to the then-current debate about why the South had lost the war.[43] Although the Fleming lectures carried an automatic guarantee of publication, Ramsdell could never bring himself to finish the editing of the lectures, which remained incomplete at the time of his death. Hence, friends completed the task, and the essays were published posthumously by LSU Press. This highlighted a basic problem with Ramsdell's approach to the research and writing of history, activities that progressed slowly for him. "The chief reason why Ramsdell did not produce was due to his method of research," one scholar later noted. "He was a perfectionist, unwilling to overlook any item in his search for knowledge."[44] His close friend Wendell H. Stephenson commented on the slowness of his writing by noting, "He needed the pressure of program committees to prepare manuscripts, the urgent solicitations of prodding editors to submit them for publication. He lacked an impelling obsession to speed his pen."[45]

Whether Ramsdell reached his full publishing potential is a matter of debate. Nonetheless, what he did write has stood the test of time and remains part of the current bibliography in southern history. His books and articles, however, are not the only legacy that flowed from his labors as a southern historian to the benefit of Texas and its history. Additionally, he was profoundly concerned with collecting library and archival materials dealing with the history of the region. This was an interest that he shared with several other Dunning students from his days at Columbia University, most especially J. R. Hamilton of the University of North Carolina, who was the motivating force behind the organization of the massive Southern History Collection at Chapel Hill. Ramsdell, in collaboration with Eugene C. Barker, did the same at the University of Texas. These efforts coalesced for Barker and Ramsdell in 1914 when University of Texas regent George W. Littlefield created a financial endowment to collect materials "bearing on the history of the South" for the University of Texas library. Although Barker, as chair of the history department, deserves credit as the individual who worked with Littlefield in crafting this significant donation, Ramsdell played a singular role thereafter as the key member of the advisory committee that disbursed these funds for library and archival acquisitions.[46] The size of the Littlefield Fund increased significantly after the death of the donor in 1920, thereby permitting increased purchases. From the very inception of the fund, Ramsdell worked closely with the university librarian and his colleagues in the history department, especially Barker, in maintaining a sound purchasing program that included both book and manuscript records. In regard to the latter, Ramsdell canvassed many of the old southern families in Texas in an effort to secure donations of manuscripts and papers to the university archives. "We wish to know if it would not be possible for you to give them," he typically wrote one such family about their papers, "or such of them as are not too personal, to the University library. We are doing everything we can to build up a great collection on southern history, and particularly the Civil War period."[47] He also tirelessly queried the publishers of the older newspapers in the state to give their runs of back issues to the university, thus creating one of the most impressive newspaper collections in the southern United States.

In the late 1930s Ramsdell embarked on two additional projects beyond the continuing acquisition of library resources as part of the Littlefield Fund activities. The first project dealt with the appearance of new microfilming technology. With the advent of photo duplication and microform, he conceived of an ambitious project that would identify, film, and deposit for researchers in the university library an array of primary source materials that were scattered all across the South, mostly in their original locations, which included courthouses, rural libraries, churches, newspaper offices, and municipalities. Most of the records filmed, according to his natural preferences, would be from the time period of the antebellum and Civil War eras. Securing support from the Littlefield Fund, Ramsdell turned to one of his graduate students, Barnes Lathrop, to undertake this project. Lathrop had come to the department in 1935 on a $200 fellowship in order to study with Ramsdell. Starting in 1937, Lathrop began to travel the South collecting and filming documents under Ramsdell's long-distance direction. Lathrop continued this activity into 1939, often traveling in the company of his wife, who served as his assistant. The Lathrops also made an additional collecting trip in 1940, eventually amassing for the University over 400 rolls of microfilm records dealing with the history of the region.[48]

The second project, conceived at the same time, involved the writing of a multivolume history of the South, with each chronological volume authored by an outstanding authority. When Ramsdell learned that Louisiana State University and its press was also contemplating a similar publication program, he encouraged both universities, typically, to join together in a single project to be sponsored by the Littlefield Fund. Starting in the late 1930s, he and his LSU counterpart, Wendell H. Stephenson, began working diligently to plan the series, choosing the authors and setting the editorial policy for this major set of comprehensive publications. Ramsdell, of course, planned to write the volume dealing with the Confederacy.[49]

The writing of this volume never occurred, as World War II and Ramsdell's declining health intervened. By late 1941, Ramsdell was clearly not feeling well. He was now in his mid-sixties, and although the years had worn well on him, he was clearly in physical decline. That year his physician had diagnosed a heart condition and recommended treatment in a Dallas hospital where more up-to-date and sophisticated procedures could be performed beyond those available in Austin. Ramsdell and his wife traveled to Dallas for this treatment during the summer of 1942.[50] It was there that he took an unexpected turn for the worse and died on July 3. He might have found it ironic that his passing occurred exactly 106 years, almost to the day and minute, after Pickett's charge at Gettysburg, the military action that established the "high water mark" of the Confederacy.

With his passing, Ramsdell left the historical profession in Texas a significant legacy. In sum, he made at least four major contributions. First, he successfully worked during most of his career to have professional historians in Texas accepted by their academic colleagues elsewhere, especially in the East at the older and more established universities. He did this with significant success thanks to his many professional associations and scholarly activities.

Second, he materially advanced the development of the University of Texas in the areas of academics and athletics, helping guide the school through its adolescence to become a mature academic institution. His insistence on fair play and sportsmanship in athletics, along with his role in creating the University Interscholastic League, greatly benefited the entire state. In coequal fashion, he labored mightily to bring academic excellence to the teaching of Texas history, both at the university and at the secondary level. A committed advocate of graduate studies, he directed the first doctoral dissertation in history at the University. He also worked diligently to improve research opportunities there.

Third, through his work with the Texas State Historical Association, he was an important influence in legitimizing the study of the state's history as a valid academic enterprise. His long career as associate editor of the *Southwestern Historical Quarterly* and his contribution to the organization as secretary-treasurer over many decades helped to make it a stable, enduring association. Moreover, the Texas history textbook that he helped to author has had an enduring impact on social studies pedagogy in the state.

Fourth, as one of the founders of the subfield of southern U.S. history and as one of its greatest motivators in the 1920s and 1930s, Ramsdell significantly advanced the viewpoint that Texas was southern in terms of its regional identity. In short, for Charles Ramsdell, Texas above all else was a southern place and anyone who wished to understand it historically had to consider its southern character. For him, the South proved to be the crucial element in understanding the nature of the Lone Star State.

SUGGESTED READING

Ramsdell, Charles W. *Reconstruction in Texas.* New York: Columbia University Press, 1910.

This book represents Ramsdell's magnum opus. It is an expanded version of his Ph.D. dissertation, which provided the first historical analysis of this important period in Texas history. Although by today's standards it manifests a marked bias toward the viewpoint of white, southern Democrats of that era, the study still contains useful information about Reconstruction and its impact on the state.

Ramsdell, Charles W. *Behind the Lines in the Southern Confederacy.* Baton Rouge: Lousiana State University Press, 1944.

Published after Ramsdell's death, the essays in this volume are the presentations he gave at the prestigious Walter Lynwood Fleming Lectures at LSU in 1937. They represent the basic ideas that would have been the underpinning of his survey history of the Confederate States of America, a project that he never completed. In these lectures, Ramsdell advanced his belief that the major reason for Confederate defeat in the Civil War was home front weaknesses in the South instead of military failures.

NOTES

1. Wendell H. Stephenson, "Charles W. Ramsdell: Historian of the Confederacy," *Journal of Southern History* 26, no. 4 (November 1960): 501–525; J. Horace Bass, "Charles W. Ramsdell," in *The New Handbook of Texas,* edited by Ron Tyler (Austin: Texas State Historical Association, 1996), 5:427. See also J. Horace Bass, "RAMSDELL, CHARLES WILLIAM," *The Handbook of Texas Online,* http://www.tshaonline.org/handbook/online/articles/RR/fra25.html (accessed May 20, 2008); Charles W. Ramsdell Vertical File, Dolph Briscoe Center for American History, University of Texas at Austin; "In Memoriam: Charles William Ramsdell," Minutes of the Faculty, University of Texas at Austin, http://www.utexas.edu/faculty/council/2000-2001/memorials/SCANNED/ramsdell.pdf (accessed May 20, 2008).

2. George W. Tyler, *The History of Bell County,* edited by Charles W. Ramsdell (1936; repr., Belton, TX: Dayton Kelley, 1966), 284, 291, 364. The home in which Charles W. Ramsdell was born still stands at this writing (2011). An edifice that once housed the Salado High School, it is a stately, two-story home locally known today as the Halley House and currently oper-

ated as a bed and breakfast establishment. See Memo from Herbert Fletcher for Mrs. Morris, July 1, 1960, in Charles W. Ramsdell Vertical File, Briscoe Center. For Ramsdell's early teaching career, see *Dallas Morning News*, June 8, 1899, and September 9, 1899.

3. Richard B. Holland, ed., *The Texas Book: Profiles, History, and Reminiscences of the University* (Austin: University of Texas Press, 2006), 106–109; Joe B. Frantz, *The Forty-Acre Follies* (Austin: Texas Monthly Press, 1983), 96–104; Margaret C. Berry, *The University of Texas: A Pictorial Account of Its First Century* (Austin: University of Texas Press, 1980), 65; Bryan A. Garner, ed., *Texas Our Texas: Remembrances of the University* (Austin: Eakin Press, 1984), 32–33.

4. Frantz, *Forty-Acre Follies*, 56–57; Richard Pennington, *Longhorn Hoops: The History of Texas Basketball* (Austin: University of Texas Press, 1998), 4–6; Jim Dunaway, "Texas Track and Field: Plenty to Brag About," *2005 Clyde Littlefield Texas Relays*, http://www.texassports.com/mainpages/txr/2004/032704_11.html (accessed May 21, 2008); "Contest at Austin," *Dallas Morning News*, October 8, 1906; "'Texas' Ramsdell in Dallas," *Dallas Morning News*, December 24, 1911; "Work of the Varsity," *Dallas Morning News*, December 12, 1908; "Says Varsity Eleven Has Good Schedule," *Dallas Morning News*, August 30, 1911.

5. William C. Pool, *Eugene C. Barker: Historian* (Austin: Texas State Historical Association, 1971), 25–31; Eugene C. Barker, "Lester Gladstone Bugbee, Teacher and Historian," *Southwestern Historical Quarterly* 49 (July 1945): 15–29; Richard B. McCaslin, *At the Heart of Texas: One Hundred Years of the Texas State Historical Association, 1897–1997* (Austin: Texas State Historical Association, 2007), 21–23; Tom B. Brewer, "A History of the History Department at the University of Texas: 1883–1951" (M.A. thesis, University of Texas at Austin, 1957); Wilbur R. Jacobs, John W. Caughey, and Joe B. Frantz, *Turner, Bolton, and Webb: Three Historians of the American Frontier* (Seattle: University of Washington Press, 1965); John Francis Bannon, *Herbert Eugene Bolton: The Historian and the Man* (Tucson: University of Arizona Press, 1978); "In Memoriam: George P. Garrison," Resolutions of the General Faculty, University of Texas at Austin, http://www.utexas.edu/faculty/council/2000-2001/memorials/AMR/Garrison/garrison.html (accessed May 21, 2008). Respect for Garrison as a Texas historian proved so enduring that over three decades after his death the U.S. Merchant Marine Commission named a liberty ship for him during World War II. The *S.S. George P. Garrison* saw active duty from its launch in 1943 to the end of the war, but was eventually scuttled in 1975 to make a fishing reef off the Virginia coast; "Liberty Ships—B," http://www.mariners-l.co.uk/LibshipsB.html (accessed May 21, 2008). His name is perpetuated to this day by the existence of Garrison Hall, the longtime campus home to the history department at the University of Texas.

6. Stephenson, "Charles W. Ramsdell," 503–504.

7. Philip R. Muller, "Look Back without Anger: A Reappraisal of William A. Dunning," *Journal of American History* 61, no. 2 (September 1974): 325–338; Bernard A. Weisberger, "The Dark and Bloody Ground of Reconstruction Historiography," *Journal of Southern History* 25, no. 4 (November 1959): 427–447; A. A. Taylor, "Historians of Reconstruction," *Journal of Negro History* 23, no. 1 (January 1938): 16–34.

8. Charles Ramsdell, *Reconstruction in Texas* (New York: Longmans, Green, 1910). It was subsequently republished without editing or updating by Peter Smith Publishers in 1964. The University of Texas Press reissued the book in 1970.

9. His son, Charles W. Ramsdell Jr., became a prominent journalist and author of popular history in Texas during the 1940s and 1950s, enjoying a long career as a newspaper reporter and feature writer in San Antonio. He wrote a history of San Antonio in the 1950s. See Charles Ramsdell, *San Antonio: An Historical Pictorial Guide* (Austin: University of Texas Press, 1959).

The son has been confused with his historian father in several bibliographies because some of the younger Ramsdell's publications did not include the designation "junior." See the two separate vertical files, "Charles W. Ramsdell" and "Charles W. Ramsdell Jr.," at the Briscoe Center.

10. Stephenson, "Charles W. Ramsdell," 507.

11. "Review by W. L. Fleming," General Correspondence 1910–1911, box 2L461, Charles W. Ramsdell Papers, Dolph Briscoe Center for American History, University of Texas at Austin (hereafter Ramsdell Papers).

12. For a more detailed analysis of these points, see Stephenson, "Charles W. Ramsdell," 307–308; Ramsdell, *Reconstruction in Texas*, 8, 146, 317.

13. Ramsdell to the Macmillan Company, June 16, 1911, General Correspondence January–August 1911, box 2L461, Ramsdell Papers.

14. Herman V. Ames to Barker, February 2, 1910, Eugene C. Barker Papers, Dolph Briscoe Center for American History, University of Texas at Austin (hereafter Barker Papers), quoted in Brewer, "A History of the History Department," 29.

15. Pool, *Barker*, 42–44.

16. Ramsdell would start teaching the course on the Old South in 1923. Ramsdell's courses proved to be very popular, eventually extending into the graduate program. In 1927 he directed the first doctoral dissertation in history written at the University of Texas: James Kimmons Greer, "Louisiana Politics, 1845–1861." Brewer, "A History of the History Department," 142.

17. Dunning to S. H. Moore, March 9, 1911, General Correspondence January–August 1911, box 2L461, Ramsdell Papers. Also quoted in Brewer, "A History of the History Department," 42.

18. Dunning to Ramsdell, March 17, 1911, General Correspondence January–August 1911, box 2L461, Ramsdell Papers.

19. Barker to U. B. Phillips, March 30, 1911, ibid.

20. Stephenson, "Charles W. Ramsdell," 507. The university's inability to promote Ramsdell or increase his salary significantly did not reflect on him personally. Instead, the university's president, Sidney Mezes, desired the construction of a new library building. The governor of Texas, in supporting this new building for inclusion in the state budget, exacted a promise from the university that there would be no salary increases for a two-year period. Brewer, "A History of the History Department," 43.

21. Dunning to Ramsdell, April 12, 1912, General Correspondence January–August 1911, box 2L461, Ramsdell Papers.

22. Ramsdell to Dunning, April 21, 1912, General Correspondence January–August 1912, ibid.

23. Beard to Ramsdell, November 12, 1912, ibid.

24. Brewer, "A History of the History Department," 43.

25. Pool, *Barker*, 45–52; McCaslin, *At the Heart of Texas*, 64; Brewer, "A History of the History Department," 89.

26. Ramsdell sometimes complained with some jocularity to close friends about the time-consuming nature of his committee assignments, which he nonetheless willingly sought and enthusiastically fulfilled. He once wrote a confidant: "I am still struggling along at the blankety-blank Athletic Council and ditto Interscholastics. . . . Once in a while I get a chance to think about doing some research but that is as far as I have got since Christmas. If I don't get relief from this trouble next year I am going to shoot up this joint. My extension work is taking almost as much time as my class yet I don't ever seem to get to the point where I

receive any fees and the time has come when they begin to bring in wheel-barrow loads of papers to grade from ambitious high school teachers who desire affiliation in American history." Ramsdell to A. C. Krey, March 7, 1913, General Correspondence 1913, box 2L462, Ramsdell Papers.

27. Ramsdell to L. F. McKay, November 22, 1912, General Correspondence August–December 1912, box 2L461, Ramsdell Papers. McKay had invited Ramsdell to attend the 1912 Texas State Teachers Association meeting to discuss regulation of high school athletics, which were then marked by many abuses and questionable irregularities across the state. Ramsdell's plan to expand the University of Texas itself into the regulation of these activities resulted from this invitation. The University Interscholastic League was created in 1913 as a result of Ramsdell's proposal to merge the Debating League of Texas with interests of the Interscholastic Athletic Association, which had written rules for high school athletics in the state. The UIL, as it quickly became known throughout Texas high schools, was structured at Ramsdell's suggestion as a division of the University of Texas Extension. Roy Bedichek, *Educational Competition: The Story of the University Interscholastic League of Texas* (Austin: University of Texas Press, 1956), 37–42.

28. Ramsdell to Professor W. T. Mather, October 3, 1912, General Correspondence August–December 1912, box 2L461, Ramsdell Papers. Bellmont's position continues today under the title Director of Athletics. For a concise early history of athletic leadership, see Bobby Hawthorne, *Longhorn Football: An Illustrated History* (Austin: University of Texas Press, 2007), 4–21.

29. His correspondence on these matters from this era is contained in box 2L467 of the Ramsdell Papers.

30. James S. Payne, "Texas Historiography in the 20th Century: A Study of Eugene C. Barker, Charles W. Ramsdell, and Walter P. Webb" (Ph.D. diss., University of Denver, 1972), 51.

31. Ramsdell to Paul L. Haworth, October 15, 1916, General Correspondence 1915–1918, box 2L463, Ramsdell Papers.

32. William Louis Braisted, "This I Remember," in *Burnt Orange Britannia: Adventures in History and the Arts,* edited by William Roger Louis (London: I. B. Taurus, 2006), 29.

33. As an example of many such activities, he wrote a letter to a Sherman, Texas, schoolteacher whose class he had recently visited, extolling the benefits of taking summer extension classes from the university. He told her, "These extension courses are designed very largely for teachers who are just in your situation and are being taken by great numbers of them. I think the university is doing a great service to the teachers of the state in this way and it is very gratifying to see the readiness with which the teachers respond." Ramsdell to Mary Crutchfield, March 6, 1913, General Correspondence August–December 1913, box 2L462, Barker Papers.

34. The preface notes: "This book aims to present in form sufficiently simple for young readers the essential facts of the history of Texas. To bring it within the grasp of fifth and sixth grade pupils and to make it a thoroughly useful tool in the hands of the teacher we have steadily sought to give it the qualities of accuracy, directness, and fairness." Eugene C. Barker, Charles Shirley Potts, and Charles W. Ramsdell, *A School History of Texas* (Chicago: Row, Peterson, 1912), v.

35. Ramsdell to Professor Carl Hartman, April 4, 1912, General Correspondence January–August 1912, box 2L461, Ramsdell Papers. To read about this controversy from Pennybacker's viewpoint, see Kelley M. King, *Call Her a Citizen: Progressive-Era Activist and Educator Anna Pennybacker* (College Station: Texas A&M University Press, 2010), 56–62.

36. Ramsdell to H. J. Lutcher Stark, July 15, 1912, General Correspondence January–August 1912, box 2L461, Ramsdell Papers.

37. McCaslin, *At the Heart of Texas,* 64, 66–67, 102.

38. The story became a fixture of the Associated Press wire for weeks and was widely reported across the entire nation. *Time* magazine also ran a short feature on the story. For selected examples of this coverage, see "Says Debt She Owed Made Girl Rob Bank: Rebecca Rogers Obligated to Historical Association in Texas," *New York Times,* December 20, 1926; "Miss Rogers Out on Bond Again," *Dallas Morning News,* December 17, 1926; "College Girl Arrested in Bank Robbery," *Hartford (CT) Courant,* December 12, 1926. Among other twists to this story, it was determined that Bradley was secretly married to Otis Rogers, then a law student at the university. "Girl Bandit Suspect Wed: Texas Lawyer Discloses Secret, College Marriage with Co-Ed Accused as Bank Robber," *Los Angeles Times,* December 14, 1926; "Rebecca Rogers Jury Discharged by Judge: Body Deadlocked to Last with Nine in Favor of Acquittal," *Washington Post,* September 21, 1929. Ramsdell's support for the young woman was featured in many of these stories; see especially "Faculty Man Testifies," *Washington Post,* December 13, 1927.

39. Brewer, "A History of the History Department," 47.

40. "The Meeting of the American Historical Association at Cincinnati," *American Historical Review* 22, no. 3 (April 1917): 529; Ramsdell, "The Confederate Government and the Railroads," *American Historical Review* 22, no. 4 (July 1917): 794–810.

41. Ramsdell, "The Control of Manufacturing by the Confederate Government," *Mississippi Valley Historical Review* 8, no. 3 (December 1921): 231–249.

42. Stephenson, "Charles W. Ramsdell," 515.

43. Ramsdell, *Behind the Lines in the Southern Confederacy* (Baton Rouge: LSU Press, 1944), 85; quoted in Stephenson, "Charles W. Ramsdell," 519.

44. Brewer, "A History of the History Department," 45. Nonetheless, his total scholarly production was not inconsiderable. During his forty-year career, Ramsdell published twenty articles in journals such as *Southwestern Historical Quarterly, Proceedings of the Mississippi Valley Historical Review, American Historical Review, North Carolina Historical Review, Southern Review,* and *Journal of Southern History*. He also contributed over a dozen entries to the *Dictionary of American Biography* and the section dealing with the Confederacy in the *Dictionary of American History*. He also edited several books in addition to his work on Reconstruction, and one may as well count in these totals the subsequent publication of his Fleming lectures.

45. Stephenson, "Charles W. Ramsdell," 523.

46. Pool, *Barker,* 58–60; Frantz, *Forty-Acre Follies,* 41–51. For analyses of Littlefield's career, see David B. Gracy II, "George Washington Littlefield: A Biography in Business" (Ph.D. diss., Texas Tech University, 1971); Evetts Haley, *George W. Littlefield, Texan* (Norman: University of Oklahoma Press, 1943).

47. Ramsdell to D. A. Nunn, April 27, 1918, General Correspondence 1918, box 2L463, Ramsdell Papers.

48. Brewer, "A History of the History Department," 104–105.

49. Stephenson, "Charles W. Ramsdell," 510–511. The LSU series on the history of the South went forward after Ramsdell's death when E. Merton Coulter joined Stephenson as the coeditor.

50. "Noted Teacher of History Passes Away: Dr. C. W. Ramsdell, University of Texas, Succumbs at Hospital," *Dallas Morning News,* July 4, 1942.

PATRICK L. COX

EUGENE C. BARKER

EUGENE C. BARKER AT THE OPENING OF THE SAN JACINTO MONUMENT, 1939

Eugene Campbell Barker rose from humble origins in the late nineteenth century to become one of the most recognized Texas historians of the twentieth century. At the end of his long career, Barker was acclaimed as "the foremost authority on Texas history and one of America's most distinguished historians" when he died in 1956. Barker achieved his dream of becoming a nationally recognized scholar and historian, but in doing so he became a controversial, combative public figure who endured both praise and criticism.[1]

Barker was born in the Piney Woods of East Texas near the small town of Riverside on November 10, 1874. He was the first child of Joseph and Fannie Holland Barker. The community of Riverside, approximately ninety miles north of Houston on the Trinity River, owed its existence to the Houston and Great Northern Railroad. Barker's father, Joseph, owned a general merchandise store in Riverside that he operated his entire life. While the Barker family may have had some economic advantages over the laborers in the lumber industry and the sharecroppers of the cotton fields, they maintained a thrifty household and were among the small merchant class of nineteenth-century rural Texas. Barker recalled that this small town consisted of "a railroad station, a water tank, one store, a saloon—called a grocery, and two or three little houses." As a child, Barker walked the railroad line to a small one-room school he attended. Joseph Barker passed away at the age of thirty-eight in 1888. Following her husband's unexpected death, Fannie Barker moved the family, consisting of Eugene and his two younger brothers and one sister, to Palestine.[2]

Young Barker quit school and went to work in Palestine for the International and Great Northern Railroad. The railroad corporations of this era offered young men the opportunity to have a more reliable income and a path out of the small towns and farms. He became an expert blacksmith and joined the National Railway Master Blacksmith's Association. He worked to support the family by day and attended school at night but never obtained a high school diploma. However, an applicant could gain admission to the University of Texas during Barker's era if he could pass an entrance examination. The university catalogue stated that candidates for admission would be accepted if they passed exams in history, English, and mathematics.

Barker traveled to Austin in September 1894 to take the required exams, but failed in English. After another year of working at the forge and attending classes at night, Barker returned in the fall of 1895 and passed the tests. He enrolled as a freshman at the University of Texas on September 23, 1895. The year he began his studies, university enrollment was 482 students with a faculty of twenty-five professors, instructors, and tutors. Barker received his B.A. in history in 1899 and his M.A. in history in 1900 from the University of Texas. His master's thesis was titled "The Unification of Public Sentiment for the Texas Revolution."[3]

Barker's entry into the field of history coincided with the development of historical professionalism in the United States. Texas and the other southern states of the former Confederacy strove to increase their higher education institutions and programs of liberal arts studies in the late nineteenth and early twentieth centuries. In addition to this new emphasis on historical writing and instruction, institutions also embarked on efforts to acquire important archival collections. These initiatives were designed to strengthen the educational institutions that lagged behind their counterparts in the North and the East. This expansion aimed to enhance and promote the research, writing, and teaching of history utilizing scientific methodology that relied on primary documents. Professional historical organizations related to the historians and their affiliated universities emerged during this time. In addition, a stronger regional and nationalistic era grew out of these initiatives, as illustrated by the careers, ideas, and historical publications of Barker and some of his fellow historians in the South.

During his years at the University of Texas, the professors who provided the greatest stimulus to Barker's intellectual growth were two colleagues in the history department: Lester Gladstone Bugbee, who taught as a tutor while he worked on his doctorate, and department chair George P. Garrison. Barker considered Bugbee "the most effective and inspiring teacher that I met anywhere during my student career." Barker commended Bugbee for involving students in lectures, encouraging scholarship and research, and working long hours to improve his knowledge and expertise. He lauded Bugbee as one of the organizers of the Texas State Historical Association and for his work as secretary and treasurer of the young organization. Barker also credited Bugbee for his labors to bring the Bexar Archives, "one of the greatest of Texas historical sources," from Bexar County in San Antonio to the university in 1899. The Bexar Archives contained over 250,000 document pages of official government records from Spanish colonial Texas as well as Mexican government records from Coahuila y Texas. In 1902, at the age of thirty-two, Bugbee passed away after an extended illness.[4]

George P. Garrison was considered a premier historian and one of the influential figures in the formation of the University of Texas. In addition to serving as a full professor of history, Garrison was one of the first Texas historians to publish in recognized national historical journals. He served as one of the founders of the Texas State Historical Association and served as the editor of its quarterly until his death in 1910. Importantly, Garrison collaborated with Bugbee to acquire the Bexar Archives for the university. Garrison also worked with Guy Morrison Bryan on the donation of the Moses Austin and Stephen F. Austin papers to the university's collections. The combined inspiration of Bugbee and Garrison would prove to have a significant impact on the life of Eugene C. Barker.[5]

Acquisition of the Bexar Archives along with the Austin and Bryan papers proved to be the impetus for Barker's first published articles. In the January 1901 edition of the *Quarterly of the Texas State Historical Association*, Barker contributed his first article, titled "The Difficulties of a Mexican Revenue Officer in Texas." Barker wrote on the resistance of Anglo settlers to the efforts of Captain Antonio Tenorio and Don José Gonzales to collect customs duties at the ports of entry in Spanish Texas. "The San Jacinto Campaign in Texas," along with "The African Slave Trade," appeared in the January 1903 issue of the association's quarterly. Additional articles on the Texas Revolution appeared in *Publications of the Southern Historical Association* in 1901. Early in his career, Barker revealed his lifelong interests in Texas history, his interest in opening new areas of historical research, and his passion for utilizing primary sources.

Barker married Matilda LeGrand Weeden on May 6, 1903. The couple had one son, David Barker. In the summer of 1901, Barker left the University of Texas to begin graduate studies at the University of Chicago. He later attended the University of Pennsylvania, where he focused on early American history. At the urging of his colleague Herbert Eugene Bolton, Barker attended the University of Pennsylvania and earned his Ph.D. in history in 1908. Barker also studied at Harvard University from 1907 to 1908. He returned to the University of Texas in the fall of 1908 to teach courses in modern European history at the behest of Chairman Garrison, but American history remained the focus of Barker's academic research and teachings. Although anxious to return to Austin, Barker had strained relations with the departmental chair over teaching assignments. Bolton, his friend and colleague at the university, left in a dispute with Chairman Garrison. However, when Barker proposed that he teach a course on Mexico and the American Southwest, Garrison conceded. Perhaps Bolton's decision prompted Garrison to retain Barker, the promising young historian, as a permanent member of the department.[6]

Barker's decision to remain at the University of Texas proved to be propitious. Garrison died unexpectedly at his home on July 3, 1910, the victim of an apparent heart attack. Shortly after Garrison's funeral, university president Sidney Mezes selected Barker to become the acting chair of the history department. Barker served as department chair for the next fifteen years. During that period, the department and the growth of its archives and publications achieved remarkable success. Barker expanded its financial support by enlisting contributions from individuals interested in history and the university. However, Barker also endured his share of criticism and became embroiled in an historic political battle between the university and the Texas governor.

Among the many initiatives Barker launched as chair, one of the most far-reaching efforts was his successful solicitation of Major George W. Littlefield. A Confederate veteran who made his fortune after the war in banking, cotton, and cattle, Littlefield became a major financial supporter and leader of the University of Texas. Following his appointment to the university's board of regents in 1911, Barker began a quest, through frequent letters to Littlefield, to obtain donations for the acquisition of historical archives. Littlefield, a strong proponent and a defender of the Confederacy, believed that educators and history books misrepresented the interests of the South. Barker told Littlefield that unless the university received money to acquire important southern historical documents, nothing could be done to provide alternative interpretations. Barker expressed his frustration to Littlefield when he stated that, without the essential primary resources combined with scholarly research, "the resolutions and protests of the South are as 'sounding brass and tinkling cymbals.'"[7]

With his appeal to sentimentality and his persistent pleas, Barker succeeded in convincing Littlefield to provide an initial $25,000 gift for the Littlefield Fund for Southern History at the University of Texas. The original committee to oversee the Littlefield Fund included Barker. The committee's mission was to purchase books, pamphlets, newspaper files, maps, manuscripts, and other materials related to the American South. The initial gift, combined with later funding of $100,000 from the Littlefield estate, established one of the premier programs for southern history archival collections that scholars continue to use to this day. The fund provided for the acquisition of hundreds of archival collections that have served as a resource for several generations of scholars to produce volumes of history, a goal that Barker and Littlefield once envisioned. These included papers and records from antebellum plantations, newspapers, correspondence, and many collections relating to the Civil War. Fortunately, the collection that began with the purpose of defending the southern slaveholding culture evolved in the modern era to produce new histories that exposed the morally corrupt slave system. Newer publications by modern historians utilize these archives to document the ongoing struggle for civil rights in the nation. Thus, Barker's collaborative efforts with Littlefield, along with his initiatives with other donors, demonstrated the growing importance of private contributions in support of the acquisition of historical archives and scholarly research.[8]

As the department chair, Barker recognized that he needed to strengthen the faculty through the addition of scholars from out of state. Only two faculty members remained on staff when Barker assumed the chair in 1910: Charles W. Ramsdell and Frederic Duncalf. As Ramsdell noted, the department was "shaken and demoralized by the departure of Bolton in 1909 and the death of Garrison."[9] Barker immediately recruited new faculty in the first two years: Thad Weed Riker, modern European history; Frank Burr Marsh, ancient history; Milton R. Gutsch, English history; Charles Wilson Hackett, Latin American history; Rudolph Biesele, American history; and Walter Prescott Webb, American history. This core group of historians remained with the university for decades and taught thousands of students who passed through the campus of the Forty Acres during the first half of the twentieth century. Furthermore, the reputation of the scholarship and teaching of this core group of historians solidified Barker's leadership at the university well beyond the walls of Garrison Hall.

Barker's departmental colleagues held him in high esteem, yet a number of them noted his somewhat brusque manner and his aloofness. Some attributed this to a self-conscious attitude. He often seemed uncomfortable in formal, social settings. Walter Prescott Webb noted that Barker "was the kindest man in the world, but almost fierce in his shyness." Dr. Milton R. Gutsch, who succeeded Barker as the history department chair, wrote, "There are those who consider Barker cold and difficult to approach. Those, however, who have worked with him or under him soon realized that the forbidding exterior concealed an unusually warm and sympathetic personality." Rupert N. Richardson recalled examples of Barker's famous temper that was often directed at students: "Once or twice I have fairly trembled at an explosion when he was vexed with some student." William J. Battle wrote of Barker's "honesty, courage and kindliness." But along with these attributes Battle stated that "with his honesty goes a courage that does not hesitate to speak out, always forcefully, often with vehemence, occasionally with temper."[10]

During a presentation honoring Barker on April 30, 1926, at Austin's landmark Driskill Hotel, historian Charles W. Ramsdell praised his colleague for his "distinguished scholarship" and stated, "No man in University circles stands higher when measured by character and services performed." According to Ramsdell, "distinguished scholarship can result only from a combination of unusual mentality and certain qualities of character." Ramsdell credited Barker with rebuilding the department in 1910 following the departure of Bolton to California and the death of Garrison.[11]

Barker accepted other professional assignments in 1910 that would shape his future career and reputation. He assumed the managing editor's position for the *Quarterly of the Texas State Historical Association*. As editor, Barker expanded the scope of articles in the publication and changed the name to the *Southwestern Historical Quarterly*, a title that has remained to this day.[12] As he expanded the scope of scholarship and teaching at the University of Texas, Barker initiated an effort to expand the horizons of the Texas State Historical Association. In addition to serving as chair of the history department in 1910, Barker assumed the position of director of the young state historical association. For several years prior to 1910, Barker and Herbert Bolton had served as coeditors of the organization's quarterly publication. Even after Bolton left for California, he remained in close contact with Barker. The two historians joined forces in redirecting and renaming the *Quarterly*. The change in the title to the *Southwestern*

Historical Quarterly reflected a desire by Barker and Bolton to expand the scope of scholarship in the journal to encompass the Spanish borderlands and articles on the American Southwest.[13]

Barker never relinquished control of the journal during his tenure, and the quarterly retained its focus on historical articles relating to Texas. "Barker took charge of the material he received and forged his own journal," historian Richard McCaslin wrote in his recent history of the organization.[14] During his long tenure as editor, Barker included articles on topics that ranged from the Spanish colonial era in Texas through the nineteenth century. Barker's own articles in the journal included pieces on the impact of slavery during the colonial era in Texas and the role of Tejanos during the 1836 Texas Revolution. In addition to expanding the study of the revolutionary era into economic and social topics, articles published during Barker's tenure as editor also focused on Texas during the period of the Republic and early statehood. They would also lay the groundwork for Barker's influential biography on Stephen F. Austin.

Early in his tenure as head of the historical association, Barker encountered a major challenge that had confronted the TSHA since it was first organized—the role of women in the organization. The confrontation reflected the changing political climate during the Progressive era in Texas and the emerging women's movement in the early twentieth century. Women played a prominent role in the Progressive movement in the late nineteenth and early twentieth centuries. They worked for prohibition and assumed very public positions in calling for significant reforms in public health and education. Many women joined organized clubs as part of the reform efforts. The Women's Clubs represented more than 5,000 women in 232 clubs by 1903. In addition, many other women's organizations were active in promoting history, notably the Daughters of the Republic of Texas, the United Daughters of the Confederacy, and the Daughters of the American Revolution.[15]

Although women participated in the TSHA and contributed articles to the *Southwestern Historical Quarterly*, conflicts arose between the predominant male leadership and the women of the organization. In 1912, Barker, Charles Ramsdell, and Charles S. Potts authored a new history text for public schools. This book replaced one written by Anna J. H. Pennybacker, a leading activist in the Women's Club movement in Texas. Once her textbook had been replaced by the all-male historians' publication, Pennebacker resigned her membership in the Texas State Historical Association. Much to the chagrin of Barker and others in the association, she became a vocal critic and led many other women out of the male-dominated organization. Seeking a way to reverse these losses and silence the women's criticisms, Barker arranged for the appointment of Adele B. Looscan as the first female president of the historical association. Looscan had outstanding credentials as a founding member of the Daughters of the Republic of Texas, an active member of the Daughters of the Confederacy and the Daughters of the American Revolution, and a charter member of the Texas Woman's Press Association. But apparently Barker failed to notify Looscan of her election. She reportedly learned of her selection from the *San Antonio Express* newspaper. Looscan told Barker she was "inexpressibly surprised" and wanted to know "how this strange thing came about."[16] Looscan, in spite of the surprise appointment that was a clumsy attempt to secure more support from women, remained president of the association from 1915 until 1925.

This incident was a reflection of Barker's controlling mannerisms and also an illustration of his views on women. While he believed that a number of women retained the necessary management, business, and academic credentials to succeed, Barker still wanted to maintain control and direction with a limited number of female historians and administrators. His aloof attitude and direct mannerisms also made it difficult for many to approach Barker. Only a relatively few women and men worked with Barker for an extended period of years. And even some of his close friends noted his standoffish manner.

As TSHA president, Looscan attempted to work with Barker for many years to increase the membership and to provide the association with a sound financial plan. However, the organization never expanded to more than one thousand members and had ongoing problems meeting its budget. These difficulties could be attributed in part to trying financial times in Texas. But, in a larger sense, Looscan and the TSHA board members were never able to alter the stringent control that Barker exerted over the association. The TSHA would fail to grow or expand its influence beyond the borders of the Lone Star State as long as it remained part of Barker's domain and relied on the University of Texas to support its operations. Nevertheless, the *Southwestern Historical Quarterly* survived the years of economic depression and limited budgets to serve as a quality academic publication.[17]

The University of Texas at Austin has a long, sometimes contentious history involving university administrators, faculty, students, and Texas government officials. As a student in the late 1800s and as a faculty member before 1915, Barker witnessed numerous confrontations between elected officials and university administrators. While he was a student, one conflict resulted in the forced resignation of a university president. But none of these incidents would compare with the public battle between the University of Texas and Governor James E. Ferguson. Much of Barker's fierce, competitive reputation is based on this epic struggle between the young historian and the popular governor.

An attorney and banker from Temple, James Ferguson had no record of public office before running for governor in 1914. Calling himself a "Hogg Progressive Democrat," Ferguson ran an energetic campaign to improve education and to institute reforms that would help agriculture and the state's rising population of tenant farmers and sharecroppers. He also opposed prohibition. Ferguson's popularity among rural Texans earned him the nickname "Farmer Jim." With his populist-style campaign, Ferguson won more votes than any prior candidate in a Democratic primary election and took office in January 1915. In his first term as governor, he persuaded the legislature to increase funding for public schools, require compulsory attendance, and enact a number of other reforms to expand the woefully inadequate services provided by the state of Texas. Notably, he also encouraged more funding for the University of Texas.[18]

Ferguson's controversy with the University of Texas began in the spring of 1915 when he questioned acting president William J. Battle over the university's annual budget. The governor also demanded that President Battle dismiss six faculty members. A year later, when the university regents named Austin Presbyterian Theological Seminary president Robert A. Vinson as the new University of Texas president, Ferguson objected and renewed his attacks. He insisted at a meeting with President Vinson and regent George W. Littlefield that the six faculty members be fired. "I am the Governor of Texas; I don't have to give reasons," Barker wrote in his account of the confrontation.[19] Ferguson also predicted that they would face "the biggest bear fight that has ever taken place in the history of the State of Texas." The fight ensued the following year when, following the legislative appropriation of 1917, Governor Ferguson vetoed the biannual funding for the university. In his veto message to the university regents, he stated, "If the University cannot be maintained as a democratic University, then we ought to have no University." As he later told the *Dallas Morning News*, "I do not care a damn what becomes of the University. The bats and owls can roost in it for all I care."[20]

While the fight between the governor and the university smoldered, Barker tangled with Governor Ferguson over an appointment to a position that most would assume would be uncontroversial: that of the state librarian. Ferguson wanted to replace state librarian E. W. Winkler with A. F. Cunningham, a devoted political supporter and Presbyterian minister. Winkler and Barker were classmates and friends at the University of Texas during the 1890s, and Barker considered Winkler a colleague. But Barker saw this as a more significant event than protecting one of his associates. At the time of the controversy, Barker, in his role as chairman of the history department, served on the board of the State Library and Historical Commission, which administered the state agency and selected the state librarian. Barker objected to "putting an inexperienced man in charge" and sent a letter to Cunningham that challenged his credentials. Barker also sent a carbon copy of the letter to Governor Ferguson. The governor quickly responded. He told Barker that the letter was "an insult to him [Cunningham] and me both." Governor Ferguson then stated, "As you have entered into a long discussion of politics in the letter, I hope that you will not hereafter complain if your wishes are not carried out." Barker undoubtedly realized that he had crossed his own Texas-style Rubicon and that he too was now in the governor's sights.[21]

When the board of the State Library and Historical Commission met in Austin on February 20, 1915, its members debated the appointment of Winkler and Cunningham for state librarian. The board deadlocked over the decision. When it reconvened on March 3, Governor Ferguson restated his position to the other board members, and they elected Cunningham. Barker resigned his board position in protest. Barker wrote to his friend Thomas M. Marshall describing the proceedings and the outcome, declaring Governor Ferguson "as devoid of general education as he is of any historical appreciation." He closed the account by stating that "the man is more than usually ignorant and self satisfied, but since the Governor had the appointment of three members of a board of five, the man was elected."[22]

As the battle between the university and the governor escalated, Barker became more involved with the university's administration and the Ex-Students Association in challenging Ferguson's accusations. The state's newspapers carried stories of the fighting in the trenches in Europe alongside accounts of the battles between the university and Governor Ferguson. Barker consulted with President Vinson during the appropriations battle and the governor's veto. Following the veto, Ferguson embarked on a statewide tour to defend his actions and continue his attacks on the university. Barker included the governor's statements in his chronology of Ferguson's attacks on the university. Between June 10 and June 18, Ferguson "made an average of three speeches a day in nearly all of which he vilified the 'University crowd.'" In Kerrville on June 10, Ferguson told his audience, many of whom were of German descent: "I have found far more disloyalty in the State University at Austin than among the Germans or the people of any nationality."[23]

In his response, Barker countered that hundreds of university students and former students enlisted in the army, purchased bonds, volunteered for the Red Cross, and allowed for the university's facilities to be used for the war effort. "The University has never to this day attacked the Governor, but has merely tried to defend itself from his vicious attacks upon it," Barker stated. In response to Ferguson's charges of misappropriated funds, professors who seldom taught class, and favoritism for wealthy students over poorer ones, Barker maintained that the governor willfully distorted the truth to impress his audiences. Ferguson had "quite surpassed his own record of vituperation, misrepresentation and libel of University, faculty, students and ex-students," Barker concluded in his review.[24]

The controversy between Ferguson and the university ultimately led to the governor's impeachment and conviction by the Texas Legislature. Although the legislature removed Ferguson for charges relating to his personal finances and refusal to disclose information, his conviction can be traced to his battle over issues involving the University of Texas. The episode undoubtedly left a profound mark on the young Barker. Only a few years into his term as history department chair, the Ferguson drama provided a clear illustration of the impact of politics on the state university and on Barker as an academic. Barker understood that a charismatic political leader could deliver a definitive strike to higher education. For those academics like Barker who chose to enter the political fray, not every outcome could be as easily analyzed or debated. Barker also discovered that the public spotlight would not always be favorable for professional academics or their institution. The episode also left him distrustful of elected officials whom Barker deemed unfit for public office or who disagreed with his vision of American society.

After the fray with Governor Ferguson, Barker returned to his professional career. The publication of *The Life of Stephen F. Austin* in 1925 brought much academic recognition for Barker.[25] The author spent years poring over the Austin Papers as the basis for his biography on Austin, known as "the Father of Texas." The Austin Papers, housed at the university since 1901, contained Austin family documents, official records, correspondence, and writings. As Barker noted, "In their entirety the Austin Papers are an absorbing human document, reflecting the life of the Austin family . . . and illuminating the social and economic history—and to some extent the political history—of the American frontier from 1789 to 1836."[26] Barker proclaimed Austin one of the "great figures of American history." "He was an unobtrusive, unassuming man, and both inclination and circumstances required him to do his work without the blare of trumpets," Barker stated in the preface to his work.[27] Barker's work on Austin became the standard not just for scholarship on the Texas pioneer himself, but also for others who followed Barker's method of constructing history as "factual and direct rather than interpretive." Subsequent printings of the work over the years established Barker as the premier biographer of Austin and early Texas history. As one historian in the next generation stated, "No other book has had as much influence on Texas historiography, and few have directed contemporary thinking about the American frontier movement to such a wide extent."[28]

Following its publication and for many years thereafter, Barker's biography of Austin stood at the epicenter of Texas history. Nearly all of Barker's peers commended his efforts with the highest praise: his book was called "the finest biography in Texas literature" and "essential to the story of American settlement; not only a biography but a history of the era." These were typical of the near unanimous accolades Barker received. Only Walter Prescott Webb, in an otherwise complimentary review, offered a dissenting view, with regard to the problem of objectivity. "Sometimes Barker fails to be objective in his support of

Austin; at other times, he tries so hard to be objective that he fails to give Austin his due," Webb noted. But even this criticism failed to dampen the enthusiasm for the Austin story.[29]

Nearly seventy-five years passed before another scholarly biography appeared on Austin, Gregg Cantrell's *Stephen F. Austin, Empresario of Texas* in 1999. Cantrell acknowledged the challenge of confronting both Austin and Barker and remarked that Barker's study of Austin "was a model of scholarly research in its presentation of the facts of Austin's public career. But in his portrayal of Austin the man, Barker essentially embraced the persona that Austin himself carefully constructed." The author concluded that Barker's Austin was "a sort of cardboard cutout, without a real life or personality of his own." The complexity of Austin's background in the context of the chaotic period in which he moved to Texas remains subdued in Barker's study of Austin. Cantrell's Austin embodied the "conflicts and contradictions of his day."[30] And perhaps Barker may have assigned some of his own character to his portrayal of Austin.

One of the more remarkable and controversial aspects of Barker's long career came from his association with J. Evetts Haley. In 1929 Barker appointed the young Haley to conduct a survey of Texas history and acquire collections for the university. Haley had studied history under Barker and received his master's of arts degree from the university. He had experience roaming the Texas Panhandle in a Model T Ford where he had collected everything from "grandpa's old branding iron to two-headed calves."[31] Once in the employ of Barker and the university, Haley brought in a treasure trove of historical records and artifacts from the state's back roads, offices, and homes. Among the collections were records from the cattle industry, railroads, county courthouses, farmers, soldiers, Texas Rangers, doctors, land speculators, and more. One collection came from James Harper Starr, a prominent West Texas physician and businessman. The massive Starr collection contained many original documents from early Texas, including the only extant portion of the diary of William B. Travis. Haley later recalled his instructions from Barker: "Here is your file and you go out there and get at it."[32]

With the onset of the Great Depression and the 1932 election of Franklin D. Roosevelt, new government programs opened up opportunities. As part of the New Deal, the Civil Works Administration (CWA) provided funds for a nationwide historical records survey. As part of his job at the university, Haley became director of the Texas Historical Records Survey. In spite of directing a very successful operation funded by the federal government, Haley began to openly criticize the Roosevelt administration. In 1934 he published an article in the *Saturday Evening Post* that blasted the administration's agricultural policies. As time passed, Haley conversed with and wrote to a sympathetic Barker as their antipathy to Roosevelt increased. Haley joined with other FDR critics in Texas to form the Jeffersonian Democrats to oppose Roosevelt's reelection. Barker sympathized with Haley. Following Haley's termination from the university after the 1936 election (which Roosevelt handily won), Barker remained one of Haley's strongest supporters. Haley also befriended conservative Wichita Falls businessman and Jeffersonian Democrats organizer Orville Bullington. A few years later, Bullington would appear as a university regent and play a significant role in the future of both Barker and Haley. Barker arranged for Haley to receive money from the university's Littlefield Fund to write a biography of George Littlefield.[33]

Barker served as mentor to a number of scholars throughout his career. One of his most distinguished former students was Carlos Eduardo Castañeda. Barker served as the young historian's most important professor at the University of Texas. Born in Mexico, Castañeda's family emigrated to Brownsville, Texas, where he graduated from Brownsville High School as valedictorian. Castañeda earned his B.A. (1921) and M.A. (1923) in history under Professor Barker's tutelage. As an undergraduate student, Castañeda provided Barker with assistance in translating Spanish documents that contributed to the professor's future biography on Stephen F. Austin. His Ph.D. dissertation was a critical edition of a long-sought eighteenth-century manuscript by Fray Juan Agustín Morfi that was later published as *History of Texas, 1673–1779*. Once again, Barker provided support and served as the dissertation committee chair. When there was an opening at the university's Genaro García Collection (now known as the Nettie Lee Benson Latin American Collection), Barker and other friends worked behind the scenes to ensure that Castañeda obtained the influential position in 1927. Castañeda later went on to publish a number of influential histories, such as the seven-volume *Our Catholic Heritage in Texas, 1519–1936* and *The Mexican Side of the Texas Revolution*. Castañeda became one of Barker's most highly acclaimed former students for his contributions to scholarship, service to the university, and his groundbreaking publications. As a member of the history department faculty during Barker's years as chair, Castañeda maintained his friendship and academic collaboration with Barker until Barker's final years.[34]

Although Barker could take pride in his many academic achievements, his strong conservative political views combined with his public criticism of the Roosevelt administration would ultimately lead to controversy. The high-profile dispute involved university president Homer Rainey and once again brought widespread news coverage and political fallout. When he took office as president of the University of Texas in 1939, Rainey engaged in a series of confrontations with the board of regents that resulted in his eventual dismissal in 1945. Rainey had taken office as president soon after the election of W. Lee O'Daniel as Texas governor. O'Daniel, a reactionary flour salesman with no experience as an elected public official, won the governor's office based on the popularity of his radio show in the 1930s. Reminiscent of Governor Jim Ferguson twenty years earlier, O'Daniel appointed several conservative political friends to the university's board of regents. O'Daniel's successor, the ultraconservative Coke Stevenson, became governor in 1941 when O'Daniel won a controversial special election to the U.S. Senate. Governor Stevenson followed a similar trend of regent selections based on political philosophy and a willingness to support the governor's agenda. As the nation's attention focused on the battlefields in Europe and the Pacific during World War II, the political battles in Texas created a firestorm at home. The university's internal divisions reflected the broader domestic schism in state and national politics that involved the role of government, the purpose of public education, academic freedom, and social issues surrounding race and economic opportunity.

The incidents that precipitated the clash between President Rainey and the regents began with attempts to remove professors in the economics department because of their teachings and, by extension, their political affiliations. A dispute also arose over the appointment of Dr. John W. Spies as dean of the medical school in Galveston. The increasing number of disagreements between President Rainey and the university faculty on one side versus members of the board of regents on the other received extensive coverage in the state's daily newspapers. Following these events, a major controversy erupted over the inclusion of John Dos Passos's *The Big Money*, a publication in the author's *U.S.A.* series, as a required text in English 312Q. While academic issues remained the center of attention, the underlying issue was unhappiness with the direction of the Roosevelt administration. The more conservative regents opposed New Deal legislation that they felt favored labor and minorities and created larger federal programs. The regents believed most faculty members at the university supported FDR and the New Deal. With Judge John H. Bickett serving as chair, the regents called a special meeting on the university campus to investigate the origins of the assignment of the Dos Passos text. The regents subsequently announced that *The Big Money* would be removed from the reading list over Rainey's opposition. Naturally the censuring of the book created an immediate demand for it as students surged to local bookstores to acquire the controversial text.[35]

Barker initially sided with the majority of the university faculty in support of Rainey. Rainey and Barker were friends and often played golf together. Barker offered resolutions of support on behalf of President Rainey for consideration by the university faculty. Given his opposition to Governor Ferguson and the regents in his early career, Barker undoubtedly understood how political entanglements could involve the university, an unfriendly governor, and an unsympathetic majority on the board of regents. However, by 1943, Barker also understood that the rift between Rainey and the regents had reached a point where it could have an impact on the future of the president and the university. Barker wrote, "There is a total lack of mutual confidence between the Board and the President."[36]

The final confrontation between the board of regents and President Rainey took place at the November 1 meeting. The board announced that Rainey had failed to abide by the regents' policies and directives, and issued a statement that he was fired. At a tumultuous meeting of the university faculty a few days later, Barker, who had defended Rainey until the very day he was dismissed, reversed course. He refused to vote with the faculty majority in a strongly worded condemnation of the regents. Barker also lost a substitute motion that would have recommended a reappointment of the former president. With these actions, Barker drove a wedge between himself and the majority of the faculty on this crucial issue. He alienated many friends in the history department, including Walter Prescott Webb, his former student and colleague in many historical initiatives. At a January 1945 meeting of the faculty, Barker opposed another resolution supporting Rainey, stating that he did not believe that "Dr. Rainey's return to the presidency would benefit the university." Barker reconfirmed his support of the regents' decision.[37]

While his years of battles within the university undoubtedly took their toll on Barker, he remained very conservative in his approach to politics and national affairs. In doing so, he often took a narrow, undisciplined view, especially when contrasted with his attitude to historical research. The careful, studied analysis that Barker relied on in his historical research was not always of value in a rapidly changing and often unpredictable contemporary political scrap. Barker also demonstrated a tendency to isolate himself from his friends and colleagues during critical stages of a controversy. His dogmatic approach would embroil him in difficulties throughout his final years at the university.

Late in his career, the University of Texas named its collections on Texas and the American Southwest for Barker. The Eugene C. Barker Texas History Center was officially dedicated in 1951.[38] Once again, the influence of the regents came into play with the creation of the new Barker Center. Barker also utilized his old friend J. Evetts Haley and his support from the regents after the Rainey affair to overcome opposition within the university administration and faculty. Regent Orville Bullington urged that the new history center be located in the Old Library Building, the home of the fine arts department. Bullington, at the urging of Barker's protégé Haley, moved the proposal through the board of regents. Bullington told President Theophilus Painter, the successor to the deposed Rainey, to oust the fine arts department from the Old Library Building.

Should the "dirt and paint dobbers" wish to study art, they should go "to a girls school, or to Paris or some other 'furrin' seaport."[39]

Barker became a professor emeritus of history in 1950. For the remaining six years of his life he maintained an office in the Barker Texas History Center. He donated all of his papers to the center, where they remain today. The Eugene C. Barker Collection remains in, and has expanded in, the newly named Dolph Briscoe Center for American History, the successor to the Barker Texas History Center. At the age of eighty-two, Barker passed away on October 22, 1956, ending a sixty-one-year association with the University of Texas.

William C. Pool, one of Barker's former students, authored the first and only biography of his mentor in 1971. Pool described Barker's role in contributing to the growth of the University of Texas as a "university of the first class." Barker was a "fine scholar, an excellent classroom teacher, a humble citizen of the University community, and a faculty power who stood for honesty and integrity above all else."[40] In his assessment of Barker's historical contributions, Pool believed that Barker utilized his professional, objective approach in the study of Texas and Mexico. "Barker approached his investigations without prejudice; he collected all the evidence available; and he formed his deductions and conclusions with a critical mind," Pool wrote. "He was intellectually honest and tolerant on matters and concerns where Texans often find objectivity rather difficult."[41] Pool and many other later historians still commend Barker's attention to detail, his ability to view complex issues from different perspectives, and his attempts to avoid the racial stereotypes that were commonplace in his era. Nevertheless, the depth of his scholarship and the strength of his interpretations made future historians reluctant to explore and evaluate his findings. As Walter Buenger and Robert Calvert concluded in their 1991 essay, the influence of Barker and other earlier historians resulted in the "arrested development" of Texas history. Contemporary historians had to challenge "the old ideas and the old purveyors."[42] Only within the past two decades has new scholarship emerged on Stephen F. Austin and the Texas-Mexico relationship during the 1820s and 1830s.

Barker stands as one of the giants and leading scholars of Texas history during the first half of the twentieth century who served as a mentor to subsequent generations of historians. He left a great legacy. His years of exhaustive research produced influential publications and articles that broke new ground in historical interpretations. He played a significant yet oftentimes controversial role at the University of Texas, at the Texas State Historical Association, in Texas politics, and in his related professional initiatives. He set the stage for the acquisition of significant historical collections that continue to serve as the basis for research for scholars of history. Notably, Barker served as a pioneer in recognizing the necessity of obtaining support from wealthy individuals, who could provide the funds that would always be in short supply from publicly funded sources. These personal initiatives increased the university's stature and collections as they enhanced Barker's own reputation.

Barker encouraged and inspired a generation of historians. Yet he often frustrated and alienated his colleagues and friends with his public stands, his controversial opinions, and his dogmatic approach. Just as he opened new areas of research on Spanish and Mexican Texans and on African Americans and slavery, he remained doggedly conservative and rigid in his political and social views. As stated in his eulogy, Barker could be both virtuous and ferocious. More than fifty years after his death, Barker's historical star may be fading, but his influence still shines. Even with his shortcomings and his temperamental personality, Barker is recognized to this day for his scholarship, his efforts to expand the role of the University of Texas and public higher education, and his vision in the field of American history.

SUGGESTED READING

Barker, Eugene C. *Ferguson's War on the University of Texas: A Chronological Outline*. Austin: Ex-Students Association of the University of Texas, 1917.

The earliest example of Barker's historical and political insights on a controversial topic.

Barker, Eugene C. *The Life of Stephen F. Austin*. Nashville, TN: Cokesbury Press, 1925.

The highly acclaimed and precedent-setting biography that stood as the model for historians and biographers of the era until modern times.

Barker, Eugene C. *Mexico and Texas, 1821–1835: University of Texas Research Lectures on the Causes of the Texas Revolution*. Dallas: P. L. Turner, 1928.

As one of the first Texas historians to attempt to examine the causes of the 1836 Texas Revolution respecting both opinions and positions within Texas, Mexico, and the United States, Barker published this series of his lectures on the controversial topic. While the lectures represented a major step forward in examining the root causes and issues of the war, they also reflect the language and sentiment of this era along with the cultural differences of the major protagonists.

Barker, Eugene C., ed. *The Austin Papers*. 3 vols. Washington, DC: U.S. Government Printing Office, 1924–1928.

As an essential source to scholars on Austin, the Austin Papers offer insight into Stephen F. Austin's contemporaries, life, and conflicts, as well as business and government in the early nineteenth century. The Austin Papers are located at the Dolph Briscoe Center for American History, University of Texas at Austin.

Barker, Eugene C., and Amelia W. Williams, eds. *The Writings of Sam Houston, 1813–1863*. 8 vols. Austin: University of Texas Press, 1938–1943.

PATRICK L. COX

An extensive compilation of Houston's public and private papers that covers his entire career as an attorney, military figure, and political leader. Barker provided introductions and oversight of the editing and commentary.

NOTES

1. *Austin American Statesman*, October 23, 1956, *Dallas Morning News*, October 23, 1956; clippings in the Eugene C. Barker Vertical File, Dolph Briscoe Center for American History, University of Texas at Austin.

2. William C. Pool, *Eugene C. Barker, Historian* (Austin: University of Texas Press, 1971), 19–21. Pool was a student of Barker's at the University of Texas, where he obtained his undergraduate and graduate degrees. Barker served as his graduate advisor. Pool remained a friend of Barker's after he went on to his own career as a historian at Southwest Texas State University (now Texas State University).

3. Ibid., 21–22.

4. Eugene C. Barker, "Lester Gladstone Bugbee, Teacher and Historian," *Southwestern Historical Quarterly*, 49 (July 1945): 1; and *Lester Gladstone Bugbee, A Memorial* (Austin: Texas State Historical Association, 1945), 1, 20, 24.

5. Margaret C. Berry, "George Pierce Garrison," in *The New Handbook of Texas*, edited by Ron Tyler (Austin: Texas State Historical Association, 1996), 3:201.

6. James Sutton Payne, "Texas Historiography in the Twentieth Century: A Study of Eugene C. Barker, Charles W. Ramsdell, and Walter P. Webb" (Ph.D. diss., University of Denver, August 1972), 102–106.

7. Don E. Carleton and Katherine J. Adams, "'A Work Peculiarly Our Own': Origins of the Barker Texas History Center, 1883–1950," *Southwestern Historical Quarterly* 86, no. 2 (October 1982): 209; Eugene C. Barker to George W. Littlefield, December 5, 1912, Barker Papers, as quoted in J. Evetts Haley, *George W. Littlefield, Texan* (Norman: University of Oklahoma Press, 1943), 219–220.

8. Haley, *Littlefield*, 210–211.

9. Pool, *Barker*, 45.

10. Ibid., 93–96.

11. Charles W. Ramsdell, "Barker as a Historian," April 30, 1926, text of speech, Barker Vertical File, Briscoe Center.

12. Ibid.

13. Richard B. McCaslin, *At the Heart of Texas: One Hundred Years of the Texas State Historical Association, 1897–1997* (Austin: Texas State Historical Association, 2007), 53–57.

14. Ibid., 58. As McCaslin points out, initial fears that the journal's name change would drive away diehard Texans proved unfounded.

15. Randolph B. Campbell, *Gone to Texas: A History of the Lone Star State* (New York: Oxford University Press, 2003), 341–342.

16. McCaslin, *Heart of Texas*, 64–65.

17. Ibid., 65–67.

18. Campbell, *Gone to Texas*, 348–351. George Taylor Winston, president of the University of Texas from 1896 through 1899, resigned following confrontations with the faculty, students, and the Texas Legislature. Barker was a student during Winston's presidency and received his B.A. in history in 1899, the year that Winston resigned.

19. Eugene C. Barker, *Ferguson's War on the University of Texas: A Chronological Outline*

(Austin: Ex-Students Association of the University of Texas, 1917), 7. Barker's pamphlet consisted of a lengthy statement of events that transpired prior to Ferguson's impeachment and removal from office. The Ex-Students Association printed the tract in time for it to be placed on the desks of legislators who had been called into session for the governor's impeachment and trial.

20. Campbell, *Gone to Texas*, 351.

21. Eugene C. Barker to A. F. Cunningham, February 19, 1915, and James E. Ferguson to Eugene C. Barker, February 20, 1915, Barker Papers, 3G 208, Classified Correspondence, 1908–1916, Briscoe Center. The letters and the account are quoted in Pool, *Barker*, 72.

22. Eugene C. Barker to Thomas M. Marshall, March 4, 1915, Barker Papers, 3G 209, Classified Correspondence, 1908–1916, Briscoe Center. The account and the letter are quoted in Pool, *Barker*, 73.

23. Barker, *Ferguson's War*, 34–35.

24. Ibid., 39.

25. Eugene C. Barker, *The Life of Stephen F. Austin* (Nashville, TN: Cokesbury Press, 1925). The highly acclaimed biography sold relatively few copies in its initial offering due to the publisher's limited interest in and pricing of the biography. In his commentary on the biography, John H. Jenkins noted that while dozens of biographies were published on Sam Houston by the 1980s, Barker's biography on Austin stood alone, as no other historian had undertaken a revised study.

26. John H. Jenkins, "Stephen F. Austin, The Austin Papers," in *Basic Texas Books: An Annotated Bibliography of Selected Works for a Research Library*, by John H. Jenkins (Austin: Texas State Historical Association, 1983), 7–9.

27. Barker, *Stephen F. Austin*, v.

28. Seymour V. Connor, introduction to *The Life of Stephen F. Austin*, by Eugene C. Barker (1925; repr., New York: Da Capo Press, 1968), viii.

29. Jenkins, *Basic Texas Books*, 14–16. Jenkins compiled a number of initial historical reviews and commentaries to Barker's biography of Austin.

30. Gregg Cantrell, *Stephen F. Austin, Empresario of Texas* (New Haven: Yale University Press, 1999), 2, 11.

31. Don E. Carleton, *Who Shot the Bear? J. Evetts Haley and the Eugene C. Barker Texas History Center* (Austin, TX: Wind River Press, 1984), 6.

32. Ibid., 7; Carleton and Adams, "'A Work Peculiarly Our Own,'" 215.

33. Carleton, *Bear*, 11–13.

34. Félix D. Almaráz Jr., "Carlos Eduardo Castañeda, Mexican-American Historian: The Formative Years, 1896–1927," *Pacific Historical Review* 42 (August 1973), 319–334.

35. Pool, *Barker*, 192–193.

36. Barker to Harbert Davenport, September 7, 1943, Barker Papers, Briscoe Center. Also quoted in Pool, *Barker*, 199.

37. Minutes of the Meeting of the General Faculty of the University of Texas, January 11, 1945, p. 2926, Briscoe Center.

38. Herbert Gambrell, "The Eugene C. Barker Texas History Center," *Southwestern Historical Quarterly* 54 (July 1950): 3–5.

39. Carleton, *Bear*, 20.

40. Pool, *Barker*, 7.

41. Ibid., 159.

42. Walter L. Buenger and Robert A. Calvert, *Texas through Time: Evolving Interpretations* (College Station: Texas A&M University Press, 1991), xxx.

MICHAEL L. COLLINS

WALTER PRESCOTT WEBB

WALTER PRESCOTT WEBB

On a dreary winter day early in 1904, a sandy-haired, fifteen-year-old farm boy hitched up a team of horses to his father's wagon and rode into the hamlet of Ranger, Texas. Along the bumpy trail that traversed the drought-scarred landscape of Eastland County, the youngster passed fields enclosed with barbed wire fences and dotted by windmills that rose above the mesquite-covered prairies. Over dry stream beds and past empty stock tanks he continued, and across the rails of the Texas and Pacific line that carried travelers to remote places he could only dream of. "It was a chance remark of my father's that sent me into the newspaper office that day," the Texan later explained. "He once said that when I grew up he wanted me to be a newspaper editor." The shy but curious and self-assured youth walked through the front door of the editor's office and gazed around the cluttered room; before him sat a graying figure working busily with pencil and notepad. As the boy fixed his attention on a stack of old newspapers and assorted magazines that had been wrapped and shoved into a corner of the shop, the elder gentleman peered up from beneath his visor and asked, in a somewhat brusque manner, what he wanted. "Emboldened by . . . efforts to find reading matter, I screwed up my courage to ask the editor if I might have some of the papers that he did not want," Webb recalled almost forty years later. The thorny and impatient newspaperman agreed, and the boy sifted through the stack, gathering up all the materials that he could carry home.[1]

In the coming days Walter Prescott Webb read and reread every newspaper and each magazine cover to cover. He was especially consumed by several issues of *The Sunny South*, a popular periodical published in Atlanta. Unable to soak up enough of the articles authored by such notables as Joel Chandler Harris (of Uncle Remus fame) and Arthur Conan Doyle, the creator of Sherlock Holmes, he determined to have more.[2]

Webb would never forget the fateful night he approached his mother, asking her for ten cents, the cost of a subscription to *The Sunny South*. The scene remained etched in his mind for decades. "Money was hard to come by," he remembered. Still, without hesitation, Mary Webb walked across the room and rummaged through a sewing box. Turning to her son, she smiled and held out a well-worn dime that had been saved for a special occasion. "I don't know what all that dime bought in its long career," Webb offered, "but I know it never bought more than on this occasion." Four decades later the internationally renowned writer and distinguished historian would muse about this defining moment in his young life: "This was the high point of the dime's career, and as it turned out, in mine."[3]

Webb aspired to become a novelist. He wrote as much in a letter to the editor of the magazine, asking for advice as to how to accomplish his goal. Soon after celebrating his sixteenth birthday in early April, Walter received in the mail an envelope with a Brooklyn return address. The letter marked not only the beginning of an eight-year friendship by correspondence but also the turning point in a life that had known little but the daily drudgery of a West Texas farm. Addressed to "Prescott," the letter began: "I am a reader of the 'Sunny South' and noticed your letter in the 'gossip corner.' I trust you will not get discouraged in your aspirations for higher things. As you know there is no such thing as fail in the lexicon of youth." The writer urged, "Keep your mind fixed on a lofty purpose and your hopes will be realized . . . though it will take time and work." Finally, the correspondent offered to send books and magazines "if you will let me know what you like." The letter was signed, "Yours Truly, William E. Hinds."[4]

Young Webb and Hinds continued to correspond, with Webb being the recipient of not merely encouragement and advice but also books, magazines, and, in the end, even money to help with the young man's expenses during his first two years as a struggling student at the University of Texas at Austin. Webb never met William Ellery Hinds, the Brooklyn toy manufacturer and philanthropist who, for some unknown reason, took such a personal interest in his education and his future. Only in time did he grow to understand how a complete stranger could "bet" on such a "dark horse" as he. And yet the answer to that vexing question was probably there all along, contained in a letter from Hinds dated January 9, 1909. Writing to inquire of the young man's plans to attend college, and what he might do to help him achieve his dreams, Hinds revealed: "The best thing in life is to help someone else. One would count it a great thing [to remember] if they had helped someone . . . that afterwards became famous or great." Then Hinds added, "Perhaps I might say that I helped Prescott Webb when he was a young man . . . and people would look on me as privileged . . . to have had the opportunity."[5]

Webb never forgot the profound influence that Hinds had on his life. When he later learned that Hinds had died in 1912 of diabetes, Webb grieved the loss as if he were mourning a member of his own immediate family. Years later he even expressed that perhaps the greatest regret of his life was not traveling to Brooklyn in 1910 or 1911 to offer in person his heartfelt appreciation for all that the benefactor's moral and monetary support had meant to him. So lasting, in fact, was Hinds's inspiration and Webb's undying gratitude that a half century later the aging professor all but suspended work on other scholarly pursuits and projects to conduct a determined quest to learn more about the benevolent gentleman from Brooklyn. His investigations resulted in the publication of an article in *Harper's* titled "The Search for William E. Hinds." Webb would describe the essay as "the most effective piece of writing I have ever done." Apparently thousands of readers agreed, as praise for what one contemporary called a "magnificent" and "beautifully written" essay poured in from around the United States and Great Britain. So popular was the inspiring account of one man's debt to another that *Reader's Digest* also picked up the article so that it might reach a larger audience and move many people to understand that philanthropy was more than only a pastime for the wealthiest in society.[6]

Perhaps longtime University of Texas chancellor Harry Ransom put it best when he observed that Webb's career should be looked upon not as the development of a great historian but as an inspirational "Horatio Alger story." And an unlikely story at that. Born on April 3, 1888, in rural Panola County, deep in the well-watered Piney Woods of East Texas, to Casner and Mary Elizabeth Webb, Walter moved with his family west of the ninety-eighth meridian to Stephens County in 1892. "I consider this move to West Texas the most important event in my life," Webb later wrote, "because it enabled me to grow up on the edge of the Great Plains . . . and gave me an understanding of the country as set forth in my book, *The Great Plains*." During the next decade the Webbs moved from one homestead to another, living as tenant farmers, working somebody else's land for somebody else's profit. While Casner supplemented the family's meager income by teaching at a series of rural schools, his only son was thus forced to assume more of the responsibilities expected of a family provider. In such a harsh and unforgiving land, young Walter therefore learned more about farming the dry, marginal lands of West Texas than he ever cared to know. "I am afraid I did not stick to it too well," he later confessed, admitting that he instead preferred the fun of hunting rabbits with his dog Bounce. Still, his childhood passed all too quickly as he experienced the daily monotony and drudgery of routine chores: watering and feeding stock, tending to the garden and peach orchard, gathering pecans, plowing and planting, and picking cotton in the fields. As Webb summarized his early years spent scratching out a hardscrabble existence from the marginal lands that lay beyond the Cross Timbers, "I never appreciated the nobility of farming. All I ever got out of it was sore fingers."[7]

Little wonder that Walter turned to reading, sometimes late into the night by the light of a coal oil lamp. He seemed to have inherited his father's innate curiosity and his love for learning. Whether the occasional copy of *Harper's* that his father carried home from trips to Ranger, Cisco, or Breckinridge, or his first bound volume, an adventure story about African explorer Henry Morton Stanley, Walter frequently longed to escape the hard realities of farm life by letting his imagination carry him into unknown worlds he discovered in books. "It was this insatiable desire to read and write that shaped the whole course of my life," he later reflected.[8]

Much like the pioneering people he later studied and wrote about, Webb was largely a product of his environment. He never forgot where he came from, and for all his days the scenes and sounds of his boyhood remained a part of him and his life's work. He lived through the Panic of 1893, and the ensuing drought years of 1896 and 1898. He witnessed one of the last long drives of cattle to the open ranges of Indian Territory. He observed men on horseback with Colt revolvers holstered, hanging from their hips. So it was not surprising that, when asked years later when he began researching *The Great Plains*, he answered with both sarcasm and sincerity: "When I was four years old."[9]

In 1898 Casner Webb moved his family from the wilds of Stephens County to the unsettled prairies of neighboring Eastland County. For the next seven years Webb attended a succession of rural schools, all the while reading and studying his favorite subjects, literature and geography. But perhaps the labors of farm life did more than anything else to convince him that his future lay in teaching rather than working the soil.

Not until 1907 did Webb decide to follow his father's path and sit for his second-grade teacher's certification exam. For the next two years he taught at five country schools, teaching children—some of them without shoes—to read and write and to dream of the greater world that awaited them beyond the grinding poverty of rural West Texas. Perhaps in the eyes of each of the children who walked into his classroom he saw something of himself. Saving his money, hoping for an opportunity to improve his lot, he moved from one temporary appointment to another. Then came another letter from William E. Hinds and the offer of assistance to pursue a college education.[10]

In September 1909 Webb struck off for the University of Texas. As he later admitted, when he stepped down from a Texas and Pacific coach early one morning and gazed out at Austin's lights, he realized that he had "made a new start, slightly below the bottom." From the first day he set foot on the campus in Austin, he was completely unprepared for the academic rigors of a university. "My first two years . . . were practically wasted," he later confessed. He first made the mistake of believing that, by taking English courses, he would learn how to write. "My sins of omission had finally caught up with me," he explained, "for I had never learned to punctuate. I have [since] found that if you can write, and you have something to say, punctuation can be provided." Admitting that he was a "persistent cuss, as well as ignorant," he enrolled in every writing course in the schedule, even a graduate seminar. "By the end I was so word conscious, so comma blind, and so sentence-structure minded that I could not write a paragraph. I not only gave up writing, but I . . . resolved not to attempt it again." To make matters worse, during his sophomore year he allowed himself to become distracted by campus social life, and his grades suffered for it.[11]

Only in his third year did he begin to find himself. He did so by signing up for the first course that truly stimulated his mind. No member of the university faculty had a greater influence on young Webb than the unconventional and even controversial professor of "institutional history" and economics, the Canadian-born, European-educated Lindley Miller Keasbey. A graduate of both Harvard and Columbia who counted among his friends the newly elected governor of New Jersey and former president of Princeton University, Thomas Woodrow

Wilson, Keasbey openly espoused socialism, his known leftist political views no doubt having led to his recent dismissal from Bryn Mawr College. But an impressionable young Webb admired Keasbey, both for his passion and the intellectual daring he exhibited. Lecturing in the new law auditorium, the largest classroom on campus, which was always filled to capacity for his classes, Keasbey challenged his students to think in the broadest of terms, and he led them to understand the importance of environmental factors upon the evolution of human institutions and ideas. "I had learned before," Webb recalled, "but now I began to think and I learned, I hope, how to think."[12]

Nothing suggests that Webb developed so much as a personal acquaintance with Keasbey, or that the eccentric yet popular professor expressed a personal interest in Webb's academic development. Nevertheless, Webb remembered always how in each lecture the brilliant and charismatic Keasbey "seemed to fit all knowledge into a single rational scheme . . . [one which students] never could find . . . in any textbook." In sum, Webb saw in Keasbey a role model, a bold, restless intellectual who stood out, above all else, as an original thinker.[13]

If Webb's boyhood and adolescence had been the story of a young man dreaming of escaping farm life and becoming a writer, perhaps one word best described his formative years between 1909 and 1918: conflicted. Drifting from one interest to another, torn between his desire to become a teacher, his ambition to write, and the necessity of making a living, he meandered through his studies. In short, he struggled to find himself.

After Webb earned the baccalaureate degree in 1913, a succession of teaching jobs presented themselves: first, at Beeville High School, then at Texas State Teachers College in San Marcos in 1914, followed by a year at Cuero High School in 1915 (he also served there as principal), and finally at Old Main High School in San Antonio the following year. Even if he failed to find himself professionally during this time, he did manage to discover the love of his life—Jane Elizabeth Oliphant. More than a year after first meeting and then courting "Janie," the daughter of his former neighbor in Austin, Walter proposed marriage. They were wed at her parent's home at 1716 Lavaca Street on September 16, 1916.[14]

After a brief honeymoon at the St. Anthony Hotel in San Antonio, Walter looked forward to his new life with Janie and, at last, to forsaking the nomadic existence that had marked his young life. With a bride to provide for now, and the happy prospect of soon raising a family, Webb resigned his position at Old Main High and went to work as a bookkeeper for a San Antonio optician. So certain was he that his frustrations with low teacher salaries and overly intrusive school administrators had convinced him never again to consider a career in education that he sold his entire library and vowed never to look back. Approaching the age of thirty, with a stable job, a steady salary adequate for a young family, and the prospect of a lucrative new career, he believed that he had finally settled down.[15]

But 1918 brought more unanticipated changes for Webb—changes that occurred either by fate or by chance. He was never sure which was the case. Just five months after going to work for the optical business, while considering the study of optometry himself, he learned that Janie was carrying their first child. Looking for guidance in a most unlikely place, Webb visited a local medium with a reputation for prophecy. A frail, wizened little German woman, known in South San Antonio as Madame Sckerles, stunned him by revealing—without prompting or prior knowledge—that his wife would give birth to a baby girl, that he should expect no riches from oil, and that she could see him soon surrounded by books.[16]

As it turned out, Mildred Alice Webb was born on July 30 of that year. Webb soon learned too that no oil had yet been discovered on the Webb homeplace near Ranger, despite the fact that gushers were blowing in all across Eastland County. Then the third prediction came to pass as well. The previous year Webb had delivered a presentation at the annual meeting of the Texas State Teachers Association on the teaching of history in high schools. The address could not have been more timely, for in the audience sat Professor Frederic Duncalf, a medieval history specialist from the University of Texas. Apparently, young Webb left such a favorable impression that, when a position opened on the Austin campus for someone to teach a course specifically designed for public school history teachers, Duncalf recommended him. Returning to the University of Texas that fall term, Webb accepted a faculty position at an annual salary of $1,500. Webb thus began what turned out to be a remarkable forty-five-year career at his alma mater.[17]

Following World War I, young Professor Webb emerged as a promising scholar and teacher but a historian still looking for an intellectual identity and a sense of direction, a niche for himself in the department, at the university and more generally in the historical profession. His interests were far-reaching, but he seemed to be adrift, and his work devoid of anything original or significant. "It was about this time that I became reconciled to the fact that I had grown up on the frontier and . . . could not rub off the evidence." Or as one colleague told him, "Webb, you are fundamentally a pioneer . . . and there is nothing you can do about it." A son of West Texas, he fully understood the significance of the reference; pioneers were supposed to venture forth, advance beyond the line of settlement, seek out and explore newer lands, discover uncharted trails and watersheds, and prepare the way for those who would someday follow. "The West had been settled," he wrote in his memoir, "and the only pioneering left was of the intellectual sort, interpreting the land and its people."[18]

It has been said that years of research often lead to a single moment of synthesis, the spontaneous flash of a simple idea. For Webb that moment happened one cold, rainy night in February 1922. While preparing another article for the *Dallas News*, he was reading Emerson Hough's *Way to the West*. A thunderstorm was rumbling through Austin when an idea struck him, as if it were a lightning bolt. "I came upon his statement that the conquest of the West had been effected with [*sic*] four instruments, the horse, the boat, the axe and the long rifle." He reread the paragraph and pondered the passage for a few minutes.[19]

Something important was missing, he thought. Then it happened. At first, what he saw clearly seemed so simple, even too obvious, he feared. Hough's words held true for the moist timberlands east of the Mississippi, "the land of rivers and trees," as Webb termed it, but not for the arid regions of the American West. To understand man's triumph over the dry, inhospitable lands of the trans-Mississippi frontier, the scholar had to search for other factors that were unique to the West. Initially, he could argue that the six-shooter, not the long rifle, was peculiarly adapted to warfare on the plains. But what about the axe if there were so few trees, and the boat in a country with so few navigable rivers? Even the horse, so important to frontiersmen in the eastern woodlands, now took on a much greater significance west of the ninety-fourth meridian, he could argue. These questions—and others—must be answered, he resolved.[20]

His ongoing research into the Texas Rangers would have to wait. But earning a doctoral degree could not. After selling to *Scribner's* an article on Samuel Colt's revolver and the famed Texas Rangers, Webb had accumulated $3,000 in savings, enough to support his family while he devoted a year to studying at a northern university. At last he decided to follow Dr. Eugene C. Barker's advice to pursue the Ph.D. degree. In September 1922 he enrolled for doctoral studies at the University of Chicago.

For the thirty-four-year-old Webb, it was the beginning of a long year of disappointment, frustration, and failure. To begin with, he settled his wife and daughter into a small apartment on Kimbark Avenue that proved comfortable enough, but too cramped for a young couple with a small child. Then Webb's mentor, Professor William Dodd, left for Austin as part of a scholar exchange at the end of the fall semester and was thus absent when Walter went before his doctoral committee for his comprehensive oral examination. Having spent years reading and studying history, preparing for written exams, it all came down to less than two hours sitting before the committee, answering questions, or not being able to answer questions, mostly on European history, which was not Webb's primary interest. Webb admittedly froze under the pressure and was informed by his graduate advisor that he had failed. That evening he walked alone along the shores of Lake Michigan and through the snow-choked streets of Chicago, contemplating the shame of his failure and the uncertainty of his future. Years later Webb confided to colleague and protégé Joe B. Frantz that, in a moment of despair, he even contemplated the unthinkable. "As he told me, that evening represented the closest he ever came to killing himself. . . . He couldn't face going home to the department or his family."[21]

Webb remained at the University of Chicago for another semester, but he made no commitment as to when he would again stand for his comprehensive exams. In fact, he never did. Not long after the beginning of the spring term Jane, then Mildred, and finally Walter came down with the flu, an especially virulent strain, leaving them weak, listless, with little energy. As soon as they recovered from their fever and regained strength, Walter put Jane and Mildred on a train to Texas. For the next several months he apparently suffered from loneliness and depression, withdrawing from his professors and fellow students, each trudging day simply going through the motions of applying himself to his studies. "I hated Chicago and the lectures I put down in notes," he later confessed. "My attitude . . . was one of bitterness for my own and their bungling. I took their notes but I would not laugh at their jokes and I would not cultivate an acquaintance." In the end, Webb summarized perhaps his greatest regret about the lost year. "I had had my year of educational outbreeding, though I had not learned anything that I could not have learned in Texas."[22]

That spring of 1923 when Webb returned to sunny Austin, he was back in his element—and back to work collecting evidence to test his thesis on the Great Plains. History department chair Dr. Eugene C. Barker, however, pressed him to continue work on his study of the Texas Rangers. So after purchasing his first automobile, a Model T Ford, with what remained of his savings, Webb determined to put the car to good use. In the summer of 1924 he hit the road, for the first time heading south to the border, then up the Rio Grande to the wilds of the trans-Pecos. Traveling through the Nueces Strip and along the meandering Rio Grande, along dirt roads and through every village and town bordering Mexico, he familiarized himself with the terrain and visited each historic sight of significance, even Ranger camps where he personally observed the apprehension of cattle rustlers and horse thieves. Like a modern-day Herodotus, he traveled to the scenes of events and interviewed Anglos and Tejanos alike, collecting remembrances that provided a vitally important context for his study.[23]

For the next several years he continued to be tugged again toward his study of the Great Plains. Not until 1931 did Webb complete work on what turned out to be, arguably, his greatest contribution to American historical literature. In a brisk, clear, and precise prose written for the general public, not merely for other scholars, the author sought to answer three central questions that had been left unanswered, even by historian Frederick Jackson Turner, architect of the seminal Frontier Hypothesis. Why was the Great Plains the last North American frontier (excluding Alaska) to be settled and conquered? What was the powerful and enduring influence of that conquest of the vast interior prairies of the

United States, for both the land and the people it changed? Was it the harsh and inhospitable conditions of the plains that, alone, halted the advance of the cotton culture of the Old South?[24]

In his introduction to *The Great Plains*, Webb observed, "East of the Mississippi civilization stood on three legs—land, water, and timber; west of the Mississippi not one but two of these legs were withdrawn—water and timber—and civilization was left on one leg—land." Little wonder, he concluded, that west of an identifiable environmental "fault line"—the ninety-eighth meridian—American life was radically different from life back east. "Practically every institution that was carried across it," he stated of the geographic fault line, "was either broken or remade or else greatly altered." Hence, this "line of semi-aridity" (running roughly along longitude 98° west) stood as an institutional fault line as well. Whether the means of travel, the weapons and tools that facilitated settlement, the ways of tilling the soil or tending to livestock, Webb's truth was born of four developments unique to the plains experience—the advent of the Colt revolver, the invention of barbed wire fencing, the development of the windmill, and the practice of dry farming techniques. Simply put, on the mostly flat, arid, treeless plains of the West, American pioneers—waves of them—were compelled by the timeless and impervious forces of nature to adapt, innovate, and invent new ways and institutions.[25]

Curiously enough, Webb prided himself on never having read Frederick Jackson Turner's "The Significance of the Frontier in American History." Yet his conclusions in *The Great Plains* rang familiar to many students of the American West, particularly those disciples of Turner's Frontier Hypothesis. Still, while admitting his discipleship, Webb went beyond Turner in arguing that Turner's thesis had applied only to the frontier east of the Mississippi, not that which lay to the west.

The book was generally well received as a major contribution to the historical literature of the American West. Not everyone, however, hailed the study as bold and groundbreaking. Eminent agricultural historian Fred Shannon reviewed the work critically, going so far as to dismiss it for "poor historical methodology" and an "unscientific" approach. When Webb read Shannon's attack, he supposedly growled, "I never looked on it as history [or science]—I always thought of it as art."[26]

At the insistence of a supportive Dr. Barker, Webb was at last awarded the Ph.D.—by his alma mater—as the graduate committee of the history department agreed that *The Great Plains* was more than sufficient for a doctoral dissertation. Feeling vindicated, Webb then pressed on to complete his history of the Rangers, his goal being to have the publication of the book coincide with the 1936 Texas Centennial celebration. He later recalled his struggle to write the history of the storied frontier institution and the greatest challenge of the project. "The Rangers had a glorious past and had performed enough exploits to fill many volumes." But "the history was episodical [*sic*]," he explained, "so it became a question of finding some thread of unity on which to hang the incidents, and the only one available seemed to be the great leaders, the captains." Tracing the origins and development of the fabled Texas Rangers, from their primitive beginnings to the emergence of a modern law enforcement agency renowned throughout the world, he offered a historian's defense of an agency that again had come under increasing attack by politicians critical of the Rangers' alleged harsh methods. With each chapter and with every subheading, the author wove his narrative around the exploits of a courageous leader who performed extraordinary feats of heroism in the service of Texas and, in so doing, contributed to the growth of a genuine Lone Star legend. John Coffee "Jack" Hays, "El Diablo" to his enemies on the border, who led Texan Rangers into the storms of the War with Mexico; the gallant Samuel H. Walker, the quintessential warrior who designed the .44 Colt revolver that revolutionized plains warfare; Ben McCulloch, famed scout, adventurer, and soldier of fortune; the irrepressible John S. "Rip" Ford, frontiersman, Indian fighter, and defender of the border; Leander H. McNelly, the fearless lawman who swept the most notorious of bad men from the Nueces Strip; and many more: together, these leaders, and those who followed in their tradition, provided Webb with a fabric of stories that could be stitched together into a continuous, dramatic weave of brave deeds and border conflicts. Fittingly, he dedicated the book to William E. Hinds.[27]

In following the trail of the Texas Rangers, Webb admittedly constructed a narrative woven around a single fabric—the heroic deeds of Anglo Texan heroes. In so doing, he failed to acknowledge a more diverse and multicolored weave of Texas history. For Texans of Mexican heritage and their kinsmen south of the Rio Grande recounted a much different story of *Los Rinches,* as Tejanos termed the Rangers. To them the Rangers rode across the pages of their history as mounted demons on horseback who terrorized the Spanish-speaking people of the border and thus earned their bloody epithet *Los Diablos Tejanos,* or Texas Devils. For many years Webb also refused to acknowledge that his history of the Texas Rangers was written with the intent of defending the world-famed law enforcement agency for its past misdeeds. After all, during the final stages of his writing, in what turned out to be largely an apotheosis of the Rangers, some lawmakers of the Lone Star State—particularly from South Texas—were advocating legislation to disband and abolish the fabled state agency. Lastly, in focusing mostly on the "great leaders," he viewed the institution of the Rangers from only the top and thus neglected a more critical view of the rank-and-file volunteers who rode in the service of Texas.

During the Great Depression years Webb, much like his American nation, was undergoing a rapid intellectual ferment. In 1937, in the midst of the Dust

Bowl years, Webb published his third major book in six years, *Divided We Stand: The Crisis of a Frontierless Democracy.* In it, he explored a controversial thesis that had been taking shape in his mind since the Great Crash almost eight years earlier. Simply put, he blamed modern corporations and the predations of capitalism for both sectionalism and the economic subjugation of both the South and the West to the industrial North and East. Then he concluded that only when available lands in the West had receded, and only when the frontier had closed, was the way open for grasping industrialists to control the nation's natural resources and thus restrain if not extinguish traditional economic individualism.[28]

Webb once affirmed that a "compelling idea" should always stand as the "essential ingredient to provide unity and inspiration in historical writing." That being the case, Chapter Six, "The Crisis of a Frontierless Society," provided the germ cell of another major study that Webb was already contemplating. The following year he organized a graduate seminar that he titled "The Great Frontier." But events both at home and abroad soon intervened and resulted in Webb's temporary detour from his next "idea book." Consequently, another fourteen years would pass before the appearance of his last major synthesis.[29]

As war clouds gathered in Europe and the Pacific, Webb understood well that the world he had known was soon to change and that nothing would ever be the same again. Although an ardent supporter of Franklin D. Roosevelt, he also expressed sadness that many of his students, and indeed an entire generation, would be summoned forth to defend the western democracies from the greatest perils that had yet faced modern man. No longer could even a distinguished scholar live out his days in the serene enclave of the Tower of Learning. In August 1942, barely eight months after the United States was awakened from the slumber of isolationism by the Japanese attack on Pearl Harbor, Webb was presented with an opportunity to serve, not in uniform but as an international ambassador of good will. While at his office in Garrison Hall, he received a telegram from the administration of Oxford University, inviting him to accept an appointment as Harmsworth Professor of American History. For a scholar given to the quieter pursuits of teaching and research, the decision proved to be an agonizing one, even though he had served as visiting Harkness Professor of American History at the University of London four years earlier. The difference was that the world was then at peace. Now Hitler's Luftwaffe and V2 rockets screamed over Britain's skies.[30]

By the time he departed for England, Webb had begun dabbling in real estate. He had never understood why some colleagues considered venture capitalism and the practice of entrepreneurial risk-taking beneath their dignity. Now his first major venture proved to be more pleasure than business, indeed nothing less than life changing. Borrowing money from an Austin bank, he purchased some 630 acres of wild lands nestled among the cedar-covered hills of northern Hays County. Situated in the limestone crags some seventeen miles southwest of Austin, the spread provided a perfect retreat, a sanctuary in the woods where he could hide out from the academic community and the celebrity he never really enjoyed. Just as important, the "hole in the mountain," as he sometimes called it, offered a precious tranquility, the perfect scene for reading, thought, study, and writing.[31]

He called his new refuge Friday Mountain Ranch, so named for the most prominent landmark in the area, a one-thousand-foot hill that towered over the rolling hills and meadows below. Soon after acquiring the ranch, Webb began work on restoring an abandoned two-story stone structure that stood like a silent sentry in the mountain's shadow, overlooking the banks of Bear Creek. More importantly, he also threw himself into a daunting task that quickly became a labor of love—restoring the land, healing the depleted soil so scarred by erosion, and returning its carpet of natural wildflowers and native grasses. He tilled the soil, planted seed, fertilized and irrigated the fields. He built barns, strung fences, tended to livestock, and in many ways returned to his own rural roots. During the next decade Webb and his wilderness retreat became one and inseparable. As J. Frank Dobie so aptly put it, the ranch "entered into his bones."[32]

In time the ranch also became the site of regular weekend gatherings of Webb's closest friends: Professor Dobie, known affectionately as "Old Pancho," folklorist Mody Boatright, naturalist Roy Bedichek, humorist and radio personality John Henry Faulk, and editor Frank Wardlaw of the University of Texas Press. The unofficial invitation list usually read like a "who's who" of Austin's intelligentsia. And the evening's fellowship and revelry inevitably included steaks on the grill and a few rounds of choice liquor and lively conversation (Webb was a moderate drinker, unlike several of his regular guests). "The talk was brisk and witty," geologist Glen Evans recalled, "and it seemed to improve steadily as the evening wore on." Students frequently entered the inner sanctum of these gatherings, both for the enlightenment provided by discussions on topics ranging from Plato to the American cowboy, and the entertainment of being regaled by their mentors and other local celebrities, who formed a collection of the greatest storytellers in all of Texas.[33]

Following World War II, Webb persuaded his friend Rodney Kidd to help him establish a boys' summer camp at the ranch, the idea being to introduce Austin-area schoolchildren to the wonders of nature and to foster in them an abiding appreciation for the environment and their own place in it. Moreover, Webb and Kidd agreed that such an experience should inculcate in youths a strong feeling of self-confidence and an enduring sense of independence as well as social responsibility. When it opened in the summer of 1947, accepting boys and girls, the Friday Mountain Ranch Camp became the first of its kind in the state.[34]

If Webb grew more cynical about academic life during his last two decades, a single series of events marked the onset of his contempt for those who would politicize the university. In 1944, months after Webb returned from Oxford, he must have felt as if he had stepped from one war zone into another. The University of Texas Board of Regents fired several economics professors for their public support of FDR's New Deal policies and even attempted to censor written materials favorable to the Roosevelt revolution. When university president Homer P. Rainey openly criticized the board's actions and spoke publicly of the sanctity of academic freedom, the board fired him. Agreeing that a university must always remain a free market of ideas, Webb joined dozens of other university faculty in defending the embattled Rainey. After the regents replaced Rainey that fall with the obsequious and highly ambitious Dr. T. S. Painter, an irate Webb became a reluctant spokesman for those faculty who demanded a vote of no confidence in Painter, who like Webb had served on the presidential search committee and had taken the same oath not to accept the university presidency. As he expressed to friend and colleague Eugene Hollon of the University of Oklahoma, "We here . . . are fighting a battle for a principle which, if preserved, will protect every educational institution in the State, but if destroyed, will unloose the forces that [have already] destroyed . . . the smaller institutions." Believing that he and his colleagues had been betrayed by Painter and the board of regents, Webb spoke for years of his bitter disappointment in the turn of events. The whole sordid affair also marked the beginning of a rift between Webb and his old chairman and mentor, Eugene C. Barker, who sided with the board and Painter during the controversy.[35]

It was almost as if the lingering Rainey affair and the festering anger resulting from it contributed to an intellectual drought in Webb's career. For the most part, Webb ceased to churn out articles for popular periodicals. He had never believed in writing for "scholarly" journals and detested the "highbrow" nature of the academy, which encouraged faculty merely to write for one another rather than reaching out to a broader audience. Other than an article in 1948 titled "How the Republican Party Lost Its Future," little else rolled off his well-worn manual typewriter.[36]

Webb was purportedly once asked by a sanctimonious colleague why he did not publish more. He responded that, unlike some in his profession, he only wrote when he had something important to say. Apparently, by 1952 Webb had something to say, this time vaulting well beyond the borders of Texas history and past the confines of regional or even national development. Not unlike the historians Oswald Spengler and Arnold Toynbee, he would undertake a most ambitious project: a sweeping examination of nothing less than the ferment in world civilizations and the dynamic changes in modern history since 1500. At the very center of the work stood what Webb called the "boom hypothesis," which held that the exploration and subsequent exploitation of the Great Frontier—by the author's definition all the new lands discovered in the age of Columbus—resulted in a 400-year age of unparalleled economic prosperity. The vast new worlds of the Western Hemisphere and Africa eventually succumbed to European proprietorship, and by the time most of these lands were heavily populated, the "boom" came to an end with the end of World War I and the resulting collapse of Old World imperialism. And thus the question, as posed by Webb, remained in the twentieth century: after the close of the "Great Frontier," what next?[37]

Webb held high hopes that *The Great Frontier* would become his most enduring work. He even commented to a friend and protégé that, if the public purchased 40,000 copies, he would at last be able to buy a luxury automobile—maybe a Cadillac or Lincoln—with more options and features than the Plymouths he had owned for years. After reviewers panned his newest book, however, and after sales lagged, falling far short of his expectations, Webb resigned himself to a major disappointment. "It looks like I'll be driving Plymouths for the rest of my life," he groaned.[38]

The year 1953 brought one of the worst droughts ever recorded on the southern plains. For Webb, that natural disaster proved cruelly ironic, yet strangely fortuitous. Already he had begun work on a short monograph that he hoped would be long in its influence on both popular opinion and public policy relating to water resource management in Texas. A mere eighty-two pages, *More Water for Texas: The Problem and the Plan*, published the following year by the University of Texas Press, traced the neglect of the dry, drought-ridden regions that had long suffered from a cyclical decrease in life-giving rainfall. Admittedly, Webb undertook the project to translate from the language of engineers to the vernacular of laypersons a December 1952 congressional report issued by the U.S. Senate titled *Water Supply and the Texas Economy: An Appraisal of the Texas Water Problem.*

Whether Webb produced the book at the behest of a fellow Texan, Senator Lyndon Baines Johnson, remains unclear. What is certain, however, is that Webb's authoritative tome failed in its chief objective: to influence the most critical public debate then before the people of Texas—how to improve the future of the arid and semiarid regions of South and West Texas. Webb proposed a plan to channel the waters of the verdant coastal regions of the lower Brazos and Colorado Rivers to the South Texas Coastal Plain by the construction of a man-made canal, running roughly in a southwesterly direction from Galveston Bay to Laredo. Perhaps Webb prophesied the continual delays, indecision, and final defeat of the idea when he wrote in the introduction of the book: "Unfortunately, a good rain washes away more than a drought. It washes away much of man's interest in providing for the next one, and washes away the support from under those who know another dry cycle is coming and who urge their fellows to make ready for it."[39]

During his last years Webb grew increasingly pessimistic and even fatalistic about the future of the arid regions of the American West. In May 1957 he unleashed some of his most caustic prose in *Harper's*. In "The American West: Perpetual Mirage," Webb divided the center of the North American continent into two categories, Desert States and Desert Rim States. He further explained that one constant, unifying force ran through the history and development of the trans-Mississippi West: the arid or semiarid climates that portended a bleak prospect for future economic and social growth. Again casting off Turner's view of the frontier movement as a process, he focused on the West as a place, a place where the impervious forces of nature—particularly the absence of water—dictated that only limited success awaited those who foolishly and stubbornly challenged what could never be changed, not even with the building of dams, the practice of irrigation and dry farming, and the introduction of new technologies to render the windmill obsolete. In sum, the West would never truly be conquered, at least not from nature's unyielding command.[40]

Webb had never been a stranger to controversy, and he expected a measure of criticism not only from the historical community but also from the public and their elected leaders throughout the West. But what happened next surprised even him. Webb's brutally honest appraisal of the plains states drew a hailstorm of stinging condemnation from public officials (including Arizona congressman Barry Goldwater) and scholars from Texas to the Dakotas.[41]

During the fourth and last decade of his tenure at the University of Texas, Webb enjoyed his status as something of an institutional fixture. The figure of the bald, bespectacled historian, with the trademark Stetson dress hat, signature bow tie, and pinched expression on his face, became one of the most familiar on the forty-acre campus. His bitterness over the turmoil of the tumultuous years of the 1940s seemed to soften, and his disposition appeared to mellow. Even so, his fame and his reputation as a leathery and grouchy old curmudgeon intimidated many students.

But those who came to know him, and truly understand him, saw beneath that gruff exterior a kind and generous man, approachable to anyone. The door to his office was always open to students, new acquaintances, new relationships, and new ideas. No one could have walked into Garrison Hall 102 without being impressed by the disheveled surroundings and scattered possessions of a man whose thoughts and class lectures were so structured. Just outside the door a large stack of books rested, there for any student to take. Inside, visitors would find a snarl of barbed wire that snared many a young man or woman who failed to take stock of its presence (Webb liked to joke about getting his students "wrapped up" in history); an ashtray shaped like a sombrero that emitted the distinct odor of cigarette butts; and strewn files, random piles of manuscript pages stacked along the walls, disorganized shelves of books, and a desk that one student described as a "surrealist's nightmare." All were pieces of a professional career known to many but a private life known only to a few.[42]

Along the way Webb always found time to contribute to his profession in ways that transcended his fame. With the help of friend Cliff Caldwell, then of Breckinridge, he founded the Junior Historians of Texas program through the University Interscholastic League (UIL). He first envisioned the idea of having students in public schools research and write on topics of local history, and he secured funding from Caldwell and others to launch a campaign to inspire young people across the state to help preserve the past of their own communities. He served as director of the Texas State Historical Association from 1939 to 1947. Later he became the driving force behind the most massive state historical project of its kind—the compilation of a multivolume encyclopedic treatment of the Lone Star State, what became *The Handbook of Texas*, first published in 1952. He also helped to establish the William E. Hinds Memorial Scholarship fund at the University of Texas (now the Hinds-Webb fund) to assist students in financial need.[43]

Webb's wry and sometimes irreverent sense of humor grew to legendary proportions. Joe Frantz liked to tell one story to illustrate that point. A "local preacher," known for being lazy and for calling upon university faculty to fill his pulpit from time to time, once asked Webb to speak to his congregation. Webb, who was about as fond of preachers as he was the predators of the legal profession, showed up on the appointed Sunday morning. Following a generous introduction, the historian strolled to the lectern with a mournful expression on his face, then looked out on the crowd and in a toneless voice announced: "I have been asked to talk to you about the cowboy and his religion. He had none." According to Frantz, Webb—without further comment—returned to his seat and sat down. "End of sermon," Frantz added. "He was never invited back."[44]

Webb's wit was often self-effacing. Never one to take himself too seriously, he often recounted the night in 1932 when he received a telephone call from a reporter with the *Austin American-Statesman*, who informed him that he had received the prestigious Loubat Award (given by Yale University) for *The Great Plains*. When asked for a reaction, he responded that he had never heard of the Loubat Award, whereupon the reporter said that, until given this assignment, he had never heard of Walter Prescott Webb or *The Great Plains*.[45]

But in time the world would come to know of Walter Prescott Webb and his works. Webb's singular contributions to the historical profession, and particularly to the study of Texas and the American West, remain unequaled, at least among historians of the Lone Star State. Historian Henry Steele Commager once called *The Great Plains* "the best single-volume contribution to American history" published between 1900 and 1950. A 1950 survey of more than one thousand members of the American Historical Association agreed, identifying *The Great Plains* as the single most significant work in U.S. history written during the first half of the twentieth century. Webb's epic study *The Texas Rangers: A Century of Frontier Defense* still stands as a landmark in the lore and literature of Texas. No matter that revisionist historians have revealed the work to be a largely sanitized history of the Rangers, one that extols the virtues of a handful of brave captains while glossing over the vices of many who served under them. The book ranks, even today, among a precious few that have served to define the Texas of popular imagination.[46]

In 1958 members of the American Historical Association honored Webb by electing him president. It was a fitting final tribute. Webb had always considered himself most fortunate, and he never feared the inevitability of death, at least his own death. But the summer of 1960 brought the most unexpected and devastating blow of his entire life. Following a brief illness, his loving wife Jane, devoted mother of their daughter, died unexpectedly. Reeling from the loss, Webb reluctantly returned to the classroom that fall, but for the next year it seemed that his passion for teaching, and maybe even his love of life, had been extinguished.[47]

The following year, however, all of that changed. Webb once argued that some of the great "dividends" in life came unexpectedly. Recently he had become acquainted with Terrell Maverick, widow of the late congressman and mayor of San Antonio, Maury Maverick. In the summer and autumn, their friendship turned into a romance that became the talk of the campus. While dining with one of his graduate students that summer, Webb asked, "Have you heard anything about me lately?" When the aspiring young historian awkwardly admitted that everyone knew of his secret courtship of the widow Maverick, the aging professor bluntly confessed that he was "in love like a schoolboy." Colleague and friend Joe B. Frantz remembered another occasion that fall, while drinking coffee with his mentor in the student center, when he bluntly inquired of Webb if the rumor were true that he and Terrell "had to get married." Frantz never forgot Webb's leering expression, followed by the broad grin that broke over his friend's wrinkled face. "You son of a bitch," Webb blurted out while fighting back a chuckle. Walter and Terrell married in a private ceremony in Fredericksburg on December 14, 1961.[48]

In the spring of 1962 Webb wrote in his last annual report to the university administration that he was "gathering up the loose ends of a long, exciting, and disorderly life." In May he left for the University of Alaska, where he served a semester as a guest lecturer in western history. As in the past, he still longed to be the frontiersman, to see what lay on the other side of the next mountain and beyond the intellectual horizons of both history and the human imagination. With boyish enthusiasm he wrote in July to his administrative assistant, Eileen Guarano, predicting "a rather exciting year ahead of us."[49]

Returning to his bride and his work, Webb looked forward to new challenges. He was even considering a revised edition of his history of the Texas Rangers. The world and Texas had changed so much during the past three decades, and so had he. He believed that a rewrite of his most popular work should treat Mexican Americans with more objectivity, balance, and sensitivity. Their story should be told, too. But that task would be left to the next generation, and the next.

As the autumn of 1962 drew to a close, and the cold north winds sweeping across Texas promised an early frost, Webb wrote Terrell that his year with her had been one of "unalloyed happiness." He admitted to being "humbled and exalted by the experience" of falling in love again in the winter of his life. With a childish enthusiasm, he confessed too that he remained "filled with amazement that life at this stage could be so new and wonderful."[50]

On February 17, 1963, while in Dallas, Webb visited journalist Lon Tinkle, author of the popular narrative *Thirteen Days to Glory: The Siege of the Alamo*. Tinkle thought that his old friend appeared tired, even fatigued. After a joint book-signing and reception, Webb unburdened himself: "I have no more books in me. At my age you live from day to day."[51]

His comment could not have been more prophetic. Three weeks later Walter and Terrell embarked on another book-signing tour, this time to promote the publication of her diary, *Washington Wife*. Webb had long dreaded such occasions. For one thing, he was naturally shy, and he admittedly never really knew what to say to people who bought his books. But this was *her* journal, even though he had edited the work. He no longer needed recognition and was now pleased to see Terrell at the center of attention, if only for a time. As he had once confided to Roy Bedichek, "I am really tired and long to get away from audiences—never liked them or the experience of amusing them by personal appearance. It ain't my forte." After a joint speaking engagement in Kerrville on a Thursday evening, Walter and Terrell drove to San Antonio the next morning to autograph books at a downtown bookstore. Late that Friday afternoon, March 8, they climbed into their 1962 Plymouth and headed up Interstate Highway 35, with Walter behind the wheel. Terrell later remembered that as they passed through San Marcos she lay her head down in his lap and fell asleep. Minutes later, near the town of Buda, some thirteen miles south of Austin, the car unexplainably veered off the road and rolled several times before coming to rest upside down in a drainage ditch. Webb was thrown from the automobile and probably killed instantly. As Terrell later wrote, "He never knew what hit him. By his own standards it was a good death." Webb was seventy-four years old. Although Terrell sustained serious injuries, including a crushed pelvis, and remained in a coma for several days before regaining consciousness, she survived.[52]

Flags across the University of Texas were lowered to half-mast the following morning—the first time a member of the faculty had been so honored. Webb's funeral was held at Austin's University Methodist Church on March 11. An estimated one thousand mourners came to pay their respects. The crowd included former students, longtime colleagues, personal friends, and admirers who had never even met him. Perhaps it was appropriate that Reverend Edmund Heinsohn, who officiated, offered his favorite Webb story to illustrate the humility of the man he had long known and admired. After all, Heinsohn began, Webb had always loved a good story. And his life was just that. "He said that when he thought of himself as a 'big shot,' all he needed to do to get himself in the right perspective was to go to San Antonio [where he was not as recognized by the public] and stand on the street corner at the Gunter Hotel and ask himself how many of the passing crowd had ever even heard of Walter Prescott Webb," much less the books he had written. Or how many "knew much of the University of Texas and had any interest in it."[53]

Fittingly, following the service Webb was interred in the Texas State Cemetery, near rows of Civil War heroes, not far from a pantheon of Texas governors, and in the company of a handful of Ranger icons he had helped to immortalize. His final resting place would be an honored one, in the shadow of the burial site of no less than the "Father of Texas," Stephen F. Austin.

One contemporary called Webb the "Texan's Texan." Another remembered him for his originality and compared him to Will Rogers, arguing that he became the favorite son of his home state and that, while imitators would soon appear, future generations would not see his like again. His friend J. Frank Dobie eulogized him with a simple observation befitting a historian and writer of international stature: "Most historians deal with the past as the past. Webb dealt with it as a guide to the future." Above all else, Webb epitomized Emerson's definition of the scholar—"Man thinking."[54]

Dobie recalled in a published memorial soon thereafter that Webb was "the most powerful thinker I have ever known." Others were quick to agree. Even a quarter of a century later, many of Webb's former students and protégés were still eager to weigh in for a special 1988 edition of the *Southwestern Historical Quarterly*, recalling their remembrances of the friend and mentor who had so profoundly influenced their lives. Running through their recollections, two aspects of Webb stood out: his brilliant mind, never at rest, and his compelling humanity.[55]

Webb wrote that over the years he had often reflected on how he could somehow repay William E. Hinds for his kindness and largesse. In preparing the 1961 article on Hinds he recalled the words of the man he never met and yet who was his benefactor: "You cannot do anything for me, but as I help you now, perhaps in time you can help someone else." Indeed, Webb's most important legacy remains not the shelf of books and articles he authored, or the awards he won, or the offices he held, but rather the students he taught, helped, and even inspired by his example. Walter Prescott Webb would have wanted no greater monument than that.[56]

SUGGESTED READING

Webb, Walter Prescott. "The American West: Perpetual Mirage." *Harper's* 214 (May 1957): 25–31.

Pessimistic about the future of the plains states and the arid Southwest, this article stirred much controversy and brought criticism to Webb.

Webb, Walter Prescott. *The Great Frontier*. Boston: Houghton Mifflin, 1952; reprint, Lincoln: University of Nebraska Press, 1986.

This work, Webb's "big idea" book, as he termed it, was the result of a synthesis of ideas that emerged from his long-standing graduate seminar by that title.

Webb, Walter Prescott. *The Great Plains*. Boston: Ginn, 1931.

Obviously this synthesis of Webb's thinking is acknowledged to be a classic, his greatest contribution as a writer and historian of Texas and the American West.

Webb, Walter Prescott. *History as High Adventure*. Austin: Pemberton Press, 1969.

A crowded volume containing addresses, speeches, and essays on Webb's philosophy of history and the meaning, relevance, and use (and misuse) of history. The title comes from his 1958 presidential address to the American Historical Association.

Webb, Walter Prescott. *More Water for Texas: The Problem and the Plan*. Austin: University of Texas Press, 1954.

Webb's appeal to his fellow Texans to grapple with the greatest problem the state was facing, and would face for generations to come, he believed—water resource management.

Webb, Walter Prescott. "The Search for William E. Hinds." *Harper's* 223, July 1961, 62–68.

Later reprinted in *Reader's Digest*, this article reveals Webb's lifelong quest to find out what happened to the man who was his benefactor a half century earlier. Poignant and revealing, Webb opens his soul in this one.

Webb, Walter Prescott. *The Texas Rangers: A Century of Frontier Defense*. Boston: Houghton Mifflin, 1935; reprint, Austin: University of Texas Press, 1965.

Webb's classic work on the institution of the Texas Rangers. He is probably most remembered by the general public for this narrative, which launched the popular idealization of the iconic frontier institution.

MICHAEL L. COLLINS

Webb, Walter Prescott. "Walter Prescott Webb" and "The Texan's Story." Typescripts, Walter Prescott Webb Papers, Dolph Briscoe Center for American History, University of Texas at Austin.

These manuscripts constitute Webb's own unfinished memoir, written during World War II while in England. Important for the candor and insight they offer.

NOTES

1. Walter Prescott Webb, "Walter Prescott Webb," typescript, 4, Walter Prescott Webb Papers, Box 2M 245, Dolph Briscoe Center for American History, University of Texas at Austin (hereafter Webb Papers); Walter Prescott Webb, "The Texan's Story," typescript, Box 2M 245, 69. Additional papers, albeit a smaller collection, relating to the life of Webb are located in the Walter Prescott Webb Collection and Mildred Webb Bugg Papers, Texas State Library and Archives, Austin.

2. Necah Furman, *Walter Prescott Webb: His Life and Impact* (Albuquerque: University of New Mexico Press, 1976), 26.

3. Webb, "The Texan's Story," 70.

4. William E. Hinds to Walter Prescott Webb, May 16, 1904, Webb Papers, Box 2M 250.

5. Hinds to Webb, January 9, 1909.

6. Webb to Dick Fleming, July 2, 1961, Webb Papers; Walter Prescott Webb, "The Search for William E. Hinds," *Harper's*, July 1961, 62–68. Webb's papers at the Briscoe Center include several files with scores of letters documenting the overwhelming positive public response to the Hinds article and the insistence of editor Dick Fleming of the *Reader's Digest* to carry the essay to a broader general audience; see Webb to Fleming, July 28, 1961; Webb to John Fischer, February 27, 1961, Webb Papers; Webb, "The Texan's Story," 125.

7. Harry Ransom to Joe B. Frantz, undated letter, Webb Papers; Webb, "Webb," 1, 7–9; Joe B. Frantz, "Remembering Walter Prescott Webb," *Southwestern Historical Quarterly* 90, no. 1 (July 1988): 18–19.

8. Webb, "The Texan's Story," 49.

9. Ibid., 157.

10. Hinds to Webb, January 9, 1909; Furman, *Webb*, 29–34.

11. Webb, "The Texan's Story," 106–109.

12. Ibid., 116.

13. Webb, "The Texan's Story," 117–118; Walter Prescott Webb, *History as High Adventure* (Austin: Pemberton Press, 1969), 7; J. Frank Dobie, "On My Friend: Walter Prescott Webb," *Houston Post*, March 17, 1963.

14. Webb, "The Texan's Story," 123–126; Furman, *Webb*, 54–55.

15. Webb, "The Texan's Story," 127–129.

16. Ibid., 127–130; Frantz, "Remembering Walter Prescott Webb," 24.

17. Ibid., 23–24; Furman, *Webb*, 71–72.

18. Webb, "The Texan's Story," 134–135; Ronnie Dugger, ed., *Three Men in Texas: Bedichek, Webb, and Dobie; Essays by Their Friends in the* Texas Observer (Austin: University of Texas Press, 1967), 111.

19. Webb, "The Texan's Story," 135–137; J. Frank Dobie to Webb, October 22, 1923, Webb Papers.

20. Dobie to Webb, October 22, 1923; Webb, *History as High Adventure*, 10.

21. Webb, "The Texan's Story," 138–145; Frantz, "Remembering Walter Prescott Webb," 25.

22. Webb, "The Texan's Story," 145; Webb, *History as High Adventure*, 11.

23. Walter Prescott Webb, *The Texas Rangers: A Century of Frontier Defense* (Austin: University of Texas Press, 1965), 549–567.

24. Webb, *History as High Adventure*, 12–15.

25. Walter Prescott Webb, *The Great Plains* (Boston: Ginn, 1931), 8–9.

26. Wilber R. Jacobs, John W. Caughey, and Joe B. Frantz, *Turner, Bolton, and Webb: Three Historians of the American Frontier* (Seattle: University of Washington Press, 1965), 78–80; Furman, *Webb*, xii.

27. Webb, "The Texan's Story," 184–185.

28. Webb, *History as High Adventure*, 17–18; Jacobs, Caughey, and Frantz, *Turner, Bolton, and Webb*, 85.

29. Jacobs, Caughey, and Frantz, *Turner, Bolton, and Webb*, 88–90.

30. Furman, *Webb*, 140–143.

31. William A. Owens, ed., *Three Friends: Roy Bedichek, J. Frank Dobie, and Walter Prescott Webb* (New York: Doubleday, 1969), 88–89; Dobie, "On My Friend."

32. Owens, ed., *Three Friends*, 84, 96–98; Dugger, ed., *Three Men*, 148–149.

33. Dugger, ed., *Three Men*, 100–102, 149–150; Dorman H. Winfrey, "Memories of J. Frank Dobie and Walter Prescott Webb," *Southwestern Historical Quarterly* 90, no. 1 (July 1988): 34.

34. Furman, *Webb*, 153–154.

35. Webb to Judge Edward Crane, October 17, 1947, Webb Papers; Webb to Eugene Hollon, as cited in Furman, *Webb*, 143; Homer P. Rainey, *The Tower and the Dome: A Free University v. Political Control* (Boulder, CO: Pruett, 1971), 56–58; Dobie, "On My Friend."

36. Dugger, ed., *Three Men*, 133; Walter Prescott Webb, "How the Republican Party Lost Its Future," *Southwest Review* 34 (Autumn 1949): 392–397.

37. Walter Prescott Webb, *The Great Frontier* (Lincoln: University of Nebraska Press, 1986), 13–28, 413–418; Dugger, ed., *Three Men*, 119, 152–155.

38. Dugger, ed., *Three Men*, 129; Joe B. Frantz, "He Took the Lead Late," *Austin American-Statesman*, June 28, 1964, 16–17.

39. Walter Prescott Webb, *More Water for Texas: The Problem and the Plan* (Austin: University of Texas Press, 1954), v, 50.

40. Walter Prescott Webb, "The American West: Perpetual Mirage," *Harper's* 214 (May 1957): 25–31; Jacobs, Caughey, and Frantz, *Turner, Bolton, and Webb*, 92–93; Dugger, ed., *Three Men*, 158.

41. Dugger, ed., *Three Men*, 118.

42. Ibid., 118, 158; Jacobs, Caughey, and Frantz, *Turner, Bolton, and Webb*, 96; Eileen Guarino, "The Excitement of Dr. Webb," *Southwestern Historical Quarterly* 90, no. 1 (July 1988): 60–64.

43. Frantz, "Remembering Walter Prescott Webb," 26–27; Winfrey, "Memories," 31–34.

44. Frantz, "Remembering Walter Prescott Webb," 17.

45. Walter Rundell Jr., "A Dedication to the Memory of Walter Prescott Webb, 1888–1963," *Arizona and the West* 5, no. 1 (1963): 1–2.

46. Dugger, ed., *Three Men*, 144.

47. Furman, *Webb*, 175.

48. Dobie, "On My Friend"; Frantz, "Remembering Walter Prescott Webb," 27; Jim Pierson, "Memories of Walter P. Webb," *Southwestern Historical Quarterly* 90, no. 1 (July 1988): 44.

49. Guarino, "The Excitement of Dr. Webb," 60.

50. Betty Hannstein Adams, ed., "Touched with a Sunset: The Letters of Terrell Maverick and Walter Prescott Webb," *Southwestern Historical Quarterly* 113, no. 4 (April 2010): 506.

51. Dugger, ed., *Three Men*, 147.

52. Owens, ed., *Three Friends*, 96; see news clippings and obituaries in Walter Prescott Webb biographical file, Daughters of the Republic of Texas Library, San Antonio; Adams, ed., "Touched with a Sunset," 507.

53. Dugger, ed., *Three Men*, 158.

54. Ibid., 97–98.

55. Frantz, "Remembering Walter Prescott Webb," 30; Dugger, ed., *Three Men*, 145.

56. Hinds to Webb, January 9, 1909, Webb Papers, Box 2M 250.

DAN UTLEY

ERNEST W. WINKLER

ERNEST W. WINKLER

Reserved, unassuming, and focused, Ernest William Winkler was a researcher's historian, dedicated to preserving records and providing access to reference materials but also to sharing his discoveries freely with others. He was a librarian, an archivist, an educator, a bibliographer, and a respected Texas historian of the highest order, known for his indefatigable and uncompromising approach to research. Although generally a quiet man who preferred to work behind the scenes in archival collections, on his own projects as well as in assistance to others, Winkler nevertheless found himself at times a somewhat reluctant leader. In that capacity, though, he set high standards and expected nothing less than the best from those with whom he worked. In the course of his lengthy and multifaceted career, he forged important friendships and collaborated with many of the leading Texas and southwestern historians of his time. As a key player during a seminal era of Texas historiography, he was often among those at the forefront of archival preservation and collection management.

Winkler's appreciation for Texas history came, no doubt, in large part from his family's rich heritage. His paternal grandparents, August and Maria Winkler, migrated to Texas from Prussia in the 1850s as part of the Wendish settlement of Serbin in present Lee County. A people of Slavic origin from the Lusatia region of what is now eastern Germany, the Wends came seeking improved economic conditions and freedom of religious (Lutheran) identity. From Serbin, many moved to other areas of the state; some assimilated into existing German communities, while others maintained distinct enclaves.[1] In the early 1870s, two of the Winklers' sons, William and Charles (Karl) August, relocated their families northwest to the rolling prairies of the Leon River valley above present-day Temple. William settled at The Grove in southeastern Coryell County, and Charles located across the river in Bell County. Given the relative isolation of the area in pre-railroad days, the Winklers found it difficult to attract a Lutheran minister for regular worship services, so instead, enlisting a German Methodist minister, the brothers established a church (now Moody-Leon United Methodist Church) of that denomination in Bell County. Over time, William's family opted for a return to the traditions of the Lutheran denomination and joined with other settlers to form a congregation at The Grove. The two churches founded by the Winkler brothers thus served as early determinants of distinct rural communities—one, primarily Wendish Lutheran, in Coryell County, and the other, largely German Methodist, nearby in Bell County.[2]

On January 21, 1875, Charles August and Kathrina Louisa Huber Winkler welcomed the birth of a son they named Ernest William.[3] The first of ten children born to the couple, he grew up on the Bell County farm and from 1883 to 1891 attended Winkler School on family land. Despite the limited educational opportunities the rural school afforded him, E. W. (Will to his family) pursued advanced studies. Influenced by his Wendish-German heritage and Methodist training, he attended Blinn Memorial College, founded by the Southern German Conference of the Methodist Episcopal Church. The coeducational academy in Brenham provided a broad-based curriculum of liberal arts, music, education, and theology. Winkler entered Blinn in 1892 and completed the normal instruction (teacher training) two years later. After teaching one year in a country school south of Brenham, he left to pursue a degree at the University of Texas in Austin, but limited resources led him to teach again the following year, at the Eden community near Seguin.[4]

Winkler returned to the University of Texas in 1897 and earned a bachelor's degree in literature in 1899 and a master's degree in history in 1900. His thesis, "The History of the Cherokee Indians of Texas," dealt with tribal land claims. At the university, he became friends with fellow student Eugene Campbell Barker, also destined to become a noted historian. Winkler's association with Barker proved to be significant throughout his life, both personally and professionally. The two shared common interests in Texas history, archival collections, libraries, and educational philosophy.[5]

Under the direction of professors George P. Garrison and Lester Bugbee, Winkler excelled in his studies and became a fellow of the department in 1899, assisting with research and tutoring. In the summer of 1900, on a project that presaged his life's work, Winkler began cataloging the voluminous Bexar Archives, acquired by the university only the year before. An extensive collection of original documents chronicling Spanish and Mexican colonial Texas, the archives figured prominently in the school's early research capabilities. The fact that Professor Bugbee entrusted such an important collection to an otherwise inexperienced young graduate reflects an abiding trust in his protégé's scholarship, diligence, and integrity. The assignment, albeit brief, afforded Winkler a unique opportunity to understand the myriad preservation issues, as well as far-reaching potential, associated with large collections.[6]

In the fall Winkler joined the faculty of Blinn Memorial College as a history instructor. During his summer vacation in 1902, he traveled to the University of Wisconsin and studied under the direction of Professor Frederick Jackson Turner, the renowned historian noted for his seminal thesis on the American frontier. Little is known of the brief assignment with Turner, but it provided Winkler opportunities to use library collections in Madison, Chicago, and St. Louis. At least part of the research related to his thesis on the Cherokee, which he reworked for publication in the *Quarterly of the Texas State Historical Association* (1903). While in Brenham, Winkler assisted the Texas State Historical Association (TSHA) by writing and editing articles and indexing early copies of the quarterly. At the end of the school year in 1903, he again returned to Austin, where he embarked on a new career path, one that marked a major turning point in his continuing growth as a Texas historian.[7]

Upon the recommendation of Dr. Garrison, Winkler joined the staff of the Texas State Library in September 1903 to translate Spanish documents and catalog manuscript collections. Although part of Texas government early on, the state library function initially received only limited direction and oversight. As a result, a number of agencies administered the library over the years before it came under the Department of Agriculture, Insurance, Statistics and History in the 1880s. Its second-class status began to change in the early 1890s through the direction of Governor James Stephen Hogg, who took a personal interest in history. To oversee the transformation he envisioned, he appointed Judge Cadwell Walton Raines, a friend from his Wood County days, to serve as state librarian. A Civil War veteran, former county judge in two counties, and a newspaperman, Raines brought key elements to the position: he was university-trained, active in TSHA leadership, interested in Texas history, aware of the scope of work required, and trusted by the governor. Due in part to his political connections, though, Raines left office at the end of the Hogg administration; he later returned as state librarian in 1899 and was in that position when Winkler joined the staff.[8]

Raines and Winkler worked well together, and the young historian respected the vision and determination of his new mentor. Although Raines "had librarianship thrust upon him," as Winkler noted, he worked hard to make "the State Library a collection of Texas books, and a reference library," and he traveled extensively to bring important collections into the public domain. Raines also understood the value of bibliographic studies, and he devoted significant time to his own research in that regard, establishing credentials as a historian in the process.[9]

Winkler again proved to be an observant student, and under Raines's tutelage quickly learned all aspects of library operations. In an effort to strengthen his particular interest in the preservation of manuscripts, Winkler sought every available resource, relying heavily on the Library of Congress in particular for direction and assistance. His enthusiasm, personal discipline, and hard work—he worked long hours daily and on weekends and preferred handling assignments on his own rather than delegating—caught the attention of Governor S. W. T. Lanham, as well as Raines, and in the summer of 1904 they authorized him to travel to Washington, DC, for further studies. There he would not only learn Library of Congress methodologies firsthand but also research newspaper collections and archives for historical data on Texas, while visiting some of the nation's grand monuments and museums. Prior to his lengthy journey, though, Winkler traveled to Lavaca County, where he proposed to Johanna Tabea Kuehne, a native of the Wied community between Shiner and Hallettsville. The couple proudly shared a common ancestral heritage, and their courtship included letters written in the German language. They married on December 22, 1904, and made their home in Austin. Adding to the significance of 1904 for Winkler, the TSHA had inducted him earlier that year as a fellow, a high honor that recognized his rapid ascendancy as a Texas scholar.[10]

Throughout 1905 and into the following year, Winkler grew in stature as an expert on Texas records. Library correspondence indicates he worked tirelessly and diplomatically to assist governmental agencies and the general public as well as researchers from other states and collections. There seemed to be no limits to his inquisitiveness and investigative determination. As a historian, Winkler understood the unique scholastic value of various manuscripts, and the agency's early and systematic acquisitions proved vital to researchers as well as to the history program at the University of Texas. "The excellent Texas collection in the State Library, together with the large collection of manuscripts in the State Department and Land Office," he wrote, "made possible the inauguration of graduate work in Southwestern history long before the resources of the University Library would have warranted such a step."[11]

The State Library gained significant identity and purpose in the Raines-Winkler years but remained a small department within a larger agency, although there were ongoing efforts by others, most notably the Texas Federation of Women's Clubs and the Texas Library Association, to establish a separate Texas Library Commission. Raines, who moved the department forward as state librarian and put it in a position to stand on its own, was not part of the eventual transition, however. He passed away on August 6, 1906, and Winkler, his friend, colleague, and student and soon to be his successor, served as a pallbearer at his funeral. With Winkler's appointment, the State Library for the first time had a trained historian and seasoned librarian to direct its various programs.[12]

Accepting his new assignment with optimism yet reluctance—he much preferred the role of archivist to that of administrator—Winkler had little time to establish his own vision for the State Library. At year's end, he experienced firsthand the politics often associated with the public realm of history. Rumors of change were spreading as Thomas M. Campbell prepared for his governorship. Winkler noted in his diary in December 1906, "Am entirely in the dark as to what changes will be made by Governor C. or the man who he appoints to the head of this Dept. Do not think the place of Librarian should go as a political plum, & have not resorted to the politician's plans to influence my retention."[13] Only a few days later, in early January 1907, he wrote, "On arriving at the Library Thursday morning I learned of the rumor published in the [Austin] Statesman stating that Judge V. W. Grubbs was slated for State Librarian. On further inquiry I could find no one who knew anything certain about the statement. It is very disconcerting to say the least."[14] While Grubbs, a former Greenville jurist and longtime advocate for vocational education, had an impressive public service record, Winkler favored credentials and professional experience over cronyism. Uncertainty continued even to the inauguration:

> Since writing last, as in fact since the nomination of Colonel Campbell last August, we of the Department have been on the *qui vive* for any clue that would inform us upon the point of our being retained or turned out; at times I felt sure of being retained, at other times as certain of being turned out. Today Colonel Campbell was inaugurated and I am yet ignorant of my fate; still hoping to be retained, without a word from Colonel [R. T.] Milner, however, that I will be.[15]

Robert Teague Milner proved to be a pivotal figure in Winkler's professional development. An Alabama native raised in East Texas, he worked as a newspaperman before election to the Texas House of Representatives, where he authored legislation requiring that Texas history be included in the public school curriculum. Appointed commissioner of the Department of Agriculture, Insurance, Statistics and History in 1907, he quickly learned, as others did, to rely on the dependable Winkler. Possibly in part to avoid the political inevitability, but also to strengthen his own administrative objectives, Milner persuaded Winkler to accept a position as chief clerk for the new and separate Department of Agriculture he would head. Admitting in his diary that he was surprised and flattered by the job offer and noting that "the increase in salary was not entirely ignored," Winkler wrote that the commissioner felt the assignment "would be for the uplift of the great mass of our people, and not confined to a few as the work of the Library was."[16]

Winkler became part of a small team charged with getting the new agency under way. His first project involved gathering production statistics from cotton ginners. His research focus told only part of the story, as the enormity of the undertaking soon overwhelmed the team. Even the normally industrious Winkler had difficulty with the workload as he endeavored to continue his own historical research. "This kind of work wrought a decided change in my habits," he observed, "which up to this time had been those of a student. I had been accustomed to reading and investigating." Obligated to the Carnegie Institute for a book on Texas public lands at the time of his transfer, he wrote, "I soon saw I could not keep up this work and, therefore, cancelled my contract." More work and job-related stress meant less reading at home as he "drifted from the student's ways and habits to those of the business man." Although Winkler enjoyed aspects of the work, he found particularly vexing the interpretation of laws, inexperience of colleagues, and interaction with farmers who refused state assistance, "rejecting it with contempt and even with insult."[17] The job was not a good fit for historian Winkler, and it grew unbearable when Commissioner Milner left in 1908 to become president of Texas A&M College.[18]

Meanwhile, circumstances at his former place of employment allowed Winkler an opportunity to resume his previous job. After years of intense lobbying by advocates for a separate library agency, Governor Campbell signed legislation in March 1909 establishing the Texas Library and Historical Commission (later Texas State Library and Archives Commission). The law provided for five commissioners: three appointed by the governor and two ex officio positions, including the chairman of the University of Texas history department. Once again, Dr. Garrison was in a position to recommend his former student, which he did, and E. W. Winkler became the first state librarian for the new agency. This time he ignored the pay differential—a twenty percent reduction. Winkler transitioned with a renewed purpose and made good on a previous pledge to "permit nothing relating to Texas to escape."[19] Sadly, his mentor, Dr. Garrison, passed away in the summer of 1910, just over a year after the appointment. His replacement as chair of the history department, and therefore as a commission member, was Dr. Eugene C. Barker. In a move that signaled important institutional support for Winkler and the agency, as well as for continued reliance on skilled leadership, Barker agreed to serve as commission chair.[20]

For Winkler, the initial years as state librarian in the new agency were productive, both professionally and personally. Only a few months into his new assignment, R. T. Milner offered him a teaching position at Texas A&M College, but he declined, content with his responsibilities.[21] At the library Winkler moved systematically to professionalize and depoliticize the staff; to address longstanding conservation, access, and storage issues; to open communication with the public and commissioners; to seek adequate funding; and to promote a broader range of programs, including extension work. Under his supervision the latter especially took on the form of a mission as he endeavored to promote development of a model public library system throughout the state. At a time when relatively few existed, he promoted public and school libraries as integral elements of community education for both young people and adults. "There are some cities in Texas where the authorities seem to entertain the idea that the public library can subsist on charity and still do valiant service in the cause of education," he wrote, adding, "Such cities need to be waked up."[22] According to historian David B. Gracy II:

> Winkler's industry in gathering, standardizing, and disseminating information on libraries in Texas through correspondence, the newsletter, and the few trips he was able to take became legendary. Missing no opportunity to promote libraries, his own in particular, in 1911 he published a series of articles

on the state library in the major Texas dailies in Galveston and Dallas, and an extended report in the Texas State Historical Association's quarterly.[23]

While he worked to bring greater order and definition to the new agency, Winkler reinvigorated his passion for research and writing. Driven by intrinsic goals and also by a commission mandate to utilize state collections, he worked on several publications while also serving as associate editor for the TSHA quarterly (*Southwestern Historical Quarterly* after 1912), a position he held until 1937. Given the broad scope of the state collections, he focused on reference books and bibliographic studies. Significant publications of the era include his edited works, *Secret Journals of the Senate, Republic of Texas, 1836–1845* (1911) and *Journal of the Secession Convention of Texas, 1861* (1912), and his articles for the *Quarterly of the Texas State Historical Association*: "The Seat of Government in Texas" (vol. 10, nos. 2 and 3, October 1906 and January 1907) and "Documents Relating to the Organization of the Municipality of Washington" (vol. 10, no. 1, July 1906).

Winkler's wife, Johanna, regularly accompanied him to the library at night to assist with his research. In 1906 the couple started their family with the birth of their first child, Johann Friedrich Wilelm, whom they called Hans. Over time, the family grew with the addition of four daughters: Lydia, Katherine, Johanna, and Helen. Tragically, a daughter they named Elizabeth died at birth. Throughout that ordeal and others, Winkler remained a devout man, following the Texas religious traditions of his family and regularly participating in the activities and leadership of University Methodist Church in Austin. The Winklers attended few social events; they much preferred the opera or traveling with their children to historic sites.[24]

Increasingly, historians of diverse topics relied on Winkler for his comprehensive knowledge of Texas archival collections and bibliographic sources. Librarians, too, recognized his contributions, and he served as president of the Texas Library Association for three terms (1911–1914), longer than anyone in the group's history. His presidency also marks the only time to date that a sitting state librarian has held the office.[25]

All looked promising for the dedicated historian and librarian until he again faced the reality of politics. The irony is that, although a Democrat, Winkler scrupulously avoided political talk at work, believing it a hindrance to his interaction with colleagues and patrons. Despite that guiding principle, and regardless of his many recognitions and accomplishments, he held a prominent position in state government unfortunately subject to political appointment. What lay ahead for Winkler this time put him and the commission at the center of a controversy that tested his resolve, challenged his professional and personal integrity, and ultimately set him on a new course that added even greater significance to his impact as a historian.

The genesis of the incident was the election of James E. "Farmer Jim" Ferguson as governor of Texas in 1914. Like Winkler, Ferguson grew up on a Bell County farm in the 1870s and 1880s. Early on, he exhibited a tenacious spirit that defined his personality and drove him throughout his life. Briefly schooled in law, he set up a practice in Belton, where he cultivated additional interests in real estate and banking. He wed Miriam A. Wallace in 1899, and in 1907 the couple moved to Temple. There, as a successful banker, Jim Ferguson involved himself in politics, although initially behind the scenes as a supporter and campaign manager. Once ready to go out on his own, he formally announced in 1913 as a Democratic candidate for governor. His chief opponent in the 1914 primary was former congressman Thomas H. Ball of Houston, a formidable challenger with an impressive record in law and party politics. A Wilsonian Progressive, Ball favored prohibition, a major divisive issue of the era. Ferguson, more of a political pragmatist on prohibition who sensed the public's weariness with the topic, campaigned with his usual tenacity and a rural, folksy personality that appealed to the state's largely agrarian voter base. Ball and his supporters clearly underestimated their competition, and the Temple banker won handily in the Democratic primary, then a clear ticket through the general election.[26]

Soon after the election and well before Ferguson took office, rumors circulated about the governor-elect's interest in politically rewarding his supporters—and conversely, punishing his detractors. One of the bureaucratic "plums" he identified was state librarian. Ferguson's interest in the position was purely for political payback, and he had neither a concern for professional credentials nor any reason to anticipate problems with his decision. He planned to appoint the Reverend Allan Ferguson Cunningham, a native of Scotland and pastor of the First Presbyterian Church in Temple, who had defended him during the campaign in a letter sent to a group of opposition ministers. Ferguson viewed Cunningham as an educated man and therefore, in his mind, qualified to be state librarian.[27]

Barker, as commission chair, moved quickly to confront the rumors and protect Winkler. For him, the battle was not just about his friend, as important as that was to him personally; it was also about the credibility of the Texas Library and Historical Commission. Seeking support within the Ferguson camp, Barker first wrote to the governor's brother, whom he knew. When that failed, he met with other commission members to draft an alternate plan of action, and it fell to him as chairman to write directly to the governor, which he did the following day, December 11, 1914:

> I am not speaking recklessly in saying that the position, when properly filled, requires a more specialized and expert training than that of any other department head in the capitol, with the possible exception of the Attorney

> General. Mr. Winkler has this training in an unusual degree. He is a trained librarian, a trained historian, an experienced editor, and a linguist. And he has a more thorough and comprehensive knowledge of every phase of Texas history than any other man living. (I say this as a historian myself, and one who knows some Texas history.) . . . From the standpoint of efficiency, in every respect, we think that the loss of Mr. Winkler's services would be nothing short of a calamity to the State Library.[28]

While Barker worked the political front, the frustrated Winkler appealed to colleagues for support, albeit in a reserved and modest manner:

> When the newly appointed Library Commission meets about February 9th [1915], it will be confronted by a recommendation from the Governor suggesting that his warm friend, Rev. Mr. Cunningham, of Temple, be elected State Librarian. I have no objection to being superseded in office, but the work to which I have dedicated years of devoted service merits a worthy successor—one who is qualified by training and experience to do it even better than I have done. . . . You can do the new administration a good turn by writing to the Library Commission . . . and urging that no change be made unless it be to choose a better qualified person than the present encumbent [*sic*].[29]

The pleas had the desired results, and letters of support soon poured in to the library and most likely to the governor. Attorney Will Hogg, son of Governor Hogg, wrote, "Mr. Winkler is peculiarly fitted for that position and it would be a sad mistake to replace him by anyone not better trained and more experienced than he."[30] Baylor University librarian Willard P. Lewis called the move a potential "death blow," and added, "No office in the State should be further removed from political influences than that of State Librarian, which demands experience and training equal to that of a college professor of the highest capacity."[31] The Daughters of the Republic of Texas chapter in Austin drafted a resolution supporting Winkler,[32] and Sherman librarian Nora Kay Weems wrote praising his assistance to small public libraries. "For my part," she pointedly stated, "I have no interest in the political side of the question, as I am not even a suffragette, and do not know anything of Mr. Winklers [*sic*] views on politics." But, she continued, "any man who can do so much for the cause he has done, could not be an offence to one even of different political views."[33]

Meanwhile, Barker and other commissioners turned up the heat by visiting with the governor in early February, but the meeting proved disappointing, although Ferguson did concede the final decision to the commission (to which he appointed three of the five members). The following day Winkler personally visited Ferguson, but was unprepared for the reprimand he faced. As he remembered the conversation:

> [The governor] said in substance: Mr. Winkler, you are the son of a farmer; you know what it costs to obtain an education; it was through the sacrifices of your father that you obtained an education. Now that you have an education and have occupied an important position, you have turned away from the teaching of your father and have gone off with the University Church crowd and supported Tom Ball, and proclaimed that a man without a college education is not fit to hold office.[34]

Dismayed, Winkler confided in friends, defending himself against the allegations. To the charge he had fallen out with his family, he said simply, "This is so far from the truth that it needs no farther [*sic*] attention." In response to the comment about his church, he explained, "Two years ago the Rev. Bob Shuler was foisted upon this congregation over the protest of the board of stewards.... I went to hear Shuler preach a few times, and hearing him detail more sensational stuff in thirty minutes than I ever read in a week I became disgusted and quit going to church. I have not heard him preach in eighteen months."[35] The fiery pastor he referenced was Robert Pierce Shuler, later known as "Fighting Bob" during his California years, who freely practiced a form of "pulpit denunciation" in campaigns against the corruption he discerned in numerous individuals, cultural groups, and social practices. He particularly disliked Ferguson and held nothing back in his virulent political attacks, thereby making his estranged congregant Winkler guilty by ministerial association in the process.[36]

Equally as frustrated as Winkler by Ferguson's unfounded charges, Barker obtained the governor's permission to write Reverend Cunningham for the express purpose of explaining the functions of the agency he would soon inherit. Instead, in the letter to the pastor (copied to the governor) he admitted that he was writing "frankly, in the hope of dissuading you from accepting the position." Barker went on to say that, if the pastor failed to meet the job requirements, "it would be a violation of the law for the Commission to elect you."[37] As anticipated, the letter brought an immediate and heated response from the governor: "As you have entered into a long discussion of politics in the letter, I hope that you will not hereafter complain if your wishes are not carried out."[38] As Barker biographer William C. Pool observed, the professor thus found himself "in the professional-occupied doghouse of the Governor of Texas"—a preview of a coming storm.[39]

With one member absent at the called library commission meeting in February, the vote for state librarian—with Winkler and Cunningham as the only choices—resulted in a deadlock. By the next meeting on March 3, the governor had his appointees in line and in place, and the commission approved Cunningham by a vote of three to two. Disgusted, Barker immediately resigned as chair. Two days later, Winkler wrote historian Herbert E. Bolton, a friend from his university days, "The Vandals have invaded the State Library. . . . The Governor does not believe in 'going hog wild over higher education' nor in efficiency in the State Library, but he is a great believer in taking care of his political friends."[40] He ended with a plea for Bolton's assistance in finding a new job. "Words cannot express my disgust at the ignorance and littleness of the politician," Bolton replied, "who has deprived an important part of the state's administration of the service of an expert."[41]

Surprisingly, after all the political maneuvering, Cunningham declined the appointment, citing privately the marginal vote of the commission and publicly his need to continue serving his church. No doubt he also had reservations about Barker's continued presence on the commission. Ferguson still refused to consider Winkler and instead settled on Bavarian-born Christian Klaerner, a county school superintendent and singing club enthusiast from Washington County. Although Barker again placed his friend's name in nomination at the following meeting, Ferguson's marginal coalition held, and Klaerner became state librarian.[42] Writing to Bolton himself, Barker soberly summarized the incident: "Winkler, as you may have heard, has been removed from the State Library, and things are in a fair way to go pretty much to smash down there."[43] A victim of political posturing for the second time in his short career, Winkler left the agency on April 15, 1915. Within months he became assistant librarian and bibliographer with the University of Texas library system. Ultimately, Barker's assessment rang true. Embroiled in a controversy that stemmed from his inability to exert his brand of political control over the University of Texas, Governor Ferguson faced impeachment charges and eventually resigned his office in 1917. The following year, against a backdrop of anti-German sentiment at the height of World War I, a special review of state agencies included an investigation of Klaerner's record and loyalty that found him unqualified for the position he held. The commission removed him soon after and considered turning to Winkler for leadership, but this time he respectfully declined.[44]

With the resilience that defined his character, Winkler put his full energies into his new assignment and continued researching and writing, completing editorial work on an important (and somewhat ironic) study, *Platforms of Political Parties in Texas*. In 1916, the year of the study's publication, he took on new responsibilities as head reference librarian and curator of Texas books at the university. Once again, he was in a position to build and acquire important collections, most notably with philanthropic support from George W. Littlefield. The celebrated Civil War veteran, cattleman, and banker began his service as a University of Texas regent in 1911. A friend of both Barker and Winkler, with whom he worked as a pre-Ferguson member of the Texas Library and Historical Commission, Littlefield had great respect for the historians. He was a dedicated student of Texas history who strongly advocated for textbooks that offered a balanced view of the South and its role in U.S. history. Frustrated by what he viewed as a northern bias in that regard and by a lack of intellectual studies of the southern "cause," he established, at Barker's suggestion, the Littlefield Fund for Southern History at the university. Through his beneficence and Winkler's administrative skills as a historian, collector, and appraiser of historical materials, the university became a national research center for southern history through acquisition of major archival collections.[45]

In 1921, when school officials learned about the possibility of purchasing the extensive Latin American collection of Mexican historian and bibliophile Genaro García, the president sent Winkler to Mexico to negotiate the deal and oversee the transfer (Winkler personally escorted the collection to Texas). With 25,000 books and publications and more than 250,000 pages of original material, it became the nucleus of what evolved into the renowned Nettie Lee Benson Latin American Collection.[46]

Two years later Winkler was promoted to the position of university librarian. Truly touched by the support and confidence reflected in the appointment, he wrote to acting president Dr. W. S. Sutton, his former teacher: "It is impossible for me to choose words to express to you the emotions of fear and happiness stirred by the appointment." He pledged, "What ability I possess, with industry and faithfulness to the trust, I hereby rededicate to my alma mater."[47] He remained in the position for eleven years, capably handling the increased demands of personnel, budgets, and administration, as well as acquisitions and cataloging, associated with a growing institution. In 1934, though, as the library program prepared to move to a new building (now Battle Hall), he believed the timing was right for a return to his professional roots among the archives. While he no doubt missed his historical investigations, there are indications of infighting within the library program that may have hastened his decision. In a letter to Phineas L. Windsor, former University of Texas librarian then at the University of Illinois, University of Texas president H. Y. Benedict confided:

> Winkler, never very desirous I think of an administrative position, is retiring as Librarian to continue as main bibliographer, etc., and the Regents desire to put in a young, active and competent head librarian who is willing to start at $2700 [annually], manage the somewhat difficult staff, and hope for a greater reward later. Winkler has not been able to keep some of his subordinates in proper relation, and the Regents, I am sure, will appoint the new librarian with all the power that is needed to get more coordinated results. The spe-

cial libraries, Wrenn, Aitken, Garcia, et al., have been the cause of friction via the vaulting ambition route.[48]

Regardless of the motivation, Winkler's return to research brought him contentment. With his desk characteristically piled high with books, periodicals, and documents in a deceptively systematic form of apparent clutter that staff members carefully avoided, he enjoyed his standing as the senior resident expert on Texas history. He continued to provide invaluable research assistance, helping on such noteworthy projects as Thomas W. Streeter's *Bibliography of Texas, 1795–1845* (1955–1960). His most significant work during this era, and arguably the most rewarding of his career, was *Check List of Texas Imprints, 1846–1860*, an impressive and extensive inventory of early Texas publications. The study first appeared as installments in the *Southwestern Historical Quarterly* in 1943 and then as a separate book in 1949. Winkler's colleague, Llerena Friend, provided final editing of a second volume in 1963 after his death. She wrote in the preface that following his investigative trail had proved challenging, as he made notes on any available ephemera and "wrote on three sides of the card."[49] A further indication of his work is the quantity of his personal papers and research materials at the Dolph Briscoe Center for American History at the University of Texas—a collection of thirty-two linear feet.

In the mid-1940s Winkler accepted modified service at the university, but his routine changed little. He maintained regular office hours and continued to work on weekends when the solitude allowed for fewer distractions. In 1950 he attended the dedication ceremony for the Barker Texas History Center, named for his valued friend Eugene C. Barker, who used the occasion to recognize him publicly for his life's work. The following year, E. W. Winkler retired with emeritus status. He died in Austin on February 8, 1960, and was buried in Buckhorn Cemetery, near where he grew up in northern Bell County. His beloved wife, Johanna, died four years later. Today Winkler's simple gravesite in its rural prairie setting provides no evidence of his life as a historian—and he may have preferred it that way, given his preference for staying behind the scenes. His more public monument remains the impressive body of work he left to future generations of researchers, who continue to consult his early foundational studies and bibliographies, ever appreciative of his range, detail, and foresight. Through the myriad investigations of his life's calling, Ernest William Winkler left a lasting mark on Texas historiography, meticulously recording the past and moving it forward.

In 1932 Winkler presented a talk to the Texas State Historical Association in which he provided an overview of historical collections in the Southwest. His opening remarks, preserved in print by Llerena Friend from his original notes, now serve as poignant context for his remarkable body of work:

When do old documents, letters, journals, diaries, etc., and newspapers, pamphlets, broadsides, [and maps] cease to be rubbish, and when do they become material suitable for historical collections? For many people regard them as much rubbish to be discarded, while, on the other hand, there are those who are continually on the alert to acquire such material for their libraries. The quality that makes the difference in their appraisal is not in the material; it is in those making the choice.[50]

SUGGESTED READING

Winkler, Ernest W., ed. *Journal of the Secession Convention of Texas, 1861*. Austin: Austin Printing Company, 1912.

As part of his efforts to make the content of original documents more readily accessible to the public, state librarian Winkler provided a verbatim account from original records of the convention proceedings without any editorial comments.

Winkler, Ernest W. *Platforms of Political Parties in Texas*. Bulletin of the University of Texas (Austin), no. 53, 1916.

Winkler divides his 700-page bulletin into three parts. The first is his historiographical treatment of the origins of political parties in the state, from the earliest days that centered primarily on dynamic leaders, rather than issues, to later years when platforms began to reflect national trends more closely. The second section shows Winkler's strength as a bibliographer, with copies of extended platforms through the years, derived from various sources, along with names of party nominees, party chairs, and committee structures. Third, the author provides even more detailed information through a statistical appendix that includes vote totals for state offices and other key information.

Winkler, Ernest W. *Secret Journals of the Senate, Republic of Texas, 1836–1945*. Austin: Austin Printing Company, 1911.

In his role as state librarian, Winkler edited this piece from original journals housed in the Texas State Library and the Department of State and prepared it as part of the biennial reports of the Texas State Library and Historical Commission.

Winkler, Ernest W. *Check List of Texas Imprints, 1846–1860*. Austin: Texas State Historical Association, 1949.

Following up on the Historical Records Survey by the Works Progress Administration, Winkler sought to provide a central collection of early bibliographical information for Texas historians. His first volume focused on early statehood with detailed references to a broad range of imprints, including newspapers, pamphlets, periodicals, and maps.

Winkler, Ernest W., and Llerena Friend, eds. *Check List of Texas Imprints, 1846–1876*. Austin: Texas State Historical Association, 1963.

Completed in association with his esteemed colleague Llerena Friend, and published three years after his death, this second volume of Winkler's 1949 work extended his original bibliographical concept through the Civil War years and the era of Reconstruction.

NOTES

1. Census of the United States, 1880 and 1900; Winkler biographical sketch, box 3K104, Ernest William Winkler Papers, Dolph Briscoe Center for American History, University of Texas at Austin (hereafter Winkler Papers); George C. Engerrand, *The So-Called Wends of Germany and Their Colonies in Texas and in Australia*, University of Texas Bulletin 3417, Bureau of Research in the Social Sciences, Study No. 7, May 1, 1934, 125 and 156; Anne Blasig, *The Wends of Texas* (San Antonio: Naylor, 1954), ii, 8, 34.

2. Moody-Leon United Methodist Church, Bell County, and St. Paul Lutheran Church, Coryell County, Official Texas Historical Marker Files, Texas Historical Commission, Austin.

3. Kathrina Winkler's maiden name is shown in various written and online records as Huber, Schott, and Schott-Huber. Additionally, her given names are noted as Catherine, Katherine, Katarina, and Louise. The name shown in the text is based on E. W. Winkler's notes and her tombstone inscription at Buckhorn Cemetery, Bell County.

4. Census of the United States, 1880 and 1900; Winkler biographical sketch, Winkler Papers; James H. Atkinson, "Blinn College," in *The New Handbook of Texas*, edited by Ron Tyler (Austin: Texas State Historical Association, 1996), 1:593 (hereafter *NHOT*).

5. Winkler biographical sketch; Llerena Friend, "E. W. Winkler and the Texas State Library," *Texas Libraries* 24 (May–June 1962): 89–90.

6. Friend, "E. W. Winkler and the Texas State Library," 90.

7. Ibid.; Winkler biographical sketch.

8. Friend, "E. W. Winkler and the Texas State Library," 90; E. W. Winkler, "Cadwell Walton Raines," *NHOT*, 5:415; David B. Gracy II, draft of manuscript on the history of the Texas State Library, chap. 1. (Dr. Gracy is preparing the manuscript for publication; his generosity for allowing a prior review of the contents is hereby gratefully acknowledged.)

9. Undated Winkler typescript titled "The Southwestern History Collection at the University," box 3K111, Winkler Papers; Llerena Friend, "E. W. Winkler's Speech on Historical Collections of the Southwest," *Southwestern Historical Quarterly* 76, no. 1 (July 1972): 75–76; C. W. Raines materials, boxes 4Q515 and 3K62, Winkler Papers.

10. Friend, "E. W. Winkler and the Texas State Library," 94; biographical materials, box 3K104, Winkler Papers.

11. "The Southwestern History Collection at the University."

12. Gracy draft, chap. 2; C. W. Raines materials, box 4Q515, Winkler Papers.

13. E. W. Winkler diary, December 20, 1906, box 3K59, Winkler Papers.

14. Winkler diary, January 3, 1907.

15. Ibid., January 15, 1907.

16. Dorman H. Winfrey, "Robert Teague Milner," *NHOT*, 4:754–755; Winkler diary, March 16, 1909. (As someone familiar with the value of personal records, Winkler maintained a widely intermittent diary at times. His entry for June 13, 1907, is "On the morning of this day, Col. Milner came." The next entry, dated March 16, 1909, begins, "After a year and six months I will attempt to take up the thread where it was snapped off so suddenly above.")

17. Winkler diary, March 16, 1909.

18. Ibid.

19. Gracy draft, chap. 2.

20. Friend, "E. W. Winkler and the Texas State Library," 104; William C. Pool, *Eugene C. Barker, Historian* (Austin: Texas State Historical Association, 1971), 71.

21. R. T. Milner to E. W. Winkler, box 3K103, Winkler Papers.

22. Quoted in Gracy draft, chap. 2, 5–6.

23. Ibid., chap. 2.

24. Friend, "E. W. Winkler and the Texas State Library," 95–107; Capitola Cannon, "Librarian Makes Collection of Printed Texas History," *Daily Texan*, April (n.d.), 1937, E. W. Winkler Vertical File, Briscoe Center.

25. Gracy draft, chap. 2.

26. Kenneth E. Hendrickson Jr., *The Chief Executives of Texas: From Stephen F. Austin to John B. Connally, Jr.* (College Station: Texas A&M University Press, 1995), 157–162; Ralph W. Steen, "James Edward Ferguson," *NHOT*, 2:979–981.

27. Pool, *Eugene C. Barker*, 71; Friend, "E. W. Winkler and the Texas State Library," 107–109.

28. Eugene C. Barker to Governor James E. Ferguson, December 11, 1914, box 2B130, Eugene C. Barker Papers, Dolph Briscoe Center for American History, University of Texas at Austin (hereafter Barker Papers).

29. Undated draft letter from E. W. Winkler, box 3K101, Winkler Papers.

30. Will C. Hogg to W. F. Doughty (state superintendent of public instruction and an ex officio member of the Texas Library and Historical Commission), February 1, 1915, ibid.

31. Willard P. Lewis to State Library and Historical Commission, February 2, 1915, ibid.

32. Resolution adopted by the William B. Travis Chapter, Daughters of the Republic of Texas, February 3, 1915, ibid.

33. Nora Kay Weems to W. F. Doughty, February 3, 1915, ibid.

34. Draft letter from E. W. Winkler to Hugh N. Fitzgerald (editor, *Fort Worth Record*), February 10, 1915, ibid.

35. Ibid.

36. Kevin Starr, *Material Dreams: Southern California through the 1920s* (New York: Oxford University Press, 1990), 136–139; David C. Humphrey, "Prostitution and Public Policy in Austin, Texas, 1870–1915," *Southwestern Historical Quarterly* 86, no. 4 (April 1983): 501, 504–505, 515.

37. Pool, *Eugene C. Barker*, 72.

38. Ibid.

39. Ibid.

40. E. W. Winkler to Herbert E. Bolton, March 5, 1915, box 3K102, Winkler Papers.

41. Herbert E. Bolton to E. W. Winkler, March 11, 1915, box 3K102, Winkler Papers.

42. Gracy draft, chap. 2; "Declines Post as Librarian," *Dallas Morning News*, March 13, 1915, n.p., E. W. Winkler scrapbooks, Briscoe Center; "Christian Klaerner," *NHOT*, 3:1134–1135.

43. Friend, "E. W. Winkler and the Texas State Library," 112.

44. Ibid., 113; Central Investigating Committee, Report of Subcommittee #5 on the Library and Historic [*sic*] Commission and the Legislative Reference Library, January 9, 1918, box 058/1963-2, Texas State Library and Archives Commission, Austin.

45. Winkler correspondence and materials on Littlefield Fund for Southern History, box 2H405, Winkler Papers; J. Evetts Haley, *George W. Littlefield, Texan* (Norman: University of Oklahoma Press, 1943), 258–271.

46. Nettie Lee Benson, "Nettie Lee Benson Latin American Collection," *NHOT*, 4:981.

47. E. W. Winkler to W. S. Sutton, June 30, 1923, box 3K114, Winkler Papers.

48. H. Y. Benedict to P. L. Windsor, June 20, 1934, box 3K105, ibid.

49. Ernest W. Winkler and Llerena Friend, eds., *Check List of Texas Imprints, 1861–1876* (Austin: Texas State Historical Association, 1963), vii.

50. Friend, "E. W. Winkler's Speech," 74.

DAN UTLEY

LLERENA FRIEND

LLERENA FRIEND

Late in her life, Llerena Friend penned the following words. I quote them here because it would be impossible for me to express these thoughts any better.

> Growing up for me did not mean living in one house in one town so long that the feel and smell and sound of a community became a part of my subconscious. It did mean living along the line of the Fort Worth and Denver Railroad in four towns in three adjacent counties in western North Texas. I mention the railroad because it had meaning. It was the way we went west to what was still frontier country when I was five and a half. My father used the railroad for travel to make our living. It was the way we made our first trip back to the town of my birth for the funeral of the aunt for whom I was named. Early each summer for a number of years, I was tagged and put on a train for Fort Worth, the center of the universe and the largest place I knew, and there the Travelers' Aid re-tagged me and sent me on to Dublin to Granny Perry's for vacation time with Granny and four aunts still living within four blocks of each other. And on that same train, when I was sixteen, Mama took me to Austin to enroll in The University of Texas. I guess I thought then I was grown up. And the world was never quite the same again.[1]

Llerena, who was destined to write what many historians believe to be the best of all the biographies of Sam Houston, was born in the hamlet of Dublin on October 19, 1903. One of her first memories was of a move from the house of her birth to a house two doors from Granny Perry's place. It was the first of what she said would be twenty-four moves in the next twenty-four years. But she wrote, "There was never an uprooting. We were always at home."[2]

The next move was a big one. The family, now consisting of Llerena, Papa, Mama, and baby brother Ben, left Dublin on the Texas Central, changed to the Denver at Fort Worth, and headed west to Chillicothe in Hardeman County. Chillicothe was at the junction of the Denver and Orient Railroads, a strategic location for a warehouse for the Waples-Platter Grocery Company, for which Llerena's father, Everest MacDonald Friend, was a traveling salesman. The family had no sooner settled in Chillicothe than Papa was off on his routes, leaving Mama and the children together but alone in a strange place. It was March and the weather was, well, Texas weather. The clouds were black and the hailstones were big, but the neighbors were kind and invited the newcomers to join them in their storm cellar.

When April came, the mesquite came out, the wild onions appeared, and life was better. Papa's friends at the warehouse gave Llerena and Ben a dime every day to buy candy, and Llerena made friends with Elizabeth Farrington while Ben found a playmate in Elizabeth's brother, Lee. One of Llerena's fondest memories of that time was their trip to Molly Bailey's Circus where the band played "Put on Your Old Gray Bonnet" and "Red Wing." That event might not have been her first introduction to music, but it certainly remained on her mind. Throughout her life she enjoyed music, but admitted to having no musical talent.

Mama had a piano, which she loved, but no sheet music. On one of his sales trips, Papa brought back sheet music so Mama could play the newest popular songs. She had always enjoyed playing, and although she was a devout Methodist, she also loved to dance. At one point in her life, a preacher took her to task for that, and she never again entered a church. But she maintained her faith and her devotion to Methodism and saw to it that the children made regular appearances at Sunday school after their weekly baths. Saturday nights were special. Not only was it bath time, but it was the time when Papa came home. He always brought the *Saturday Evening Post* and Llerena learned to read from it. Once Papa came home with books. For Ben it was a collection of Robert Burns, for Llerena it was Longfellow's collected works, and for Mama it was Kipling's *Barrack-Room Ballads*. Llerena memorized Kipling.

Llerena's second brother, Everest MacDonald, was born in March 1910, and a few months later the family moved from Chillicothe to Vernon in Wilbarger County. At first they could not find a house, so they lived at the Bailey Hotel. Proprietors Bill and Pearl Bailey became family friends and remained close to the family for the rest of their lives. The move to Vernon brought other changes. Papa was now traveling for Carroll-Brough-Robinson-Gates of Wichita Falls, and he soon bought a car. He went by train to Dallas to get it and proudly drove it home over miles of unpaved country roads. It was well dented by the time he got back, but it was also famous. It was one of the first cars in Wilbarger County. Of course it was a Ford.

Llerena's formal education began in Vernon at the same school where she would later begin her teaching career. She completed the first grade and started the second in Vernon, but in September 1911 things changed. Oil had been discovered at Electra, twenty-five miles farther east on the Denver line, and Papa's bosses thought a retail store was in order. So the newborn firm of Friend and Puckett rented a store site and was in business. The store was in a building originally built by the Waggoner Ranch as a supply depot near the railroad. Unfortunately, it was next door to a saloon and had been in operation only two months when a drunk knocked over a lamp in the saloon and started a fire that burned down the entire block. There was a bucket brigade, but it failed because there was no water.

During the Electra oil boom housing was hard to find, and the best Papa could do was a four-room structure that Llerena remembered as the "Club House." She never knew why it bore that name. In any case, she spent a lot of time there helping to care for her brothers. Mama needed the help but was also leery of the neighborhood, for next to the "Club House" was a big tent featuring rows of cots inhabited twenty-four hours a day by oil field workers. The proprietor, Mr. Powell, never said anything to cause Llerena to be afraid, but sometimes at night, after a "disturbance," she would hear him call out to Mama, "Don't worry Mrs. Friend, I've got him."

At the time the store burned, the Masonic Lodge was putting up a new two-story building, so Friend and Puckett made a deal and reopened their store on the lower floor. There was no such thing as adequate refrigeration, so they featured only staples, such as crackers, tobacco, coffee, coal oil, and canned goods. Of course, the family needed more, so they bought eggs and milk from local farmers and fresh meat from a butcher whose establishment was known as Mr. Delashaw's Tuff Steak Meat Market. The family had an icebox with a drip pan, but considered it better and safer to buy fresh meat. The water from the drip pan was used to wash the children's hair because it was the softest and cleanest water available. Drinking water came to Electra in tank cars on the railroad and was purchased by the barrel. They stored it in a tin cistern that also served to catch what little rainwater came along. Wash water, bath water, and dishwater was never put down the drain; all were saved to put on the ground outside to dampen the dust.

The first sojourn of the Friend family in Electra came to an end when Papa traded the farm near Dublin for a house in Wichita Falls at the corner of Eighth and Broad Streets, right across from Bellevue Park. There they had running water, an indoor bathroom, and gaslights, but it was lonely because Papa remained in Electra to tend the store. It was as if he were still on the road, although he did come home on weekends. Llerena had vivid memories of that year in Wichita Falls. She got her first pair of ice skates for Christmas. She and her friends rode the elevator in the Kemp and Kell Building. They watched Mrs. Frank Kell drive her Detroit Electric Brougham. (Later the Kell family would make significant contributions to the Texas Collection at the University of Texas.) She and her friends played Indians on the bluffs near Riverside Cemetery, unaware that it was a real Indian campground and that Jesse James had once found sanctuary there. It was also in Wichita Falls that Llerena encountered her first library, made up of three rows of books in a small anteroom in the Methodist Church on Tenth Street; little did Llerena know that she would later make her career in the library of a major university.

Llerena attended Alamo School during that year in Wichita Falls and enjoyed living in the "Big City" (Wichita Falls had a population of about 10,000 at that time), but business was good in Electra and Papa wanted his family back with him. So he bought a Hudson Super Six touring car and off they went to Electra in style. The house they lived in had burned down so they were back in a rental briefly, but Papa soon bought a new place on Cleveland "Avenue," which was in reality a dirt road on the edge of town. Those were the summers, just before the nation entered World War I, that Llerena vacationed in Dublin. She would sleep at Granny Perry's and spend each day with one or another of her four aunts. She passed her time playing with her cousins, reading, and going to prayer meetings on Wednesday nights and church on Sunday. She remembered that each time she arrived in Dublin, the aunts would immediately wash all her clothes—at night. Her garments were dingy from the incessant sandstorms and poor water in Electra, and the aunts could not bear for the neighbors to see them on their clothesline, so they would wash and wash; by the end of the summer her clothes would be bleached. That did not matter because when they were not washing, the aunts were sewing, and they always sent her home with a new wardrobe.

In 1917 Electra built a new high school, and the Friend family moved into a new home only two blocks from the school. It had three bedrooms and indoor plumbing that worked only occasionally, so Llerena remembered preferring the outdoor facility. Before long, a series of tragedies befell the family. Llerena's younger brother, Everest, accidentally set the house on fire while playing with matches. Only the roof was destroyed, but the family had to find shelter with friends while the house was repaired. They were back home by Christmas, and into the rebuilt house two more Friend children were born. Emma Perry, Llerena's first little sister, lived only eighteen months. Five months after her death, Baby Brother was born dead. Both were buried in the cemetery at Vernon where Mama and Papa would later be laid to rest.

Llerena completed high school in Electra during World War I. The classes she remembered most clearly were Latin, math, English, history, and home economics. She and Mama both thought that the last was a waste of time. What was "economical" about requiring Llerena to buy new material to make a cup towel when she could do just as well with a flour sack or a feed sack? There was also a little music, but no art or physical education. They got their exercise, she remembered, by running up and down the sidelines at football games. She also remembered that the track team won the interscholastic meet in Austin. Their uniform pants were made from an American flag, and she wondered later if that was such a good idea.

During the second decade of the twentieth century Electra was still a raw frontier town with major growing pains and no physical beauty, but it had good people with civic pride and school loyalty. Mama helped organize the parent-teacher association, and Papa helped organize the Business League, which grew into the Chamber of Commerce. Electra was still competing with Wichita Falls for area dominance, and the local folks did everything they could to promote their town. On one occasion, the Chamber of Commerce sponsored a special train from Dallas and Fort Worth to bring visitors to a big barbeque to show off the oil industry and the economic development it had spawned. But Llerena remembered that the elements showed off instead. A thunderstorm doused the outdoor barbeque pit and a bolt of lightning struck an oil tank farm. The resulting fire spoiled the party, but gave the visitors an opportunity to see a spectacular conflagration.

Llerena and her friends were aware that the nation was at war. They bought thrift stamps and tried to practice conservation. At home Llerena learned to mix wheat, rice, and barley flour to make a strange biscuit. She did not know exactly how that promoted conservation, but she wrote a paper about it for an essay contest. Papa was a "Ten Minute Man," and one Sunday he was on stage at the theater selling savings bonds when someone rushed in with the news that his store was on fire. (The structure was badly damaged, and he was forced to start over once again.) Llerena and her friends sang war songs such as "Over There" and "Tipperary," and her declamation for the Interscholastic League contest was on Newell D. Hillis's "The Woes of Belgium." She was proud of it, but did not win first place. Then came November 11, 1918, and the armistice. Classes were canceled and businesses closed and Electrans paraded through the streets. In the excitement a button on Llerena's petticoat broke and her skirt fell off.

Llerena was a senior during the 1919–1920 academic year and graduated with the largest class in the history of Electra High School—thirteen girls and five boys. The following September seventeen of the eighteen went to college; the only one who did not was the class valedictorian. Also, in September, Llerena and Mama set out on one of their last train rides together on the Fort Worth and Denver, bound for Austin where Llerena would enroll in the University of Texas. The first part of growing up was over.[3]

In her freshman year Llerena took history classes from men who were to become legends. These included Eugene C. Barker and Walter Prescott Webb. In her junior year Barker, impressed with her ability, gave her an assistantship in a modern European history class taught by Professor Frederick Duncalf. The shelves of his office held copies of a magazine called the *Quarterly of the Texas State Historical Association,* which at the time meant nothing to her. The following year she became a grader for Webb and also attended his education course, How to Teach History. She was always glad that she did. At that time, Webb shared an office with Charles Ramsdell, who was secretary-treasurer of the Texas State Historical Association. There were more copies of the *Quarterly* in that office, and she began to suspect that the association might be important.

After graduation, she took a teaching job in Vernon and stayed there for two years. The fall of 1926 found her in Wichita Falls to begin a teaching job at

Wichita Falls High School that would last, on and off, for eighteen years. She was awarded a University Fellowship at the University of Texas for the 1927–1928 academic year, so she went to Austin and completed her M.A. degree, writing a thesis in the field of Texas history while learning the subject material on the side. She returned to Wichita Falls and taught English, civics, and general history until the early 1930s brought plans for the Texas Centennial. One summer prior to 1936, she went to the University of California and took two courses from Herbert E. Bolton. Her seminar paper was on the Tovayas Indians. When she returned, she was told that a new course in Texas history was to be offered and she was to teach it. Because of the approaching centennial, the newspapers were full of articles on Texas history, so she clipped them out and put together several scrapbooks filed according to topics on the subject.

At about the same time, she received word from Austin that Webb wanted her to organize a chapter of Junior Historians, and she did it by conducting club activities along with her class. She introduced her students to the *Quarterly*; they made reports from the magazine and were impressed when she could tell them personal things about the authors. With the help of colleagues Louise Kelly and J. W. Williams, Llerena took some of her students to annual Junior Historians meetings and sometimes submitted papers that won prizes. Each year she also took the Junior Historians to some historic spot in the area—Fort Belknap, Fort Griffin, Spanish Fort—and to commemorate the only event that took place on home ground, they raised money to erect a monument to the Texas–Santa Fe Expedition of 1841. The monument was dedicated in 1941, and Walter Prescott Webb came to town to make the banquet speech.

Meanwhile, Webb had persuaded the university administration and the Texas Legislature to support the first *Handbook of Texas* project, and it was underway. Llerena was asked to begin work on the *Handbook* in the summer of 1943. Her task was to start a list of "Tentative Subjects." She returned to Wichita Falls to teach the fall semester and then went back to Austin in February 1944 to continue work on the *Handbook*. Her last stint of high school teaching came in the 1944–1945 academic year, after which she returned once more to Austin where she would remain until 1975. For the next few years she worked on the *Handbook* project and proofread manuscripts for the *Quarterly*. She also taught an occasional class in American history.

When Llerena moved to Austin she had no interest in pursuing an advanced degree, but when she discovered that university policy allowed employees to take one course each semester on university time, she succumbed and went to work on her Ph.D. Eventually she completed her course work, the *Handbook* project came to an end, and she wondered what she would do next. When she went to seek advice from Webb, he told her that she would soon be asked to become the librarian of the soon-to-be-established Eugene C. Barker Texas History Center. And so, at the age of forty-seven, she launched herself into a new career and began to think about a dissertation topic.[4]

Her primary responsibility in her new job was to assist head librarian Ernest W. Winkler with the administration of the Texas Collection. At that time, the Texas Collection and the Eugene C. Barker Texas History Center were affiliated with the university library. They were not separated until 1991. The collection includes books, printed materials, pictures, manuscripts, and scrapbooks covering not only most of Texas history but also the greater Southwest and the Old South. It began shortly after the founding of the university but owes its successful early development mostly to the efforts of Winkler. At first, the Texas Collection consisted primarily of law books, sets of statutes, digests, and *Texas Reports*, but over the years various people and organizations made gifts and contributions and the collection grew steadily but slowly. In 1897, the collection consisted of about 283 volumes and just under 100 newspapers. In 1898 came the gift of Governor Oran M. Roberts's library and, in 1899, Colonel Ashbel Smith's library. At about the same time the Commissioners' Court of Bexar County transferred the Spanish Archives to the university. As the years passed, the library purchased new materials to the extent allowed by the meager budget, but relied heavily on gifts for its development. The establishment of the Littlefield Fund for Southern History by George W. Littlefield in 1914 and the arrival of the Genaro García Collection on the history of Mexico in 1917 both enriched the collection. The former furnished the American background of Texas and the latter the Spanish and Mexican background.

As the 1920s dawned and Llerena arrived in Austin to further her education, the catalogue department of the university library began sending more and more material to the Texas Collection. Included were University of Texas publications, state publications, publications of religious groups in Texas, publications of all organizations having state or local chapters in Texas, periodicals published in the state, books by Texans, and books about Texas written by non-Texans. By 1934, the size of the collection was estimated at 22,514 pieces; with the appointment of Marcelle Hamer in 1935, the Texas Collection had its first special librarian.

The collection had to be broadened to include material on the Southwest for use in J. Frank Dobie's popular course Life and Literature of the Southwest and Walter Prescott Webb's course on the Great Plains, which encompassed a wide geographical base. By 1939, the collection consisted of more than 25,000 items, including all things pertaining to the life of Texas: history, biography, natural history, geography, geology, botany, government, business, folklore, education, archeology, and religion. And major gifts continued to arrive. Late in 1941, Blanche McKie, as a memorial to her father, W. J. McKie, presented the library with the W. A. Philpott Jr. Collection, which consisted of first-edition mint copies of 2,500 Texas books. With this and other acquisitions, the space in the library allocated for Texas books had become crowded by the early forties, and in 1945 the university's board of regents decided to return a structure known as the Cass Gilbert Building (now Battle Hall) to its original library use and to house in it all the books, archives, historical manuscripts, and other items relating to Texas and Southwest history. Henceforth, the collection, including the offices of the Texas State Historical Association, was to be known as the Eugene C. Barker Texas History Center. At the April 1950 meeting of the Texas State Historical Association, the center was dedicated to be the location on the campus of "a corner forever Texas."[5]

Between the time that the Barker Texas History Center was authorized and the facility opened, two major additions were made to the collection. In 1948 came the Earl Vandale Collection, an impressive combination of printed and manuscript material, including many rare books, and a significant amount of German material, but with an emphasis on the history of the Panhandle area. Even more impressive, however, was the Kell Collection. Frank Kell, who died in 1941, was a wealthy Wichita Falls businessman, who for years had collected books on the frontier—not only the frontier of settlement, but of enterprises in mining, milling, and railroading. Several of his children, including Sadie—the wife of Orville Bullington, a University of Texas regent—had attended the university. Bullington had been instrumental in the establishment of the Barker Center, and in the summer of 1945 he discussed the disposition of the Kell family library with Dr. Barker, suggesting that some 200 books, mostly Texas items, might be given to the university. Ernest Winkler went to Wichita Falls to examine the books and chose those destined to go to Austin. His original list contained not merely 200 items, but rather 608, for which he apologized to Bullington—who then encouraged him to ask for more. It was obvious that Bullington wanted all the Kell books to go to the Barker Center, and before very long the family agreed to donate the entire collection, some 2,000 volumes. In addition, they created the Kell Fund, the proceeds of which were to be used for the purchase of additional books.[6]

The Texas Collection was thus a large and continually growing project when Llerena took her new job, and administering it was a time-consuming task. Nevertheless, she was determined to finish her Ph.D., so she consulted Barker and Webb about a dissertation topic. Much to her surprise, they proposed that she focus her research on Sam Houston. She responded that Houston had been "done"—and by experts like Marquis James, whose biography of Houston, *The Raven,* had won a Pulitzer Prize. Barker replied that, in fact, no major biography of Houston had been written since the compilation of Houston's papers, and that a new documented biography was needed.

So Llerena went to work, spending every spare moment delving into all the printed material about Houston, his own writings, documents showing what his contemporaries thought about him, the archives of the Republic, and many other sources, such as the university archives and the state archives, in addition to microfilm and photocopies obtained from other institutions. The Daughters of the Republic of Texas gave her the Clara Driscoll Scholarship for Research in Texas History, which enabled her to spend time in Washington to examine relevant holdings in the Library of Congress and the National Archives. As her research progressed, Llerena decided that her work would deal principally with Houston's activities in national politics. She would not ignore his unusual and colorful personal life, nor his monumental contributions to Texas, but she would concentrate on his significance to the national scene during the critical years between the Texas Revolution and the outbreak of the Civil War.

Guided by Barker, Llerena finished her dissertation and was granted her Ph.D. in the spring of 1951. Both Barker and Webb were so pleased with her work that they urged her to submit it to the University of Texas Press for publication. So Llerena plunged into the difficult task of converting a dry, scholarly piece to a book that would be, while still factual, appealing to the general public. She succeeded. Even before the book was released in December 1954, she received the distinguished Summerfield G. Roberts Award from the Sons of the Republic of Texas for what was judged to be the best book of the year mirroring the characters and characteristics of the founders of Anglo-American Texas.[7]

Llerena titled her book *Sam Houston, the Great Designer* in reference to the fact that her emphasis was on Houston's work as a practical politician and statesman. He was, after all, a political planner, thinker, and perhaps even a schemer. And yet, even Llerena, after all her deep and methodical research, could not provide definitive answers to some of the questions that had puzzled Houston's friends, detractors, and biographers since before the Great Designer died. Concerning the question of why Houston came to Texas, she told Stanley E. Bebb, book review editor of the *Galveston News*:

> I have not been able, had it been my wish, to prove that Houston came to Texas as Jackson's tool to win the area for the United States or that he was involved in a capitalist conspiracy to speculate Texas lands as a corporate lawyer. The Texas Revolution was inevitable with or without Houston. He was there to make a living and to make a name for himself. His separation from his wife (Eliza Allen) had shattered his personal life and his political future. Timed with that shock was the invitation to Texas. . . . Texas was adjacent (to Arkansas) and offered a chance political and financial. A political change was inevitable there, and he had political experience which he might use to advantage, but in what direction he was not sure. Above all, he was an opportunist.[8]

As to Houston's career in the Senate, Llerena said:

> To say that Sam Houston was colorful as a United States Senator is as trite as it is true. Measured against Clay, Webster, and Calhoun with whom he served his first years in the Senate, he perhaps did not prove their equal in statesmanship. He was always personal, he was vindictive, he dramatized himself, he used sarcasm and even vulgarity to make his point. He could be small in small things, but he was always right on fundamental issues, and he was, regardless of what his enemies said, entirely consistent.[9]

Of course, there were many reviews of Llerena's book in newspapers, magazines, and scholarly journals, but the best one, the one that most effectively captured the essence of Llerena's great work, was the one offered by Professor Rupert N. Richardson:

> It is calculated to change one's conception of Sam Houston. The picture is still blurred in spots, but the features of the man are clearer than we have ever seen them before. There is the Houston of contrasts: the man who might appear dressed in the best taste or, more likely, wearing a panther skin vest or some other token of his love of the bizarre; who could, on one occasion, harass his host and landlady by spitting on her clean porch and having his servant cut off the posts of a fine old bed and, on another, move from his presidential "mansion" to make room for a needy widow and her children; who could hurl at his enemies the bitterest of sarcasm and address his friends and family with the gentlest words. Here is set forth the Houston who could rise from the gutter to the presidency of a republic, who could play the politician so deftly and then, as a statesman, fighting to the end and go down so magnificently with the great cause of unionism, prompted by a prophetic vision to believe that history would vindicate his course.
>
> This biography, the most nearly definitive that has yet appeared, suggests that Sam Houston must be remembered with the great.[10]

Llerena was pleased with the reception of her book, but when asked what her next project would be, she replied that she would never write another monograph or biography. She was content to devote herself to her career as a librarian. She did that, but at the same time she did not entirely give up her scholarly pursuits. She edited three books, *Check List of Texas Imprints, 1861–1876* (1963), M. K. Kellogg's *Texas Journal, 1872* (1967), and *Talks on Texas Books* by Walter Prescott Webb (1970). She also published numerous articles in such journals as the *Southwestern Historical Quarterly, Texas and the West, Library Chronicle of The University of Texas, West Texas Historical Association Yearbook,* and others. And, of course, there were many book reviews. Llerena also taught the United States Survey and Texas History from time to time as an adjunct member of the University of Texas history department.

In addition to the Summerfield Award, other honors were bestowed upon her. She was elected to the Texas Institute of Letters and was made a fellow of the Texas State Historical Association, and all the while she continued her work in the Barker Center until her retirement in 1969. After that she remained in Austin until 1975, when she moved back to Wichita Falls. Shortly after that I met her.[11]

Llerena was seventy-two when she arrived in Wichita Falls, but she was still vigorous and had many interests. She began to attend lectures and other events at Midwestern State University, where I was head of the history department, and we soon got to know each other. Occasionally, we would get together and talk about history, Sam Houston, current events, and other things. At the university we were trying at the time to develop a small archive and rare book room in our library, and she became interested in the project. One day she called and asked me to come over to her apartment; she said she had something to give me. When I arrived, we talked for a little while and then she produced a box. She said it was mine, but suggested that I put it in our new rare book collection. I said of course, and then I opened the box. It contained the research notes for her book, *Sam Houston, The Great Designer*.

As Llerena grew older, I wanted to do something to honor her before it was too late. So, with the help of the Midwestern State University administration, I planned a dinner party for her to be held at the Wichita Falls Country Club. One of her old friends was Frank Vandiver, who was chancellor of the Texas A&M University system. He accepted an invitation to speak at the party and flew up to Wichita Falls on the Texas A&M plane. She beamed as he gave a wonderful talk reminiscing about their friendship and her career. That evening was one of the last times Llerena and I were together. She died on September 8, 1995, at the age of ninety-two. I still miss her.

SUGGESTED READING

Friend, Llerena. *Sam Houston, the Great Designer*. Austin: University of Texas Press, 1954.

Llerena's biography of Sam Houston was her only book. However, she edited three books for the University of Texas Press in 1963, 1967, and 1970. She was also the author of several scholarly articles that appeared in various journals, including *Southwestern Historical Quarterly*.

NOTES

1. Llerena Friend, unpublished autobiographical essay, typescript, Llerena Beaufort Friend Papers, 1918–1986, box 3F403, Dolph Briscoe Center for American History, University of Texas at Austin (hereafter Friend Papers).

2. Ibid.

3. Ibid. Early in her biographical essay Llerena writes that the family made twenty-four moves during her childhood, but she does not discuss every move the family made.

4. Llerena Friend, "Me and the 'Hysterical' Association," unpublished essay, typescript, box 3F403, Friend Papers.

5. Friend, unpublished autobiographical essay.

6. Llerena Friend, "The Texas Collection," unpublished essay, typescript, box 3F403, Friend Papers.

7. *Houston Post,* December 12, 1954.

8. *Galveston News,* December 19, 1954; *Little Rock Gazette,* February 20, 1955.

9. *Galveston News,* December 19, 1954.

10. Rupert N. Richardson, "Review of *Sam Houston, the Great Designer,*" *Southwestern Historical Quarterly* 58, no. 4 (April 1955): 568–570.

11. Laurie E. Jasinski, "Llerena Friend," in *The New Handbook of Texas,* edited by Ron Tyler (Austin: Texas State Historical Association, 1996), 3:3–4.

DON GRAHAM

J. FRANK DOBIE

J. FRANK DOBIE, 1957, AT JOE SMALL'S BARBECUE

Where history is doubtful, legend is assured.

J. FRANK DOBIE, "THE LEGEND OF THE SAN SABA OR BOWIE MINE," *Legends of Texas*

James Frank Dobie, dubbed "Mr. Texas" by his biographer, Lon Tinkle, was once among the most famous names in the Lone Star State, but as the years pass that fame has lessened.[1] Today's generation of students at the University of Texas, where he taught, have hardly any inkling of who he was. Some believe that he must have had something to do with Dobie Mall, a commercial and residential high-rise at Twenty-First and Guadalupe that opened in 1967. And indeed the name was selected because at that time, three years after his death, Dobie was still the university's best-known faculty member, despite the fact that he had not been on the faculty since 1947. Others think he was a Texas politician, and still others a Texas Ranger. But mostly the students say they are clueless.

Still, there are Dobie memorials on and off campus that keep his name green. His home on Dean Keeton Street, across from the Law School, is listed in the National Register of Historic Places and is a designated Texas Historic Landmark, although the house is now primarily known for being the headquarters of the Michener Center for Writers. Perhaps the most visible sign of Dobie's onetime importance in the community is the *Philosophers' Rock* statue installed near the entrance of Barton Springs Pool in Zilker Park. Here for eternity, or close to it, may be seen the three friends credited with "inventing" Texas literature—Dobie, Roy Bedichek, and Walter P. Webb. Engaged in bronzed discourse, they carry on their dialogues on this simulacrum of Bedi's rock. (The actual rock, located in or beside the water, was swept away in a flood.) But even with this stone salute, the identity gets blurred; once, on site, a visitor was heard to remark that the statue was a depiction of Lyndon B. Johnson.

Another Dobie memorial is Paisano Ranch, fifteen miles southwest of Austin, where each year two recipients of Paisano Fellowships enjoy a six-month stay in creative solitude. (This site, however, is not open to the public.) In Austin there is a J. Frank Dobie Middle School (as there are other schools named for Bedichek, Webb, and Américo Paredes). Finally, there are Dobie's books, numerous titles of which are available in paperback from the University of Texas Press. Without such writings, of course, Dobie's legend would never have been born in the first place.

His lifelong interest in books, in reading, grew naturally from his family background. Born in Live Oak County on September 26, 1888 (the same year as Webb and T. S. Eliot), Dobie, the eldest of six children, received the imprint of four influences: rural ranch life, Methodism, Victorian culture, and the Old South.[2] He eventually abandoned both the strict religious certitude of his rancher father and the Rebel sympathies of his maternal grandfather, who inculcated in the young Dobie a reverential idealization of General Robert E. Lee and the Lost Cause. But Dobie's interest in ranching never flagged, nor did his love of books. If his father emphasized one book, the Bible, his mother read aloud to her children such classics as *Treasure Island, Ivanhoe,* and *The Swiss Family Robinson.* (Perhaps Stevenson's novel of buried treasure influenced Dobie's interest in the subject decades later, resulting in two books.) In a late essay Dobie remarked that when he was growing up, people in the country "who read books at all read good ones — mostly. Drugstore literature was as unknown as drugstore cowboys."[3]

The story of how Dobie became a writer and what kind of writer he became — and remained his whole life — begins with his early enthusiasm for reading and listening to his mother read, and continues with his college years at Southwestern University in Georgetown. Dobie matriculated as a freshman in 1906 and graduated four years later. In an autobiographical essay tellingly titled "Prose and Poetry," Dobie recounted his experiences at Southwestern. It was there that he met R. S. Hyer, the university president, who much impressed the young freshman by telling him that he had always read a book a week, whereupon said freshman vowed to do the same. The professor who made the biggest impact on Dobie was, perhaps not surprisingly, an English teacher, Albert Shipp Pegues. In Pegues's class Dobie studied the history of English poetry through Tennyson, and Tennyson is just about where Dobie's knowledge of poetry stopped. As with the Modernist prose masters whom he appears not to have read, he appears likewise not to have read T. S. Eliot, Wallace Stevens, Ezra Pound, or William Carlos Williams, all of whom were producing their greatest work during the 1920s when Dobie was an instructor in the English department at the University of Texas. Dobie kept his gaze on the past. As he recalled his days at Southwestern, he stated, "I was my essential self when I walked alone up the San Gabriel River with a volume of Wordsworth."[4] The imprint of English poetry was so strong that Dobie claimed that he "drifted into teaching solely because I had fallen in love with English poetry and wanted to continue and communicate that love."[5] At Southwestern he also met a classmate, Bertha McKee, whom he would eventually marry.

After college Dobie pursued his twin vocational goals: teaching and writing. In 1910 and 1911 he worked summers on newspapers in Galveston and San Antonio, and in 1910 he also took a job as principal and teacher at the high school in Alpine, way out in the Big Bend country. In addition, Dobie directed plays and edited the school newspaper.

Dobie also apparently taught the theory of evolution to his students in Alpine. In a letter to her son written in 1911, Dobie's mother sarcastically criticized him for his belief in the "precious doctrine of evolution" and implored him thus: "Oh. My son it is bad enough to fill your own mind with poison but for God's sake and for my sake don't try to shake any child's faith in God and God's word."[6] In 1911 the heretic moved back to Georgetown, where he taught for the next two years in a preparatory school for Southwestern.

In January 1913 Dobie went to New York to attend Columbia University. Letters from this period and entries in a journal that Dobie kept offer windows into his feelings and aspirations as he struggled, in his mid-twenties, to define himself. Dobie spent a lonely year and a half there, earning an M.A. and conclusively deciding that he did not want to pursue a Ph.D. New York made Dobie feel even more intensely aware of his southern roots, as had a brief trip to Chicago that he had made while still at Southwestern. A notice in *University Notes* (Southwestern) in 1909 highlighted how the young Texan—namely, Dobie—might feel upon encountering the North: "He dodged all the isms and heresies promulgated by the Chicago University and absorbed only the good. He avoided negro equality up there and came back to dear old Texas without a scalp in his belt."[7]

Dobie's youthful Confederate sympathies were much influenced by the years he had spent living with his grandfather, Friendly Dubose, from age sixteen to eighteen. Dubose revered Robert E. Lee and refused to celebrate the Fourth of July.[8] In a letter to his mother, dated January 19, 1913, Dobie professed, "I have cried many times because I was born too late to fight with these [Lee and other Southern generals], but I know now that there are battles to be fought for the same sweet land, as hard, as glorious, as decisive as they fought."[9] Dobie later recanted these Rebel sentiments, yet he remarked in one of his autobiographical essays, "Sometimes when I see the small Confederate flags that people stick on their automobiles—more through hate than love—I remember how the blood rushed to my head and tears to my eyes when I heard 'Dixie' played in a New York theater while I was attending Columbia University."[10] In another telling sentence, the elder Dobie, looking back on his younger self, summed up the two main loyalties of his youth: "I was disappointed with life because I had been born too late to help Grandpa fight the Yankees, and too late also to drive up the Trail with him and Papa and uncles on both sides of the house."[11]

In New York Dobie often seems to have felt or been made to feel provincial—and homesick. In a letter to his mother of June 29, 1913, he wrote of how the city seemed to him a "hell-hole of noise, colors, sophistication and vulgarity."[12] Nor was he happy with his lot as a graduate student. On February 16, 1913, he wrote his mother, "A look at this graduate work assigned is purely pedantry and foolishness of no practical worth."[13] Throughout his career Dobie would never cease to rail against pedantic Ph.D.'s.

It was the theater that proved to be the most positive and lasting experience in his New York stay. In his diary, which upon its completion he pronounced dull, Dobie kept a strict accounting of the plays that he saw during that year and a half. He mostly commented on the actors rather than the plays themselves. He saw a dozen or more productions of Shakespeare, as well as dramas by modern playwrights such as George Bernard Shaw, Somerset Maugham, and many other lesser lights. Attending plays and concerts seems to have been his chief form of entertainment and escape from the boredom and irrelevance of his graduate classes. He also attended performances of Richard Wagner's operas and heard, on another occasion, Enrico Caruso, the most popular tenor of the day.

In a later essay, Dobie declared that "New York gave me more than the university gave me."[14] He also stated, "I am sure that I received more from New York theaters than from Columbia professors."[15]

In June 1914, Dobie returned to Texas and began what would be a long, successful, and at times tempestuous teaching career in the English department at the University of Texas. That same year he learned a new word, folklore, and joined the Texas Folklore Society, an organization that would provide a network of affiliated interests in the study of regional history and culture that would propel him to the publication of his first book and beyond. All during this period he continued a courtship, mostly epistolary, with Bertha McKee and edged closer to marrying her, which he finally did in 1916.

In 1917 Dobie joined the U.S. Army and served in a field artillery unit. Although he arrived in France just at the war's end, he remained in Europe for over a year, returning in 1919 when he was discharged. After resigning from the university, he spent the following year managing his uncle Jim Dobie's ranch in South Texas. This was where enlightenment struck; Dobie vividly described the epiphany in his essay "How My Life Took Its Turn." Listening to old vaqueros around campfires tell of the days of the open range, Dobie "seemed to be seeing a great painting of something I'd known all my life. I seemed to be listening to a great epic." From these impressions he arrived at his destiny: "One day it came to me that I could collect and tell the legendary tales of Texas as Lomax had collected the old-time songs and ballads of Texas and the frontier."[16]

From then on, Dobie's career had a direction it had previously lacked. He returned to the University of Texas, resumed his teaching career, took up the position of secretary of the Texas Folklore Society in 1922—a post he would hold for twenty-one years—and saw the first book with his name on it published in 1924, *Legends of Texas,* which he edited. The volume contained sixty-six pieces, among which were two by Walter Prescott Webb, three by Bertha McKee Dobie, and thirteen by Dobie himself. Dobie's entries included several that would reappear in his breakthrough book of 1931, *Coronado's Children,* including "Treasure Legends of McMullen County" and "The Nigger Gold Mine of the Big Bend."

In the "Editor's Preface" to *Legends of Texas,* Dobie listed his academic affiliation as Oklahoma Agricultural and Mechanical College, Stillwater, Oklahoma, where he had assumed chairmanship of the English department in 1923. He left Texas because the university would not promote him without a Ph.D. and because he needed more money. One way he increased his income was by writing articles for a popular magazine of the day, *Country Gentleman*. Dobie was at Oklahoma A&M for only two years, returning to the University of Texas on the basis of a small promotion.

In 1929 Dobie published his first authored book, *A Vaquero of the Brush Country,* and herein lies a tale worth retelling. The title page read, "Partly from the Reminiscences of John D. Young." It also contained a preface by Dobie titled "A Necessary Explanation." Everybody considered the book to be Dobie's. Lon Tinkle stated unequivocally that it was "Frank's first book that was all his own."[17]

And so things stood until 1998, when the University of Texas Press released a paperback edition of *Vaquero* that listed not one but two authors: John D. Young and J. Frank Dobie. Removed was the reference to "Partly from . . ." and there was also a subtitle where none had been before: "The Life and Times of John D. Young." Thus, in one stroke, Dobie was demoted from sole author to supporting author behind Young, the reference to the use of Young's reminiscences was dropped, and the title was altered with the addition of a subtitle. Suddenly it was no longer Dobie's book.

This surprising change in authorship has gone almost totally unnoticed in the scholarly community. It is hard to say whether anybody is paying attention or whether it is simply that nobody cares.

But it does seem important, and a review of Dobie's claim, apparent in both his preface to the 1929 edition and in the letters he exchanged with John D. Young, leads one to conclude that Dobie was the sole author of the book. Dobie's preface written for the first edition makes it clear that he considered himself the sole author. Young provided the raw material—but not all of it—and Dobie provided everything else. According to Dobie, in a telling phrase, Young "has never made any pretensions to being a writer." Dobie then explains that he changed Young's "arrangement" of material, and his language as well, in order to "give his style a pitch in unity with my own."[18] Lawrence Clark Powell, a leading authority on western writing, in a preface to the 1957 edition declared that the book "was unmistakably Dobie on every page, in every paragraph, sentence, and word, its prose permeated with the flavor of the writer I have called the best Southwesterner of them all."[19]

Dobie's letters to Young give a very full picture of Dobie's role in the making of the book. The evidence for designating Dobie as the author of *Vaquero* is very strong. On July 30, 1926, Dobie explained what remained to be done: "Now

I must make all the joints fit in together so that the narrative will flow in a smooth, uninterrupted way."[20] In a sense Dobie was babysitting Young at the same time that that he was doing the hard, grinding work of getting the book fleshed out and replete with all the virtues that Dobie demanded of historical writing: reality, vividness, authenticity, readability. The goal, he wrote on August 2, 1928, was to create "something new in cowboy literature."[21]

Once the book was published and the sales proved disappointing to Young, Dobie allowed a note of vexation to creep into his correspondence with Young, who appears to have been pressuring Dobie to sell, sell, sell. Wrote Dobie on December 9, 1929, "As for taking some months off to sell the book. You must not realize my position. I am engaged here to teach in the University and am being paid a starvation salary to do so. I can't get up and leave when I want to. Furthermore, I am not worth a dern as a salesman."[22]

Young died in 1932 and so ended the Dobie-Young relationship. *Vaquero* went through many editions in the years to come, which brings us back to the question of why the authorship was changed in 1998. The answer, one might easily guess, is that Young's heirs went to court, and that answer would be correct. On June 6, 1994, John D. Young's heirs filed a petition with U.S. District Court, Western District of Texas, Austin Division. Their claim was that John Young was coauthor with Dobie, and the basis for their claim, attached with the petition, was a contract between Dobie and Young dated March 17, 1928. This contract made null and void an earlier one, dated February 14, 1927. A judgment was handed down on February 28, 1995, saying that any new publication of the book had to display the following: "The Life and Times of John D. Young by John D. Young and J. Frank Dobie" immediately below the title of the book.[23]

The demotion of Dobie's authorship runs contrary to Dobie's preface, the judgments of western scholars such as Lawrence Clark Powell, the Dobie-Young correspondence, and the unmistakable Dobie "voice" that resonates through the prose. And again, why this change of authorship seems to bother no one is rather mystifying.

Nineteen twenty-nine was important for Dobie in another respect because that was the year he invented his famous course, English 342, Life and Literature of the Southwest. As soon as he proposed the course, he ran into opposition from the senior professors who ran the shop. As the story goes, the Ph.D.'s solemnly declared that there was no such thing as southwestern literature. Dobie carried the day by countering that, in any event, there was plenty of life and he would teach that.

To be fair, however, the old dons in the English department had a point. In 1929 American literature as a whole was only beginning to cut into the dominance of British and classical literature in colleges and universities around the country. Certainly the Southwest as a literary region would seem a hard sell to professors skeptical of adding national literature to the curriculum. Dobie well understood what he was up against: he was quite familiar with the disdain that many faculty held for the region where the University of Texas was located. Folklorist John A. Lomax had run into the same kind of elitist cultural assumptions when he proposed to collect cowboy songs. He had to go to Harvard to find faculty who appreciated the importance of regional culture.

Happily, Dobie's proposal coincided with a burst of creative literary energy in the Southwest that received national attention. In 1930, for example, two southwestern books racked up Pulitzer Prizes: Santa Fe–based author Oliver La Farge's novel *Laughing Boy* and Marquis James's biography of Texas hero Sam Houston, *The Raven*. In Texas things were astir as well. Katherine Anne Porter's *Flowering Judas* was published in 1930 to widespread acclaim, and Dobie and Webb both published significant regional works in 1931: *Coronado's Children* and *The Great Plains*.

In the end Dobie prevailed and got his course up and running in the spring semester of 1930. He would offer it regularly for the next two decades, and it would continue in other hands through the century and into the next. The manner in which Dobie taught the class can be gleaned from a surviving document from the spring semester of 1940—a compilation of the best work done by members of the class. In May the students put together a bound mimeographed anthology with a title in the form of a cattle brand: "E342" (the *E* is on its back with the three lines sticking up—the lazy *E*). The title page described the work as "A Collection of Stray Mavericks Caught, Roped, and Branded by Members of the 'Big Corral' (English 342: Life and Literature of the Southwest)." A student named William H. Cleveland Jr. was listed as the "Foreman," and the "Boss o' the Outfit" was, naturally, J. Frank Dobie. Sixty-nine pages long, the anthology brought together the work of 39 student contributors from a total of 107 class members.

In a brief preface, Dobie stated the rationale for studying the art of a particular region: "I have not ceased to din into your ears the idea that any literature, art, architecture, or even music that the Southwest can hope to achieve, will, if it is 'authentic,' reflect the backgrounds of its setting."[24] Then he took a familiar swipe at the Littlefield Fountain on the South Mall of the campus, arguing that the sculptor should have depicted burros or mustangs instead of winged horses.

Student work was arranged in categories that might have come from a Dobie book: "Critters in the Southwest"; "The Pioneers"; "Those Hero Folks"; "Dust, Quartz, and Bullion"; "Ridin' Herd"; and "Hunter's Stew." As for his students' scribblings, they all sounded like little Dobies. The titles of the individual pieces included "Cougar Tales My Grandma Told," "The Story of Juan Torres," "Dulco, the Cutting Horse," "Down the Road Lived Bigfoot Wallace," "Buried Treasure in Central Texas," and "The Cowboy's Philosophy."

Dobie the literary and curriculum pioneer was leading his charges into the still-fertile field of frontier folklore. His students could interview grandparents and other old-timers who went right back to the thrilling days of yesteryear. Nineteenth-century history was as close as Granddad's rocking chair.

Because of the newness of the subject and the scarcity of texts—this was long before the paperback revolution—Dobie did not have a core set of works, a canon that everybody read. In effect, he was trying to figure out if there *was* a canon, a generally agreed upon consensus as to the best works. To this end Dobie assembled and added to, as the years went by, an annotated list of books that he considered relevant.

One such mimeographed compilation, for example, was put together in 1936 under the title "Life and Literature of the Southwest: An Incomplete Guide to Books on Texas and the Southwest." Here Dobie made the case for his subject in his usual combative manner. Castigating Harvard and the "sheep-like makers of textbooks" for emphasizing Puritan writers whom he considered "dreary creatures," he wrote, "I rebel at having the tradition, the spirit, the meaning of the soil to which I belong utterly neglected by academicians and at the same time having the Cotton Mather kind of thing taught."[25]

Just twenty-six pages long, the "Incomplete Guide" emphasized the western side of the Southwest almost exclusively. Divided into topic categories, the list included only one item that dealt with life east of IH 35: "Negro Folk Songs and Tales in the Southwest." There was also scant attention paid to fiction, as might be surmised from the title "The Fictional Betrayal of the Wild West." Similar categories would reflect Dobie's constant emphasis on the West to the near exclusion of the South when the compilation was published in book form as *Guide to Life and Literature of the Southwest* (University of Texas Press, 1943), followed ten years later by a second edition "Revised and Enlarged in Both Knowledge and Wisdom."

Dobie came fully into his own in the 1930s. He did it his way, by working hard, publishing steadily, and achieving a growing reputation that stretched far beyond the boundaries of the Forty Acres. He saw his work appear in such national publications as the *Saturday Evening Post*, the *Nation*, and the *American Mercury*. And in Texas he seemed to be everywhere. In 1932 he began regular appearances on a radio program originating from San Antonio, "Longhorn Luke and His Cowboys." More and more he cultivated a public persona and could be counted on for a frank comment on just about any subject. In 1933 Dobie was promoted to full professor, the first non-Ph.D. Texan to receive such an honor. And throughout it all, Dobie continued to publish steadily. In 1934 *Tongues of the Monte*, an account of a sojourn in Mexico, was released to disappointing reviews. This book was the closest that Dobie came to writing fiction, and despite Larry McMurtry's favorable opinion of it, *Tongues* remains more problematical than admired. In 1939 came *Apache Gold and Yaqui Silver,* another assemblage of treasure-hunting tales. It holds a special place in the very small world of Texas literary culture because it beat out Katherine Anne Porter's great *Pale Horse, Pale Rider* for best book of the year, awarded by the fledgling Texas Institute of Letters. In 1941 Dobie published the first of his critter books, *The Longhorns.*

This was followed by the intermittently interesting *A Texan in England* (1945), a collection of essays drawing on the two years (1942–1944) that Dobie spent at Cambridge University in wartime England lecturing on American history. While Dobie was in England, all hell broke loose at the University of Texas. During his absence the university became embroiled in an internecine war between an obtrusive board of regents and university president Homer P. Rainey. The regents ordered Rainey to fire four economics professors for teaching "Communist" theories, and they also went after the English department for including John Dos Passos's *U.S.A.* on a reading list. When Rainey refused to act, the regents fired him. From afar, Dobie followed the back-and-forth and, through letters to friends like Roy Bedichek, played an active role in defending Rainey. When Dobie asked for another leave, the new president saw a good opportunity to get rid of Dobie as well, and the regents passed the "Dobie rule," which is still in effect at the university: faculty leaves of absence are restricted to two years. Dobie appears to have liked the "martyrdom" and may well have provoked the severance, as he was now making enough money from his writings to be able to relinquish his long association with the university. At his house at 702 East 26th Street (formerly Park Place, now East Dean Keaton Street), he began to maintain a kind of one-man salon for writers and intellectuals either living in Austin or passing through.

A curious artifact from Dobie's teaching career can be seen in a 1951 Bantam Books paperback edition of *Apache Gold and Yaqui Silver.* The promotional material on the back cover, including a miniature of a Tom Lea drawing of Dobie, contains this description: "THE MAVERICK PROFESSOR is only one of the titles accorded author J. Frank Dobie by students at the University of Texas where his course 'Life and Literature of the Southwest' has been packing classrooms for more than 15 years." In 1951, however, Dobie hadn't taught at the University of Texas since 1942 and would never teach there again.

Dobie's political activism in the Rainey case was in line with his political conversion from ranch conservatism to New Deal liberalism. His change of heart happened in the late 1930s. John Henry Faulk often claimed that he was the agent of change in persuading Dobie to become a liberal Democrat, and maybe he was. In any case, Dobie began to speak out on such public issues as segregation and academic freedom.[26] Using his weekly newspaper columns as a forum for contemporary political commentary, Dobie lost some followers and probably gained some others. In 1945, for example, he advocated the proposition that blacks should be given full voting rights, and in a speech in Fort Worth he declared that he would welcome qualified black students to the University of Texas. Such progressive stands drew fire from citizens around the state. One anonymous letter was addressed to "Mr. Dopey," calling him a "decrepit, good-for-nothing old fossil and fool."[27] When he died, Kate Stoner O'Connor, wife of a famous South Texas rancher and at one time a supporter and friend of Dobie (he had written part of *The Longhorns* while staying at the O'Connor Ranch on the San Antonio River), wrote in her inscribed copy of *The Longhorns*: "J. Frank Dobie died in Austin, Texas, Friday, Sept. 18, 1964—unloved and unmourned—because he defected to the enemy—communism."[28]

After Dobie left the university, the books continued to pour out, including two critter books in three years: *The Voice of the Coyote* in 1949 and *The Mustangs* in 1952, probably the most thoroughly researched work that Dobie produced. But he also continued to write about human critters: one of his strangest books is *The Ben Lilly Legend* (1950), an uncritical account of a hunter obsessed with slaughtering wildlife in Texas. The body count of vanquished animals in this book is astounding. To the modern reader, the work appears to be a celebration of a psychopath. Lilly's biographer reports the following fact without censure: "Any hunting dog that proved lazy, he clubbed to death."[29] To such behavior, Dobie turned a blind eye.

Dobie was writing right up to the end. *Cow People*, published just before his death, brought together some salty portraits of cattlemen, from Shanghai Pierce to Charles Goodnight. Dobie's last critter book, *Rattlesnakes*, appeared posthumously in 1965, as did *Some Part of Myself*, an interesting collection of mostly autobiographical essays containing some of his best, most salient writing.

One interesting facet of Dobie's last few years is the degree to which he kept up with breaking news on the Texas literary scene. He read books by new authors such as Larry McMurtry, Edwin Shrake, Billy Lee Brammer, and John Graves. His annotations of his copies of these books, following a lifelong practice of commenting on what he had read, offer valuable insights into Dobie's tastes and judgments. Of McMurtry's *Horseman, Pass By*, Dobie proclaimed: "If 'ripeness' were all, Larry McMurtry wouldn't get much of a grade. Picture of old cowman is good in places."[30] Of McMurtry's second, *Leaving Cheyenne*, he sniffed, "I could read this but prefer *The World of Herodotus*."[31] Shrake's *But Not for Love* drew criticism for its "over drinking of everything but water. Prolonged drunk talk gets boresome . . . Lacks art of omission."[32] Nor did Dobie like the frank realism of Brammer's *The Gay Place*: "We are in the middle of politics for 175,000 words and nobody actually every [*sic*] does anything but drink and drink & drink to boredom & screw, & screw & screw to death."[33] But Graves was a different matter. Dobie wrote a very positive review of *Goodbye to a River* and became friends with the author. It is easy to understand why Dobie admired

Graves's book. First of all, it was nonfiction, and, second, it brought together the three strands of the Dobie-Webb-Bedichek approach to Texas culture: folklore, history, and nature.

In fiction, Dobie remained firmly attached to nineteenth-century novels, and although he did admire the great pre-Modernist Joseph Conrad, one of his aesthetic weaknesses is that he never appeared to be interested in or even aware of the central literary movement of his lifetime, the period of Modernism through which he himself was coming to full educational consciousness (1914–1929). Ernest Hemingway, William Faulkner, James Joyce, and Virginia Woolf all published important novels in the 1920s, but there is scant evidence that Dobie read them or admired them. One searches in vain through his extensive remarks on books for any comments on these writers or others in the vanguard of American and British fiction. Faulkner, in particular, could have been a useful model for Dobie. Stories like "Spotted Horses" revealed just how a folkloric tale could be expanded into great art. But Dobie, in most of his writing, was content to string together a series of brief anecdotes instead of selecting the richest one and exfoliating it into a well-told tale.

One exception to Dobie's ignoring modern writing was D. H. Lawrence's *Lady Chatterley's Lover*, but Dobie's interest in that book (he owned several editions) seems to have owed more to his dogged concern with literary censorship than to his appreciation of avant-garde writing. He was also probably interested in the sensational sexual content of Lawrence's novel, as evidenced by an aborted project late in his life, a compilation of smutty stories and outhouse humor in a volume titled "Piss and Vinegar."[34]

For the first fifty-odd years of his life Dobie focused on the past; then, during World War II, when he went overseas to England, he became, he said, a contemporary of himself. But he never became a contemporary of the best writers of his lifetime.

When Dobie died, the *Texas Observer* devoted a whole issue (July 24, 1964) to his memory, and appreciative books soon followed: Ronnie Dugger's *Three Men in Texas: Bedichek, Webb, and Dobie* (1967), Winston Bode's *J. Frank Dobie: A Portrait of Pancho* (1968), and William A. Owens's *Three Friends: Roy Bedichek, J. Frank Dobie, and Walter P. Webb* (1969). But there were also dissonant voices that offered a fresh and generally unfavorable assessment of the body of work. Foremost among these was Larry McMurtry, who in 1968 published a searching piece titled "Southwestern Literature?" in which Dobie and his followers were cut down to size. McMurtry's second and even more scathing assessment of Dobie appeared in 1981. Wrote McMurtry: "Dobie's twenty-odd books are a congealed mass of virtually undifferentiated anecdotage: endlessly repetitious, thematically empty, structureless, and carelessly written."[35] Other negative reevaluations came along in the years afterward. Greg Curtis, editor of *Texas Monthly,* declared Dobie's writings to be little more than "bedtime stories for boys in junior high";[36] even that is probably no longer true because boys in junior high are watching YouTube or playing video games.

Similarly negative portrayals of Dobie began to appear in Texas fiction. In Andrew Jolly's *A Time for Soldiers* (1968), Dobie is dismissed as a "professional Texan,"[37] and in Américo Paredes novel, *George Washington Gómez,* written in the late thirties but not published until 1992, Dobie is roundly caricatured in a character named H. Hank Harvey, a racist blowhard.

The most recent reassessments, in a special Dobie issue of *Southwestern American Literature* (2006), generally concede the fading of Dobie's star, especially in the academy, but grant him lasting importance in other venues. Paul Stone points to Dobie's influence on folk and blues musicians, finding traces of his imprint in the life and works of such figures as Townes Van Zandt, Tracey Nelson, and Ramblin' Jack Elliott; in cowboy poets such as Ian Tyson and Don Edwards; and even in Bob Dylan. But Stone also points out that "it is possible to graduate from any major American university where either Western American or American cultural history is taught never having heard of James Frank Dobie."[38]

Tom Pilkington suggests that the downturn in Dobie's reputation and relevance is almost inevitable given the sociological changes that have remapped Texas, turning the state into essentially an urban/suburban society whose demographics consist of generations of native Texans divorced from the land and of newly arrived pilgrims from California, the Midwest, and the East Coast who have no knowledge whatsoever of Texas history and its earlier land-centered ethos.[39] Pilkington argues, as does Stone, that future generations, if they become interested in the past, may well turn to Dobie to find out how those ancient peoples—Texans—lived. If so, they could find, scattered through Dobie's prose, many examples of a vanished discourse. Here, for example, is a passage picked almost at random from "Northers, Drouths and Sandstorms" (in *Tales of Old-Time Texas*):

> It was in the same part of Texas that a certain rancher who was better at raising children than calves went out one September night soon after dark and began throwing handfuls of pebbles on the roof. His wife ran out and asked him what in the world he meant.
>
> "Why," he said, "it's lightning in the west and might rain. The drought has got to end sometime. That's certain. I thought it would be a good idear to kinder break the kids into hearing something fall on the roof. Then if it ever actually rains, they won't stampede."[40]

A century from now, the works of Dobie and all of the Texas writers whose stories sprang from rural traditions of farming and ranching may well require annotations as copious as those for Chaucer and Shakespeare to bring to light what the old phrases and words might possibly have meant. Already this is happening. Dobie and his tradition are an endangered species in the suburban/urban landscape of twenty-first-century Texas.

SUGGESTED READING

Dobie, J. Frank. *A Vaquero of the Brush Country.* Dallas: The Southwest Press, 1929.

In Dobie's first book he used the adventures of John D. Young, a much-traveled cowboy, to form the narrative basis of an extended examination of life in the cattle industry of the post–Civil War era. The best part is Dobie's account of the undeclared war between Anglo ranchers and Mexican bandits in South Texas in the 1870s. Of late, Dobie's authorship has been called into question by an edition that credits authorship to John D. Young and J. Frank Dobie, in that order.

Dobie, J. Frank. *The Longhorns.* Boston: Little, Brown and Company, 1941.

Dobie, J. Frank. *The Mustangs.* Boston: Little, Brown and Company, 1952.

Which of these two books a reader prefers will probably depend on whether one prefers cattle or horses. In any event each book is representative of Dobie's interest in iconic Southwestern animals, and they both proceed by a mix of historical research and anecdotes of varying interest regarding said animals. Dobie produced similar books on coyotes and rattlesnakes. All of these animals, the good, the bad, and the ugly, represent for Dobie freedom and liberty in a wild land.

Dobie, J. Frank. *Cow People.* Boston: Little, Brown, 1964.

Essays on such outsized figures as Ab Blocker, Shanghai Pierce, and Charles Goodnight are featured alongside examples of Dobie's ability to spin tall tales, as in "Bogged Shadows," which records the whoppers told by Findlay Simpson on the O'Connor Ranch, and "The Drouthed," a lively look at folk attitudes toward that old perennial in Texas, droughts. Dobie is always good on weather.

Dobie, J. Frank. *Some Part of Myself.* Boston: Little, Brown, 1967.

The several personal essays collected here are among the most intriguing writing Dobie ever did. Sketches of his father and mother are of interest, but even more compelling are such autobiographical pieces as "Prose and Poetry," a vivid account of his undergraduate experiences at Southwestern University in Georgetown, and both "No Idea Where I Was Going" and "How My Life Took Its Turn," which tell of early work experience and the discovery of his life's mission.

NOTES

1. Lon Tinkle, *An American Original: The Life of J. Frank Dobie* (Boston: Little, Brown, 1978), 154–177. Tinkle devotes a chapter to Dobie's ascension in the 1930s to the unofficial title "Mr. Texas."

2. Francis E. Abernethy, "James Frank Dobie," in *The New Handbook of Texas*, edited by Ron Tyler (Austin: Texas State Historical Association, 1996), 2:662–663.

3. J. Frank Dobie, "Prose and Poetry," in *Some Part of Myself* (Boston: Little, Brown, 1967), 140.

4. Ibid., 145.

5. J. Frank Dobie, "A Schoolteacher in Alpine," in *Some Part of Myself*, 169.

6. Quoted in Catherine Supple and James Supple, "J. Frank Dobie at Columbia University, 1913–1914: His Letters and Diary," *Southwestern American Literature* 32, no. 1 (Fall 2006): 17.

7. Ibid., 13.

8. J. Frank Dobie, "His Looks and My Ways Would Hang Any Man," in *Some Part of Myself*, 122.

9. Supple and Supple, "J. Frank Dobie at Columbia University," 9.

10. Dobie, "His Looks and My Ways Would Hang Any Man," 122–123.

11. Ibid., 123.

12. Supple and Supple, "J. Frank Dobie at Columbia University," 13.

13. Ibid., 16.

14. J. Frank Dobie, "Columbia University in the City of New York," in *Some Part of Myself*, 184–185.

15. Ibid., 185.

16. J. Frank Dobie, "How My Life Took Its Turn," in *Some Part of Myself*, 236.

17. Tinkle, *An American Original*, 123.

18. J. Frank Dobie, "A Necessary Explanation," preface to *A Vaquero of the Brush Country* (New York: Little, Brown, 1957), xi. Oddly, the University of Texas Press edition of 1998 includes "A Necessary Explanation" without a word of new necessary explanation.

19. Lawrence Clark Powell, "The Time, the Place, and the Book," preface to *A Vaquero of the Brush Country* (Austin: University of Texas Press, 1957), vii–viii. This preface also appears in the 1998 edition. Thus both prefaces, reprinted in the new edition, refute what the new edition claims.

20. Quoted in Don Graham, "Who Wrote *A Vaquero of the Brush Country*? A Strange Case of Demoted Authorship," *Southwestern American Literature* 32, no. 1 (Fall 2006): 73.

21. Ibid., 74.

22. Ibid.

23. J. Frank Dobie's letters to John D. Young, J. Frank Dobie Collection, Harry Ransom Center, the University of Texas at Austin. For a full discussion of the legal aspects and the University of Texas Press's decision to yield in favor of Young, see ibid., 76–77.

24. The "E342" document bears the "publication" date of 1940. A copy is in the author's private collection.

25. J. Frank Dobie, "Life and Literature of the Southwest: An Incomplete Guide to Books on Texas and the Southwest" (Austin: University of Texas, 1936), 1.

26. Steven L. Davis, in a new biography, *J. Frank Dobie: A Liberated Mind* (Austin: University of Texas Press, 2009), focuses most of his attention on Dobie's journey from southern

conservatism to post–New Deal liberalism. In his view Dobie's main accomplishment lies in his advocacy of liberal Democratic causes.

27. Anonymous letter to Dobie, J. Frank Dobie Collection, Harry Ransom Center, the University of Texas at Austin.

28. First edition of *The Longhorns,* in personal library of Kate Stoner O'Connor, O'Connor Ranch.

29. Tinkle, *An American Original,* 146.

30. J. Frank Dobie's Ranch Library, Harry Ransom Center, the University of Texas at Austin. Quoted in Don Graham, "J. Frank Dobie: A Reappraisal," in *The Texas Book: Profiles, History, and Reminiscences of the University,* edited by Richard A. Holland (Austin: University of Texas Press, 2006), 15.

31. Ibid., 16.

32. Ibid., 15.

33. Ibid.

34. For a fuller account of this project, see Graham, "Pen Pals," 112–115.

35. Quoted in Tom Pilkington, "J. Frank Dobie's Reputation and Influence: A Brief Overview," *Southwestern American Literature* 32, no. 1 (Fall 2006), 60.

36. Ibid., pp. 60–61.

37. Quoted in Don Graham, "J. Frank Dobie: A Reappraisal," 17.

38. Paul Stone, "Whatever Happened to J. Frank Dobie?" *Southwestern American Literature* 32, no. 1 (Fall 2006): 66.

39. Tom Pilkington, "J. Frank Dobie's Reputation and Influence: A Brief Overview," *Southwestern American Literature* 32, no. 1 (Fall 2006): 57–64.

40. J. Frank Dobie, *Tales of Old-Time Texas* (Boston: Little, Brown, 1955; repr., Austin: University of Texas Press, 1984), 105.

B. BYRON PRICE

J. EVETTS HALEY

J. EVETTS HALEY, 1931

During a lifetime that spanned much of the twentieth century, J. Evetts Haley wrote five major books of history and biography, a colorful family chronicle, many shorter works—including scores of essays and articles for newspapers, magazines, and academic journals—and a controversial political polemic that almost overshadowed them all. Despite his historical training and prodigious output, Haley, for most of his career, pursued the past only part-time, usually while managing one or more far-flung cattle ranches and engaging in intense partisan political activity on behalf of conservative causes and candidates.

Most of Haley's writing related in some way to Texans and Texas history. With one notable exception he wrote about people he admired, even idolized; he was especially drawn to "men of fiber," resolute figures who exhibited uncommon and laudable strength of character. Nature and place, enduring and unyielding, also inspired his prose and the powerful lyrical style that marked his work.[1]

J. Evetts Haley's interest in history was rooted in the Southwest, shaped by his southern ancestry, and leavened by the reminiscences of the old-timers he encountered in search of the past. Haley himself was a master storyteller who knew how to entertain as well as inform his audience. The irony, gallows humor, and range lore that laced his narratives gave them bite and charm in equal measure.

During the course of his historical research Haley interviewed hundreds of western pioneers, carefully jotting down their recollections in his own distinctive shorthand or relying on stenographers and mechanical recording devices. Although eyewitness testimony lent color and life to his work, Haley proved adept at distinguishing fact from fiction and was rarely, if ever, taken in by a tall tale.[2]

He also understood the value of historical documents and artifacts and proved adept not only in ferreting them out of attics, basements, and vaults but also in talking their owners into depositing them into libraries and museums. And while reviewers and critics have sometimes disputed Haley's interpretation of the evidence he uncovered, factual errors seldom disfigured his work.

Born in Belton, Texas, on July 5, 1901, Haley soon moved west with his family to the Permian Basin. He landed in Midland in 1906, where his enterprising parents John Alva and Julia Evetts Haley eventually launched a hardware store and, later, a hotel. They also invested in ranchland near Midland and on the Pecos River.[3]

When Haley was eight years old, a book on Kit Carson introduced him to the world of history. In school and out, he read voraciously, mostly novels and short stories with historical settings. Tales both read and told stimulated the youngster's imagination and helped develop an awareness that the past did not always happen somewhere else.[4]

Reading also stimulated Haley's desire to express himself through writing. As a youth he began to keep a diary, a practice he continued off and on throughout his life. In 1916 the scouting magazine *Boy's Life* published Haley's first article, an illustrated, six-sentence "how-to" piece on the field refrigeration of milk and drinking water.[5] Four years later, a historical article on a local cowboy and rancher carried the young writer's byline in the *Midland Reporter-Telegram*.[6]

By then Haley was himself an aspiring cowboy who worked on his family's ranches and made a hand for sixteen dollars a month on local cow outfits during summers as a teenager. He also competed in riding events at local rodeos.[7]

After graduating from high school in 1920, Haley enrolled briefly in Midland Christian College, but when the hometown school closed in 1922 he transferred to West Texas Normal College in Canyon. He intended to major in science but, lacking the required math credits, settled on history instead. At West Texas Haley excelled as a student, served as senior class president, edited the college yearbook, and wrote the column "West Texas Breezes" for the school newspaper while serving as its business manager. He also played football with reckless abandon until a knee injury ended his athletic career.[8]

In 1921, the year before Haley's arrival in Canyon, a group of historically minded citizens, led by college history professors Hattie M. Anderson and Lester M. Sheffy, formed the Panhandle-Plains Historical Society. The group hoped to preserve the memories of early settlers in the Panhandle, who were rapidly dying off, and, eventually, to write a history of the region and establish a museum.[9]

At annual gatherings of the society, Haley's intelligence, interest, and ability so impressed its leaders that they hired him as a field collector upon his graduation in 1925. That summer the energetic young historian crisscrossed the Texas Panhandle and South Plains gathering memberships, documents, artifacts, and interviews. Traveling in a secondhand Ford touring car purchased by the society, he often slept in a bedroll under the stars.[10] One June night, in the shadow of the crumbling walls of old Fort Elliot, near Mobeetie, he wrote his future wife, Vernita Stewart: "My fancy carried me back fifty years to the times when the soldiers paced their guard upon that same spot, when buffalo and Indians were upon the plains, and I thought 'What changes a relatively short time bring.' Visions of tramping troops filled my mind, while several small ants belligerently tramped down my side and began to sting."[11]

After a summer of collecting, Haley sought a master's degree in history from the University of Texas in fall 1925. Native-born Texans, led by Dr. Eugene C. Barker, dominated the history department at the time. Barker, the biographer of Stephen F. Austin, directed Haley's master's thesis, "A Survey of Texas Cattle Drives to the North 1866–1895," and became the young scholar's mentor and lifelong friend.[12]

Armed with his new degree, Haley resumed his field duties with the Panhandle-Plains Historical Society in summer 1926 with renewed vigor and success. An article in the college newspaper, the *Prairie*, opined that the historian's charismatic personality, historical training, and cowboy background were key in getting "the close-mouthed pioneer to talk freely where one less versed in the life of the west would only antagonize."[13]

That fall, representatives of the Capitol Freehold Lands company of Chicago hired Haley to write a history of the famous XIT Ranch. With readily available published sources in relatively short supply, Haley crafted much of his narrative from interviews with some seventy former employees and other knowledgeable informants, scattered from Texas to California. An early draft of the manuscript, however, disappointed the project's sponsor, John V. Farwell. "We want to get the general high-spots and let the details go," the Chicago tycoon wrote the author. "I do not believe anyone else will care about reading too much of that sort of thing either."[14]

By February 1928, Haley had revised his text to accommodate Farwell's desire for "a rather romantic, casual and general treatment" of the subject while preserving the demands of scholarship.[15] The resulting manuscript pleased his sponsor, who wrote approvingly of the "atmosphere" that the author had infused into the work.[16]

At Haley's suggestion, company officials had hired University of Texas professor J. Frank Dobie to review the manuscript for style and content. Farwell also asked former president William Howard Taft, now chief justice of the Supreme Court, to read Haley's chapter documenting the roles the Capitol Reservation Lands and XIT Ranch had played in the settlement of a important boundary issue between Texas and New Mexico.[17]

In October 1928, while in Chicago seeing to last-minute publishing details, Haley learned that the Capitol Reservation Lands intended to incinerate a vast archive pertaining to the XIT Ranch. Acting quickly, Haley secured the collection, including 166,000 letters dating between 1885 and 1912, for the Panhandle-Plains Historical Society.[18]

While Haley awaited publication of his first book, he married his fiancée, Vernita Stewart, at Alpine, Texas, and edited the first volume of the *Panhandle-Plains Historical Review*. The publication's inaugural issue contained "Charles Goodnight's Indian Recollections," a result of Haley's fortuitous 1925 encounter with the famous Texas frontiersman during his first season of fieldwork for the historical society. In the interim, Haley's friendship with Goodnight had blossomed, and in August 1928 the historian had accompanied the retired rancher-frontiersman and his wife, Corrine, on a visit to the Pueblo Indian tribe at Taos, New Mexico. By December, Haley had begun work on Goodnight's biography, a task that would take him eleven years to complete.[19]

J. EVETTS HALEY

The publication of *The* XIT *Ranch of Texas and the Early Days of the Llano Estacado* in spring 1929 garnered the author lavish praise from reviewers.[20] J. Frank Dobie declared in the *Dallas News* that Haley's volume had "set the standard for ranch histories that will probably never be reached by another recorder in that particular field."[21] Eugene C. Barker, who had consumed his protégé's book in one sitting, called it "a fine piece of writing and an excellent example of descriptive historical narration."[22] Barker passed the volume on to his colleague Walter Prescott Webb, who was completing his own historical masterpiece, *The Great Plains.*

No one was more effusive or prophetic in his praise than John L. McCarty of the *Amarillo News,* who wrote: "Haley has made his debut as a writer in an impressive manner. If his work improves, as it must, his products will be classical and great. He deserves all the praises a grateful country can give. He needs no other monument for greatness."[23]

Not everyone, however, applauded Haley's interpretation of the past. His account of lawlessness on the XIT, for example, rankled Fred Spikes, a respected Lubbock businessman who, along with two of his brothers, had been portrayed as cattle thieves. During the summer of 1930, Spikes and several members of his family filed libel suits against the author and the Capitol Reservation Lands seeking $2.2 million in damages. The company refused to settle the matter out of court and prepared for a jury trial.[24]

By this time Haley had relocated to Austin, where he was employed by the University of Texas, under a grant from the Laura Spellman Rockefeller Foundation, to establish a field program similar to that he had pioneered so successfully in the Panhandle. With the trial looming, Haley took leave from the university for several months to assist in locating witnesses and help defense lawyers prepare their case. On June 19, 1931, after a sensational and widely publicized trial held in state court in Lubbock, Haley and his fellow defendants were acquitted of libel in the first of nine suits. A few months later the remaining actions were settled out of court for a total of $17,500 and an agreement by the publishers to suppress the remaining copies of the book.[25]

Exonerated of the charges against him and something of a celebrity as a result of his ordeal, Haley resumed his duties as collector of research at the University of Texas. His efforts yielded a torrent of books, broadsides, manuscripts, maps, photographs, and newspapers for the university's archives. More than 50,000 manuscript pages alone arrived during the fiscal year ending August 31, 1931, and nearly five times that amount the following year.[26]

Although often on the road pursuing the past and the proud father of a new son and namesake born in 1931, the energetic historian still found time to pen articles for newspapers, regional academic journals such as the *Quarterly of the Texas State Historical Association* and *Southwest Review,* and popular magazines that ranged from *Nature* to *Ranch Romances*. He also contributed articles to the *Cattleman*, the trade journal of the Texas and Southwestern Cattle Raisers' Association, and in 1931 was named that organization's official historian.[27] Haley described collecting the raw materials of history in terms a cowboy could understand when he wrote, in "Back-trailin' with the Old Timers," that "unlike the man who makes history, the one who collects it must ride at an easy, moderate gait. And the back-trail, in contrast to the out-trail, will not be as straight as an old pony's tracks headed toward home, but will leisurely circle and turn like those of a 'finicky' old cow hunting 'taller weed' in the cactus."[28]

By late 1934, Haley had also completed all but two chapters of his biography of Charles Goodnight. A grant from the Rockefeller Foundation enabled him to take a six-month leave from the university in 1935 to complete the work and arrange for publication.[29]

He had already begun sharing sample chapters with East Coast publishers, and while several had expressed initial interest, none had committed to publish his work and several had rejected the idea. Boston publisher Houghton Mifflin, however, proved receptive and in spring 1935 offered Haley a contract and a modest advance for his completed manuscript. The company also released Walter Prescott Webb's celebrated study *The Texas Rangers: A Century of Frontier Defense* later that year in hopes that interest in the Texas Centennial celebration in 1936 would help drive sales of both books.[30]

Although Haley had turned down an offer to work for the Texas Centennial Commission, he had been given the task of mounting the university history department's exhibitions for the celebration. Not surprisingly, perhaps, ranching and range life took center stage in the final product, including a stunning display of cowboy photography by Erwin E. Smith.[31]

With the approach of the presidential election of 1936, Haley, a conservative Democrat, actively opposed the candidacy of President Franklin D. Roosevelt. Although he headed the Texas historical records survey, a Depression-era federal work program, in the early 1930s, Haley became increasingly disenchanted with Roosevelt's New Deal when the administration abandoned the gold standard in 1933. The government's agricultural policies especially galled him, and he constantly lobbied leading western livestock organizations to oppose what he and others of his ilk called the "Raw Deal." Haley's talented pen was soon producing forceful, caustic, and widely circulated editorials and essays with such catchy titles as "Cows in the Cotton Patch" and "Cow Business and Monkey Business," the latter published in the December 8, 1934, issue of the *Saturday Evening Post*.[32]

Haley's collecting work brought him into contact with many influential and like-minded conservatives with whom he exchanged ideas and political strategy. Around the university, Haley's political views and outspokenness often spawned rancorous exchanges with the more liberal members of the faculty. "The more I saw of the average run of University people," he wrote J. Frank Dobie in retrospect, "the more my soul rebelled, until, during the last year or so, I found them almost intolerable. In turn, I made myself intolerable to them, I suppose, for my contempt was rarely concealed."[33]

In August 1936 Haley joined with other party mavericks to form the Jeffersonian Democrats of Texas in hopes of derailing Roosevelt's reelection. Elected chairman of the new organization, Haley requested a leave from his university duties to devote full time to political activities. A few days later, however, Haley found himself out of a job when the grant that had funded his collecting activities at the university expired and was not renewed. Haley made a cause célèbre of this turn of events and went to his grave believing that he had been "fired" for his political views.

After FDR defeated Republican candidate Alfred M. Landon in the November election, Haley, exhausted and disappointed, found himself back in Canyon eying the future. Despite recent political and economic reversals, he was not without prospects. *Charles Goodnight, Cowman and Plainsman* had been released the previous May to overwhelmingly positive reviews, and two more books were in the offing.[34]

In early 1936 Houghton Mifflin officials had expressed interest in Haley writing a biography of Jefferson Davis Milton, a retired western lawman now living in Tombstone, Arizona. Haley, who had met Milton briefly three years earlier at a Texas Rangers reunion near San Angelo, was eager to discuss the project in person. Politics and economics, however, delayed a face-to-face meeting until late February 1937.[35]

By this time, Haley had agreed to write a biography of Texas rancher and banker George W. Littlefield. Eugene C. Barker had arranged the modest commission for his former student with the trustees of the Littlefield Fund for Southern History at the University of Texas. The terms of the agreement paid the author $3,600 in quarterly installments, allotted another $1,600 for expenses, and allowed him two years to complete the manuscript.[36]

Because neither book project was lucrative enough to permit him to conduct research and write full time, Haley welcomed an unexpected opportunity to manage the Zeebar Ranch in northeastern Arizona for Dallas businessman Louis L. Dent. In time, the young rancher would add the Atarque and Clochintoh Ranches in New Mexico to his growing list of responsibilities. The tally grew even longer in the summer 1937, when Haley purchased 4,000 acres of his own on the Canadian River in Hutchinson County, Texas. He christened the new ranch the JH.[37]

Haley relished his return to outdoor life and the physical labor that ranching in some of the remotest reaches of the Southwest entailed. "And while I find that I am not the resilient cowpuncher that I once was," he admitted in a letter to Dobie in June 1937, "I find that I can work down most of the younger men who are with me on the range, and who have not suffered the enervating effects of fifteen years at an academic pursuit."[38]

Although the demands of whipping the widespread ranches in his charge into shape dominated his time and energy, Haley set aside blocks of time for research and writing. Support from the Littlefield Fund and another grant from the Rockefeller Foundation, facilitated in part by J. Frank Dobie, helped support travel and stenographic expenses in connection with these historical investigations.[39]

Oral history was the sinew that would knit the Milton and Littlefield biographies together, as it had Haley's previous books on the XIT Ranch and Charles Goodnight. Although George Littlefield was long dead, J. Phelps White, Littlefield's nephew and confidant, who lived at Roswell, New Mexico, proved a valuable source of information and leads to family, business associates, and cowboys who had worked the LIT, LFD, and other outfits the Austin banker had once owned. By December 1937, Haley had conducted two dozen interviews and had secured thirteen ranch daybooks, numerous photographs, and more than 300 letters connected to Littlefield.[40]

One of Haley's most memorable interviews occurred the previous summer, south of Fort Sumner, New Mexico, with three, down-on-their-luck, ex-Littlefield cowhands. All were named Walker, but only two were brothers. As was sometimes his practice, Haley kept the reminiscences flowing with the help of a bottle of whiskey, and while stenographer Brockman Horne took down the often ribald tales of cowboy life and trail driving, Haley periodically snapped photographs of the trio with a small box camera held unobtrusively between his legs.[41]

Haley's meeting with Jeff Milton and his wife Mildred in Tombstone earlier that spring had proved equally fruitful. Drawn by Milton's southern charm and dangerous reputation, Haley agreed to write his biography, provided he could take all the time he needed to complete the task. In return for their cooperation, he also offered to share half the royalties from the publication with the Miltons, the same split he had worked out with Charles and Corrine Goodnight nearly a decade before.[42]

Haley warmed to the old lawman immediately but feared at first that some of his lively and sometimes graphic tales were "better told than written."[43] "Western history has for me been shot through with adventure," he wrote Ira Rich Kent, his editor at Houghton Mifflin, "and this association with Mr. Milton promises to be on the same happy plane. So far as the writer is concerned, however, I hope the shooting is wholly vicarious instead of real, even though a few good deaths would elevate the writing profession."[44]

To economize on expenses Haley conducted research on both Littlefield and Milton simultaneously, often while traveling among the ranches in his charge. Between 1937 and 1939 the interviews conducted in connection with Jeff Milton's saga alone resulted in more than 600 typed pages.[45]

Somehow Haley still found time to write historical sketches for newspapers and magazines and to lambaste Roosevelt and the New Deal in print as well. And, as though he had time to spare, Haley in 1938 bought stock in the company that published the *Amarillo Times* and for a time became the newspaper's business manager and editorialist![46]

The following year, Haley left Louis L. Dent's employ to accept a more lucrative offer to manage the ranches of James M. West. A Houston business tycoon, West shared his new ranch manager's political conservatism and hatred of the New Deal and had helped bankroll the Jeffersonian Democrats in 1936.[47]

For the next two years, overseeing ranching properties that stretched from Houston to the lower Rio Grande to the Big Bend kept Haley continually on the road and in the saddle, leaving little time to write history. His deadline for completing the Littlefield biography came and went, but its sponsors were understanding and granted him an extension. Finally, in January 1941, Haley completed the last chapter of his long-awaited manuscript.[48]

While Panhandle artist Harold D. Bugbee prepared pen and ink illustrations for the new volume, as he had for *Charles Goodnight*, Eugene C. Barker, representing the Littlefield trustees, and the author sought a publisher. Houghton Mifflin expressed early interest but declined, as did Alfred A. Knopf, both houses believing the subject too narrow to be commercially viable. Knopf also objected to comments in the text critical of the New Deal, calling their inclusion "a mistake" and recommending their removal from the final draft. "They are calculated, I think," wrote the publisher, "to irritate even readers who would agree with you."[49]

Overall the book pleased both Barker and the Littlefield trustees. After reading the completed manuscript for the second time, the old professor pronounced it "an excellent book, and one, I think that the Major would have approved. Nobody else could have done the job with the relatively scant material that you obtained; and yet the scantiness of material is not obtrusive. The man really lived in the setting of his environment."[50]

Shunned by commercial publishers, the Littlefield Fund trustees offered university presses in Louisiana and Oklahoma a substantial subsidy to underwrite the publication. Savoie Lottinville, director at the University of Oklahoma Press, expressed immediate and unqualified enthusiasm for the project and by August 1942 had submitted an acceptable proposal to publish Haley's manuscript.[51]

Critical response to the publication of *George Littlefield, Texan* in fall 1943 was generally positive. Writing in the *Dallas News* on November 14, Herbert Gambrell praised Haley's "capacity for straightforward writing and his knack of using the right word in the right place" and his use of oral sources to "supply salty phrases and enlivening anecdote." Gambrell called *Littlefield* "a scholarly study in the best sense of the term—which means that the paraphernalia of scholarship is so unobtrusive that it will not bother the most untutored reader, while the best bifocals of the academic historian will be unable to find an important statement unsupported by admissible evidence."[52]

Although more than one reviewer thought *Littlefield* better written than his highly touted *Charles Goodnight*,[53] some critics questioned the absence of the main character for long stretches of text. Others, who had known Littlefield personally, could see, too, that the author had glossed over his subject's flaws. "Some critics will insist that [Haley's biography] omits shady personal details," E. C. Barker wrote one of Littlefield's detractors, "but I am inclined to think Shakespeare was a little in error: Unless a man was a villain on a grand scale the good that he does is really more significant than the evil."[54]

Between the time Haley completed his manuscript on Littlefield and the time it was published, J. M. West had died and Haley had left West's employ and returned to the Panhandle. By then the onset of World War II had compounded the usual difficulties of running a cattle ranch. Labor, gasoline, and livestock feed were scarce and costly. Water and grass were often in short supply as well.[55]

Haley, who persevered and even thrived during hard times, kept up his usual relentless pace. In a series of essays published in the *San Antonio Express*, Haley defended the University of Texas regents in a squabble over academic freedom and governance that led to the firing of the school's president, Homer P. Rainey, in 1944. The following year he released *The University of Texas and the Issue*, a pamphlet detailing the fight from the regents' perspective.[56]

The controversy effectively ended Haley's close friendship with Dobie, who took Rainey's side in the matter.[57] After Barker had given him a copy of Dobie's recently published *Guide to Life and Literature of the Southwest* in 1943, Haley replied: "Frank is a great authority on folklore. I imagine he knows literature, but when it comes to life, he is the worst confused individual who is supposed to have reached maturity that I know."[58]

While the Rainey affair raged, Haley managed to complete *Charles Schreiner, General Merchandise: The Story of a Country Store*, a brief appreciation of a colorful Hill Country rancher-businessman. Published by the Texas State Historical Association in 1944, the thin volume marked the first of several fruitful collaborations between its author and the celebrated El Paso book designer Carl Hertzog.[59]

Although Haley had completed most of the research for Jeff Milton's biography before the advent of World War II, he did not complete the first chapter until February 1943. Ranching, politics, and other writing projects continued to delay his progress. At one point in 1945, he had not produced a single chapter for eight months. Finally, in 1947, the task was complete. A few weeks later, on May 7, Jeff Milton died in Tucson at the age of eighty-five.[60]

Revisions to the manuscript would still require several months when Haley headed east, eager to finalize publishing arrangements with Houghton Mifflin. His meeting in New York with Paul Brooks, Houghton Mifflin's editor-in-chief, proved chilly, however, as irresolvable differences arose over matters of design and a clause in the contract regarding the author's responsibility for libelous statements in his work. Although Houghton Mifflin attempted to revive the stalled negotiations, Haley withdrew his manuscript from the Boston house and promptly concluded a publishing deal with Savoie Lottinville and the University of Oklahoma Press.[61]

Although disappointed that his book would not have the distribution and marketing muscle of Houghton Mifflin, Haley was delighted to work again with Lottinville. In a letter to Harold Bugbee, who would illustrate Milton's biography, Haley praised the Oklahoma Press director as "a young man with a lot of drive and imagination and genuine scholarship."[62] Lottinville did not disappoint. The cleverly titled *Jeff Milton, a Good Man with a Gun* made its long-awaited debut on October 23, 1948, and was the best-seller on the publisher's fall list.[63]

Even before he had completed Milton's story, Haley had accepted a commission from Houston Harte, publisher of the *San Angelo Standard-Times,* to prepare a history of Tom Green County, Texas. Over time, the project evolved into a more ambitious regional study published in 1952 under the title *Fort Concho and the Texas Frontier.* Always anxious to communicate the lessons of history to his readers, Haley peppered the story of a famous West Texas military post and its untamed surroundings with asides on contemporary issues ranging from politics to race, often delivered with biting sarcasm. The finished product wowed the Sons of the Republic of Texas, who rewarded *Fort Concho* with the organization's Summerfield G. Roberts award for the best book of the year on the Texas frontier.[64]

The year 1952 also saw the appearance of Haley's *Life on the Texas Range,* an homage to cowboy photographer Erwin E. Smith. The handsome boxed volume would be the author's first and only University of Texas Press publication.

During the early 1950s, Haley, an active supporter of the Panhandle-Plains Historical Society since his days as its field representative, served a two-year term as president of the organization. In 1953 Texas Technological College in Lubbock named him the first director of the Institute of Americanism with the rank of distinguished professor. He resigned the position in 1955 but subsequently accepted Governor Allan Shivers's appointment to the Texas Tech board of regents. During his tenure as regent, Haley was again embroiled in controversy over academic freedom and the dismissal of several professors but also was instrumental in establishing and funding the Southwest Collection, an important regional history archive at the college.[65]

Haley ran a colorful but unsuccessful campaign for governor in 1956. His platform championed individual and states' rights, supported segregation, and opposed labor unions and federal price controls on natural gas. On the stump and in campaign literature Haley reminded voters of his historical writing and vicarious connections with legendary Texas heroes and patriots. "I have chronicled their glorious deeds in passion and in pride," read one brochure, "and have tried to live in keeping with their finest principals [*sic*] and traditions. . . . Again the time has come to draw the valorous line."[66] Haley's allusion to William B. Travis's fabled line in the sand at the Alamo suggested both the righteousness and the hopelessness of his candidacy.

Undaunted in defeat, Haley and other Texas conservatives formed the political action group Texans for America. Elected state chairman of the anticommunist organization, Haley regularly railed against "subversive" and "anti-American" textbooks at public hearings of the State Textbook Committee in Austin. He was also a featured speaker at the "National Indignation Convention" held in Dallas the following year, in the wake of John F. Kennedy's election as president.[67]

During the presidential election campaign of 1964 Haley directed his wrath at Kennedy's successor, Lyndon B. Johnson, in a privately published polemic, *A Texan Looks at Lyndon: A Study of Illegitimate Power*. In the book's introduction Haley stressed his historical research and offered more than 800 footnotes to substantiate his accusations that Johnson's rise to power had been accompanied by wholesale corruption, fraud, and even murder. The president's supporters struck back, portraying the author as a right-wing "crackpot" whose charges more often than not were based on flimsy evidence and hearsay. Haley responded that if the charges were not true, then he should have been sued for libel. Before public interest waned, more than a million copies of the book had been printed and distributed throughout the United States.[68]

In contrast to his other biographical subjects—Goodnight, Littlefield, and Milton most prominent among them—Lyndon B. Johnson was the only figure that J. Evetts Haley did not admire or make allowances for with respect to questionable behavior. His assertion in the introduction to Jeff Milton's biography that "human tolerance and critical historical appraisal can and should go together" clearly did not apply to LBJ.[69]

Although Haley continued to write articles and essays on history and politics and to edit historical documents and the reminiscences of others, more than a decade passed between *A Texan Looks at Lyndon* and Haley's last major book, *Rough Times—Tough Fiber*, published in 1976. The poetic family chronicle was also Haley's loving tribute to the Southwest, the land that had produced and shaped him.

The year 1976, the year of the American bicentennial, also marked the opening of the Nita Stewart Haley Memorial Library in Haley's hometown of Midland. Named for Haley's first wife, who had died of cancer in 1958, the new facility would house and make available for research not only the historian's substantial reference library and personal papers but also the collections of others.[70]

In the waning years of his long life, Haley received many honors for his work on behalf of Texas and western history. He was named a Knight of San Jacinto by the Sons of the Republic of Texas in 1978, received an Award of Merit from the American Association of State and Local History in 1981, was inducted into the Hall of Great Westerners at the National Cowboy Hall of Fame and Western Heritage Center in 1990, and was named to the Heritage Hall of Fame at the State Fair of Texas four years later. The historian died in Midland on October 9, 1995, and was buried with other members of his family in Belton.[71]

Although J. Evetts Haley belongs in the first rank of Texas writers and historians of the twentieth century, the emergence of the New Western History and the prevailing climate of political correctness have sometimes denied him his due. Yet no one has written with greater knowledge of and empathy for the ranch and range in Texas and the Southwest, nor produced a better written or more magisterial biography of a westerner than *Charles Goodnight, Cowman and Plainsman*. In 1982 *Dallas Morning News* columnist A. C. Greene ranked *Goodnight* among his list of the fifty best books on Texas.[72] Novelist Larry McMurtry, who borrowed freely from Haley's biography of Goodnight for his own 1985 Pulitzer Prize–winning novel, *Lonesome Dove*, agreed with Greene. In his 1999 book *Walter Benjamin at the Dairy Queen*, McMurtry praised Haley as "a brilliant historian and master of a considerably more graceful prose than Webb's—or J. Frank Dobie's, either. Haley's biography of Charles Goodnight remains the single best biography of a cattleman—perhaps of a Western figure of any kind. That book is as good a place to start as any if one seeks to understand the attitudes and philosophies of the people such as my grandparents who settled the west Texas frontier."[73]

Revisionist studies of Lyndon Johnson in the 1980s and early 1990s, most notably the publication of *Means of Ascent*, Robert Caro's critical look at Johnson's controversial rise to power, have even prompted a reappraisal of Haley's *A Texan Looks at Lyndon*.[74] Interviewed for *Texas Monthly* three years before

Caro's book, Haley contemptuously dismissed latter-day critics of Johnson with the curt observation: "Everybody wants to write about the sonofabitch now that he's dead."[75]

In the final analysis, few historians have written as tellingly about Texas or have done more to further the cause of Texas history than J. Evetts Haley. He was not only a superb researcher, gifted writer, and distinctive interpreter of the past but also a persuasive collector and promoter whose efforts at preserving, organizing, and housing the raw materials of the past in libraries and archives provided a firm foundation for future historical studies.

Historian Melvin E. Bradford has compared Haley's approach to history to that of the ancient Greek historian Plutarch.[76] Though separated by time and space, both men believed that history taught immutable lessons and provided worthy role models for the edification of present and future generations. The rigidity and severity of Haley's worldview, his racial intolerance, justification of violence, and tendency to romanticize the past have proved troublesome to many modern historians who consider both his subjects and his approach to the past increasingly passé and irrelevant. Yet his best work endures and, thanks to his powerful prose and the larger-than-life characters that inhabit his biographies, continues to attract new readers with each succeeding generation.

SUGGESTED READING

Haley, J. Evetts. *Charles Goodnight, Cowman and Plainsman.* Boston: Houghton Mifflin, 1936.

Described by critics as one of the best biographies of the legendary cattlemen of the American West. A vivid work about the life of Goodnight and the open-range and barbed-wire ranching era.

Haley, J. Evetts. *Fort Concho on the Texas Frontier.* San Angelo, TX: San Angelo Standard-Times, 1952.

Described by Eugene C. Barker as a "history of West Texas in its heroic age," this work began as a project about the history of Tom Green County by newspaper publisher Houston Harte.

Haley, J. Evetts. *George W. Littlefield, Texan.* Norman: University of Oklahoma Press, 1943.

Biography of the renowned Confederate veteran, rancher, and Austin banker who played a significant role in the development of the University of Texas and who was also known for his support for historical research and the preservation of archives.

Haley, J. Evetts. *Jeff Milton, a Good Man with a Gun.* Norman: University of Oklahoma Press, 1948.

Biography of a legendary Southwestern lawman based largely on oral histories, conducted by Haley with Milton and those who knew him.

Haley, J. Evetts. *Life on the Texas Range*. Austin: University of Texas Press, 1952.

Haley's essay on photographer Erwin E. Smith accompanies a portfolio of images on Texas cowboy life originally assembled and exhibited at the Texas Centennial in 1936.

Haley, J. Evetts. *Rough Times—Tough Fiber: A Fragmentary Family Chronicle*. Canyon, TX: Palo Duro Press, 1976.

The family chronicle that was also Haley's loving tribute to the Southwest, the land that had produced and shaped him.

Haley, J. Evetts. *A Texan Looks at Lyndon: A Study in Illegitimate Power*. Canyon, TX: Palo Duro Press, 1964.

Haley's controversial political tract on the business history and backroom dealings of Lyndon B. Johnson. The book gained attention during the 1964 presidential election campaign.

Haley, J. Evetts. *The XIT Ranch of Texas and the Early Days of the Llano Estacado*. Chicago: The Lakeside Press, 1929.

Haley's first book profiled one of the West's largest and most famous cattle ranches. His account of cattle theft on the mammoth spread resulted in a sensational libel suit and trial.

NOTES

1. For Haley's views on human character and the role of nature in shaping it, see J. Evetts Haley, *Men of Fiber* (El Paso: Carl Hertzog, 1963); and J. Evetts Haley, *Rough Times—Tough Fiber: A Fragmentary Family Chronicle* (Canyon, TX: Palo Duro Press, 1976).

2. J. Evetts Haley, taped interview by B. Byron Price, August 2, 1986, Midland, in the possession of the author.

3. Chandler A. Robinson, *J. Evetts Haley, Cowman-Historian* (El Paso: Carl Hertzog, 1967), 5; Haley, *Rough Times*, 150–151.

4. Myra McIlvain, "Bell, Book, and Cowboys," *Texas Highways* 34 (March 1987): 30; J. Evetts Haley, Diary, December 12, 1919–March 20, 1922, entries for January 20, 1920, December 11, 1920, and February 1, 1921, Notebooks, Diaries, and Tally Books, the J. Evetts Haley Collection, Nita Stewart Haley Memorial Library and J. Evetts Haley History Center, Midland (hereafter NSHML); Linda T. Bond, "J. Evetts Haley: Historian on Horseback," *Midland* 5 (Third Quarter 1983): 3.

5. Evetts Haley, "A Camp Refrigeration," *Boy's Life* 6, no. 5 (September 1916): 26.

6. J. Evetts Haley, interview by B. Byron Price, July 31, 1986, notes in possession of the author; Bond, "J. Evetts Haley," 3.

7. Gerry Burton, "Haley: He's Known It All," in *J. Evetts Haley and the Passing of the Old West*, edited by Chandler A. Robinson (Austin: Jenkins Publishing, 1978), 77.

8. B. Byron Price, "J. Evetts Haley: Southwestern Historian," *Continuity* 9 (Fall 1984): 189–190.

9. For a history of the Panhandle-Plains Historical Society, see Joseph A. Hill, *The Panhandle-Plains Historical Society and Its Museum* (Canyon: West Texas State College Press, 1955).

10. J. Evetts Haley, "Report of the Field Representative, Sept. 14, 1925," in Panhandle-

Plains Historical Society, Minutes of the Annual Meeting of the Panhandle-Plains Historical Society, February 12, 1926 [p. 2], Annual Meeting Files, Panhandle-Plains Historical Museum, Canyon (hereafter PPHM); Minutes of the Panhandle-Plains Historical Society, February 15, 1925, PPHM; J. Evetts Haley to My Dearest Nita, June 10, 1925, Amarillo, Texas, Letters, J. Evetts Haley to Nita, 1924–1929, the J. Evetts Haley Collection, NSHML. See also Price, "J. Evetts Haley," 190, 192; Hill, *Panhandle-Plains Historical Society*, 31.

11. J. Evetts Haley to My Dearest Nita, June 18, 1925, Mobeetie, Texas, Letters, J. Evetts Haley to Nita, 1924–1929, the J. Evetts Haley Collection, NSHML.

12. For a discussion of the background of the University of Texas faculty during the period, see Joe B. Frantz, *The Forty-Acre Follies* (Austin: Texas Monthly Press, 1983), 3. Haley's warm relationship with Eugene C. Barker is recounted in J. Evetts Haley, "The Eugene C. Barker Portrait Presentation, Acceptance, and Acknowledgments Address," *Southwestern Historical Quarterly* 46, no. 3 (January 1943): 301–312.

13. "Haley Valuable Aid to Work of History Group," *Prairie* (Canyon, TX), June 22, 1926, 1.

14. John V. Farwell to J. Evetts Haley, December 1, 1927, J. Evetts Haley Correspondence, 1927, box 1, 1924–1928 (Mi-Mo), J. Evetts Haley Correspondence 1924–1934, PPHM.

15. J. Evetts Haley to James D. Hamlin, November 3, 1927, copy in J. Evetts Haley Correspondence 1927, box 1, 1924–1928 (Mi-Mo), J. Evetts Haley Correspondence 1924–1934, PPHM.

16. John V. Farwell to J. Evetts Haley, n.d. [1928], J. Evetts Haley Correspondence 1928, box 1, 1924–1928 (Mi-Mo), J. Evetts Haley Correspondence 1924–1934, PPHM.

17. J. Frank Dobie to J. Evetts Haley, May 2, 1928, XIT Reviews File, the J. Evetts Haley Collection, NSHML; J. Evetts Haley to My Dearest Nita, June 26, 1928, Canyon, Texas, Letters, J. Evetts Haley to Nita, 1924–1929, the J. Evetts Haley Collection, NSHML.

18. J. Evetts Haley to My Dearest Nita, October 23, 1928, Chicago, Illinois, Letters, J. Evetts Haley to Nita, 1924–1929, the J. Evetts Haley Collection, NSHML; J. Evetts Haley to Samuel H. Roberts, copy in J. Evetts Haley Correspondence 1928, box 2, 1928 (N) — 1929 (Hoo-Hu), J. Evetts Haley Correspondence 1924–1934, PPHM; Hill, *Panhandle-Plains Historical Society*, 44; "XIT Records Are Turned Over to History Group," *Prairie*, November 20, 1928, 1, 4.

19. B. Byron Price, *Crafting a Southwestern Masterpiece* (Midland, TX: Nita Stewart Haley Memorial Library, 1986), 1, 9–10; J. Evetts Haley, "Charles Goodnight's Indian Recollections," *Panhandle-Plains Historical Review* 1 (1928): 3–29; Hill, *Panhandle-Plains Historical Society*, 48–49.

20. John L. McCarty, "J. Evetts Haley's History of the Famous XIT Ranch Is Out!" *Amarillo Sunday News and Globe*, April 7, 1929, 9; "Amarillo News Gives Praise to J. E. Haley," *Prairie*, April 16, 1929. See also Mildred W. Cheney to J. Evetts Haley, June 4, 1929, XIT Reviews File, the J. Evetts Haley Collection, NSHML.

21. Quoted in Hill, *Panhandle-Plains Historical Society*, 51. See also "Dobie Praises Haley's XIT Ranch History," *Prairie*, May 14, 1929, 1.

22. Eugene C. Barker to J. Evetts Haley, April 18, 1929, XIT Reviews File, the J. Evetts Haley Collection, NSHML.

23. Quoted in "Amarillo News Gives Praise to J. E. Haley," *Prairie*, April 16, 1929. See also "Haley Ranch History Now on Sale Here," *Prairie*, April 2, 1929, 1.

24. For an account of the libel suit in connection with Haley's book on the XIT, see James D. Hamlin, *The Flamboyant Judge* (Canyon, TX: Palo Duro Press, 1972), 235–256.

25. Robinson, *J. Evetts Haley, Cowman-Historian*, 10; J. Evetts Haley to Curry [Holden], December 21, 1931, William Curry Holden Papers, 1934–1941 and undated, Southwest Col-

lection, Texas Tech University, Lubbock (hereafter SWC); Hamlin, *The Flamboyant Judge,* 235–256.

26. J. Evetts Haley, "Annual Report of Project No. 12 Collector in Research in the Social Sciences 1930–1931, in J. Evetts Haley, *Annual Reports of Project No. 12 for the Collection of Historical Materials for the University of Texas, 1930–1936,* 5, box 2R28, J. Evetts Haley Papers, 1930–1936, the Dolph Briscoe Center for American History, University of Texas at Austin (hereafter DBCAH); J. Evetts Haley, "Report of Project No. 12 Collector in Research in the Social Sciences [1931–1932]," in Haley, *Annual Reports of Project No. 12.*

27. Robinson, ed., *J. Evetts Haley and the Passing of the Old West,* 151–175.

28. J. Evetts Haley, "Back-trailin' with the Old Timers," *Cattleman* 19 (March 1933): 11.

29. J. Evetts Haley to W. E. Gettys, April 29, 1936, copy in Haley, *Annual Reports of Project No. 12.*

30. Price, *Crafting a Southwestern Masterpiece,* 33.

31. J. Evetts Haley to L. W. Kemp, September 9, 1935, copy in Correspondence 1935–36, K, box 2D263, Haley Papers, DBCAH; Price, "J. Evetts Haley," 38; J. Evetts Haley to Erwin E. Smith, June 19, 1936, Erwin E. Smith Collection, NSHML.

32. See J. Evetts Haley, diary entries for December 15, 1933, and June 13, 1934, J. Evetts Haley, Diary 1933–1934, pp. 21, 52, J. Evetts Haley, Diaries and Notebooks, the J. Evetts Haley Collection, NSHML; Price, *Crafting a Southwestern Masterpiece,* 25; Don E. Carleton, *Who Shot the Bear?* (Austin: Wind River Press, 1984), 6.

33. J. Evetts Haley to Mr. Frank [Dobie], December 4, 1936, J. Frank Dobie Collection, Harry Ransom Center, University of Texas at Austin (hereafter HRC).

34. E. C. Barker to Mrs. [Nita] Haley, November 4, 1936, copy in Correspondence, General, June–December 1936, box 2B100, E. C. Barker Papers, DBCAH; Haley to Mr. Frank [Dobie], December 4, 1936, Ira Rich Kent to J. Evetts Haley, December 28, 1936, Milton Correspondence File, Jeff Milton Collection (Book Files), NSHML; E. C. Barker to H. Y. Benedict, November 17, 1936, copy in Correspondence, General, 1936, box 2B99, Barker Papers, DBCAH.

35. Jeff Davis Milton's more than fifty-year career as a western peace officer included duty as not only a Texas Ranger but also a Pullman Company detective, a Wells Fargo agent, an immigration inspector, and the El Paso chief of police. J. Evetts Haley, interview by B. Byron Price, June 6, 1985, Midland, tape in possession of the author; J. Evetts Haley, *Jeff Milton, a Good Man with a Gun* (Norman: University of Oklahoma Press, 1948), viii, 402; Jeff Milton to J. Evetts Haley, March 16, 1936, Correspondence 1935–1936, M, box 2D264, Haley Papers, DBCAH.

36. "General Terms of Agreement between the Trustees of the Littlefield Fund for Southern History and J. Evetts Haley," General Correspondence, 1936, box 2B99, Barker Papers, DBCAH. See also J. Evetts Haley to J. Frank Dobie, June 21, 1937, and September 21, 1937, Dobie Collection, HRC; J. Evetts Haley to Jeff Milton, June 21, 1937, copy in Milton Book Files, NSHML.

37. Haley, interview by Price, June 6, 1985. Dent owned the Atarque and Clochintoh in partnership with fellow Texan W. A. Wrather. See Kent to Haley, December 28, 1936, Milton Correspondence File, NSHML; J. Evetts Haley, foreword to *Adventuring with the Old-Timers: Trails Travelled—Tales Told,* by Hervey E. Chesley (Midland, TX: Nita Stewart Haley Memorial Library, 1979), xi–xii.

38. Haley to Dobie, June 21, 1937.

39. Ibid.; Evetts [Haley] to Frank [Dobie], April 3, 1937, Dobie Collection, HRC; J. Evetts Haley to My Dear Mamma and Papa [Julia E. and John A. Haley], August 3, 1937, Letters to and from J. E. H.—Julia E. Haley, 1923–1945, the J. Evetts Haley Collection, NSHML; Brock-

man Horne to Haley, April 22, 1941, J. Evetts Haley Correspondence, 1941, the J. Evetts Haley Collection, NSHML.

40. J. Evetts Haley to Dr. [E. C.] Barker, December 12, 1937, copy in Eugene C. Barker Biographical (Interview) File, the J. Evetts Haley Collection, NSHML.

41. Evetts [Haley] to Frank [Dobie], September 21, 1937; C. W. (Charlie) Walker, W. W. (Walter) Walker, and W. D. (Bill) Walker, interview by J. Evetts Haley, Dunlap, New Mexico, August 5, 1937, typescript, Walker Biographical (Interview) File, the J. Evetts Haley Collection, NSHML.

42. J. Evetts Haley to Ira Rich Kent, March 19, 1937, copy in Milton Correspondence File, Jeff Milton Collection (Book Files), NSHML.

43. J. Evetts Haley to Ira Rich Kent, February 1, 1938, Milton, Jeff File, Jeff Milton Collection (Book Files), NSHML.

44. Haley to Kent, March 19, 1937.

45. Haley to Barker, March 18, 1944, Correspondence, General, January–June 1944, box 2B101, Barker Papers, DBCAH; see also J. Evetts Haley to Dr. Barker, February 26, 1944, box 2B101, Barker Papers, DBCAH; J. Evetts Haley letter to Dr. [E. C.] Barker, February 15, 1945, Correspondence, General, January–May 1945, box 2B102, Barker Papers, DBCAH.

46. J. Evetts Haley to Messrs. Stone and Guleke, February 24, 1938, copy in Amarillo Times, Editorials, etc. File, the J. Evetts Haley Collection, NSHML.

47. Haley, *Jeff Milton*, 34.

48. West owned the Clear Lake Ranch in southeastern Texas, the Chupadero on the lower Rio Grande, and the Figure 2 near Van Horne. J. Evetts Haley to Mr. and Mrs. [Jeff D.] Milton, February 7, 1943, copy in Milton Book Files, NSHML. See also J. Evetts Haley to My Dear Mamma, January 30, 1943, Letters to and from J. E. H.—Julia E. Haley, 1923–1945, "Family Files," the J. Evetts Haley Collection, NSHML; Donald C. Coney to Eugene C. Barker, January 27, 1941, copy in Littlefield—Correspondence, Reviews, etc., Littlefield Papers, NSHML.

49. Alfred A. Knopf to J. Evetts Haley, March 4, 1941, Littlefield Fund, NSHML.

50. E. C. Barker to [J. Evetts] Haley, May 26, 1942, J. Evetts Haley Correspondence, 1942, the J. Evetts Haley Collection, NSHML.

51. Donald Coney "Changes in Oklahoma Press Contract for Littlefield," November 25, 1942, copy in Correspondence, General, April–December, 1941, box 2B101, Barker Papers, DBCAH; E. C. Barker to J. Evetts Haley, March 3, 1943, Littlefield—Correspondence, Reviews, etc., Littlefield Papers, NSHML.

52. Herbert P. Gambrell, "Evetts Haley's Life of Littlefield Illuminates Era of Texas History," *Dallas News*, November 14, 1943, copy in Littlefield—Correspondence, Reviews, etc., Littlefield Papers, NSHML.

53. Ibid.; J. L. McC. [John L. McCarty], "Evetts Haley Adds Another Book to List," *Amarillo Globe*, November 9, 1943, 2.

54. E. C. Barker to [John] Lomax, December 4, 1943, Homer P. Rainey Controversy File, box 2E379, John Lomax Papers, DBCAH.

55. West died in Kansas City, Missouri, on August 24, 1941. See Claudia Hazelwood, "West, James Marion," *The Handbook of Texas Online*, http://www.tshaonline.org/handbook/online/articles/WW/fwe33.html (accessed January 23, 2010).

56. B. Byron Price, "When a Good Man with a Gun Met a Good Man with a Pen: Writing Jeff Milton's Biography," *Journal of Arizona History* 33, no. 1 (Spring 1992): 11; Evetts [Haley] to Dr. [Eugene C.] Barker, January 4, 1945, Correspondence, General, January–May 1945, box 2B102, Barker Papers, DBCAH; J. Evetts Haley, *The University of Texas and the Issue* (Amarillo, TX: Miller Printing, 1945).

57. Evetts [Haley] to Dr. [Eugene C.] Barker, January 21, 1945, Correspondence, General, January–May 1945, box 2B102, Barker Papers, DBCAH.

58. Evetts [Haley] to Dr. [Eugene C.] Barker, April 4, 1943, Correspondence, General, January–May 1943, box 2B101, Barker Papers, DBCAH.

59. J. Evetts Haley to Dr. [Eugene C.] Barker, January 21, 1945, Correspondence, General, January–May 1945, box 2B102, Barker Papers, DBCAH.

60. Haley, interview by Price, June 6, 1985.

61. J. Evetts Haley, interview by B. Byron Price, July 25, 1989, Midland, Texas, tape in possession of the author.

62. J. Evetts Haley to Harold Bugbee, December 29, 1947, Harold D. Bugbee Papers, 1900–1963, PPHM; Haley, interview by Price, July 25, 1989.

63. University of Oklahoma Press, "Statement of Sales" [semiannual], Jeff Milton Collection (Book Files), NSHML.

64. Robinson, *J. Evetts Haley, Cowman-Historian*, 22–23.

65. [Biographical Sketch], [ca. 1955], J. Evetts Haley File, Past Presidents Correspondence, Panhandle Plains Historical Society Papers, PPHM; William Curry Holden, interview by Jimmy M. Skaggs, December 15, 18, 1967, Holden Papers, SWC.

66. J. Evetts Haley, "States Rights—The Issue! Interposition the Way to Preserve them [.] Announcement for Governor" (brochure), copy in Haley-Bugbee Correspondence 1918–1963, Harold D. Bugbee Collection, PPHM.

67. "10 Textbooks Attacked by Haley-Texas Group," *Victoria Advocate*, October 6, 1960, 9. See also Price, "J. Evetts Haley," 199; Robinson, *J. Evetts Haley, Cowman-Historian*, 20–22; Rick Perlstein, *Before the Storm: Barry Goldwater and the Unmaking of American Consensus* (New York: Hill and Wang, 2001), 151.

68. Robinson, *J. Evetts Haley, Cowman-Historian*, 26–31; Joseph Warren, "Suppression of a Book," in Robinson, ed., *J. Evetts Haley and the Passing of the Old West*, 111–115; J. Evetts Haley, *A Texan Looks at Lyndon: A Study in Illegitimate Power* (Canyon, TX: Palo Duro Press, 1964).

69. Haley, *Jeff Milton*, ix.

70. J. C. Barnes Jr., "Friend and Library Builder," in *What a World of Wonder!*, edited by J. Evetts Haley Jr. (Midland, TX: Nita Stewart Haley Memorial Library, 1990), 29–31.

71. J. Evetts Haley Jr., "Epilogue," in ibid., 73–79; "J. Evetts Haley Receives Award of Merit," *Haley Library Newsletter* 3 (Winter 1981): n.p.; "Haley Chosen for Induction into Heritage Hall of Fame," *Haley Library Newsletter* 15 (Fall 1993): 3.

72. Don Graham, *Giant Country: Essays on Texas* (Fort Worth: Texas Christian University Press, 1998), 106; A. C. Greene, *The Fifty Best Books on Texas* (Dallas: Pressworks, 1982), 35.

73. Larry McMurtry, *Walter Benjamin at the Dairy Queen* (New York: Simon and Schuster, 1999), 94.

74. "The Original LBJ Critic—Caro Trilogy Furor Revives Interest in Book Shunned in '64," *Dallas Morning News*, July 17, 1990, 21A.

75. William Adler, "A Texan Looks at Lyndon," *Texas Monthly* 14, no. 9 (September 1987): 114.

76. Melvin E. Bradford, "The Care and Keeping of Memory: J. Evetts Haley and Plutarchian Biography," *Southwestern American Literature* 3 (Spring/Fall 1973): 69–76.

ARCHIE P. MCDONALD

ROBERT MAXWELL

ROBERT MAXWELL

Divinely tall and built to please
He's very helpful and loves to tease!

Robert Sidney Maxwell's evaluation in *The Highlander*, the annual published by the senior class of Highlands High School in Fort Thomas, Kentucky, in 1930, remained remarkably accurate throughout his life, though his high school nickname, "Shorty," did not.[1] (Maxwell measured nearly six feet four inches at maximum height at a time when most American males averaged approximately five feet ten.) Throughout his career he did his best to be helpful to friends, colleagues, and especially younger scholars; he enjoyed all sports, but participated vigorously in basketball, tennis, and later golf; and he enjoyed a wide range of friendships in both academic and lay communities. He also earned national status as a historian, first in the field of Progressivism and, after he moved to Texas, as founder of the study of forest history there.

Robert Sidney Maxwell was born on November 11, 1911, in Danville, Kentucky, to William Samuel and Ida Maxwell. His middle name honored an earlier Kentuckian, Albert Sidney Johnston, Confederate commander of the Western Theater until his death on June 6, 1862, from a wound suffered during the Battle of Shiloh. In later years Maxwell enjoyed showing visitors the portrait of his martial namesake on display in the Senate chamber in the Texas Capitol in Austin.[2]

Maxwell and his older brother Samuel grew up in several cities in Kentucky because William Maxwell was a United Methodist minister and district superintendent, and that denomination requires most of its clergy to accept reassignment every few years.[3] But Maxwell did get to complete four years at Highlands High School in Fort Thomas. His participation in sports earned him three letters in football and basketball, and he took an active part in the Hi-Y Club, the Boy's Athletic Club, the French Club, and the Bible Study Club. He also played the taxi driver in *The Whole Town's Talking*, the school's senior class play. A portrait of Maxwell clad in a basketball uniform in *The Highlander* annual shows a tall, thin, and pleasant-looking young man of nineteen. Maxwell's team, the Bluebirds, won the championship in Class B of the greater Cincinnati area and the Twenty-Second District Tournament with a record of twenty-three wins against only two defeats, but lost to a team from a high school in Lexington in the Sixth Regional Tournament.[4]

Maxwell enrolled in Kentucky Wesleyan College in Winchester, Kentucky, in the fall of 1930 and received his baccalaureate degree with a double major in history and chemistry in 1934. He played center on the school's varsity basketball team and won the privilege of wearing a *W* on his school sweater.[5] Maxwell crossed the Ohio River to enroll in the graduate program at the University of Cincinnati and received a master's degree in history in 1937. He later taught history and served as assistant basketball coach at Campbell County High School in Alexandria, Kentucky, helping Coach L. E. Woolum and his Camels win seventeen consecutive games one season in the Suburban Conference.[6]

When the United States entered World War II in December 1941, Maxwell, thirty years of age and single, entered the U.S. Army. He completed officer training school and served as a company commander in the European Theater. Although he did not take part in the landing at Normandy, France, in 1944 Captain Maxwell participated in the remaining campaigns of the war in Europe. In a letter addressed to "Rev. W. S. Maxwell, 545 E. Main St., Danville, Kentucky," from the Netherlands on February 15, 1945, he wrote, "Dear Father and Mother, The days seem to fade into weeks—a little progress is made here & there,—the news of the Russians is good, the air fleets go & come, yet still the Krautheads fight on. Perhaps they will quit before Christmas." (Maxwell's pessimism must have improved when Germany surrendered several months later, in May 1945.) Maxwell told his parents that he was well, "with the exception of a bad cold," but enjoyed "almost normal living conditions,—food, beds, and private home, regular washing & shaving, and such." He added, "After that stretch in Belgium these things seem like luxuries." And, as always, sports: "By the time you get this the basketball tournaments will be on and the baseball teams will start spring training. Tell me the news. Love, Bob."[7]

When Maxwell returned from military service, he enrolled in the doctoral program at the University of Wisconsin, one of the nation's premier programs in graduate history studies. Merle Curti, Maxwell's major professor and director of his dissertation on the career of Robert M. La Follette, directed Maxwell's study of twentieth-century U.S. history. While in Madison, Maxwell met and married Margaret Dunning of New York City, a graduate of Hunter College and a teacher in the University of Wisconsin's school of social work. Their daughter, Elizabeth Gail, was born on September 19, 1958.[8]

Maxwell remained in residence at the University of Wisconsin from 1946 through 1948 and received his Ph.D. in 1949. He accepted a teaching post in Lexington at the University of Kentucky in 1948 and taught recent American history there until 1952, when the "bubble" of the GI Bill generation of students had passed through educational preparation to become part of the workforce. Retrenchment—known by its army term as a "riff"—forced Maxwell to seek other employment. In September 1952 he joined chairman Fletcher Garner and historians C. K. Chamberlain and James L. Nichols as an assistant professor in the history department at Stephen F. Austin State College in Nacogdoches, Texas. Nichols, also a veteran of World War II, and Maxwell became leading scholars in their respective fields of Civil War studies and recent American history.

Maxwell's post at SFA broadened in 1954 when he won promotion to the rank of associate professor and was appointed director of the Bureau of East Texas Research. Under Maxwell's direction the bureau gathered data about the economy of the region, an economy heavily invested in forests and the forest products industries. Maxwell traveled extensively in the East Texas region, visiting the headquarters of railroads and lumber companies and becoming familiar with their historical records and the individuals who ran the various enterprises in those industries. Maxwell's letter to Emmie M. Muenker, county clerk of Kerr County, gives insight into this quest: "As a part of the program of the Bureau of East Texas Research we are making a study of the old Houston, East and West Texas Railway, now a part of the Southern Pacific System. The H.E. & W.T. Railway was one of the pioneer railroads of East Texas and has had an interesting and significant history. One facet of the program involves the study of land grants received by the railroad." Maxwell explained that he had learned from Texas land commissioner Earl Rudder that one such grant had been awarded in Kerr County and inquired, "Can you tell us what happened to it?"[9]

Maxwell had developed an interest in Paul Bremond's railroad, which connected Houston with Shreveport, Louisiana, to provide the first meaningful transportation outlet for the 300 million board feet of southern pine lumber growing for nearly 100 miles on either side of its tracks; eventually his first book in forest history, a field he pioneered in Texas, dealt with that rail line. But before that he published two books, essentially prepared in Wisconsin and Kentucky before coming to Nacogdoches, on turn-of-the-century Progressivism that established him as a leader in that field. The first, *La Follette and the Rise of Progressives in Wisconsin*, published in 1956 by the State Historical Society of Wisconsin, is still cited over half a century later as a milestone in the study of Progressivism. The second book, *Emanuel L. Philipp: Wisconsin Stalwart*, also published by the State Historical Society of Wisconsin, followed in 1959. Maxwell joked that everyone connected with the book on La Follette—publisher, designer, illustrator, etc.—won an award for their role in its publication except him! Nevertheless, *La Follette* established Maxwell's national reputation as a distinguished historian long before his work in forest history made him a leader in that field as well.

Maxwell's activities for the Bureau of Research led to a great deal of travel throughout East Texas and elsewhere. A partial review of his official state travel forms and vouchers for 1954–1960 gives an indication of his busy schedule: he traveled to Diboll, Texas, to discuss the history of the Southern Pine Lumber Company with company officials; to Hemphill, Texas, "to interview Judge Minton concerning early history of Kirby Lumber Company"; to Center, Texas, to interview W. I. Davis concerning the Pickering Lumber Company; to Houston to examine records of the HE&WT Railway; to Dallas to "pick up for deposit in the library papers of the Chronister Lumber Company"; to Keltys, Texas, to talk with E. L. Kurth and officials of the Angelina County Lumber Company; to Diboll again, to confer with Arthur Temple; to Camden, Texas, to observe logging operations of the Carter Lumber Company; and to Silsbee, Texas, to inspect "the new electric saw mill of the Kirby Lumber Company and interview veteran employees about operations." He also took numerous trips throughout Texas to attend semiannual meetings of the Lone Star Athletic Conference as SFA's faculty representative, and headed to various destinations to attend annual meetings of the Mississippi Valley Historical Association, Southern Historical Association, and Texas State Historical Association. This represents a remarkable amount of travel for a professor employed at a regional state-supported university where the emphasis remained on classroom instruction. All of Maxwell's classes were covered by colleagues who joined administrators in encouraging the expansion of his professional opportunities and achievements.[10]

Maxwell received appointment as a senior Fulbright scholar for 1960–1961, and he and his family spent the academic year at the University of Southampton. The Maxwells crossed the Atlantic aboard the *Queen Elizabeth* in September 1960; they showed four-year-old Elizabeth the sights of London before Maxwell assumed his duties in Southampton, though he reported that they had "barely scratched the surface of that marvelous city."[11] During the academic year they lived at 26 Pentire Avenue, Shirley, Southampton.

In a letter to the Conference Board of Associated Research Councils, headquartered in Washington, DC, Maxwell disclosed that he was the third American scholar to hold the post. In addition to lecturing to three classes on American history, Maxwell also organized a continuing program for the American history option and selected library books to support the program. He gave guest lectures in a variety of venues, including locations in London, Birmingham, and Falkenstein, Germany, and participated in the summer revision school in history sponsored by the British Historical Association, the first such offering in American studies in the program's history.[12] Maxwell's papers include a newspaper clipping showing him marching with other robed scholars from Southampton University to Highfield Church to participate in the annual commemoration service for the university. Before Maxwell returned to Nacogdoches, he received a letter from Vice Chancellor D. G. James expressing "how much we have enjoyed having you here this session, and how much we feel you and Mrs. Maxwell have contributed to the life of the University during your stay with us . . . and we could not have had more welcomed visitors from the academic life of the States than you and Mrs. Maxwell."[13] Maxwell utilized the back flyleaf of his copy of the University of Southampton calendar for 1960–1961 to record addresses of colleagues with whom he wished to remain in contact, and often spoke fondly of his tenure at Southampton.

The year in England made Maxwell a confirmed Anglophile, internationalist, and international traveler for the remainder of his life, and he encouraged others to go and do likewise. In a May 1962 letter to a friend identified only as Wayne, Maxwell congratulated his colleague on receiving a similar appointment, urging him to follow his own example of visits to London to attend plays and concerts or travels to Canterbury and Land's End. Maxwell said that the entire family had traveled for approximately twenty dollars per day and had budgeted twenty-five dollars each month to "keep as warm as we do in the United States"; they considered the money "well spent." He concluded, "You will find the weather cold and wet but no colder than Iowa."[14]

When Maxwell returned to Nacogdoches from England, he assumed an interim chairmanship of SFA's history department during the second summer session while the chairman, C. K. Chamberlain, vacationed. Maxwell prepared a report for Chamberlain on the summer's activities, assuring him that things had gone "smoothly." Maxwell reported that Dean Joe Gerber had authorized a new teaching post in the department and that he had hired Carl L. Davis, a Ph.D. candidate at Rice University; had revised the fall schedule to include Davis; and had made appointments for graduate assistantships. Maxwell reported laying in supplies for the fall semester, though he proudly reported that a "substantial" sum remained in the department's account.[15]

Beginning in the 1960s, Robert Maxwell's career proceeded on parallel paths of academic teaching/administration and scholarship. He remained comfortable in each path, moving from one to the other as opportunities presented themselves. Shortly after arriving at SFA, department chairman Fletcher Garner asked each department member to prepare a statement—in two paragraphs—of his philosophy of history. Typically, Maxwell groused about such compaction, pointing out that Arnold Toynbee had taken twelve volumes and Spengler and Henry Adams at least two volumes for such a chore. But good soldier that he was, Maxwell complied.

> Philosophy:
> The study of History is a well-recognized branch of knowledge, which dates back to the ancient Greeks. As a separate discipline it has developed special tools and techniques of teaching, research and interpretation that may be described as the "historical method." The historian seeks to encompass all phases of significant human experience, political, social, economic, intellectual and cultural. By studying the past we hope to give meaning to the present and give purpose to the future.
>
> Goals:
> The Department of History seeks to impart to the students of this college a fundamental knowledge of man's achievements, problems and development.

> As this is a regional college the principal concentration of the department is upon the more recent past and to some degree upon our own national development. The department seeks to arouse in the student an enthusiasm for historical study and a desire to delve further into the aspects of man's past that particularly interest him. It also seeks to provide the student with the basic tools for further study and interpretation that would make independent work profitable.
>
> As a secondary goal the department of history actively encourages advanced study and research not only on the part of its own members but by other members of the faculty and outside qualified persons. The department seeks to build up at this college a center for regional historical studies that will add meaning and understanding of this area and its history.[16]

Maxwell summarized his personal philosophy of history as "idea-centered, progressive, optimistic and Christian" and assured his boss, "Like Chaucer's Clerk, I would gladly learn and gladly teach."[17]

On the teacher/administrator path, Maxwell passed on an invitation from Thomas H. Barland, president of the Texas State Historical Society, to apply for the position of director of that association after its previous director, Leslie H. Fishel, retired. Maxwell declined, stating, "I am certain that this would not be the kind of work that I do best. It is a challenging opportunity for an enterprising scholar with a flair for organization and promotion, but for me it would be a sure route to a stomach ulcer."[18]

Maxwell did agree to succeed C. K. Chamberlain as chairman of SFA's history department in 1969. The department moved from the second flour of the Birdwell Building to new quarters in the T. E. Ferguson Liberal Arts Building at the same time, further symbolizing the transfer of leadership. Maxwell never ceased his scholarship, balancing administrative duties against research and writing by relying on an elected executive committee of faculty members and an excellent secretary, Jeanne Attaway. He remained available to students and faculty most mornings, but by midafternoon one could see him in the hall, perhaps swinging an umbrella upside down in a practice golf swing, and announcing that it was time to "change base of operations," a reference to his days as a company commander in World War II. Faculty members never knew if this predicted a visit to Piney Woods Country Club for a round of golf or to his study in the Maxwell home, located at 423 Parker Road.

In 1972 Maxwell's standing in forest history led to his appointment to the board of directors of the Forest History Society. That same year, SFA's president, Ralph W. Steen, called on Maxwell to serve as the school's representative to the executive committee for the Texas College and University Bicentennial Program to plan the 200th anniversary of the nation's birth in 1976. Maxwell also headed a local bicentennial committee, which presented a series of lectures on the SFA campus by distinguished scholars on the American Revolution. In that same year, Maxwell delivered the principal address at the dedication of SFA's new library, named in honor of Dr. Steen, who was retiring from the university's presidency. And in the profession Maxwell accepted numerous positions of responsibility, including service on program and nominating committees for the Forest History Society, the Southern Historical Association, the Southwest Social Science Association, and the Texas State Historical Association; he also served as president of the East Texas Historical Association in 1973–1974. He often reviewed books for professional journals or quarterlies and presented papers, especially on forest history, at their annual meetings.

Maxwell navigated the tightrope of departmental chairmanship—which in SFA's system was part faculty and part administrator—with skill. He always remained accessible to students and faculty, frequently visiting colleagues in their offices and occasionally hosting social events at his home. He supported members of his faculty in their quest for professional advancement and always found time to provide recommendations for younger scholars seeking grants or employment.[19] Maxwell's annual administrative evaluations of members of the history department were supportive, encouraging, and, in at least one case, revealed his own values (he reported that "Mr. Cooper has been so dedicated to finishing his doctorate that he has allowed his golf game to deteriorate. This should be corrected next year").[20]

When Maxwell gave up the chairmanship of the history department in September 1977, SFA's vice president for academic affairs, Dr. John T. Lewis III, sent him a handwritten note that said, in part, "I want to thank you for the fine leadership you have given to the History Department. I think you can look with justifiable pride upon your accomplishments. You have been a good department head, a gentleman in all our relationships, and a fine example for those in your department. I appreciate what you are, a good man."[21] Other previous departmental chairmen then invited Maxwell to join them in an exclusive campus organization known as the "Were-Heads." Their constitution stated that a member could be any person who had served as head of a department; prohibited the election of officers, committees, or regular meetings, and even, when assembled, meeting agenda; and confirmed the privilege of sitting "in unofficial judgment on administrative actions and decisions."[22]

In the classroom Maxwell expected competence and achievement, but he retained the goodwill of most students, one of whom wrote, "Just a note of thanks for all your help and consideration during my graduate years and all my time in the history department. Someone who shows interest and understanding is more appreciated than you know. Thanks for the patience you showed me during my comprehensive examination."[23] And, after four decades of teaching, Dr. William Brophy, Maxwell's successor as chairman, commented on Maxwell's teaching in his annual evaluation: "Dr. Maxwell probably has more knowledge of his field than any other member of the department. His students receive a sound consensus view of the American experience."[24]

In scholarship Maxwell had established a national reputation in the study of Progressivism before coming to SFA in 1952. Far from Wisconsin and the resources he had utilized to write on the careers of Robert La Follette and Emanuel Philipp, he embraced a new topic of study, forest history. As director of the Bureau of East Texas Research, he turned to this unexplored field—unexplored in East Texas, at least. With the support of SFA presidents Paul L. Boynton and Ralph W. Steen, he convinced officials of the Angelina County Lumber Company, Frost-Johnson Lumber Company, W. T. Carter Lumber Company, Lutcher Moore Lumber Company, Temple Industries, Kirby Lumber Company, W. Goodrich Jones, and other forestry pioneers to make the SFA library the depository of their business records no longer required for current operations. Using those papers, and others collected later, Maxwell began to write in—and establish—a new avenue of scholarship in East Texas.

First came *Whistle in the Piney Woods: Paul Bremond and the Houston, East And West Texas Railway*, published by the Texas Gulf Coast Historical Association in 1963, because, said Maxwell, "The history of the railroad and of the lumber industry were inseparable."[25] The 192-mile rail line of the HE&WT, nicknamed "Hell Either Way Taken," connected the port cities of Houston, with its access via ship channel to the Gulf of Mexico, New Orleans, and Shreveport, Louisiana, a pathway to the continent's midsection by the Red River to the Mississippi River and by rail east and west on a more northerly route. This connection opened the vast timber and timber products resources of the East Texas region to the world. Maxwell's presentation explored social developments as well as business development, and, among other things, helped revive interest in a song titled "Teneha, Timpson, Bobo and Blair," a reference to four stops on the HE&WT.

In 1964 Maxwell wrote "The Pines of Texas: A Study in Lumbering and Public Policy" for the *East Texas Historical Journal*, in which he called attention to such giants of the industry as John Henry Kirby and the father of forest conservation in Texas, W. Goodrich Jones.[26]

Maxwell addressed a national audience in 1965 in "Lumbermen of the East Texas Frontier," published in *Forest History*.[27] Maxwell reminded readers that all of Texas was not what they usually saw in motion pictures; instead, Texas also had miles and miles of trees, mostly pine trees, in its eastern portion, where Henry J. Lutcher, G. Bedell Moore, William H. Stark, John Henry Kirby, and others had made fortunes and also altered the landscape. He wrote dozens of articles and spoke to scores of audiences about the careers of such lumber barons and their impact on the lives of nearly every East Texan.

With Robert D. Baker, formerly with the College of Forestry at SFA but by 1983 on the forestry staff at Texas A&M University, Maxwell published *Sawdust Empire: The Texas Lumber Industry, 1830–1940*, touted accurately as the "first comprehensive story of logging, lumbering, and forest conservation in Texas."[28] Their study remains the standard work in its field and is Maxwell's major contribution to the study of the forest industry. *Sawdust Empire* presents the story of the East Texas forest itself, from the days of "virgin pines" shading a parklike understory through the "cut and get out" and clear-cutting eras. Maxwell and Baker examine the mills, the timber barons, and the workers in company towns with equal interest and intensity.

In 1985 Maxwell joined others in preparing *This Well-Wooded Land: Americans and their Forests from Colonial Times to the Present*, published by the University of Nebraska Press, and three years later he and Baker joined other scholars to write *Timeless Heritage: A History of the Forest Service in the Southwest.*

Robert S. Maxwell retired from teaching in 1983, but he remained a vital citizen and an active member of the academy until his death on December 29, 1990. He and Margaret roamed the world, often in the company of friends and sometimes on golf outings to such places as Spain, and he remained active in forest associations, Texas organizations, and southern historical associations. Governor Julian M. Carrol appointed him an official "Kentucky Colonel" in honor of his retirement as departmental chairman, and he was pleased, but in reality Bob Maxwell never really ceased being what he had been since 1946—teacher, friend, and historian.

Writing to J. C. Green, another departmental chairman retiring in 1978, Maxwell observed, "SFA is a considerable university now, larger than the University of Kentucky was when I left in 1952 to come here. But I think it has retained some of the personal characteristics which we remember from the earlier days when the faculty was a small compact group."[29]

Even so, Maxwell was part of a larger group of teachers who became outstanding historians in the years after World War II, and he became a bridge to the Vietnam generation. James Fickle said in tribute, "In the ideal world, academe is supposed to be inhabited by a community of scholars. Bob Maxwell, through his work and his personal warmth and generosity, demonstrated to me that the ideal world can sometimes be real."[30]

Bob Maxwell and I traveled and roomed together frequently to attend historical meetings, and I came to know him as well as I knew anyone in the history profession. I recall most vividly one of our last trips, to Lexington, Kentucky, to attend a meeting of the Southern Historical Association. In some ways, it was a disappointing homecoming for Bob—the town where he had studied and taught before moving to Texas had changed so much, and not all for the better. As we walked the streets of its dying downtown, in his memory a vital center of business during the 1940s, he was saddened. Then, on the last day of the meeting, his brother came from Cincinnati to collect him for a visit. I remember the tenderness with which these two older men greeted each other, and I was glad that his bittersweet visit "home" would have a happy ending. I trust that Bob is home again.[31]

SUGGESTED READING

Maxwell, Robert S. *La Follette and the Rise of Progressives in Wisconsin.* Madison, WI: State Historical Society of Wisconsin, 1956.

Still cited over half a century later as a milestone in the study of Progressivism. *La Follette* established Maxwell's national reputation as a distinguished historian preceding his landmark works in forest history.

Maxwell, Robert S. *Whistle in the Piney Woods: Paul Bremond and the Houston, East and West Texas Railway.* Houston, TX: Texas Gulf Coast Historical Association, 1963.

Maxwell's presentation explored social and business relationships and the railroad's role in the development of East Texas, and helped revive interest in a song titled "Teneha, Timpson, Bobo and Blair," from the names of four stops on the HE&WT.

Maxwell, Robert S., and Robert D. Baker. *Sawdust Empire: The Texas Lumber Industry, 1830–1940.* College Station: Texas A&M University Press, 1983.

This remains the standard work in its field and is Maxwell's major contribution to the study of the forest industry.

NOTES

1. *The Highlander*, vol. 14 (Fort Thomas, KY: Highlands High School, 1930): 37.

2. Maxwell's birthday appears on his Texas driver's license, box 1–2, Maxwell Papers, East Texas Research Center, Ralph W. Steen Library, Stephen F. Austin State University, Nacogdoches, Texas (hereafter Maxwell Papers). The author accompanied Maxwell to the Senate Chamber on many occasions while attending annual meetings of the Texas State Historical Association in Austin.

3. Interview with Margaret Maxwell, Houston, TX, June 4, 2008.

4. *Highlander*, 37, 66, 68, 79, and 91.

5. *Porphyrian* 12 (1933): 40, 58 (published by the senior class of Kentucky Wesleyan College).

6. Undated newspaper clipping, box 1–2, Maxwell Papers.

7. V-E Letter, copy in box 1–2, Maxwell Papers.

8. Maxwell interview.

ARCHIE P. MCDONALD

9. Maxwell to Emmie M. Muenker, January 8, 1957, box 1–2, Maxwell Papers.

10. Maxwell's copies of travel applications and some vouchers, box 1–2, Maxwell Papers.

11. Alberta Rich (travel editor), "Traveler's World," *Nacogdoches Daily Sentinel*, n.d. (clipping), box 1–2, Maxwell Papers.

12. Maxwell to Conference Board of Associated Research Councils, October 12, 1961, and Maxwell's nomination form for a Piper Professor award, n.d., box 1–2, Maxwell Papers.

13. D. G. James to My dear Maxwell, July 10, 1961, ibid.

14. Maxwell to Wayne, May 4, 1968, box 1–2, Maxwell Papers.

15. Maxwell to C. K. Chamberlain, August 18, 1962, box 1–2, Maxwell Papers.

16. Maxwell to Fletcher Garner, n.d., box 1–2, Maxwell Papers.

17. Ibid.

18. Maxwell to Thomas A. Barland, December 18, 1968, box 1–2, Maxwell Papers.

19. Maxwell to Maurice A. Crouse (regarding the candidacy of James E. Fickle, a young scholar in the field of forest history), October 2, 1979, box 1–2, Maxwell Papers.

20. Maxwell evaluation of George F. Cooper Jr., filed May 16, 1975, box 1–2, Maxwell Papers.

21. John T. Lewis to Robert S. Maxwell, n.d., box 1–2, Maxwell Papers.

22. Were-Heads Constitution and Bylaws, copy in box 1–2, Maxwell Papers.

23. Sylvia Sessions to Robert S. Maxwell, July 13 [no year], box 1–2, Maxwell Papers.

24. James E. Fickle, "The Legacy of a Gentlemanly Scholar: Dr. Robert S. Maxwell and His Contributions to Forest History," *East Texas Historical Journal* 32, no. 2 (1993): 7. Fickle became a protégé of Maxwell, and his evaluation of Maxwell's work in forest history is authoritative. The author is deeply indebted to Professor Fickle for his insight into this aspect of Robert Maxwell's career.

25. Robert S. Maxwell, "The Pines of Texas: A Study in Lumbering and Public Policy, 1880–1930," *East Texas Historical Journal*, Vol. 2, No. 2 (October 1964): 77–86.

26. Robert S. Maxwell, "Lumbermen of the East Texas Frontier," *Forest History* 9 (April 1965): 12–17.

27. Robert S. Maxwell and Robert D. Baker, *Sawdust Empire: The Texas Lumber Industry, 1830–1949* (College Station: Texas A&M University Press, 1983).

28. Robert D. Baker, Robert S. Maxwell, Victor H. Treat, and Henry C. Dethloff, *Timeless Heritage: A History of the Forest Service in the Southwest*, Publication FS-409 (Washington, DC: U.S. Department of Agriculture, Forest Service, August 1988); Thomas R. Cox, Robert S. Maxwell, Phillip Drennon Thomas, and Joseph J. Malone, *This Well-Wooded Land: Americans and Their Forests from Colonial Times to the Present* (Lincoln: University of Nebraska Press: 1985). James E. Fickle called these publications the capstones "for Bob Maxwell's distinguished career as a forest historian." *Environmental Review* 10 (Winter 1986): 314–315.

29. Robert S. Maxwell to J. C. Green, May 3, 1978, box 1–2, Maxwell Papers.

30. Fickle, "Legacy of a Gentlemanly Scholar," 12.

31. Andre P. McDonald, "East Texas Colloquy," *East Texas Historical Journal* 29, no. 2 (1991): 72–73.

FÉLIX D. ALMARÁZ JR.

CARLOS E. CASTAÑEDA

CARLOS E. CASTAÑEDA, 1940

As a mature scholar, Carlos Eduardo Castañeda always considered himself a second-generation Boltonian. His affiliation with Herbert Eugene Bolton, distinguished founder of borderlands history, stemmed from a pre–World War I introduction at the University of Texas in Austin to Professor Charles Wilson Hackett, who had studied under Bolton in California. Castañeda's relationship with Hackett, solidified by the commonality of their first names, gradually broadened his interest in southwestern history to the extent that much later he claimed to be Bolton's "intellectual grandson."[1] In 1946, after twenty years of productive scholarship and the publication of several volumes of the famed *Our Catholic Heritage in Texas*, Castañeda expressed his disappointment to Bolton for "not being one of your boys by rights." But with superb agility, Carlos upheld his identity by asserting he was Bolton's "adopted boy."[2] This unique bond, separated by the space of one generation, originated in the mid-twenties when Castañeda underwent transformation from professor of Spanish to librarian, culminating in his induction into Clio's fraternity.

In 1927, at thirty years of age, Castañeda assumed the curatorship of the Latin American Collection at the Austin campus of the University of Texas. By then he had successfully passed through the formative stages of methodology. First, after changing his planned career from one in civil engineering to one in history, he earned a B.A. and a Phi Beta Kappa key in 1921, and two years later an M.A., both degrees under the principal guidance of Eugene Campbell Barker at the University of Texas. Next, he gained valuable teaching experience in the public schools of Beaumont and San Antonio as an instructor of Spanish. On the personal side, during the Christmas holidays in 1921 he married Elisa Ríos, whom he had known since adolescence in his hometown of Brownsville. A year later they became parents with the birth of a daughter, Irma Gloria. Then he prepared a detailed classification and calendar of the Spanish and Mexican documents in the Bexar County Courthouse, an achievement subsequently published by the Yanaguana Society of San Antonio and described by Bolton as "an admirable piece of work" in that it revealed "a surprising amount of important materials." Finally, in 1923 he accepted an associate professorship of Spanish at the College of William and Mary, where for three years he combined a linguistic capability with history-oriented projects that resulted in modest publications.[3]

The formative period ended at William and Mary in 1926. Castañeda, having used language instruction as an avenue to teaching at the college level, searched diligently for the opportunity that would allow him to return to Texas and its history. Although he had found the Williamsburg experience meaningful in terms of pedagogical improvement, he never really enjoyed living so far away from home. To him the borderlands represented an area where he could expend his restless energy in work and study. There was no doubt in his mind about the place where he preferred to further his education. In a letter to F. O. Adam Jr., a friend and graduate student in Mexico, he wrote: "South of Chicago and East of California, I think the University of Texas ranks as the best in the southwest."[4]

Meanwhile, in Austin, two independent decision-making processes evolved that presented to Castañeda the opening he needed. In June the state deputy of the Knights of Columbus, Joseph I. Driscoll, informed him that the Texas Council had decided to sponsor the research, writing, and publication of a full-length study of Catholicism as a historical movement in Texas "from the earliest days to the present time." When completed, this history would be the Catholic Church's contribution to the 1936 Texas Centennial celebration.[5] To carry out this monumental task, the Columbian leadership had established the Texas Historical Commission, with the Reverend Dr. Paul J. Foik, C.S.C., of St. Edward's University in Austin as chairman.[6] Driscoll, aware of Castañeda's interest in archival materials relating to Texas history, invited him to submit suggestions on procedural methods for the project.[7]

Not only was Castañeda's response to Driscoll prompt and enthusiastic, but it clearly showed that the young scholar had a firm conceptual grasp of the undertaking: "It seems to me that the work naturally divides itself into distinct periods such as the early missionary work under the Spanish Regime, the abolition of the missions, the church from 1810 to 1836, covering both the revolutionary period and the period after independence was obtained from Spain, ... [then] from this point on the modern history of the church in Texas would begin." On the question of procedure, Castañeda suggested appointing an individual to collect the primary sources for later evaluation and organization by the commission. "But coming to the point," he declared, "someone has to get the material together, devoting, if not all, at least the greater part of his time to this task, if it is to be accomplished by 1936." Sensing the timeliness of the moment, Carlos added: "I am more than willing to cooperate with you in any way possible. I am a graduate of the University of Texas, and though a Mexican by birth, I feel that I am a Texan in spirit." Castañeda then departed for a summer teaching job in Mexico City, advising Driscoll that he would stay at Hotel Metropolitano. The state deputy of the Knights of Columbus acted quickly. "It is gratifying," he answered, "to see your willingness to assist us, and I feel free to authorize you for the Commission, to secure and send such materials as you may find while in Mexico City bearing on our subject, not covered in the secondary sources of history already available."[8] With respect to the first process of decisions, the die was cast, although it would be several years before a precise working relationship developed.

The second set of resolves occurred at the University of Texas library after Castañeda's trip to Mexico, when Ernest Winkler offered Carlos the curatorship of the Genaro García, or Latin American, Collection at an annual salary of $1,800 for a seven-hour workday. As in other matters of personal importance, Castañeda turned to his mentor, Professor Barker, explaining that while in Mexico City he had met Hackett, with whom he had discussed the possibility of pursuing doctoral studies. His first choice would be to return to Texas, "provided I can do some work there towards my degree." Winkler's job offer was appealing, he admitted, but not at the salary level cited, which fell below the $2,400 he earned at William and Mary for a three-class load, supplemented by an additional $300 for extension work. If Texas would increase the salary to $2,400.00, he would accept Winkler's offer. Carlos solicited Barker's assistance, stating that he strongly desired to come home "even at a sacrifice." Salary negotiations notwithstanding, there was another obstacle in the path, namely, giving the college "sixty days notice" to hire a replacement. Even under ideal circumstances, the earliest date of arrival in Texas would not occur "before December 1st."[9]

At the Austin campus, Barker carefully weighed the options on behalf of his former student. No doubt Barker recalled the years before World War I when Castañeda as an undergraduate assisted him in translating Mexican documents for his definitive biography of Stephen F. Austin. Without question, as Barker acknowledged later, Castañeda was "an altogether exceptional" man, and a scholar endowed with "rather extraordinary equipment."[10] Although Barker in midcareer was an influential member of the faculty, he exercised discretion in handling Castañeda's case so as not to jeopardize the negotiations. "Winkler wants more time to consider," he advised his former student, allowing that the librarian had correctly evaluated Carlos as being "too good a man to stay with that job permanently at a salary of $2,400." Since the final decision rested with Winkler, Barker proceeded slowly, but he promised Castañeda that he would reconcile the librarian "to the better salary." At this juncture, more important to Barker than salary was the problem of coordinating Castañeda's full-time schedule with graduate study for the doctorate. Barker counseled:

> It will take you a long time to work out the doctor's degree under such an arrangement, and you can't save any money on the salary so as to take a leave of absence and hasten the degree. . . . In some ways it would be wiser to save enough, if possible, from your present income to take a year off. The thing would drag out interminably if you busied yourself for seven hours a day over eleven months in the year in the Library job. Think soberly about the matter and let me have your conclusions while Winkler is puzzling over it.[11]

Castañeda valued Barker's advice. He fully realized the librarianship would indeed demand constant attention to endless detail. Moreover, if he included the responsibility of graduate work to an overcrowded schedule, there would be limitations placed on the degree program and "very little energy to do it with." All the same, Castañeda's "chief inducement" was the opportunity of studying for the doctorate. He considered the options available to him. If the possibility for graduate work was "non-existent," or incompatible with the position of librarian, then it would be disadvantageous for him to leave William and Mary. On the other hand, if being in charge of the García Collection gave to him "a good start," he would not hesitate to move. Cognizant of the fact that on November 11 he would be thirty years old, Castañeda emphasized to Barker that the longer he delayed enrolling in a doctoral program, the more his chances for making this important commitment decreased.[12]

There were times when Castañeda seemed despondent, but like a Spanish tornado (as he referred to himself in later years), he would strike out boldly in another direction. Manifesting unbounded optimism, he mentioned to Barker that he would give himself one year in which "to canvass all the possibilities" at other universities because he had "determined to get a start somewhere next fall at all costs." In fact, he continued, he had received a job offer from University Junior College of San Antonio "at $2,500 in the history department," but he had politely rejected it because it would have been a temporary appointment. Even so, the inquiry from San Antonio reinforced Castañeda's confidence. "I have a feeling," he told Barker, "that once back in Texas something else may turn up that will give me the desired opportunity." Then he unfolded a few details of the Knights of Columbus history project, including the names of the principal leaders, Driscoll and Foik. Castañeda asserted: "Now my idea is to try to do the actual work of getting the material together, copying, rewriting, etc., the real grind. I wonder if I could get that job with a reasonable remuneration to make it worth my while to work full time on this job during the summers? I don't particularly care to be editor, call it clerk of the commission, or any other name, the question for me would be the money in it. I would be willing to do the work."[13]

Assuredly, the information was merely for Barker's consumption, because Castañeda did not ask the professor to intercede with the Texas Historical Commission. Perhaps it was a gentle probe on Castañeda's part to determine whether Barker had established contact with the Catholic historians. In any event, the impact of this report on Winkler is difficult to ascertain, but probably it influenced him in reaching a final decision. Barker was prompt in transmitting the good news to Castañeda: "Winkler tells me that he has offered you the place. I hope we can help you toward the Ph.D. in history. You are right in thinking that something may turn up if you are on the ground. I recommended you for the San Antonio place. It would probably have been permanent."[14]

Barker's letter and Winkler's offer arrived simultaneously in Williamsburg. Castañeda, having made up his mind to return to Texas, accepted the librarianship on the terms he had specified. The only problem that remained was arranging an amiable resignation from William and Mary. Two weeks before his birthday, Castañeda conferred with the college president, who viewed the situation "in the proper light" and agreed to release him on the first of January, if absolutely imperative, or preferably at the close of the semester on January 24. From Castañeda's vantage point, the latter date was more practical because it would eliminate the inconvenience to his students of having a different instructor to conclude the classes. Moreover, considering Castañeda's restricted financial resources, since the nine months' salary was paid in twelve installments, the slight delay would make him eligible to receive one half of the summer income, or $300, which he would forfeit if he resigned before the end of the semester.[15]

The decision to leave Williamsburg positively lifted Castañeda's spirits. He shared the news with Professor Havila Babcock, a friend and former colleague in South Carolina. Alluding to a passage in Shakespeare's *Julius Caesar*, Castañeda declared philosophically: "It seems that a tidal wave has suddenly arisen on my barren shore of life, and it threatens to sweep my frail bark into unknown and trackless seas." Referring specifically to the librarianship and the opportunity to study for the doctorate, he admitted: "This is the tidal wave that has practically swept me off my feet."[16]

The thrust of Castañeda's allegorical tidal wave was that the lines of the decision-making processes in Texas had figuratively converged. In late October the chairman of the Knights of Columbus Historical Commission, Father Foik, invited Carlos to St. Edward's University for an interview on "the important work in which the commission is at present engaged." The invitation undoubtedly pleased Castañeda, who informed Foik of his "good fortune" in being appointed librarian of the García Collection. Aware that the Holy Cross priest was the guiding force behind the project, Castañeda, with humility and chivalry, used a direct approach: "I am highly honored to have you consult me in any way on this work, and I assure you that I have no other qualifications for offering suggestions than my life-long interest in the early history of Texas and particularly the early missionary movement in Texas, which I feel is a great epic in the gallant efforts to spread our holy faith to the farthermost ends of the trackless wilds of New Spain."[17]

During the first week of November, Castañeda charted a course of action for moving from Virginia to Texas. To Adam in Mexico he reviewed the long chain of events, particularly the conversations with Hackett that led to the librarianship, commenting: "Well, those interviews have borne fruit at last." Since Castañeda was not expected in the Lone Star State until February 1, he concluded that he had sufficient time in which to make the trip if he left at the end of the semester, perhaps a day or two earlier. Characteristically, he had a farewell audience with the college president and the chairman of the modern languages department, both of whom were extremely courteous and "we outdid each other in mutual compliments on the pleasantness of the work at William and Mary."

As the November days unfolded, Castañeda's plans took on greater detail. While his wife and daughter traveled safely on the train, he would drive the family car. "It is going to be a long and tiresome ride," he complained to his friend in Mexico. Then in a fashion typical of most professors on the threshold of making an important relocation, he became sentimental: "As the time approaches, I cannot help but feel a tinge of sadness in giving up my work here, for I really enjoy it. I look upon the Spanish Library of this college as my own creation and I have become attached to the old place in many ways in spite of the little appreciation I have encountered from administrative sources. But perhaps the change will turn out . . . for the best. I have taken a decision, and will try to make the best of it."[18] At approximately the same time as Castañeda finalized his travel plans, Father Foik informed the members of the Texas Historical Commission about Castañeda's keen interest in their project and that he would soon take up duties nearby as librarian of the Latin American Collection.[19] Clearly the two sets of decisions had intermingled in Castañeda's favor.

On Saturday, January 22, 1927, Castañeda left Williamsburg and headed for Texas and the job he viewed as "a promotion for me."[20] Upon arriving in Austin, the Castañedas rented a house on Red River Street near the university. After customary introductions and initial briefings with the library staff, Carlos plunged into his work. Three weeks later, writing to Adam in Mexico, he assessed the new situation: "This is no soft job, I want to tell you, yet I like the work much more than teaching and I will soon get it well in hand."[21] At this point in his career, Castañeda probably enjoyed the library more than the classroom because it had united him with historical documents and an opportunity to pursue the doctorate. He disclosed to a social worker in Baltimore: "My work here is wonderful for it is just what I love, books, and the opportunities for study and research could not be better."[22]

As the spring days lengthened into summer, Castañeda adjusted comfortably to the duties of librarianship, graduate study, and family life. Confident that he had mastered the routine of administering the García Collection, like a skillful juggler he increased the tempo of his activities. "Thank goodness," he confided to Adam, "I am *al corriente,* as they say in Spanish," signifying that he had everything under control. Glimpses of Castañeda the parent occasionally crept into his voluminous correspondence, as when he commented about his five-year-old daughter: "Gloria is a big girl already. She goes to school everyday, but she does not learn much for most of her time is spent in playing."[23] On the surface the remark about Gloria revealed paternal pride, but underneath it manifested Castañeda's dedication to work and scholarship. For instance, when he learned of the election of a former associate at William and Mary to Phi Beta Kappa, he extended congratulations and advice. Good teachers, he said, particularly those in Spanish, were "as rare as *garbanzos de la libra.*" Therefore, he counseled, "if you are sincere in your work, enthusiastic, fair, and painstaking, it will not be long before opportunities which you never expected will open before you."[24]

In full accord with this commitment to honest toil, Castañeda often pushed himself to the limits of physical endurance. Joe B. Frantz recalled his own experiences as a graduate student in the Latin American Collection. "Castañeda's life was cluttered. It was just like every morning somebody took it all, threw it up in the air and let it scatter. It landed where it could. He did *everything* [at] just a racetrack pace. There wasn't any time to put up or clean up or tidy up."[25] Aside from complexities of character, one probable explanation for Castañeda's "cluttered" lifestyle was the sudden discovery that the administrative side of librarianship required patient consideration. He described the situation to a William and Mary professor: "My work here is very pleasant but it certainly takes a great deal more time than I imagined. It is the most curious phenomenon to me. I thought I would have a great deal of time to read and study while in the Library but I find that being librarian means an endless amount of unavoidable routine and trifling duties that take up all the time and leave very little to show for your pains. Nevertheless, I like the work and I am learning . . . about library work and bibliography in general."[26] Routine tasks notwithstanding, on the positive side Castañeda, following what he called "the usual tactics," succeeded in garnering for himself "quite a little publicity."[27] First, the Texas State Historical Association, in recognition of Castañeda's translation of Juan N. Almonte's "Statistical Report on Texas, 1834," published in the *Southwestern Historical Quarterly*, conferred on him the distinction of fellow in the society. Unquestionably, Barker's influence was paramount in this selection. Next the Knights of Columbus historical group elected him a corresponding member for "conspicuous service you have rendered, are rendering, and will render to the Commission."[28]

In other matters, Castañeda, having successfully completed one course in the doctoral program in the spring semester, spent the summer acquainting himself with the manuscript holdings in the Latin American Collection, no doubt in preparation for assisting the Knights of Columbus in the multivolume history project. Almost with prophetic insight he predicted to Babcock: "I will very likely edit the first volume on the missionary period."[29]

Aside from the usual seven-hour workday, in the fall semester Carlos endeavored to translate and edit four books for publication the following spring. Furthermore, he enrolled in two graduate courses, complaining after a while that he found himself "literally swamped with the amount of work I have on hand." Even as pressures mounted he refused to slow down.

Instead, he began formulating plans for the summer of 1928, thinking seriously of leading a student group in "a new invasion of Mexico." However, because of recent political unrest surrounding Plutarco Calles's administration and because summer was months away, Carlos recommended caution. All the same, with optimism and imagination, he forecast that his group would "sally forth as the knights of old in the spring."[30]

For someone who maintained an extremely rigorous schedule, Castañeda was hardly in a position to recommend moderation. Yet to fellow graduate students who were struggling through the research phase of their theses, he was a fountainhead of good counsel. To the longtime friend in Mexico City he gave this advice: "Do your best, but do not kill yourself, for after all the prime duty of any man is self preservation." On another occasion he warned Babcock in South Carolina to temper his "too restless spirit" lest it should lead him "in a mad rush to accomplish the impossible by killing yourself."[31] Llerena Friend, then a relative newcomer to the Texas history field in 1927, experienced difficulty writing the introductory chapter of her thesis. She recalled in particular the assistance Castañeda extended:

> Carlos had a desk in the back end of the catalogue room and I was working in the Archives Room, which adjoined. Perhaps I came to know him in the Graduate History Club. Anyhow, I remember I was having a hard time getting off the ground—simply could not begin with sentence 1 in the thesis, and so I complained to Castañeda. In his excitable volubility he said—'Why just say'—and went on improvising an opening. I laughed and was able to start. Oh, Dr. Barker had me redo that initial start, but at least I had started—and to Carlos I was eternally grateful.[32]

In the midst of multiple activities, Castañeda apparently allowed himself one indulgence—cigar smoking. Acknowledging receipt of a Christmas package from a former student at William and Mary, he became serenely poetic: "Those good cigars arrived safe and sound and every ring of blue smoke that curls up in gentle curbs [*sic*] and floats away into space, leaving behind the fragrant aroma of the magic-weed, brings back sweet memories of not forgotten 'bull-sessions' in sleepy old Williamsburg. Now, I think that sentence is a masterpiece, and I will not spoil it by writing another one like it. Enough is as much as a feast."[33] In sharp contrast to the foregoing, Joe Frantz remembered a fast-moving scene featuring Castañeda and his contest with cigars. "He was always running into his own cigar ashes. You know, there wasn't time. [There was] no such thing as a leisurely cigar. This was furious puffing. He didn't have time to knock the ashes off; he used to let them dribble down . . . [in] front. Too big a hurry."[34]

At the outset of 1928, Castañeda revived his plan for leading a student group into Mexico. Confident of the outcome and with logistical details plotted minutely, he invited his South Carolina friend to join the expedition. In an effort to give the educational venture the "stamp of international cooperation" he initiated discussions with university officials. Much to Castañeda's chagrin, the administration disapproved his proposal, forcing him to remark caustically: "It is Hell to be poor but worst [*sic*] to be unable to act even when you have a good idea and know that you can swing it."[35]

With his spirit undaunted by this setback, in the spring Castañeda was ready to charge in different directions. Foremost among several activities was a paper, titled "Santa Anna as Seen By His Secretary," to be presented at the thirty-first annual meeting of the Texas State Historical Association.[36] On April 3, a few days before the history group convened in the auditorium of Garrison Hall on the university campus, Carlos sent another invitation to Babcock in South Carolina outlining the details of his next venture. "Well, I am ready to sail for Panama! What do you say? Will you join my pleasure tour to the Caribbean? . . . It will be the best trip in the world for you, 16½ days of which 11 will be spent on board a boat in the utmost comfort and luxury. Boy, I assure you there is nothing like it."[37] The Panama trip was for Castañeda a way of celebrating the upcoming publication of his first book, *The Mexican Side of the Texan Revolution*. Years later, in accepting the coveted Serra Award from the Academy of American Franciscan History, he reflected on that singular experience: "The thrill of that first book will ever remain a treasured and vivid memory. Only those who have had a first book printed can understand this strange sensation of elation. It is akin to the joy of bringing a new being into this world. My line of future endeavor was now clearly drawn. I would continue to work in the field of history, more particularly the early history of Texas and Mexico."[38]

The Mexican Side of the Texan Revolution was the beginning of a series of publications. He disclosed to Babcock that he had signed a contract for a second book and that he had two manuscripts in Spanish "practically ready for the press," one of which would be sponsored by the Mexican government through the department of education. With tongue-in-cheek, he asked, "How is that for a lazy, easy-going Latin-American?"[39]

As the summer months approached, Castañeda's extensive activities dispelled the notion, if it ever existed, that he was casual and indolent. To supplement his library income, he secured a visiting instructorship in Spanish literature at Our Lady of the Lake College in San Antonio, an appointment that included on-campus housing for the family.[40] Then he consented to supervise the translation of Mariano Cuevas's *Historia de la Iglesia en México*.[41] Finally, in partnership with a fellow librarian, Winnie Allen, he established the Mexican Photo Print Company to undertake an ambitious program of copying documentary materials south of the border. By mutual agreement, Allen furnished the working capital and Castañeda directed field operations.[42] In the absence of relatively complete business ledgers it is difficult to analyze the company's financial structure; generally speaking, it was a private enterprise with an unpretentious budget that produced a significant body of archival data.

From his temporary headquarters at Our Lady of the Lake, Castañeda, like an opera house impresario, coordinated manifold duties in his efforts to photostat the archives in Matamoros, Tamaulipas, across the Rio Grande from Brownsville. The first task was to negotiate a deferred-payment contract with the Photostat Corporation of Rochester, New York, for the purchase of a copying machine, Model L with book holder, for $675.[43] Castañeda then arranged with the U.S. vice consul in Matamoros for his brother, Fernando—in charge of the actual copying—to use the facilities of a bathroom in the consulate to wash the photostat negatives. Castañeda wrote Vice Consul Leonard, "I shall appreciate your showing my brother the premises and explaining to him about the wind mill. He will attend to everything and will very likely have to go in twice a day, once at noon and once at five in the afternoon. He will have to return about nine o'clock to hang the proofs to dry. I sincerely hope that they will not inconvenience you too much."[44]

In the meantime, while awaiting official permission from Mexican authorities, Castañeda prepared detailed guidelines to assist Fernando in copying the materials. Obtaining formal approval from Mexico was a most delicate matter involving several layers of bureaucracy on both sides of the river. Castañeda anticipated all emergencies. He drafted letters in Spanish addressed to Emilio Partes Gil, governor of Tamaulipas, explaining the purpose of the project, and sent them to Allen for typing on the stationery of Texas governor Dan Moody, University of Texas president H. Y. Benedict, and librarian Ernest Winkler.[45] Within a week, Allen forwarded the letters, adorned with appropriate seals and signatures, to Castañeda with the comment that they indicated how the project stood "in the 'favor of the mighty.'" As opening devices, however, the letters proved unnecessary, because Portes Gil, before their arrival, granted permission for the copying to begin. Not to be outdone by this lack of protocol, Winkler advised Castañeda to post the letters in the gubernatorial office in Ciudad Victoria "for future reference."[46]

After several errors of a technical nature, Fernando Castañeda and a young assistant began copying the archives on the feast day of St. Anthony, June 13. In five days they had processed a thousand negatives and needed an additional two hundred to complete the first volume. To expedite matters, Castañeda hired his sister, María, to help Fernando in arranging, packing, and transporting the materials through customs. As the company's representative in Matamoros, Fernando earned an average of ninety dollars a month, out of which he paid fifteen dollars to his assistant.[47] Castañeda summarized the scope of the Matamoros project to Sister Angelique, academic dean of Our Lady of the Lake College.

The entire archive, bound and calendared, would consist of "about 10,000 pieces comprising the dates from 1797 to the late 1870s."[48]

Whenever photostat negatives arrived at Our Lady of the Lake, Castañeda carefully appraised the results and removed imperfections for recopying. Afterward he either mailed or delivered the documents to St. Edward's University, where Allen assumed responsibility for the next phase of the program. Previously, Castañeda had arranged with the Reverend Peter P. Forrestal, C.S.C., to hire two college students to make positive prints, paying an hourly wage of fifty cents to the machine operator and thirty cents to the helper.[49]

Attending to details of the Matamoros project and teaching a survey course in Spanish literature filled Castañeda's workdays at Our Lady of the Lake. But not content to be idle on weekends, Carlos agreed, among other things, to give an illustrated lecture focusing on the special holdings in the Latin American Collection.[50] Toward the end of the summer session, Castañeda's publisher in Dallas released *The Mexican Side of the Texan Revolution*. Anxious to examine his first book, which had arrived in Austin, Castañeda wrote to Maurine Wilson, his temporary replacement in the García Collection, "I am glad that my work will be over next week, for I certainly want to get back to my old corner again. I have lots of things which I want to do and I am literally itching to get back to Austin for good. The change has been pleasant, but I really miss the quiet of my little corner which you have been enjoying in my absence."[51]

On Saturday, July 14, Castañeda completed his teaching commitment at Our Lady of the Lake and returned to the University of Texas library. He advised Fernando of the relocation and encouraged him to continue the current level of productivity on the border archives.[52] As the summer months yielded to autumn, Castañeda and his associates finished the twelfth volume of documents from Matamoros and estimated that six more volumes would be processed by December.[53]

With the photocopying project well under way, Castañeda turned his attention to other engagements. For the initial drafts in the translation of Father Cuevas's *Historia de la Iglesia en México*, Carlos obtained the services of Jovita González. Under this arrangement, he revised the composition and forwarded it for editing to Sister Mary Angela at Our Lady of the Lake College. By early October, as the translation progressed into the second volume, Cuevas arrived in Austin to assess the results. The Mexican Jesuit historian, eager to satisfy his printer's demands, insisted on accelerating the work schedule. He authorized Castañeda to pay the typists thirty-five cents an hour and to hire an extra clerk if necessary to type the finished copy. Responding to Father Mariano's tight deadline, Castañeda urged Sister Angela to conclude the editing and copying at the earliest possible date, preferably the end of November. In turn, the Divine Providence nun, by devoting eight hours a week to the manuscript, completed several chapters of the volume by the early part of December. But much to Cuevas's disappointment, the translation proceeded slowly. Castañeda, the general editor, offered sage advice to his associates: "I know from experience that translation work requires lots of time and infinite pains to attain the best results." A further delay occurred unexpectedly during the Christmas holidays, when Castañeda hurried to Brownsville to attend the funeral of one of his eldest sisters, ending the year on a note of sadness.[54]

When the new year of 1929 began, Castañeda in all probability examined his financial status, prompted by the knowledge that the legislature had kept his salary at the same level at which he started in 1927. In fact, his wages would remain static for the next biennium, ending August 31, 1931.[55] This development explained Castañeda's hectic activities to supplement his income. As he revealed to Babcock, "I have kept so busy trying to 'keep the wolf from the door' since I came to Texas or as you might say 'making hay while the sun shines' or again trying to provide for a rainy day that I have advanced but slowly on the way to my ultimate goal, my Ph.D."[56] In spite of these setbacks, Castañeda maintained an optimistic attitude. To remind the Knights of Columbus of his availability to write even part of the Texas history project he addressed the Austin chapter in a speech titled "College Life in Mexico in the Sixteenth and Seventeenth Centuries,"[57] a topic inspired by the forthcoming publication of *Historia de todos los Colegios de la Ciudad de México desde la conquista hasta 1780*, a nineteenth-century manuscript by Félix Osores that Castañeda edited for the Mexican ministry of education. The book on Mexico City's colleges was a continuation of a documentary series begun in 1913 by Genaro García, *Nuevos documentos inéditos o muy raros para la historia de México*. Castañeda, aware of his own limited resources and the fact that the publication was an inexpensive edition, remarked wryly to an Incarnate Word nun in San Antonio that he was a poor librarian who could not "afford to dress his intellectual children in the garb they deserve."[58]

Although Castañeda involved himself in a number of new activities of an ephemeral nature, such as representing the National University of Mexico on the Austin campus in the recruitment of summer school exchange students,[59] his main concern outside of graduate study and the library was expanding the photocopying enterprise. By mid-March, work on the Matamoros project had surpassed initial expectations with thirty volumes finished and more in the process of completion. Meanwhile, the Mexican Photo Print Company successfully negotiated with the University of Texas, the University of California, and the Newberry Library for a continuing subscription to the photostat documents. Castañeda estimated that the entire series would comprise "a little over seventy volumes" valued at three thousand dollars. Looking beyond the anticipated termination of the Matamoros activity, he drafted plans for copying the Monclova

Archives, "where there is a great deal of material concerning the early history of Texas and of the Spanish Southwest."[60]

In the summer of 1929, after submitting a manuscript on the *corregidor* to the *Hispanic American Historical Review*, Castañeda took his wife and daughter into Mexico on a trip that was partially a vacation but also an opportunity to examine the archives in Coahuila and Nuevo León. So preoccupied was Carlos on the archival trail that he did not bother to read the galley proofs of his article. Winnie Allen, who corrected the proofs for him, said the contribution was "a learned and most erudite article for the consumption of the chosen few."[61]

Using Bolton's *Guide to Materials for the History of the United States in the Principal Archives of Mexico* as a springboard, Castañeda moved from one repository to the next, secure in his conviction that writing a history of Texas as a borderland frontier could not be undertaken without reference to the documentary wealth he was uncovering.[62] Reporting from Saltillo in the first week of July, he informed Allen: "I had complete success in Monterrey. They gave me every facility and we can get anything we want from the crowd there. . . . Here in Saltillo everything is going on fine. I am getting a list of documents as long as from here to New York. Bolton did not list half of the materials and though Dr. Barker used most of what he was interested in, he did not copy everything and we should have a complete copy of everything in the Archives here on Texas."[63] Intending to remain in Mexico for another two weeks, Castañeda then proceeded to Monclova. At the end of the month, the Castañedas returned to the United States by way of Brownsville. Within days of their arrival, tragedy overtook them. On Sunday, July 28, six-year-old Gloria was suddenly taken from their midst, a victim of encephalitis.[64] A mournful Castañeda wrote to Adam, who had known the child: "I am too much moved by the irreparable loss which I have just suffered. . . . dear little Gloria, she passed away to a better world. . . . My heart bleeds."[65] Of all the condolences Castañeda received, perhaps he found the most comfort in the words of Winnie Allen: "Will it be any comfort in your sorrow to have the thought that you have known the most beautiful human relation in the love and devotion you felt for Gloria—always anxious to do everything for her at no matter what cost to yourself and deriving only pleasure from serving her. . . . If you can but feel that the relation has been translated from a human [form] to a spiritual one, then it will be with you always and will continue to grow and thrive as in life."[66] After the funeral in Brownsville, Castañeda and Elisa returned to Austin in time for the fall semester. Searching for solace in work, he gradually resumed his active schedule. To Sister Angelique of Our Lady of the Lake he described the archival discoveries he had made in Saltillo, Monterrey, and Monclova, announcing that photocopying of the Saltillo archives would begin shortly. "The material," he said, "is of the most vital nature for the history of Texas, as Saltillo was the capital of Coahuila and Texas." In other matters, remembering the hardships he had endured as an undergraduate, he assisted Spanish-speaking students trying to find employment at Seton Infirmary.[67]

As the 1929–1930 academic year opened, Castañeda reviewed his record of progress in the doctoral program. No doubt the financial burden lessened somewhat with the aid of a Farmer Foundation scholarship. Reminding Professor Barker that all course work for the degree would be completed at the end of the current year, Castañeda asked him to schedule the preliminary examinations.[68] For the remainder of 1929, Carlos concentrated on the immediate tasks at hand, allowing for periodic contacts with the Knights of Columbus Historical Commission and with the Catholic Association for International Peace, for which he translated the pamphlet *Latin America and the United States* into Spanish for widespread distribution.[69]

The year 1930 was a milestone in Casteñeda's career. Little did he realize as the new year unfolded that he was on the brink of uncovering a significant contribution to borderlands history, a windfall that would definitely transform him into a Boltonian scholar. For the first five months of the year he prepared himself for the doctoral examinations, a task that he accomplished with minimal difficulty. Then he reapplied for an extension of the Farmer Foundation fellowship to complete the dissertation requirement.[70] In the meantime, he devoted attention to other endeavors, such as encouraging Sister Angelique to seek external resources by which Our Lady of the Lake might purchase a photostat edition of the Matamoros and Saltillo Archives.[71] As if Carlos did not have enough to do, he responded to a plea from friends in the Lower Rio Grande Valley town of Mercedes for assistance in establishing a Spanish-language newspaper,[72] and on campus he served as faculty moderator of the Club Latino Americano.[73] In addition, with financial support from Ignacio Lozano, influential publisher of *La Prensa* in San Antonio, Castañeda edited and published another volume of Mexican history documents, *La guerra de reforma: según el archivo del General D. Manuel Doblado, 1857–1860*.[74]

Most important of all, in April Castañeda went to Mexico City for initiation into the Sociedad de Geografía y Estadística. On this occasion he learned for the first time that the National Library had acquired the extensive archive of the old Convento Grande de San Francisco, the mother house of the Franciscan order in colonial New Spain. Through personal contacts Castañeda obtained permission to make "a hurried investigation" of the archival contents. He estimated that among the more than one hundred *legajos* (bundles) there were approximately 500,000 pages of "new and unexplored documents," many of which related to Texas and the other interior provinces. He promptly arranged with library directors to come back in December to conduct a thorough inspection of materials dealing with the history of Texas. In the event he could not return at the end of the year, Carlos made "a verbal agreement" with Professor France V. Scholes of the University of New Mexico, who was in the area searching for primary sources pertaining to his own state, to set aside and copy the Texas documents.[75] To be sure, this archival windfall elated Castañeda; the impact was an emotional experience. For the moment he was content to return home.

In the summer, Carlos and Elisa went on a much-deserved vacation to Charlottesville, Virginia, happily combining business and pleasure. Castañeda, representing the National University of Mexico, had consented to speak at a meeting of the Institute of National Affairs at the University of Virginia. On the day of the conference, misfortune struck a minor blow to their plans. Instead of delivering his prepared text, Carlos entered a local hospital as a typhoid patient. Doña Elisa, aware of her husband's determination to appear at the meeting, went to the hospital and found him, dressed in pajamas and robe, sitting in a wheelchair waiting for someone to take him to the convention. But this was one address that Castañeda failed to give. For three weeks he convalesced in the Charlottesville hospital, inducing him to comment to Winnie Allen: "My illness in Virginia has thrown me back some, but I dug into my little pile and have done the best I could." Upon returning to Texas, he confided to a Brackenridge High School teacher in San Antonio that he was "not as vigorously active" as in earlier days. "I haven't that inexhaustible energy," he wrote, "of which I prided myself. Still, I am trying to keep up the thousand and one things I have on hand."[76]

Castañeda's allusion to a "thousand and one things" centered on the archival project of the Convento Grande de San Francisco. The National Library of Mexico, in making the Franciscan documents available to the public, invited Latin American specialists in the United States to participate in sorting, organizing, and copying the archive.[77] Castañeda prepared to attend this important gathering of scholars and notified Father Foik that the University of Texas would pay his roundtrip expenses to Mexico City. However, since Guadalajara was another major depository of materials relating to Texas history, Castañeda asked the Knights of Columbus to defray the additional expenses of travel to that city in the amount of $150. Foik sent a telegram to Driscoll in El Paso advising that in his judgment the request was a reasonable expenditure. Driscoll replied: "APPROVE CASTAÑEDA PROPOSAL KINDLY FORWARD VOUCHER AND DIRECTIONS FOR PAYMENT." Pleased with the support of the Texas Historical Commission, Castañeda departed for Mexico on Wednesday, December 1. So determined was he to get to the archives that he canceled a presentation before the American Catholic Historical Association in Boston, where he was to have read a paper titled "Earliest Catholic Activities in Texas," which was subsequently published in the organization's journal.[78]

Arriving in Mexico City, Carlos secured quarters on Calle Moreno in Colonia del Valle. On December 9 he reported to Foik that he had obtained authorization to copy new materials on Texas ahead of the Library of Congress representative. "My friends are all here," he declared, "and in influential positions."[79] Among those of "influential" status in Mexico was Herbert Eugene Bolton, whom Castañeda met for the first time. "We were all given tables by the librarian and instructed to pick out a bundle of documents at random from the immense heap on the floor and proceeded to find out what it contained, sort out the documents and put them in some kind of order."

On Thursday, December 11, shortly before noon, Castañeda discovered the *History of Texas* by Fray Juan Agustín Morfi, an eighteenth-century manuscript that had eluded scholars for decades. Overwhelmed with his finding, Carlos took the afternoon off to celebrate.[80] The next day, the anniversary of the Virgin of Guadalupe, he explained the significance of his windfall to Father Foik:

> Your heart will dance with glee when you see the complete calendar of the material I have found. I almost had heart failure yesterday when I unexpectedly ran into the long lost and much searched after *Historia de la Provincia de los Tejas* by no other than Father Morfi. This is a real find. There are two other works of Morfi known. *The Diary* published in the Third series of *Documentos*, and the *Memorial* . . . but this *history* I have discovered is the one that was found in his cell after his death with eight or ten other works, the list of which is given by Bolton but the originals of which have been lost ever since. Bolton will be surprised to hear I have found it.[81]

Upon receipt of this report, Foik sent another telegram to Driscoll: "RUSH DRAFT TO CASTAÑEDA RECEIVED GOOD NEWS TODAY LETTER FOLLOWS." The priest at St. Edward's, a historian in his own right, then answered Castañeda: "You have anticipated my feelings when you said the news . . . would make my heart leap with joy. Carlos, I am proud of your work and I hope that you will continue to reveal documents that will amaze the mightiest. . . . I speak as if this were a triumph for the Commission. You see how envious I am for some of the glory that must surely come to you among the scholars when you return."[82]

Indeed, Castañeda did return triumphantly to his library at the University of Texas. As he resolved that Morfi's *Historia* would be the dissertation project, an idea that Barker quickly approved,[83] the transitional period in his career was in its final stage. He devoted the following year and part of the next to translating, editing, and annotating the Franciscan manuscript. In the spring of 1932 he submitted the finished draft to a seven-member committee that included, besides Barker as chairman, Charles Wilson Hackett, Castañeda's connecting link to the Boltonian school of history.[84] On the night of June 6, Castañeda received the doctoral degree,[85] thus formally closing the transition. The Quivira Society, recognizing the merit of his contribution to southwestern history, offered to publish the dissertation as a handsome and artistic two-part edition under the title *History of Texas, 1673–1779*.[86]

Having accomplished the goal of establishing his academic muniments as historian, and being professionally secure as the university's Latin American librarian, Castañeda now turned to a project that would consume much of his time over the final two decades of his life. In his ongoing discussions with the Knights of Columbus over his role in the preparation of a history of Texas emphasizing the role of the Catholic faith, it had become increasingly clear that no one was better suited to do the work, at least on the early part of the story, than Carlos. Emulating the knights he admired, he readily accepted the challenge and prepared for the monumental charge of writing *Our Catholic Heritage in Texas, 1519–1936*.[87]

Between 1936 and 1942 Castañeda published the first five volumes of *Our Catholic Heritage*, bringing the history of Texas from 1519 up to 1810. The two remaining volumes, which would bring the story up to 1936, would have to wait. Already in his forties, Castañeda knew it was not reasonable for him to play an active military role in the the war effort; he might, however, be of service to his country on the domestic front. His opportunity came in summer 1943 with appointment as associate director of the Dallas office of the Fair Employment Practices Committee. His devotion to the work of the committee, which investigated discriminatory practices against Hispanics and blacks in the workplace, led to his promotion to regional director in February 1945 during the last year of the regional office's existence. In early 1946 Carlos returned to work, both at the university and on Volume 6 of *Our Catholic Heritage*, which appeared two years later. Volume 7, the one that should have brought the story up to the centennial of Texas independence, did not appear for another decade, a few months after Castañeda's passing. By then the church in Texas had changed so much that it made little sense to conclude the work in 1936, so the title of the volume became *The Church in Texas since Independence, 1836–1950*.

The transition of Carlos Eduardo Castañeda from professor of Spanish to borderlands historian signified the unflinching commitment of one man to an ideal. The hardships and disappointments that he suffered and overcame sustained him in his conviction that the role of historian, although difficult to achieve, was a noble profession having the dual responsibility of the search for truth and the reconstruction of the past from fragmentary and elusive documents. As a second-generation Boltonian, Castañeda limited his sphere of activity mostly to Spanish Texas, but to gain insight and understanding he made the expansive borderlands his province. In turn, Texas, rich in archival documentation, rewarded him with an opportunity to devote a lifetime to its early history.

SUGGESTED READING

Castañeda, Carlos E., trans. and ed. *The History of Texas, 1673–1779, by Fray Juan Agustín Morfi, Missionary, Teacher, Historian*. Albuquerque: Quivira Society, 1935; repr., New York: Arno Press, 1967.

Almost as important for the interpretation of early Texas history as *Our Catholic Heritage*, Morfi's *History of Texas* represents the most learned and systematic contemporary interpretation of Texas.

Castañeda, Carlos E., trans. and ed. *The Mexican Side of the Texas Revolution*. Dallas: P. L. Turner, 1928.

In this collection of primary documents from Mexican sources, Castañeda brought many Texans their first glimpse into an alternative interpretation of the struggle for Texas independence.

Castañeda, Carlos E. *Our Catholic Heritage in Texas, 1519–1936*. 7 vols. Austin: Von Boeckmann-Jones, 1936–1958; repr., New York: Arno Press, 1976.

Volumes 1–5 cover the history of Texas from the earliest explorations until the outbreak of the Mexican War of Independence. Volume 6 treats Texas from 1810 until Texas independence. Volume 7 narrates the story of the Catholic Church in Texas until the middle of the twentieth century. The work remains a principal source for understanding the storyline of Spanish Texas in detail.

NOTES

1. Carlos E. Castañeda, "Why I Chose History," *The Americas* 8 (April 1952): 476; Charles A. Bacarisse, "Dedication to Carlos Eduardo Castañeda, 1896–1958," *Arizona and the West* 3 (Spring 1961): 2; Carlos E. Castañeda, "In Memoriam: Charles W. Hackett, 1888–1951," *The Americas* 8 (July 1951): 83.

2. Castañeda to Bolton, October 11, 1946, Bolton Papers, Bancroft Library, University of California, Berkeley (hereafter BPBL).

3. Félix D. Almaráz Jr., "Carlos Eduardo Castañeda, Mexican-American Historian: The Formative Years, 1896–1927," *Pacific Historical Review* 42 (August 1973): 319–334; Bolton to Frederick C. Chabot, February 25, 1937, Yanaguana Society Papers, Daughters of the Republic of Texas Library, San Antonio.

4. Castañeda to F. O. Adam Jr., December 17, 1926, Carlos E. Castañeda Papers, Nettie Lee Benson Latin American Collection, University of Texas at Austin (hereafter CP).

5. Driscoll to Castañeda, June 4, 1926, Knights of Columbus Correspondence File, Catholic Archives of Texas, Chancery of Austin (hereafter KCCF).

6. Mayellen Bresie, "Paul J. Foik, C.S.C., Librarian and Historian" (master's thesis, University of Texas, 1964), 93–94.

7. Driscoll to Castañeda, June 4, 1926, KCCF.

8. Castañeda to Driscoll, June 12, 1926; Driscoll to Castañeda, June 22, 1926, KCCF.

9. Castañeda to Barker, September 13, 1926, CP.

10. Castañeda, "Why I Chose History," 477; Barker to Thomas M. Knapp, S.J., May 24, 1934, Barker Papers, Dolph Briscoe Center for American History, University of Texas at Austin.

11. Barker to Castañeda, September 18, 1926, CP.

12. Castañeda to Barker, September 23, 1926, CP.

13. Ibid.

14. Barker to Castañeda, October 14, 1926, CP.

15. Castañeda to Barker, October 18, 1926, CP.

16. Castañeda to Havila Babcock, October 28, 1926, CP.

17. Paul J. Foik to Castañeda, October 28, 1926; Castañeda to Foik, November 5, 1926, KCCF.

18. Castañeda to Adam, November 5 and 17, 1926, CP.

19. Minutes of the Second Meeting of the Texas Knights of Columbus Historical Commission, Austin, Texas, November 23–24, 1926, 15, KCCF.

20. Castañeda to Babcock, January 11, 1927; Castañeda to American National Insurance Co., April 29, 1927, CP.

21. Castañeda to Adam, February 19, 1927, CP.

22. Castañeda to Lillian Berlin, March 4, 1927, CP.

23. Castañeda to Adam, May 3, 1927, CP.

24. Castañeda to K. R. Addington, June 17, 1927, CP.

25. Quoted in Félix D. Almaráz Jr., *Knight without Armor: Carlos Eduardo Castañeda, 1896–1958* (College Station: Texas A&M University Press, 1999), 51.

26. Castañeda to Babcock, June 17, 1927, CP.

27. Ibid.

28. Castañeda, "Why I Chose History," 478; Foik to Castañeda, November 2, 1927, KCCF.

29. Castañeda to Babcock, June 17, 1927, CP.

30. Castañeda to Babcock, October 13, 1927, CP.

31. Castañeda to Adam, October 25, 1927; Castañeda to Babcock, October 28, 1926, CP.

32. Llerena B. Friend to author, March 17, 1973.

33. Castañeda to Addington, December 29, 1921, CP.

34. Almaráz, *Knight without Armor*, 52.

35. Castañeda to Babcock, January 19 and February 9, 1928, CP.

36. "Affairs of the Association," *Southwestern Historical Quarterly* 32 (July 1928): 100.

37. Castañeda to Babcock, April 3, 1928, CP.

38. Castañeda, "Why I Chose History," 479.

39. Castañeda to Babcock, April 3, 1928, CP.

40. Castañeda to Sister M. Angelique, April 25 and May 1, 1928; Sister M. Angelique to Castañeda, April 30, 1928, CP.

41. *Southern Messenger*, May 24, 1928.

42. Winnie Allen to Castañeda, June 11, 1928, CP; Castañeda to Allen, June 12, 1928, Castañeda Biographical File, Dolph Briscoe Center for American History, University of Texas at Austin (hereafter Castañeda Biographical File).

43. Castañeda agreed to pay $285 upon receipt of the equipment, plus transportation costs, and $100 every month for four months. Purchase Agreement, Castañeda and Photostat Corporation, in H. G. Holden to Castañeda, May 26, 1928, Castañeda Biographical File.

44. Castañeda to H. H. Leonard, June 2, 1928, Castañeda Biographical File.

45. Castañeda to Fernando A. Castañeda, June 12, 1928; Castañeda to Allen, June 15, 1928, Castañeda Biographical File.

46. Castañeda to Allen, June 18,1928, Castañeda Biographical File; Allen to Castañeda, June 21, 1928, CP.

47. Castañeda to Allen, June 18, 1928; Castañeda to Manas (his sisters in Brownsville), June 28, 1928; Castañeda to Fernando Castañeda, July 2, 1928, Castañeda Biographical File.

48. Castañeda to Sister Angelique, June 12, 1928, Castañeda Letter File, Office of the Academic Dean, Our Lady of the Lake College, San Antonio (hereafter Castañeda Letter File).

49. Castañeda to Allen, July 2, 1928; Castañeda to Reverend P. P. Forrestal, n.d. (ca. July 10, 1928), Castañeda Biographical File.

50. *Southern Messenger*, June 28, 1928.

51. Castañeda to Maurine Wilson, July 6, 1928, Castañeda Biographical File.

52. Instrucciones Que Debe Seguir Fernando A. Castañeda en el Trabajo de Copiar de Documentos para la Universidad de Texas, typescript, n.d., Castañeda Biographical File.

53. Castañeda to Sister Angelique, September 30, 1928, Castañeda Letter File.

54. Castañeda to Sister M. Angela, October 9 and December 4, 1928; Sister Angela to Castañeda, October 12, 1928; Castañeda to Georgie Armstrong, January 9, 1929, CP.

55. General and Special Laws of Texas, 40th Legislature, First Called Session, 1927, 362; General Laws of Texas, 41st Legislature, Second and Third Called Sessions, 1929, 330.

56. Castañeda to Babcock, January 22, 1929, CP.

57. *Southern Messenger*, January 31, 1929.

58. Castañeda, "Why I Chose History," 479; *Diccionario Porrúa: Historia, Biografía y Geografía de México* (Mexico City: Editorial Porrúa, 1964), 2:1541; Castañeda to Sister M. Adriana, April 15, 1930, CP; Charles W. Hackett, review of *Historia de todos los colegios de la Ciudad de México, Southwestern Historical Quarterly* 35 (July 1931): 86.

59. Castañeda to H. H. Avants (*The Texas Outlook*), February 4, 1929; E. A. Fan (Missouri Pacific Lines) to Castañeda, February 14, 1929; Henry DeWitt Phillips (East Texas State Teachers College) to Castañeda, March 13, 1929; Sarah L. Thaxton to Castañeda, March 26, 1929; Julio Jiménez Rueda (Departamento de Intercambio Universitario, Universidad Nacional Autonoma de México, to Castañeda, March 1 and April 23, 1929; Jiménez Rueda to Enrique Santibañez, n.d.; Castañeda to Jiménez Rueda, April 30, 1929; *The Texas Outlook* (March 19, 1929): 71; Texas Outlook Advertising Department, invoice, March 1, 1929; "Universities, Two Nations Co-operate," March 19, 1929, University of Texas Students' Clipping Bureau, CP.

60. Castañeda to Sister M. Angelique, March 19, 1929, Castañeda Letter File.

61. Castañeda to Allen, July 8, 1929, CP; C. E. Castañeda, "The Corregidor in Spanish Colonial Administration," *Hispanic American Historical Review* 9 (November 1929): 446–470.

62. Castañeda to Frank C. Ayres (Business Historical Society), April 10, 1930, CP.

63. Castañeda to Allen, July 8, 1929, CP.

64. Almaráz, *Knight without Armor*, 71.

65. Castañeda to Adam, August 2, 1929, CP.

66. Allen to Castañeda, n.d. (ca. August 1, 1929), CP.

67. Castañeda to Sister Angelique, September 5, 1929; Priscilla H. Buckley (General Land Office) to Castañeda, November 22, 1929; Castañeda to Sister Agatha, September 11 and 24, 1929, CP.

68. Castañeda to H. Y. Benedict, February 20, 1930; Castañeda to Barker, September 30, 1929, CP.

69. Castañeda to Foik, December 24, 1929, KCCF; *Southern Messenger*, December 8, 1929.

70. Castañeda, "Why I Chose History," 479; Castañeda to Benedict, February 20, 1930, CP.

71. Castañeda to Sister Angelique, February 1, 1930, CP.

72. Castañeda to Barnhart Brothers and Spindler, February 25, 1930; Castañeda to Fred Dye (Associated Press, *Dallas Times-Herald*), March 11, 1930, CP.

73. *El Universitario* (journal of Club Latino Americano), April 1930, CP.

74. Hackett, review of *La guerra de reforma*, 35, 86.

75. Castañeda, Report (draft) to the Knights of Columbus Historical Commission, Austin, Texas, January 20, 1931, KCCF.

76. Castañeda to Adam, August 2, 1929; Winnie Allen to Mr. and Mrs. Castañeda, August 18, 1930; Castañeda to Allen, September 10, 1930; Castañeda to Armstrong, October 18, 1930, CP; Elsie Upton, "A Knight of Goodwill," *St. Joseph Magazine* 44 (June 1943): 14, in Castañeda Biographical File.

77. Castañeda, "Why I Chose History," 479; Bacarisse, "Dedication to Castañeda," 2.

78. Foik to Driscoll, November 30, 1930 (telegram); Driscoll to Foik, December 1, 1930 (telegram), KCCF; "Miscellany: The Eleventh Annual Meeting of the Catholic Historical Association, Boston, Massachusetts, December 28–31, 1930," *Catholic Historical Review* 17 (April 1931): 45.

79. Castañeda to Foik, December 9, 1930, KCCF.

80. Castañeda, "Why I Chose History," 479–480.

81. Castañeda to Foik, December 12, 1930, KCCF.

82. Foik to Driscoll, December 15, 1930 (telegram); Foik to Castañeda, December 16, 1930, KCCF.

83. Castañeda, "Why I Chose History," 481.

84. Carlos Eduardo Castañeda, "Morfi's History of Texas: A Critical, Chronological Account of the Early Exploration, Attempts at Colonization, and the Final Occupation of Texas by the Spaniards, by Fr. Juan Agustín Morfi, O.F.M., Missionary, Teacher and Historian of his Order, 1673–1779" (Ph.D. diss., University of Texas, 1932).

85. Francis Oliver to author, June 22, 1972.

86. Castañeda, "Why I Chose History," 481.

87. The full story of Carlos E. Castañeda's rise to prominence, both on the campus of the University of Texas in Austin and in historical circles generally, is fully realized in my biography of him, *Knight without Armor*.

MARY L. SCHEER

ROBERT COTNER

ROBERT COTNER (*RIGHT*), WITH T. S. PAINTER AND IMA HOGG, 1951

On March 24, 1958, Governor Price Daniel Sr. accepted on behalf of the State of Texas the Varner Plantation, near West Columbia in Brazoria County, a gift from the estate of Governor James S. Hogg (1851–1906). Given by daughter Ima Hogg on the anniversary of her father's birthday, the land and buildings would be utilized as a future state park and museum. At the dedication ceremony Governor Daniel remarked, "Just as he believed in the future, Governor Hogg believed in preserving the history of Texas. He encouraged the division of the Department of Insurance, Statistics and History, out of which division developed the Texas State Library." He further credited Hogg as a progressive reformer who stimulated "the collection and preservation of Texas' priceless records." For University of Texas professor Robert Crawford Cotner, who was completing his monumental 617-page biography of Hogg, the dedication ceremony affirmed his many years of research "to delineate the life of James S. Hogg"—the People's Governor. He further confirmed Hogg's ranking as one of the four prominent statesmen in Texas history.[1]

Robert C. Cotner was born in Cleveland, Ohio, on November 1, 1906, the year of Hogg's death. His father, Thomas Ewing Cotner, worked in retail sales while his mother, Nina Dot Crawford Cotner, sold real estate. In 1908 the family moved to Dallas, the same year that a disastrous flood destroyed parts of the city. Nevertheless, Dallas prospects in the first decades of the twentieth century were promising for a struggling salesman and his young family. As the world's leading inland cotton market and an emerging commercial center, its population in 1900 stood at 42,638. Local businessmen had formed the 150,000 Club, aimed at boosting the city's population, using the slogan "Dallas: The City of Splendid Realities." As a result, ten years later the number of residents had doubled, the city had built its first steel skyscraper, and its area had grown to 18.31 square miles. By the 1920s Dallas leaders had implemented a city plan for orderly growth, initiated the Trinity River levee project for flood control, and built the Houston Street viaduct, at the time the longest concrete structure in the world. The city's population continued to soar; the census of 1920 confirmed that Dallas had reached nearly 159,000 residents, making the city the forty-second largest in the nation. Adding to the demographic and economic surge was the young Cotner family, including parents Thomas and Nina and sons Robert Crawford (1906), James Allen (1910), and Thomas Ewing Jr. (1916).[2]

Cotner grew up in Dallas, where he seemingly enjoyed a happy childhood and adolescence. He attended the local Baptist church, but later joined the Methodist church after his marriage in 1943. In 1926 he enrolled at Southern Methodist University because he could attend school while living at home, but he later transferred to Baylor University in Waco, receiving his B.A. in history in 1928. The next year Cotner graduated from Brown University in Providence, Rhode Island, completing the requirements for the M.A. degree in record time.[3]

By the summer of 1929, Cotner, like many Texans, was optimistic about the future. The recent oil boom in the state had expanded opportunities both in education and industry. The University of Texas benefited from royalties that flowed from the sensational oil discoveries in West Texas, while increased industrialization and urbanization led to expanding cities with increasing school populations. As a consequence, school districts consolidated across the state, bringing uniformity and efficiency to the state's educational system. Sweeping reforms such as better salaries, free textbooks, and improved teacher training upgraded the quality of the public schools. But by 1929 only 50 percent of teachers had graduated from a normal school, college, or university, meaning degreed teachers were in heavy demand. For twenty-two-year-old Cotner, having successfully completed two educational degrees and about the enter the job market, the future seemed promising. His thoughts turned toward the public schools in Texas, and after a brief search he secured a teaching position in the Midland public schools beginning in the fall of 1929.[4]

On October 29, 1929, known as Black Tuesday, all such optimism ended. The stock market crash sent the nation and then the state into an economic tailspin. At first Texans persisted in their optimism that "prosperity was just around the corner." But as the crisis deepened across the United States in the early 1930s, public and private relief agencies became stretched, many even closing their doors. In Midland, where Cotner taught history and coached the high school debate team, the discovery of the Permian Basin oil fields at first did much to ease the strain on unemployment. But as the nation decreased its demand for oil and an East Texas oil boom glutted the market, sending petroleum prices spiraling downward, many businesses faltered, throwing their employees out of work. By 1932 one-third of Midland's workers were unemployed, and both the state and federal governments necessarily intervened with relief efforts. Despite the economic crisis, public schools did not close, although many cut teacher salaries and reduced appropriations. While conditions were harsh and immediate improvement seemed distant, Cotner was one of the fortunate few; he had employment.[5]

The Great Depression had a profound impact on Cotner both personally and professionally. He observed firsthand the hardships endured by his family and others, which influenced his attitudes toward money, work, and government. Never a spendthrift, he constantly pinched pennies and worried about opportunities for summer teaching employment and financial research assistance. Convinced that government should take a strong role in lessening the effects of the depression, he became an advocate for the New Deal programs, especially those that benefited Texas communities. Later, as a history professor, he believed that lessons could be learned from the crisis and instituted an urban history course on the University of Texas campus. Its emphasis was a study of the varying impacts the Depression had on Texas cities. Students read local newspapers, checked city council minutes, consulted school board records, and interviewed civic leaders across the state, including those in Temple, San Marcos, San Antonio, Midland, Kilgore, Dallas, Galveston, and Austin. They also interviewed community and church leaders to determine their level of assistance to those in need. Cotner explained that "enough information was gleaned to indicate that declining incomes for churches forced cuts in relief work." By the election of 1932 many private resources were "virtually depleted" and federal relief was welcome. The result of his efforts was a 215-page volume of twelve student essays titled *Texas Cities and the Great Depression* (1973), published by the Texas Memorial Museum in Austin.[6]

While Cotner's teaching career began in the Midland public schools, he quickly progressed into higher education. Typical of many teachers at the time, he stayed in the public schools only a few years before moving in 1932 to Arkadelphia, Arkansas, where he secured a better-paying position at Henderson State College as dean of men. Then five years later he moved to Stetson University in DeLand, Florida, as a professor of history and government, as well as dean of men. During those years Cotner also enrolled at Harvard University to pursue a doctorate, receiving an Austin Scholarship (1933–1934) and a Rosenwald Fellowship (1939–1940). There he fell under the academic sway of several prominent historians in the field, including Arthur M. Schlesinger Sr., Samuel E. Morison, and Frederick Merk, a western historian who would direct Cotner's dissertation: a biography of Texas governor James S. Hogg. By 1940 he had completed all course requirements for the doctorate except the exams and dissertation. With a strong record as an outstanding teacher, Cotner then accepted a position with the University of Texas at Austin. As one of six instructors hired at the university, his employment was ostensibly to "reverse the large lecture policy." History sections were divided into more manageable classes of thirty-five to forty students with full-time instructors. But with the attack on Pearl Harbor on December 7, 1941, and the subsequent outbreak of World War II, enrollments declined, and only Cotner and Barnes F. Lathrop, another newly hired instructor, continued on contract.[7]

In 1942 the war interrupted Cotner's professional career. On April 1 he reported for active duty as an assistant to the Fleet Personnel Officer of the Service Force in the Atlantic. After eight months he transferred to the Bureau of Naval Personnel and was responsible for enlistment requirements for selective service calls. Later, as a commander in the U.S. Navy, he was assigned to the staff of the Chief of Naval Operations for personnel plans, where he subsequently aided in the demobilization program. On January 30, 1943, however, he took time away from his military duties to marry Elizabeth Marie Breihan, an Austin public school teacher. With Cotner stationed in Washington, DC, the couple moved to Arlington, Virginia, to start their married life together. Children Catherine Elizabeth and Robert Crawford Jr. were born in 1947 and 1949 respectively. By that time, Cotner had already returned to the University of Texas campus, but remained active in the naval reserves until the late 1960s.[8]

With the exception of his naval service from 1942 to 1946, Cotner continuously pursued a career as a teacher, scholar, and historian that spanned three decades. He rose through the academic ranks at the University of Texas from instructor (1940) to assistant professor (1949), associate professor (1960), and then professor (1969). A dedicated teacher, his life belonged to his students, who often stopped by his office to chat and seek advice. At the same time he maintained an active research and writing regimen while completing his doctoral degree at Harvard University. As an uncommonly diligent member of the history department, he served on numerous departmental, college, and university committees, from the Faculty Council and Budget to Space and Curriculum. His longtime association with the university prompted some within the larger academic community to observe: "He *is* the Department of History at the University of Texas."[9]

In the fall of 1946 Cotner returned to his teaching duties at UT. As many servicemen and women took advantage of the GI Bill following World War II, enrollment increased at such institutions of higher learning. Cotner stated that he "felt some obligation to return" to the university, where classes once again returned to large lecture halls. But the large postwar classes created a shortage of available library resources. Cotner therefore interested Houghton Mifflin Company in publishing a two-volume anthology, *Readings in American History* (1952), edited with University of Texas professor Rudolph L. Biesele and University of Oklahoma professors John S. Ezell and Gilbert C. Fite. Its primary purpose was "to provide an interesting and convenient source of collateral reading in American history," as well as to serve as a supplement to basic college textbooks. Since such book ventures were typically "a north or eastern monopoly," Cotner and the other editors were particularly pleased when advisory editor John D. Hicks favorably reported that he had "no better selections to suggest" and the two volumes filled "a real need" within the discipline. Adoptions of the texts within the first year of publication were robust, reaching about fifty colleges and universities, and sales amounted to approximately $7,000 to $8,000 per volume.[10]

The decision to return to full-time teaching and pursue the *Readings* project had a negative impact on the completion of his doctoral degree and publication of the Hogg biography. Cotner would now have to balance his teaching obligations, typically three classes, with a book contract and research on the Hogg papers, consisting of approximately 50,000 items housed at the Eugene C. Barker Texas History Center on the University of Texas campus. This delay also affected his standing at the university, where an "up or out" policy existed. Although Cotner was on the university teaching staff prior to the adoption of the rule, he had resigned his position when he entered military service. Upon his return in 1946 the regulation technically became applicable to him. But his record as a "very good teacher" who took "more than ordianry [*sic*] interest in his students" convinced the university administration to extend his current status until he completed the degree or "for another three year period." Nevertheless, the message was clear: if Cotner wanted to rise in rank and salary, he must finish the degree.[11]

During his tenure at the University of Texas, Cotner, whose interests included social history, urban history, and American biography, initiated several teaching innovations. One significant contribution was his willingness to offer the first course in U.S. social and intellectual history as an alternative to traditional political and military history. Harvard historian Arthur M. Schlesinger Sr. had pioneered the new social history, and Cotner had studied under Dr. Schlesinger, which uniquely prepared him to teach such a class. He also introduced urban history as a subspecialty within the University of Texas history department and offered the first biography course, American Leaders, which "filled the room assigned each year." Furthermore, Cotner was an early advocate of interdisciplinary studies, and frequently invited faculty from various departments to speak to his classes on their areas of specialization. Unfortunately, since funding was not available for the invited lecturers, Cotner reluctantly ended the practice, complaining that "I have no way to pay them. It became embarrassing to ask them time and again."[12]

More than just opening up new vistas to his students, Cotner was known for his friendly yet dignified demeanor. Physically an imposing man — six feet tall, fair-skinned, blue-eyed, and balding — he arrived for class in professorial attire: conservative dark suits, ties, and frequently sporting a fedora. Described by former students as generally reserved, quiet, yet warmhearted, he always had a kind word for his students "to let them know he appreciated their individuality." History chairman Lewis Gould observed that Cotner spent countless hours with his students, advising them in their course work and supervising completion of numerous master's theses and doctoral dissertations. Whenever he identified particularly promising students, he encouraged them to pursue graduate work and invited those who made A's on his exams to lunch with him. Several students remembered that he "always had time to listen" and wrote countless letters of recommendation on their behalf. His students returned his kindness by selecting him as an honorary Texas Cowboy, naming him as a bench coach of the week for the Longhorn football team, and presenting him with a service award from the Student Union.[13]

Cotner was also active in university life. Early in his career he was an undergraduate advisor within the dean's office and helped plan the first campus-wide student-teacher evaluations. He also served as chairman of the Pre-Law Advising Committee and helped many successful students prepare for and obtain admission to law schools. At other times he willingly accepted numerous other assignments, including service on the American Studies Committee, the Naval Scholarship Committee, and the Commencement Committee. Always interested in student life, Cotner was a member of the Student Union Board, which was responsible for the day-to-day campus activities of students, faculty, and alumni. Often Cotner found himself embroiled in some controversy concerning the use of the Student Union facilities, especially during the protest movements of the 1960s and 1970s. Another university activity—the Fortnightly Club—was particularly rewarding to Cotner. An interdisciplinary organization on campus, the club was founded in 1906 for the purpose of encouraging the writing of scholarly papers. Composed primarily of language and social science professors, the members met twice a month at the University Club to hear and discuss their colleagues' research. The discussion was "always friendly, frequently witty, sometimes facetious." Cotner believed that such friendly criticism helped improve academic papers prior to their formal delivery or publication and agreed to serve as the club's president (1952–1953).[14]

In addition to his departmental and university service Cotner performed numerous professional duties. He was active in many organizations, serving on the executive committee of the Southern Historical Association and maintaining active membership within the Texas State Historical Association (TSHA) and the Southwestern Social Science Association. Cotner was also the book review editor for the *West Texas Historical Yearbook* (1955–1972) and the *Southwestern Historical Quarterly* (1966–1969), at a time when the *Quarterly* was "known for sloppy documentation with a touch of cronyism in its publication." Under his guidance and that of others, the scope of the books reviewed broadened, the list of reviewers grew, and the style and accuracy of footnotes improved. He was also president of two learned societies, the East Texas Historical Association (1971–1972) and the West Texas Historical Association (1975–1976), an unusual accomplishment since those two regional organizations were quite different. In addition, Cotner held membership in the prestigious Texas Institute of Letters and was a TSHA fellow, an honor bestowed on only a few deserving individuals.[15]

Politically, Robert Cotner was a conservative Democrat who maintained a strong interest in politics and current events. Living and working in Austin, the state capital, he knew most of the elected officials and observed firsthand the actions of the state legislature. He often consulted with the party leadership, such as Lieutenant Governor Ben Barnes, and was personally acquainted with Governor Price Daniel and President and Mrs. Lyndon B. Johnson. When the legislature was in session, he was particularly vigilant about educational bills. For example, in 1969 SB 474 was introduced, which would repeal the requirement to study Texas and U.S. history for graduates from state-supported colleges and universities. At that time the proposed bill never made it out of committee, but it was reintroduced in 1971. Cotner was "one of a few who realized its potential harm and significance to UT history." He joined with TSHA and others in a letter-writing campaign to defeat it, although the issue would resurface again later.[16]

By all accounts Robert Cotner was a kind, gentle, well-liked professor who never sought out controversy, yet he frequently expressed his opinions on a range of issues from class sizes to teacher training to academic freedom. With increasing enrollment at the university, Cotner worried that large history sections would "decrease individual involvement." He also sought to upgrade teacher requirements for UT graduates. In 1970 he weighed in, if indirectly, on the dismissal of John Silber, the dean of the College of Arts and Sciences, by regents' chairman Frank C. Erwin Jr. The firing was the result of the continuing battle over the reorganization of the College of Arts and Sciences, the largest at UT, into three separate units—the humanities, the social and behavioral sciences, and the natural sciences. A controversial figure, Silber was a bit of an empire builder, and publicly opposed attempts to dismantle the college, which would have diluted his power. His firing during the summer of 1970, when many faculty and students were gone, led to over 300 professors signing petitions protesting the "atmosphere of intimidation and distrust" at UT. The faculty was especially upset by the proposed reorganization of the college without their consultation, and by the potential for future firings of individuals who incurred Erwin's wrath. While it is unclear whether Cotner signed the petition, he did recognize "the hornet's nest" stirred up by the issue, and steadfastly opposed any threats to academic freedom or shared governance. Nevertheless, the regents prevailed and the UT history department was reorganized under the College of Social and Behavioral Sciences.

Despite his considerable interests and responsibilities, Cotner found time to be a productive scholar. Among his many publications were numerous scholarly articles, book chapters, and edited books. For example, in 1948 he authored "The Intellectual Opposition to Juan Manual de Rosas" in *The Historian*. He also wrote the introduction and a chapter titled "Attorney General Hogg and the Acceptance of the State Capitol" for *The State Capitol* (1968), a book that he edited. Based on his earlier research, he argued in his essay for *The State Capitol* that, despite his detractors, Jim Hogg had secured a better capitol for Texas by working to obtain compliance with the terms of the contract. Then, in 1969, he edited *Norris Wright Cuney: A Tribune of the Black People*, a brief book about a black Republican boss and customs collector at the Port of Galveston. It was followed by *Texas Is the Place for Me* (1970), the autobiography of a German immigrant youth edited by Cotner. In 1973, along with the publication of *Texas Cities and the Great Depression,* he worked with Ezell, Fite, and Joe Frantz of the University of Texas, who had replaced Biesele, on another edition of *Readings in American History,* which was published in 1975. Altogether Cotner produced over thirty scholarly publications and numerous book reviews in approximately thirty-seven years.[17]

While Cotner's historical contributions were many, none were more important than his publications on Governor James Stephen Hogg of Texas. In 1951 University of Texas president T. S. Painter had promised Ima Hogg, daughter of Governor Jim Hogg, that "something would be done for the Centennial of her father's birth." Since the dissertation and anticipated biography of Hogg was not yet complete, Cotner offered to edit the volume *Addresses and State Papers of Governor James Stephen Hogg* and to write a brief biographical sketch for the anniversary. The University of Texas Press published *Addresses* in 1951, which was then distributed to more than 1,000 Texas high school libraries. It received the Texas Heritage Foundation National Medal Award, and the reading room of the Texas Collection of the Barker History Center was officially renamed the James Stephen Hogg Room. On December 8, 1951, President Painter presented a copy of *Addresses* to Ima Hogg with historian Robert Cotner standing by her side. Subsequently, Miss Ima made "a most substantial bequest to the University," which Cotner believed was in appreciation for publication of the book.[18]

The long-awaited book *James Stephen Hogg, a Biography,* which began as a doctoral dissertation in 1939, ultimately took two decades to complete. The topic dated back to the years that Cotner had grown up listening to stories about Texas heroes and their larger-than-life exploits. In Dallas he had attended a grammar school named after John H. Reagan, the first railroad commissioner and a personal friend of Jim Hogg. "It was through my close contact with people who knew these men," he recalled in 1954, "that I became interested in the biographies of great American leaders." While Stephen F. Austin and Sam Houston had already found their biographers and John H. Reagan had left an autobiography, no definitive book existed on the life and times of Governor Hogg. A monograph about Hogg by George M. Bailey, a reporter for the *Dallas-Galveston News,* had appeared earlier, but it had none of the scholarly documentation required of a respected biography. The Hogg family copyrighted it to "keep it for limited use because it was not satisfactory in many places." The only other existing record of Hogg was his official addresses, state papers, and three brief essays. Consequently, Cotner had resolved to correct the oversight with a full-length biography of a man he admired and a governor whose policies, he believed, made him the forerunner of the Progressive movement.[19]

Completion of the Hogg biography, which would be Cotner's magnum opus, would be no easy task. A thorough and painstaking researcher, Cotner embarked on this massive undertaking to chronicle both the life and times of this reform-minded Texas governor (1890–1894). At times burdened with "extraneous minutiae," the dissertation and subsequent book sought to refute several charges directed against Hogg. In the October 1951 issue of the *American Historical Review*, Reinhard H. Luthin had placed Hogg on a list of southern demagogues who rose to power from the farmers' revolt by exploiting the race issue, which Cotner emphatically denied. Hogg's honesty, character, and public-spiritedness, Cotner wrote, steered him away from the radical rabble-rousers of the day. Hogg espoused the unpopular side of an issue only when he believed it was right. Cotner also wanted to correct the view of historians C. Vann Woodward and James Tinsley that Hogg deserted the forces of reform after leaving public office to pursue oil profits. Cotner argued that, after eight years in public office, Hogg's bank balance of $135 was insufficient to meet his existing obligations. In fact, he had to borrow $100 just to move out of the Governor's Mansion when his term ended. He therefore necessarily turned to earning money to pay off his debts. And while he did amass a substantial oil fortune after Spindletop in 1901, he continued to champion liberal causes such as the improvement of education and measures to outlaw permanent lobbyists in Austin. Hogg also supported progressive candidates such as Thomas Campbell and William J. Bryan.[20]

Over the years Ima Hogg provided necessary support for the completion of the Hogg biography. She permitted Cotner unlimited access to the Hogg Collection at the University of Texas library. In 1947 she escorted Robert and Elizabeth Cotner through East Texas to meet persons connected to the family and to hear stories that were "not revealed in books or letters." In 1952 she donated the desk and two chairs used by the late Governor Hogg to the Barker Texas History Center (now the Dolph Briscoe Center for American History), which Cotner at times used to conduct his research. That same year Cotner reported that he received approximately $683 from Hogg "to continue work on the biography," which enabled him to research and write free from teaching duties during the summer terms.[21]

Cotner's close association with Ima Hogg, who reviewed the early drafts of the manuscript, caused some to question the objectivity and scope of the biography. In 1955 Professor Frederick Merk, who directed his dissertation, cautioned Cotner about the "God Almighty problem," which made Hogg appear "incapable of mistakes." It was, he continued, a "crusading biography . . . rather than an analytical one." Moreover, Merk complained that his study was "rather political" in emphasis and provided "no graphic picture of Texas society" at the time. Furthermore, at over 700 pages (later edited down to 617 pages) the biography simply contained "too much detail." These and other concerns required Cotner both to revise and expand the manuscript, leading to editorial changes and publication delays.[22]

From 1955 to 1958 Cotner, facing increasing pressure to complete his doctorate, made plans to finish his degree at Harvard University. Having already passed his general examination, he prepared for a "special" examination, which included not only a comprehensive bibliography but an additional reading list comprising approximately 100 books and monographs. A concentrated reading period of four months prior to the exam would be required. Additionally, he would have to complete and defend the dissertation, which he accomplished by the spring of 1958. But due to his heavy teaching and university duties, as well as the illness of his editor, Kathleen Sproul, which delayed the galley proofs and release date of the Hogg biography, he had not had time to prepare for the exam. Once again another postponement seemed the only alternative.[23]

By 1958, after many delays and setbacks, Cotner was eager to have the biography published as soon as possible. Sixty-six years old, Ima Hogg was experiencing failing health, and Cotner wanted to do anything to bring about its early publication. "She deserves to see this in print," he commented. Moreover, advancement in his career required that the project be completed. Cotner, now fifty-two years old, still had not completed his exams for the doctorate. Only the completion of the degree and publication of the biography would finally put to rest questions about his future.[24]

In 1959 Robert C. Cotner achieved his longstanding goals. In June the University of Texas Press published *James Stephen Hogg, a Biography*. Cotner had originally submitted the manuscript to Houghton-Mifflin, which had published *Readings in American History*. Cotter believed that, as a nonacademic press, it could advertise and distribute the book more easily, but the company rejected it as "too regional" for its trade book department. Several other presses expressed an interest in the biography, but the University of Texas Press recognized its value to the university and to the large readership in Texas history. Besides, the Hogg family held strong ties to the school with a long history of financial support. To launch the long-awaited biography Governor Price Daniel held a reception at the Governor's Mansion to introduce the author and the book. Later that same year Cotner successfully completed his final examinations and at last earned his Ph.D. from Harvard University. Now, at last, it seemed that his dogged persistence had been rewarded.[25]

Reviewers of *James S. Hogg, a Biography* both praised and criticized the volume. Most lauded the scholarship, thoroughness, and literary style of the author, noting the years of research and preparation that had gone into the book.

They also credited Cotner with identifying Hogg as a reform governor, while chronicling the difficult transition of Texas from a predominately agrarian state to an industrial one. Although sometimes "heavy and slow-moving," Herbert Gambrell of Southern Methodist University described the volume as "the best account of Texas politics from Reconstruction to the turn of the century." Ralph Wooster of Lamar University praised the book as a "vivid and powerful" chronicle of the nineteenth century that depicted Hogg as "a giant among men." Critics, however, often viewed the book as an overly sympathetic treatment of a political figure who didn't always represent "the noblest example of Southern progressivism." The "partiality and near reverence" toward Hogg caused some to complain that Cotner ignored contradictory evidence or told "only one side of the story." Others suggested that Cotner overstated his case by defending Hogg's oil speculation activities, citing his close associations with the "new leviathans — oil companies," who were more interested in exploiting than developing Texas's natural resources.[26]

Whatever the critical assessment of *James Stephen Hogg, a Biography*, it represented the first comprehensive, full-length study of the Texas reform governor. Well written and exhaustively researched, the biography revealed Hogg as an honest, popular, yet moderate reformer, what Cotner described as a "middle-of-the-roader, leading the 'vital center.'" The creation of the Railroad Commission was his principal achievement, but he also championed other progressive reforms such as the passage of regulatory laws aimed at curbing the power of corporations. Fifty years after the publication of the book, it still remains the definitive account of the first native-born governor of Texas.[27]

Publication of the Hogg biography garnered Cotner numerous awards. It won the Summerfield G. Roberts Award of the Sons of the Republic of Texas and the American Association for State and Local History Award. In 1957 Cotner was the recipient of the Texas Heritage Foundation Award for "distinguished and meritorious public service in preserving the Texas heritage." Described as "the man who probably knows more about Texas' first [native] Governor Jim Hogg," Cotner was one of the honorees at the eleventh annual Writers Roundup. In 1970 his alma mater, Baylor University, honored him with a doctor of literature degree, citing him as "an authority on southern and southwestern history." Then, nine year later, the East Texas Historical Association awarded Cotner the Ralph W. Steen Service Award for "excellence in educating the public about the history and culture of east Texas." Such recognition surely marked Robert C. Cotner as one of the preeminent historians of Texas.[28]

As the leading authority on James S. Hogg, Cotner was in demand to give lectures and appear at banquets. He received numerous invitations from civic organizations to speak about the governor. For example, he served on many academic panels of the Texas State Historical Association, the West Texas Historical Association, and the Southwestern Social Science Association. His topics ranged from "Hogg and the Election of 1892" to "Kilgore, Texas, and the Oil Boom." In addition, Cotner was a sought-after speaker by patriotic societies, such as the Daughters of the Texas Revolution and the Daughters of the American Revolution, where he expounded on Hogg as a progressive Texas governor.[29]

Robert C. Cotner retired from the University of Texas in 1977 and was given the title of professor emeritus of history. While his distinguished career spanned thirty-seven years, his retirement would last only three years. On September 23, 1980, Cotner died at his home from heart failure at the age of seventy-three. Students, colleagues, and friends genuinely grieved his passing. Not only was he a respected historian but also a fine teacher and a loving father to his children. The university's General Faculty organization eulogized Professor Cotner, citing his devotion to his students. Many graduates, they noted, had "an understanding of the richness of American history because of having studied with Robert Cotner." But, equally important, they had "an understanding that human concern, dignity, and involvement have been wonderfully present in his classrooms." Colleagues and associates remembered his courteousness and thoughtfulness, which marked him as "a gentleman of the old school." History department chairman Lewis Gould described him as "a valued and dedicated professor" whose students "were always his first concerns." In addition to his magisterial biography of James Stephen Hogg, Robert C. Cotner will be remembered for the many well-trained historians he sent into the profession.[30]

SUGGESTED READING

Cotner, Robert C., ed. *Addresses and State Papers of James Stephen Hogg*. Austin: University of Texas Press, 1951.

The public papers of Governor James Hogg, well annotated and indexed, with documents, speeches, proclamations, debates, and interviews.

Cotner, Robert C. *James Stephen Hogg, a Biography*. Austin: University of Texas Press, 1959.

Utilizing the Hogg Papers, Cotner authored an award-winning biography of this influential Texas governor and progressive political leader. The governor's daughter Ima Hogg worked closely with Cotner on the research. The Hogg biography is still a recommended source for information on Hogg and the Populist and Progressive eras.

Cotner, Robert C., et al. *Texas Cities and the Great Depression*. Austin: Texas Memorial Museum, 1973.

A published collection of essays that cover the impact of the Great Depression on the larger cities of Houston, Dallas, and San Antonio and smaller ones such as Midland, Kilgore,

San Angelo, and San Marcos. While the oil booms of the 1930s mitigated some of the impact of the Great Depression, the essays reveal economic, social, and political unrest throughout the state's metropolitan areas.

Cotner, Robert C., ed. *The Texas State Capitol.* Austin: Pemberton Press, 1968.

A history of the planning, financing, and construction of the Texas State Capitol during the 1880s. Construction problems, labor strife, and the political leaders of the era are covered in this study of the largest state capitol building in the nation.

NOTES

1. The other prominent statesmen of Texas include Stephen F. Austin, Sam Houston, and John H. Reagan. Robert C. Cotner, *James Stephen Hogg, a Biography* (Austin: University of Texas Press, 1959), vii, 585.

2. Michael V. Hazel, "Dallas," *The New Handbook of Texas,* edited by Ron Tyler (Austin: Texas State Historical Association, 1996), 478–481; Michael V. Hazel, *Dallas: A History of "Big"* (Austin: Texas State Historical Association, 1997), 27–36; Robert C. Cotner Jr., interview, June 25, 2008, in possession of author.

3. Curriculum Vitae, box 3N341, Robert Crawford Cotner Papers, Dolph Briscoe Center for American History, University of Texas at Austin (hereafter RC Papers).

4. Gene B. Preuss, "Public Education Comes of Age," *Twentieth-Century Texas: A Social and Cultural History,* edited by John W. Storey and Mary L. Kelley (Denton: University of North Texas Press, 2008), 358–386.

5. Robert C. Cotner et al., *Texas Cities and the Great Depression* (Austin: Texas Memorial Museum, 1973), xi–xiv, 91–104; John Leffler, "Midland," *The Handbook of Texas,* 706–707.

6. UT Press release, Cotner Bio File, Briscoe Center; Archie McDonald interview, February 4, 2008, in possession of author; Cotner interview.

7. Curriculum Vitae; *Who's Who among Authors and Journalists,* box 3N389; Cotner to Silber, February 4, 1968, box 3N341; Cotner to Dr. John K. Weiss, June 12, 1953, box 3N341, RC Papers; *Directory of American Scholars* (Lancaster, PA: Science Press, 1942), 174–175.

8. Cotner to Weiss, June 12, 1953, box 3N341, RC Papers; "In Memoriam: Robert Crawford Cotner," Cotner Bio File, Briscoe Center.

9. Curriculum Vitae; *Southwestern Historical Quarterly* 72, no. 4 (April 1969): 535.

10. Cotner to Weiss, June 12, 1953, box 3N341; Cotner to Webb, April 25, 1953, box 3N341, RC Papers; Cotner et al., eds., preface to *Readings in American History,* 3rd ed. (Boston: Houghton-Mifflin Company, 1964).

11. Cotner to Webb; Webb to Ransom, March 3, 1955, box 3N341, RC Papers.

12. Curriculum Vitae; Cotner to Lois H. S. Murray, June 10, 1969, box 3N341; 1975 Annual Report, box 3N343, file 3, RC Papers.

13. "Robert Cotner," box AR 81–115, East Texas Historical Association Papers, Stephen F. Austin University, Nacogdoches, Texas (hereafter ETHA Papers); University of Texas news release, September 24, 1980, Briscoe Center; *Southwestern Historical Quarterly* 84 (April 1981): 444; Jo Ann Stiles interview, January 19, 2008, in possession of author.

14. Curriculum Vitae; "The Fortnightly Club," *Alcalde,* June 1937, 207.

15. Curriculum Vitae; Richard B. McCaslin, *At the Heart of Texas: 100 Years of the Texas State Historical Association, 1897–1997* (Austin: Texas State Historical Association, 2007), 177.

16. Box 3N332, file 2; *Dallas Morning News*, April 2, 1971, box 3N332, file 3; box 3N343, file 8, RC Papers; Cotner interview.

17. Some of Cotner's other publications include scholarly articles in the *West Texas Historical Association Yearbook*, *The Handbook of Texas*, and the *East Texas Historical Journal*. Chapters appeared in *Theodore Foster's Minutes of the Convention Held at South Kingston, Rhode Island, in March, 1790* (1929; 1967), *The Teacher's Yoke* (1964), and *History of Baylor University* (1972). Cotner also edited several books, including *A Debate Handbook* (1938), *Addresses and State Papers of James Stephen Hogg* (1951), and *Eagle Pass, or Life on the Border* (1966).

18. Cotner to Weiss, June 12, 1953, box 3N341; Cotner to Webb, April 25, 1953, box 3N341, RC Papers; *Daily Texan*, February 21, 1952, and October 7, 1959.

19. Eugene Barker wrote *The Life of Stephen F. Austin* (1925), James Marquis wrote *The Raven: A Biography of Sam Houston* (1929), and John H. Reagan published his *Memoirs* (1906). Cotner to Kathleen Sproul, January 21, 1958, box 3N328, General Correspondence January–July 1958, RC Papers; Cotner, *James Stephen Hogg*, vii; *Daily Texan*, April 29, 1954.

20. See Reinhard H. Luthin, "Some Demagogues in American History," *American Historical Review* 57 (October 1951): 44–45, and Cotner, *James Stephen Hogg*, vii–x; James A. Tinsley, book review, *Mississippi Valley Historical Review*, (1960): 537–539; James C. Bonner, book review, *Georgia Historical Quarterly* (March 1960): 107–108.

21. Cotner, *James Stephen Hogg*, xi; *Austin American*, November 20, 1952 (clipping), box 3N389, file 3, RC Papers.

22. Merk to Cotner, January 1955, box 3N327; Official Memorandum by Governor Price Daniel, June 8, 1959, box 3N389, RC Papers.

23. Cotner to Ransom, March 19, 1959, box 3N341, RC Papers.

24. Cotner to Sproul, January 21, 1958, box 3N328, General Correspondence January–July 1958, RC Papers.

25. The book's original title was *James Stephen Hogg: Spokesman for the New Southwest*, and the dissertation was "James Stephen Hogg: Forerunner of the Progressive Movement." Cotner to Dr. Lewis, October 10, 1956, box 3N341, RC Papers.

26. Henry Stroupe, book review, *North Carolina Historical Review* (October 1960): 583–585; Bonner, book review, 107–108; Herbert J. Doherty Jr., book review, *American Historical Review* (January 1960): 394; Tinsley, book review, 537–539; Herbert Gambrell, book review, *Southwestern Historical Quarterly* (1960): 480–481; O. Douglas Weeks, *Southwestern Social Science Quarterly*, vol. 4 (September 1960): 169–170; Ralph A. Wooster, book review, *Beaumont Journal*, July 3, 1959; Cotner, *James Stephen Hogg*, vii, x.

27. Cotner, *James Stephen Hogg*, 556–586.

28. *Daily Texan*, September 25, 1980; *Austin American*, February 16, 1957, and October 13, 1959; East Texas Historical Association, Minutes, 1979, ETHA Papers.

29. Curriculum Vitae, October 1972.

30. Cotner interview; "Robert C. Cotner," box AR 81-115, ETHA Papers; *Southwestern Historical Quarterly* 84, no. 4 (April 1981): 443–444; In Memoriam, Bio: Robert C. Cotner, RC Papers; *Daily Texan*, September 25, 1980.

CAROLINA CASTILLO CRIMM

AMÉRICO PAREDES

AMÉRICO PAREDES, 1962

Américo Paredes, Mexican American folklorist, author, scholar, teacher, singer, and songwriter, dedicated his life and his scholarly career to exploring the experiences of the Mexican American people of the Rio Grande Valley, both their resilience and strength, and the difficulties they faced in the prejudiced world of nineteenth-century Anglo American society. Because he had grown up in South Texas as a Mexican American, he was able to describe the internal conflict faced by his people, a conflict in which the love of their centuries-long Spanish heritage, learned at their parents' knee, struggled to survive in a world where their Anglo teachers taught only negative views of the Mexican culture. His straightforward, clear, honest, humorous, and lyrical prose and poetry evoked pride and pleasure among Mexican Americans in Texas, as well as a growing sympathy and a new understanding from a slowly growing number of Anglos who read his work with admiration and, perhaps, surprise. Although he never picked up a placard or walked a protest line, he inspired a generation of young Chicano scholars to activism with his gentle but deadly wit, his rigorous scholarship, and his painstaking knowledge of the fields of history, folklore, literature, and anthropology. His books and short stories, wonderfully written and entertaining to read, are as insightful and true to human character as those of Dickens or Dostoyevsky, while, like a burr under the saddle, they embarrass and irritate some Anglo readers as Paredes exposed the violence perpetrated by the Texas Rangers and the racist attitudes still prevalent in Texas during the 1950s and 1960s.

Américo Paredes was born in Brownsville, Texas, on September 3, 1915, as the third son of Justo Paredes Cisneros and Clotilde Manzano Vidal. The couple had married just prior to the turn of the century and settled in the town of Brownsville, on the Texas-Mexico border. Clotilde gave birth to eight children: Eliseo in 1899, Isaura in 1902, Lorenzo in 1904 (who died at birth), Clotilde in 1906, Blanca in 1910, Justo Jr. in 1912, Américo in 1915, and twin boys Amador and Eleazar in 1920. Américo later grew particularly close to two of his nieces, Clotilde's daughter, Patti Padron, and Isaura's daughter, Odilia Galván Rodríguez, both of whom became faithful correspondents. The large family, further expanded by aunts, uncles, and numerous cousins, provided a powerful support network for young Américo in the growing Anglo world.

Américo's family had a long history of which they were justly proud. Justo Paredes had been a rancher and descendant of Spanish Jews who had come to the New World in 1590. After being exiled from Spain by the Inquisition, the Paredes family had joined other *conversos* (converted Jews) who settled in the area around Monterrey, later moving to the Río Bravo del Norte (Rio Grande). His mother, on both the Manzano and Vidal sides, was a descendant of settlers who had arrived along the Río Bravo with José de Escandón during the 1740s. For the next hundred years, the settlers in the Rio Grande Valley, including the

Paredes, Cisneros, Manzano, and Vidal families, expanded and created a powerful interlocking network of relationships using intermarriage and *compadrazgo*, or godparenthood, to survive in the face of droughts, Indian raids, and hard times occasioned by high taxes on goods from central Mexico.

Young Américo was influenced by the conflicts that had grown up between Mexicans and Anglos in the valley of the Rio Bravo/Rio Grande. Almost as soon as the Treaty of Guadalupe Hidalgo was signed in 1848, Anglos had begun to move in and settle south of the Nueces River, drawn by the rich soil, the abundant water, and the pleasant weather. The treaty had guaranteed protection of Mexican ownership of ranches and farms. Attempting to prevent land fraud in the Republic of Texas, the newly established General Land Office sent representatives to review the deed records for the lands in question. Regrettably, the ship carrying the deeds back to Austin went down in a storm, and many of the irreplaceable land records were lost. When the new Anglo arrivals settled on land claimed by the original Mexican families, the owners of the property had lost their proof of ownership.

Prejudice, whether toward Mexicans by Anglos or by Mexicans against their own people, was already well known on the border. Opposition to *fuereños*, or outsiders, had long been a trait of the Spanish settlers of the Rio Grande. The Spanish, who had become Mexicans after 1821, like the Paredes family, had always considered themselves Europeans and saw themselves as "white" in comparison to the Mexican Indians and the mixed-blood mestizos, who were relegated to subordinate positions as peons, farmers, and day laborers. In the *corrido* "The Undying Love of 'El Indio' Córdova," the hero, named Córdova, perhaps a mixed-blood mestizo or an Indian with telltale dark skin, was snubbed by a local Spanish family when he tried to marry their daughter. The line had been drawn centuries earlier between the "pure," light-skinned Spaniards—tall, thin, often hook-nosed—and the short, swarthy, shaggy-haired, dark-skinned natives.

The descendants of the Spanish "dons," who considered themselves every bit as "white" as the new arrivals, were understandably nonplussed by the prejudice of the incoming Anglo settlers who looked down on all the Mexicans, regardless of their skin color. The Anglos harked back to the treatment of black slaves in the South and used their control of both legal and financial power, as well as the newly created Texas Rangers, to punish any Mexican, no matter how white his skin, who refused to "stay in his place." Understandably, the Mexican Texans remained defiant and obstinate in their refusal to submit to Anglo dominance.

For Mexican Americans, the ownership of land had always been part of their Spanish heritage. Their land grants had come, via the viceroy, directly from the Spanish king. Vast ranches extended for thousands of acres, and since cattle ranged freely on the land, there was no need to fence the ranches or quarrel over boundaries. Those Anglos who wanted access to the large tracts of land, much of it carefully protected with titles and deeds that went back two hundred years, realized that one way of acquiring the land was to marry into the Mexican families and become cattle ranchers on the vast Spanish ranches. It was not long before the acquisitive new Anglo arrivals, however, began expanding their ranches at the expense of their Mexican neighbors. By the time barbed wire became available in the 1870s, Anglos had begun fencing off the precious water sources and barring their Mexican neighbors from access to the rivers. This injustice, flying in the face of Spanish legal traditions that protected the rights of all to the water in the rivers, inevitably led to bloody gun battles and fierce reprisals, stories that the Mexicans preserved in their oral tradition of *corridos*, or ballads.

Américo Paredes was most perhaps most influenced by a *corrido* about Juan Nepomuceno Cortina, who from 1859 to 1870 defended the Tejano families who were being dispossessed of their lands by the newly arrived Anglos. Cortina, a border rancher and descendant of the oldest Spanish families, had shot Robert Shears, the Brownsville city marshal, for beating one of Cortina's mother's ranch hands. Cortina, soon branded an outlaw, used the upheaval of the American Civil War and the French invasion of Mexico to harass the American ranchers from across the border. Frustrated by their inability to catch the elusive border raider, the Texas Rangers began to shoot, hang, and torture any Mexican who might be associated with Cortina. Cortina was eventually jailed by Mexican president Porfirio Díaz, but the conflicts between Mexicans and Anglos escalated during the 1870s and 1880s, leading to more shootings, more reprisals, and more *corridos*, songs with which the young Américo became bitterly familiar.

The railroad into the Rio Grande Valley was completed in 1904, and Américo's family and the Mexicans of South Texas were overwhelmed by Anglo American Midwesterners who swarmed into the valley on the newly completed railroad. The new arrivals, uninterested in cattle ranching, saw the farming possibilities for the land if it could be cleared and irrigated. With the support of the federal government, the new Anglo residents installed steam pumps and irrigation lines, bought up land, and diverted water from the Rio Grande onto the newly cleared chaparral to create a paradise of cotton, sugarcane, vegetables, and citrus crops, which could be transported quickly to the Northeast on the new trains. The Mexicans, particularly the old ranching families, long dedicated to cattle, saw little of interest in the new methods and could not join the new society as anything other than day laborers on the new farms, something their pride forbade.

From south of the border, meanwhile, the Mexican Revolution of 1910 erupted against the aging dictator Porfirio Díaz. Justo Paredes, Américo's father, like many of the Mexican Texans, joined the armies of the revolution and left his growing family in Brownsville. The inspiring ideals of the revolution infected the Mexican Americans, who bitterly resented the loss of their lands to the giant Anglo American conglomerates. In 1915, just as Clotilde gave birth to young Américo, a group of Mexican Texans, led by Aniceto Pizaña and known as the *sediciosos*, or seditionists, declared the Plan of San Diego. They proposed to revolt against Anglo American authority in Texas, New Mexico, Arizona, Colorado, and California to reclaim Mexican lands and create a separate country that would recognize freedom for all the races, including Mexicans, Negroes, Japanese, and Indians. The more extreme elements intended to kill every Anglo American male over the age of sixteen.

The *sediciosos*, by using Mexico as their haven—where the revolution had left the land in a lawless state—raided across the border, destroying Anglo homes and businesses in Texas, and derailed the Brownsville train. The Anglos deputized their own posses and called on the Texas Rangers to suppress the raids in South Texas. As often happens when bandits can blend into the local population, it was almost impossible for the Texas Rangers to distinguish the bandits from the honest citizens. The Rangers, however, adopted the method of shooting first and asking questions later, leading to an orgy of killing in which thousands of innocent Mexican Americans were murdered in cold blood, while the bandits were almost all safe across the border in Mexico.

Immersed in the bloodbath of the border, Américo learned to sing the *corridos* that he heard sung around campfires at the ranches of family and friends, stories that described in vivid detail the conflict between the Anglo Americans and the Tejanos. The *corridos* affected young Paredes deeply and became a fundamental influence throughout his life, as they would for most of the Tejanos who grew up in the racist world of the Rio Grande Valley during the first decades of the twentieth century.

Clotilde, Américo's mother, encouraged education for her children. She had instilled in young Américo an appreciation for the history and traditions of Mexico, Mexican Texas, and the Mexican Americans. Under his mother's tutelage, Américo could read and write in Spanish before he entered the segregated American educational system. This skill enabled him to learn to read English well, and it was not long before he was surprising his Anglo teachers by writing poetry in English as well as Spanish. He dates his decision to write poetry from 1924 or 1925, at the age of ten, when one of his teachers, a Miss McCollum, read one of his poems in class. His skill at writing continued to build, and he was fortunate to have a number of excellent Mexican American teachers, including the sisters of the Texas historian Carlos E. Castañeda, who encouraged him in his writing and his poetry. Américo wrote many of his poems in English beginning in 1930 at the age of fifteen. Within two years he won a high school poetry contest and represented Brownsville High School on the state level. He also began to write poetry in Spanish in 1932, blaming the delay to write in Spanish on the English schools and the lack of books available *en la lengua de Cervantes* (in the language of Cervantes).[1]

Singing and songwriting were a common pursuit along the border, but Don Justo, Américo's father, opposed the musical traits displayed by his son. Although Paredes found out years later that his father both played the guitar and sang, it was with his mother's support that he learned to play the piano. His father feared that Américo would become a drunk and a derelict like the composer of the famous Mexican song "Sobre las Olas," whom Don Justo had seen years earlier in a gutter in Monterrey. Young Américo, frustrated by his father's refusal but frightened of disobeying, expressed his anger in a story he called "Over the Waves Is Out," which he did not publish for almost forty years. He also bought a guitar on the sly and learned from his friends to play and sing.

Paredes credited his creative abilities to his training in songwriting when he wrote lyrics to put to music as well as when he wrote music for his poetry. He also acknowledged the necessary boyhood skill of verbal sparring in Spanish when he had to "improvise insulting quatrains" to defend himself among his Mexican friends.[2] He was influenced by the classic authors such as Longfellow, Poe, Emerson, and Bryant, but he found that the "bored, gum-chewing sweater girl who was my high school English teacher was not much help."[3]

Between 1930 and 1936, as he moved through his teenage years, he was torn between his two cultures and his two languages. The Anglo American culture dominated his school days, but afternoons and evenings were bound to the Mexican American traditions of the songs and stories that he had learned from the *corridos* on the Mexican ranches. As he says, these years formed a time of transition, as if he was a butterfly emerging from a cocoon—"son los años ciegos y desequilibrados de metamorphosis . . . se sintió un momento netamente mexicano y al otro puro yanqui."[4] These years were "the years of blindness and imbalance where he felt, at one moment, totally Mexican and at the next pure Yankee." As he became more aware of the prejudice and racial bias against the Mexican Americans—and as the truth of the *corridos* he continued to sing became more evident—he developed a love-hate relationship with the local Anglo American culture, in which the Mexican Americans were despised and the educational system conveniently ignored the all-too-racist history of the Anglo Americans in Texas and the United States. He expressed his feelings in a semihumorous poem, "The Mexico-Texan," in which he used his dry wit to focus on the mistreatment of Mexican Americans. He later said that he had composed it during the spring of 1934 "while walking the twenty-one blocks home from school one afternoon and written down—with revisions—shortly afterward."[5]

The Mexico-Texan, he's one fonny man
Who lives in the region that's north of the Gran';
Of Mexican father, he born in these part.
For the Mexico-Texan he no gota lan';
And sometimes he rues it, deep down in hees heart.
He stomped on da neck on both sides of the Gran';
The dam gringo lingo he no cannot spick,
It twista da tong and it maka heem sik;
A cit'zen of Texas they say that he ees!
But then,—they call heem da Mexican Grease?
Soft talk and hard action, he can't understan';
The Mexico-Texan, he no gotta lan' . . .[6]

It was his first attempt at exposing the political injustices done to the Mexican Americans in the Valley, and the poem would become an inspiration for the Chicano movement.

Although he had begun working at fifteen at a local grocery store, the young scholar continued to suffer from lack of funds as he tried to help support the family. Years later he remembered not being able to buy membership pins for honorary organizations that he had been invited to join or to purchase his high school graduation ring.[7] During his last semester at Brownsville High School, he entered his poem "Night" in the Trinity University Scriptscrafters' Club competition. In May of 1934, he was notified that his poem had been chosen as the best in the state of Texas. J. W. Irvine, the high school principal, wrote to congratulate him: "You were not only a consistent student but a boy with great potential," he wrote. "The initiative which you displayed in entering the poetry contest . . . deserves special recognition."[8] With such statewide success, he was able to avoid the fate of most young Mexican Americans, who were told to attend technical school since Mexican Americans did not go to college.

By the fall of 1934, he had begun to make arrangements to go to the University of Texas in Austin. He worked during the summer to buy clothing and borrowed money for his expenses. He also found a job as a janitor at a boardinghouse in Austin where he could work for his keep. As he admitted later, it wounded him deeply to have to lower himself to the menial job, but if it was for his education, he was willing to sacrifice. By this time, however, the Depression had reached deep into the Lower Rio Grande Valley. His father supplied food for the household from the small family ranch, but his elder brothers, burdened with families and debts of their own, could not help his mother. He realized that if he left for Austin, his younger twin brothers would have to drop out of high school to support the family. Just as he gave up his dream of a college degree, Irvine, his high school principal and the dean of the local community college, offered him a student assistantship. Américo gratefully accepted and enrolled at Brownsville Junior College.[9]

At the junior college throughout 1935 and 1936, he continued to work at various jobs while attending classes. He struggled to find his place in the Anglo society, angered by segregation and racial bias, and finally chose not to write poetry in English anymore. He wanted so badly to be proud of his Spanish heritage, but realized that he was also a creature of the Anglo school system. His poem "¡Soy pocho!," scribbled on a scrap of paper, expressed his desire to be admired, not for his English writing but by others like him who faced the conflict of not being accepted in the United States for their Mexican heritage. He desperately needed to feel pride in being part of both cultures.

> ¡Soy pocho! Dios me haga
> Orgullo de los pochos
> Así como los pochos son mi orgullo.
> Quisiera llegar a ser
> el orgullo de los pochos.
> (I'm Pocho! May God make me
> the pride of the Pochos
> Just as the Pochos are my pride.
> I would like to become
> the pride of the Pochos.)[10]

During his years at Brownsville Junior College, he continued to struggle with this dichotomy as he explored and expanded his knowledge. He reveled in his studies of the English writers of the eighteenth and nineteenth centuries, but he had also at last found the Spanish classics. He won an award for his essay on Miguel Cervantes de Saavedra, author of the classic *Don Quijote*. He polished his writing as a reporter and proofreader for the *Brownsville Herald* and published his Spanish poetry in Matamoros and in San Antonio's *La Prensa*.

In 1937, writing his poetry almost exclusively in Spanish now, he collected his poems and published them as *Cantos de adolescencia* in San Antonio. The small book was an instant success. The collection won him acclaim from businessmen and writers from both sides of the border. He was honored in Matamoros at a literary banquet as "El joven bardo" and received a letter of congratulations from the well-known Texas historian Carlos E. Castañeda, who predicted he would "obtain the success he deserves and will vindicate the reputation of his people."[11] He was soon corresponding with the members of the Lower Rio Grande Writers Circle, almost all Mexican Americans, who exchanged poetry, discussed philosophy, and shared the problems of living among Anglo Americans. He hoped to publish more of his poetry, but it would be almost thirty years before he finally collected his work into *Between Two Worlds* (1991).

During this time, twenty-two-year-old Paredes wrote his heartfelt first and only novel, *George Washington Gómez.* Although not autobiographical, Paredes used his experiences and his profound knowledge of the border to write a story that traces the life of a young Mexican American boy growing up in Brownsville in the 1920s and 1930s. His father gives him the name George Washington and has high hopes for his son's future as a leader of his people (much like Don Justo's hopes for Américo). Young Guálinto—the Mexican grandmother's mispronunciation of Washington—is raised by his uncle and educated by his mother when his father is killed by the Texas Rangers during the "border troubles" of 1915–1917. With deep insight, sympathy, and a wry humor, Paredes describes the challenges faced by the young boy as he struggles to understand the cultural conflicts in his border society, even as he succeeds brilliantly in the segregated school system thanks to the early training in Spanish he received from his mother, a direct reference to his own experiences at home.

Although Paredes tried to publish his novel at the time, he encountered only rejection, perhaps in part because of its bitingly honest portrayal of the racist Anglo American world of the Valley. He put the manuscript away for more than thirty years and unearthed it some fourteen years after his retirement. It would finally be published in 1990, near the end of his life, at which time Paredes had added a bitter last few chapters in which Guálinto, now an Americanized George W. Gómez, returns to the Valley during World War II, not as a leader but to spy on his own people as part of his job in counterintelligence for the U.S. military.

By the end of 1938, perhaps because of his failure to find acceptance for his novel and his growing fear that life was passing him by and that he would not be able to attend the University of Texas, Paredes entered a period of deep depression that he expressed in a series of notes that are preserved among his papers. Throughout his life, he had faithfully kept a record of his thoughts and ideas on scraps of paper, but he found that he did not have the time to develop them fully. His frustration, with which any writer or artist can empathize, is best described in his own words:

> How I would like to sit down with these that still breathe life, and with the zeal of a doctor beside his dying patient, of the husbandman before a broken plant, nurse them slowly back to life—expanding, enlarging, perfecting, until they are what I first intended them to be. It is this that makes me grieve. It is this that gives me a desperate feeling of futility and emptiness. For I know that I cannot revive them, that I cannot give to these dying thoughts the

growth that will make them live. I am too occupied in other things, the result of which is the adding of more scraps of paper, more scraps of thought, in the pile that is covering me slowly.

For it has not been enough that my self be bifurcated by two languages and two cultures, but that I must divide my energies into so many pursuits that I can master none. . . . And the seconds tick away into hours, the hours into years. Time glides by like a fox, scarcely seeming to move, yet traveling at a lightning pace. And I am standing still. Each minute throws a silk-like thread around me, tying me down more firmly to the place where, Gulliver-like, I sprawl. It is futile that I strain at my bonds, so tenuous and yet so strong. It is useless to fret against the inevitable.

But I do. I know that these scraps must die with me because I shall never have time to give them autonomous life. For I cannot withhold the march of time. I cannot live forever. I know that every moment I am living I am also dying. I know that I shall pass from the world as passes a boat over the waters, scarcely stirring the waves by its passing.

And these thoughts do but hasten my end.[12]

The depression in these thoughts remained with him, but like many frustrated artists, he continued to write poetry, sing the *corridos* of the border, and play the guitar, entering the boisterous bohemian world of the bars and *cantinas* just as his father had feared. In 1939, during one of his jobs as a disc jockey for the local Mexican American radio station, he invited Consuelo Silva, an up-and-coming young seventeen-year-old singer, to appear on the show. The twenty-four-year-old Paredes became enamored of the beautiful young singer, better known by her nickname "Chelo," and they were married within the year. Chelo gave birth to their only child, Américo Paredes Jr., in 1940. The couple became well known as they sang together throughout South Texas, but sometime during the next year, Paredes was forced to give up the road life. He hints at legal problems ("primero tuve mi lío con la ley") that may have cost him all the money he had.[13] By the end of 1941, he had found a job with Pan American Airways in Brownsville as his marriage fell apart. The couple were divorced, and Chelo Silva took the baby, Américo Junior, with her and went on to have a brilliant international singing career, which included several major hits when she signed with Columbia Records.

In 1944, as World War II was winding down, Américo Paredes at last enlisted, perhaps influenced by his two younger brothers who had both joined the army. Just as the war ended, he was sent to the Pacific Theater where his writing skills stood him in good stead during the U.S. occupation of Japan. He was assigned to edit and write the army's *Stars and Stripes* and later the *Armed Forces* magazine. He covered the Japanese war crimes trials and wrote for other army publications, later joining the Red Cross in its public relations department. He also began to send a weekly column to *El Universal*, a newspaper in Mexico City, and published a scholarly article titled "The Mexico-Texan *Corrido*" in the *Southwest Review*.

Paredes was particularly interested in the cultural conflict between the Japanese and the U.S. Army and felt a deep compassion for the defeated Japanese. Moved by what he had seen, he expressed his feelings in several painfully poignant and tender short stories, as well as two rollicking and witty tales about army life in Japan that he later added to a growing collection of stories published late in life as *The Hammon and the Beans* (1994).

In the army Paredes found a number of friends who shared his ideas, in particular a German American named Horst Maximilian Albert de la Croix. Paredes and Horst de la Croix both shared writing assignments in the Far East, and both would marry Japanese women and eventually become university professors, Paredes in Texas and de la Croix in California. They continued their friendship and their correspondence for the next thirty years. De la Croix teased Paredes about "propagandizing his people,"[14] but the two men understood the difficulty of life in a prejudiced society. They also shared the challenge of finding women to date in the very small world of the U.S. military occupation forces. As a major assigned to the Red Cross in Korea, Paredes complained to de la Croix that a young woman of his acquaintance had "told me she had been briefed by you bastards about me before she came."[15]

On October 13, 1947, while in Tokyo, Paredes was introduced to a young woman who, to his surprise, spoke Spanish. Amelia Sidzu Nagamine was the daughter of Naoya Honda Nagamine, a Japanese diplomat who had lived in Argentina, and his wife, María Julia Sidzu, an Uruguayan. Amelia and her younger brother had been born and raised in Latin America, and the family had returned to Japan just prior to the outbreak of hostilities between the United States and Japan. They suffered from a lack of food and supplies throughout the war, and then, after 1946, they faced racism from the Americans during the occupation. Amelia had married Paul, an American GI whose last name she did not mention and who left his young bride behind when he was transferred after less than a year of marriage.

Paredes, aware that he was dating a married woman, could not stop his growing affection and, ultimately, overwhelming love. In a letter reminding Amelia of their first meeting, he reminded her that when he had taken her out on October 22, neither had been seriously interested in a relationship. Two weeks later, however, after their first kiss, he "accepted he loved her," regardless of her married state.[16] He had known Amelia, whom he called "Nena," for only two months when he, like the absent husband Paul, was transferred to China and then back to Korea.

In December of 1947 he wrote to Amelia and admitted to having taken a picture of her with him. "Llevo esta foto conmigo como lleva un ladrón una joya robada. Y en esta, mi noche triste, la contemplo a solas. A solas y escondido, ya que nuestro amor es furtivo y avergonzado. Yo no lo quisiera así."[17] (I carry this picture with me like a thief carrying a stolen jewel. And in this, my sad night, I gaze on it alone. Alone and hidden away, since our love is furtive and shameful. I would not have it that way.)

He received her letter by return mail, in which she warns him that they must be careful. "Los dos tenemos una equivocación en nuestras vidas, así que esta vez tenemos que estar bien seguros que lo que sientes por mi no es una pasión repentina y pasadera. Piensa bien que vamos a tener que esperar mucho tiempo y que vas a necesitar mucha paciencia."[18] (We both have mistakes in our lives, so this time we need to be very sure that what you feel for me is not a passing fancy. Think hard about the fact that we are going to have to wait a long time and that you will have to have a great deal of patience.) She then concludes by admitting, "Y ahora te voy a decir un secreto muy grande—estoy enamorada de un pochito de ojos verdes y lo extraño muchísimo."[19] (And now I am going to tell you a very big secret—I am in love with a *pochito* [Mexican American] with green eyes and I miss him very much.) She still worried about being seen with him in public and had a difficult time showing her sentiments when they were together at parties.

During the following months, their romance progressed only through correspondence, letters that Paredes preserved among his papers. In January of 1948 Paredes received news that his father had passed away and that his mother was ill, so he flew back to the United States, landing in San Antonio, where he hired a private plane to reach Brownsville. The family, amid the sorrow of the funeral, celebrated being back together. The burial took place not in Brownsville, but on the Mexican side of the border in Matamoros. The five brothers, Eliseo (forty-eight), Lorenzo (forty-four), Américo (thirty-two), and the twins Amador and Eleazar (twenty-eight), together for the first time in almost ten years, shared their experiences and reveled in reuniting with their extended family and dozens of old friends. Américo admitted to Eliseo, who had taken the place of their father, that he had plans to marry Amelia. When Américo told his mother, he reported that she was pleased that Amelia was Catholic, although Américo himself had followed in his father's anticlerical beliefs. At least Américo had found a Spanish-speaking wife.[20]

When Paredes returned to Tokyo in March of 1948, Nena and Américo had a brief reunion before he returned to Korea for two months. Amelia had worked with a local priest and a lawyer to complete the annulment proceedings from her first marriage as they discussed their own future plans. Américo still wanted to become an English professor, and Amelia supported him in this hope. He had sworn he would never return to the racism and bigotry of Texas, but if he wanted to continue his studies at the University of Texas, they would have to move to Austin. He worried about their finances, and she insisted that she would get a job to support him.

The major problem for the young couple, however, was the opposition by President Truman to Japanese wives entering the United States. In 1949 and 1950, laws against war brides were slowly changing as the United States grudgingly gave up its prejudice against the foreigners. Amelia suggested that she enter as a student or as an Uruguayan, for which there was no quota. Other problems cropped up. Amelia's father was ill and needed someone to care for him. Her mother hated being in Japan and wanted to return to Uruguay. Paredes, discharged from the military after being recalled from Korea in 1948, would not leave Amelia and Japan. He accepted a job as the editor for a small weekly army journal in Tokyo.

At last, however, in May of 1948 Horst de la Croix received a letter:

> Hey Horst,
> You bareheaded bastard, how about getting back here as quick as you can, at least by the 26th of this month. This, if you haven't figured it out, is a wedding announcement. We went to the consulate this morning, and we are set to get married 28 May, not 28 June. This change was due to circumstances beyond our control . . . and it's not what you think either, you dirty-minded bum. We wrote you down as a witness and need your date and place of birth.
> You unsociable son of a bitch,
> Yours breathlessly, A[21]

The marriage, with Horst in attendance, took place in Tokyo on May 26, 1948. The happy couple spent a week at an army-leave hotel in Tokyo for their honeymoon at a rate of $2.50 a day, something that the money-conscious young groom noted. For the next two years Américo and Amelia remained in Japan while she cared for her parents and he continued his job as editor of the magazine. The job gave him time to enroll in the U.S. Armed Forces College, better known to the soldiers as Tokyo College, where he continued work toward his degree in English and American literature. By 1950, Amelia, fully supporting her husband's desire to become an English professor, agreed to return to Texas where Paredes could complete his bachelor's degree in English. The couple had to obtain a temporary visa for Amelia and spend six months in Matamoros with Américo's brother Lorenzo. By September, Amelia had at last received permanent residency status, and they finally moved to Austin.

In August of 1950 Horst de la Croix wrote with considerable concern over the return to Texas:

> I was glad . . . that you like it back home. Wait a minute, am I really? By God, when I read the first part of your letter over again, I had the uneasy feeling that it might take very little to get you back into the same old rut from which the Army forcibly uprooted you back in 1944–45. This business of the "roots from which one sprang" is all very well and good, if you realize that separatism, race-hatred, prejudice, nationalism and many other forms of ignorance are springing from those very same roots. Only individuals who sever themselves from those roots . . . can lay claim to being fully alive.[22]

Paredes, however, was very much alive, back amid the segregation and racism of Texas. The prejudice irritated him, since there were still segregated barbershops, restaurants, and stores in Austin, but he was determined to correct the stereotypes about his people. He worried constantly about finances, about the demands of his new family, about the success of the University of Texas football team, and about the pressure of his studies. He listed his capital and his *gastos* (expenses) in April of 1949. He had left $2,000 with his eldest brother Eliseo, he had $310 in the bank, he would receive $1,580 from the GI Bill for schooling, and he had $1,200 in savings for a total of $2,050, which he believed would allow him to cover the expenses for two semesters and two summer sessions in Austin.

Money would remain an ongoing worry, but he discovered he could make money by entering his short stories in contests. He won first place ($500 worth of books) in the *Dallas Times Herald*'s short story competition for "Border Country," and $500 cash for his book *The Shadow* from the D. A. Frank writing contest.[23] What mattered most, however, was that he was back in the field he loved, and for the first time in fifteen years, he felt that achieving his dream of a doctorate was a very real possibility.

During his first year at the University of Texas, Paredes focused on his schoolwork, leaving the household chores to Amelia. He was able to transfer many of his credits from Brownsville Junior College and Tokyo College, and completed his bachelor's degree in English within one year, graduating with highest honors. His professors encouraged him to continue for the master's degree and eventually the doctorate. Continuing would be difficult because Amelia had given birth to their first son, Alan, born July 13, 1951. As part of the master's program, Paredes received income from teaching assistantships in the English department to help defray the expenses of the new baby.

In the field of folklore, rather than English, Paredes found an ideal niche for his studies of the Mexican Americans and the cultural conflict of the border. Although Anglo American folklorists such as John Lomax and J. Frank Dobie studied Mexican folklore and presented papers and published articles through the Texas Folklore Society, their views of both the Mexicans and Mexican Americans were condescending in the extreme. Their "folk" subjects were always illiterate and docile, usually cruel and cowardly, and often silly or superstitious. The attitudes of these folklorists infuriated Paredes, who dedicated himself to using scientific studies to change the negative stereotypes. With the *corridos* he focused on the successful resilience of the Tejanos and Mexican Americans who had defied the *rinches* (Texas Rangers) and found ways to retain their culture and survive within the oppressive border society. He spent his life "countering the negative attitudes and prejudicial views toward the Mexican American people and offering what he considered to be a more objective assessment of the matter, . . . celebrat[ing] the spirit, wisdom and dignity of his people."[24]

As a master's candidate, he found two professors who became major influences in encouraging his study of balladry as folklore. Dr. Robert Stephenson, a professor of both English and Spanish who also taught folklore, was particularly interested in Paredes's ideas about the performance of the *corridos*. The other professor who influenced him was Dr. Stith Thompson, an internationally renowned visiting scholar in the field of folklore who encouraged the determined new scholar and joined Paredes's dissertation committee.

By 1953 Paredes had graduated from the master's program, having published "The Love Tragedy in Texas-Mexican Balladry," which appeared in *Folk Travelers: Ballads, Tales, and Talk*, edited by Mody C. Boatright, the chairman of the English department. He moved immediately into the doctoral program and completed his course work in 1955. On January 9, 1955, Amelia gave birth to their second son, Vicente. Américo, in the middle of research for his dissertation, had received a grant to go to the border and into Mexico to collect stories that summer. He felt he had no choice but to accept, and he left Amelia to care for the two babies while he began the arduous task of finding Gregorio Cortez *corridos*. Writing the dissertation, titled "El Corrido de Gregorio Cortez, a Ballad of Border Conflict," took up the better part of the next year, and with the support of Stephenson and Thompson, Paredes received his Ph.D. from the University of Texas in May of 1956. A shortened version of the dissertation appeared as "The Legend of Gregorio Cortez" in Boatright's *Mesquite and Willow* the following year.

Paredes had hoped to stay on at the University of Texas as one of the faculty, and there had evidently been some indications that he would be made an assistant professor. The university, however, refused to keep him on, maintaining that it would be detrimental to the institution to hire its own graduates, although his letters to friends at the time indicate that he believed there was racism involved in the decision. He was offered a position in the English department at Texas Western University in El Paso for 1957–1958 as an instructor for nine months at $4,400. He was furious when he learned that all the other new

Ph.D.'s in his department had been offered assistant professorships at $4,800. To compound the insult, the chairman recommended he take a year's leave for the 1958–1959 school year and passed him over for a promotion. Paredes seriously considered leaving the field of academia.

With the time off, however, Paredes was able to rewrite the dissertation into a book, published in 1958 by the University of Texas Press as *"With His Pistol in His Hand": A Border Ballad and Its Hero*. In the very first chapter he took the renowned Texas historian Walter Prescott Webb to task for his racist views of the Mexicans. In his *Texas Rangers*, Webb had stated, "Without disparagement, it may be said that there is a cruel streak in the Mexican nature," along with a string of more disparaging remarks.[25] Paredes, with a healthy dose of sarcasm, countered with "One wonders what his [Webb's] opinion might have been when he was in a less scholarly mood and not looking at the Mexican from the objective point of view of the historian."[26] In the same chapter he spent almost a dozen pages describing the atrocities committed by the Texas Rangers in the years from 1859 (and the Cortina wars) to 1915–1917 (and the revolts of the *sediciosos*).

For a newly minted, wet-behind-the-ears Ph.D. to suggest feet of clay for the great Walter P. Webb and the Texas Rangers sent a ripple of shock through the intellectual community at the University of Texas and throughout Texas. Webb had been a professor in the history department at the University of Texas for twenty-six years, from 1931 until 1957. He had, admittedly, failed to receive his Ph.D. from the University of Chicago in 1931, but was granted his degree by the University of Texas the following year for his book *The Great Plains*, which received national acclaim from historians and social scientists. Webb had gone on to become one of the best known of Texas scholars and a jewel in the crown of the University of Texas. Paredes did not hesitate to take on the glorified professor emeritus, who would pass away in 1963.

Paredes also tore into the Texas Rangers and attacked Webb's book on the Texas Rangers. With undisguised contempt, he pointed out the fallacies, lies, and deceptions and suggested that the Rangers had "created in the Border Mexican a deep and understandable hostility for American authority . . . [and] added to the roll of bandits and raiders many high-spirited individuals who would have otherwise remained peaceful and useful citizens."[27] He accused the Rangers of cowardice, terror, murder, and the habit of "shooting first and asking questions afterward."[28] His attack on the Rangers struck at the heart of Texan folklore and gained him the enmity of many at the University of Texas.

Perhaps understandably, the University of Texas Press initially hesitated to publish the manuscript and sent Paredes a "number of revisions."[29] With the intervention of Dr. Stith Thompson, however, the Press published the book, although the university refused to hold a book signing, as was traditional for other authors when their works were published, and one retired Ranger is said to have come to the Press asking for the author's address and threatening to shoot Paredes.

With this galling reminder of the racism still rampant at the University of Texas, Paredes wrote to his friend at El Paso, Jerry Langford, about "inquiring about a government job as a cultural affairs officer abroad."[30] Langford counseled against leaving teaching, especially since the university at El Paso had a "definite wish to bring you back, ya know!"[31] By the spring of 1958, Dr. Stephenson, his mentor and friend, had decided to retire from the University of Texas, leaving open a position as folklorist. The head of the English department, Mody Boatright, sent Paredes a card indicating that Texas was low on oil money but that the university would be willing to hire Paredes as one of two Ph.D.'s hired at the lower rank of instructor, although "we can't promise raises or promotions."[32] Evidently, Paredes, incensed at the demeaning offer, refused to accept. After some negotiating and perhaps some interference from his supporters in the field of folklore, he was finally hired as a tenure-track assistant professor. He would teach Stephenson's two folklore classes, a senior course on ballads, another senior course on folktales, and two classes of short-story writing, as well as still find the time for a Folklore Archive project.[33] He and Amelia used the GI Bill to buy a house in Austin for $13,000, and the couple settled in at the University of Texas, where he would remain for the next twenty-six years (as long as Webb) until his retirement in 1984.

Once installed in the English department, Paredes began at once to publish on Mexican folklore. In 1958 he published articles titled "El Corrido de José Mosqueda" and "The Mexican Corrido: Its Rise and Fall." He also became involved in the creation of the Folklore Archive at the University of Texas, which he oversaw, and met other Mexican Texans on the campus, including the outspoken "maverick and non-conformist" George Sánchez, who chaired the Department of History and Philosophy of Education. Paredes, in a tribute written in 1971, suggested that Sánchez enjoyed being the "thorn in the side of those who favored the academic status quo" and making his academic colleagues "extremely uncomfortable by saying exactly what he thought."[34] Paredes learned much from Sánchez about teaching courses in Mexican American studies, and the two men made common cause in the face of the often blatant racism. He recalled that when he visited with Sánchez in his last days, his colleague's final advice to him was "Give them hell!"[35] And he did.

In 1959 personal affairs intervened. Clotilde Manzano Vidal, Américo's mother, passed away in Brownsville. As he had after his father's death, Américo grieved deeply, but it was a chance for the family to gather once again and share their experiences. The family was pleased and proud of Américo's successes, and it was at this time that he became acquainted with his two nieces, Patti Padron and Odilia Galván Rodríguez, with whom he continued to correspond the rest of his life.

In August, after their return from the Valley, Amelia was involved in an automobile accident in Austin. She was pregnant with their third child and had Vicente, their second son, in the car with her. Both Amelia and Américo did not want to "make the driver of the other car liable for any medical expenses."[36] Amelia was checked at the hospital, but there seemed to be no injuries. The couple just hoped that the other driver would pay for the damages to the car, which he did, perhaps to their surprise. The following year, however, when their baby daughter, Julie, was born, it became apparent that there had been injury to the little girl.

By the time the baby was twenty-two months old, she was diagnosed with schizophrenia at the state institution in Austin. The couple took it hard and blamed themselves for the baby's problems. They spent hours trying to get the baby to respond, but with no success. Amelia would spend the rest of her life working in support of agencies to help children like Julie, although there was nothing they were ever able to do to help the little girl, who was eventually institutionalized in Austin.

Paredes, meanwhile, was not happy at the University of Texas. His book had irritated the establishment and resulted in bitterness and discord with his colleagues in the English department. He continued his work in folklore, producing the articles "Folklore and History" and the "Folklore Bibliography for 1960." His biting wit also became evident in his semihumorous article "On Gringo, Greaser, and Other Neighborly Names," in which he once again exposed the racism in Texas.

During the summer of 1961, he was offered a position as associate professor with a $1,000 raise at the University of West Virginia in Morgantown. He left Amelia in Austin to try out the position for the summer but returned in the fall, having decided to stay on at the University of Texas. Since he disliked the atmosphere at the university, he spent much of the next few years doing research away from campus as a Fulbright scholar in Barcelona, Spain. The couple bought a new four-bedroom house in northwest Austin and continued to "try to do something about our little girl."[37]

Amelia's brother, Hideo, wrote in January of 1962 from South America where he was caring for their mother in Uruguay. Hideo asked if it would be possible for Julia Nagamine to be with Amelia and the family in the United States. Amelia, concerned over the growing problems with Julie, had hidden the letter and not told Américo about her brother's request. Américo, unaware of the problem, received a Guggenheim to study in Mexico and South Texas, New Mexico, and California for the fall of 1962 and the spring of 1963. At Amelia's insistence, he once again left her alone with the children and went to Mexico to carry out his fieldwork collecting jokes and stories about North Americans.[38]

The trip proved particularly fruitful, although he reported that "collecting is more work than people think."[39] Paredes soon realized that he could either stay in Mexico for four or five years collecting a few jokes a week, or he could "establish contacts to get the feel of the place and then correspond with people while I do library research in Austin."[40] He began making contacts but found that many of the Mexican scholars working in fields related to his were particularly jealous of their work. "These scholars," he said, "fear and mistrust each other so that each one hugs his little findings to his bosom for fear someone will steal them."[41] Although the scholars and other contacts whom he met were nice, they "bought me dinner and then forgot about me."[42] He did, however, find two Americans who proved to be of the "Horst de la Croix type, open, frank, and cooperative."[43] Joseph Hellmer, the folklore collector for Bellas Artes, the cultural center in Mexico City, and Thomas Stanford, the archivist for the Muséo Nacional de Antropología, both of whom had married Mexican wives, became fast friends and provided him with the kind of material he needed.

The following year Américo was on the road again. While he presented papers in Ann Arbor, Michigan, and at the Kinsey Institute at Indiana University, Amelia took Julie to Chicago to determine what could be done to help their daughter. The prognosis was not good, and Amelia returned to Austin deeply distressed. When another letter came from her brother in Paraguay asking about bringing her mother to Austin, this time she shared the request with Américo. The couple realized that having her mother with them would considerably ease the burden for Amelia as Américo became more involved in international conferences and foreign travel.

In April of 1964 Amelia's mother arrived from Paraguay to join the family. The boys, who were not used to dealing with older people since the death of Américo's mother in 1959, were pleased with the new addition. Américo, grateful to have his mother-in-law to help with Julie, accepted the offer of a Fulbright to spend the summer in Barcelona, Spain, and to attend a conference in Argentina. Amelia, meanwhile, continued to carry on his correspondence, read and answer letters, and type his diary while complaining about "Alan at his worst, Tito his usual self, and Julie wouldn't walk."[44]

In spite of the family problems and the increasing number of international conferences, Paredes continued to write. In Argentina he presented "Folk Medicine and the Intercultural Jest," and published such articles as "The Ancestry of Mexico's Corridos: A Matter of Definitions" and "El cowboy norteamericano en el folklore y la literatura"; he also published "Texas' Third Man: The Texas-Mexican" in *Race: The Journal of the Institute of Race Relations,* among other articles, as well as *Folklore Bibliography* for 1961, 1962, and 1963. In 1965 he wrote "Vicente T. Mendoza, 1894–1964," published in the *Journal of American Folklore*. The following year, he joined George Foss in publishing the results of his trip to Mexico in "The Anglo-American in Mexican Folklore." In 1966 he wrote and published "The Décima on the Texas-Mexican Border" and, again with George Foss, "The Décima Cantada on the Texas-Mexican Border." His publications, although they continued to be very abrasive to the mainstream at the University of Texas, began winning him attention and prizes.

During the spring of 1967, Paredes's growing fame led to an invitation from the University of California at Berkeley to come out to teach for a summer in California. While there, he had a chance to visit with his old friend Horst de la Croix, a reunion that both men enjoyed immensely. He taught classes for the department of anthropology, although he reported that his high standards and strict rigor, and the demands he placed on the students, were more than they were used to. As opposition to the war in Vietnam escalated and the civil rights movement exploded, Paredes reported witnessing two demonstrations on the campus, although he himself did not take part.[45]

Perhaps influenced by his time in California, Paredes took a half-time appointment in the anthropology department at the University of Texas and became determined to take on the Old Guard, this time in the form of Mody C. Boatright, the chairman of the English department. Folklore and the Texas Folklore Society had been a very small part of the English department at the University of Texas. With Richard Bauman and Roger D. Abrahams, Paredes worked to establish folklore as its own field. By 1967, Paredes had succeeded in creating the Center for Intercultural Studies in Folklore and Oral History, for which he served as director for the next three years.

By 1969, as activism on campuses across the country reached a crescendo, he joined George Sánchez and the students petitioning for a Mexican American studies program. By January of 1972, the program faced opposition by the administration at the university, which had been perfectly content with an ethnic studies major that was mediocre at best. Sánchez and Paredes wrote eloquent letters in support of a strong program, and when Sánchez passed away that year, Paredes and the students established one of the top ethnic studies centers in the country in his honor.[46]

Paredes was deeply influenced by the death of his mentor and colleague. In a retrospective collection of articles completed in 1977 about George Sánchez, or, more respectfully, Jorge Isidoro Sánchez y Sanchez, Paredes looked back at the difficulties faced by those who had fought for the rights of the Chicanos. He caustically quotes Edward Simmen, who reported, "That lazy bandido sleeping beneath the big sombrero in the shade of the adobe hut has suddenly awakened."[47] Paredes pointed out that men such as George Sánchez proved that the

Mexican had not been asleep but that the WASP majority had at last awakened to the realization of the racism inherent in the culture. He worried that the reaction against the activism of the 1960s was setting in during the 1970s and that "we may be entering again into times when we will be able to inch forward toward our goals only at the cost of great effort and much frustration. In such times we will need men patterned after Jorge Isidoro Sánchez y Sanchez."[48] Paredes, perhaps intentionally, took on the role left by his friend.

Paredes may not have been an activist, but his words inspired a whole generation of young Chicano scholars as he published dozens of articles expressing his opposition to the overt racism he found everywhere. José A. Limón would later argue that Paredes helped form the Chicano movement when young Mexican Americans adopted his book *"With His Pistol in His Hand"* as their inspiration for a new "socio-educational reality."[49]

A favorite topic was the concept of "machismo," which Paredes described in "Estados Unidos, Mexico y el machismo," which first appeared in the *Journal of Inter-American Studies* and was translated by Marcy Steen for the *Journal of the Folklore Institute* three years later. He explored the concept by suggesting that it was much more than just a Mexican stereotype, but a universal manifestation, found among many peoples, including the Anglo Westerner, the frontier Mexicans, the inner-city blacks, the Eskimos, and others. He suggested there were two kinds of machismo, one exemplified by the authentic honest hero and the other by the false braggart covering up an inferiority complex. He again took on the mighty Walter Prescott Webb and exposed him for his racist stereotypes. Paredes adeptly proved that machismo is a product of a frontier in which men, whether Mexican or American, must battle for survival and display true courage. Only after the frontier ends does machismo decline into false braggadocio. He pointed out that the machismo adopted by the Chicano bully is not a Mexican concept but one foisted on young Chicanos by social scientists who have exaggerated the term and applied it to Mexicans as a stereotype. True machismo is "simply courage of a high order and has been admired by many peoples in many ages."[50]

With the success of the Mexican American Studies Program, for which he became director in 1970, Paredes became a cult hero for young Mexican Americans. He had published "Folk Medicine and the Intercultural Jest" two years earlier, in which he once again skewered the social scientists who were oblivious to the nuances of the jokes that were being played on them as they collected stories along the border, stories that they used to continue to stereotype the Mexicans. In 1969, "Tributaries to the Mainstream: The Ethnic Groups" and "Concepts about Folklore in Latin America and the United States" followed the same theme and continued to expose the fallacies of the stereotypes applied to the Mexican people by social scientists. Not all his articles attacked social scientists, however. In 1970 he published a preface to *Bibliografía del folklore chileno* and "Las miniaturas en el arte popular mexicano" as well as an article titled "Proverbs and Ethnic Stereotypes." The following year he published "Folklore e historia—Dos cantares de la frontera del Norte" and the foreword to *The Concept of Folklore*. With his colleague Raymund Paredes he edited a book on Mexican American authors, and with Richard Bauman the article "Toward New Perspectives in Folklore."[51]

By the end of the 1970s, Paredes had become well known both on and off campus. His major work—*"With His Pistol in His Hand"*—had found an audience among the restive Chicano minority to whom he became an iconic hero, much to his own amusement. He had also become a popular teacher on the University of Texas campus, a director for the Mexican American Studies Program, and a leader in the field of folklore. Influenced by his participation in 1966 at the Thirty-Seventh International Congress of Americanists in Argentina, Paredes recognized the many changes he had seen over the years in the field of folklore. In 1972 he and Richard Bauman brought together a group of articles representing "a summation of past achievements, surveying present orientations, and attempting to define new perspectives." Paredes showed that there had been a major shift in the field, a "reorientation from traditional focus upon folklore as an 'item'—the things of folklore—to a conceptualization of folklore as 'event'—the doing of folklore."[52] His 1973 article, "José Mosqueda and the Folklorization of Actual Events," explored the same theme, as did his speeches and articles during the remainder of the decade, in particular the 1976 article "The Role of Folklore in Border Relations" and *A Texas-Mexican Cancionero—Folksongs of the Lower Border*. In 1978 he published "El Romance de la Isla de Jauja en el suroeste de Estados Unidos" and "The Problem of Identity in a Changing Culture: Popular Expressions of Culture Conflict along the Lower Rio Grande Border," which he followed up the following year with "The Folk Base of Chicano Literature."

By the 1980s, the sixty-five-year-old had begun to consider retirement. Always gracious, dignified, and witty, now carrying the honorific of Don Américo, he continued to meet with his students and to inspire many of them to distinguished careers. After articles on folklore, "Lo Mexicano" and "Proverbs in Aztlán," which came out in 1982, and articles the following year titled "The Corrido: Yesterday and Today" and "Nearby Places and Strange-Sounding Names," Paredes at last retired from the University of Texas in 1984. He continued to visit the campus weekly to meet with students and friends. With time to spare, he finally returned to the writings of his boyhood. He published "The Undying Love of 'El Indio' Córdova: Décimas and Oral History in a Border Family"; he at long last published his 1955 novel, *George Washington Gómez: A Mexicotexan Novel*, in 1990, as well as *The Shadow*, his collections of early poetry, and in 1991, *Between Two Worlds*. In 1993 he wrote "Folklore and Culture on the Texas-Mexican Border" and published two witty and entertaining books, *Uncle Remus con Chile* and a collection of short stories, *The Hammon and the Beans and Other Stories*. His final works, published posthumously in 1998 and 1999, "Mi Tia Pilar—Reflexiones" and "Mr. White," closed a career that had spanned more than seven decades and had included hundreds of articles, books, and manuscripts defending and supporting Mexican Americans.

By the 1990s, he had at last begun to receive the praise and honors that he had earned during his career as an academic. His caustic wit did not abate, however. In his acceptance speech for the Aguila Azteca, Mexico's highest honor for foreigners, he excoriated the American society for its racism and denigration of all things Mexican. He received the Charles Frankel Prize from the National Endowment for the Humanities as well as honors from the American Folklore Society, the North American Academy of the Spanish Language, the Sociedad Folklorica de Mexico, and the Western Literature Association. An endowed professorship in folklore was established in his honor at the University of Texas, and a lecture series was named for him, as well as an Austin middle school.

Américo Paredes passed away on May 5, 1999, followed soon thereafter by the death of his beloved wife Amelia. He left a legacy that inspired hundreds of students and thousands who read his works. Although he always maintained a calm and gentlemanly demeanor, he never failed to express his anger at the racism and mistreatment of Mexican Americans through his wit and sarcasm. As Richard Bauman wrote, "We who lack his magnificence of talent and spirit can best honor his memory . . . by schooling ourselves . . . in the willingness to listen, to hear the voices that sang through him . . . from anywhere in the world that people stand up for their right to live in freedom and dignity."[53]

SUGGESTED READING

Paredes, Américo. *Between Two Worlds*. Houston: Arte Publico, 1991.

A collection of poems written during the 1930s and 1940s, many of which were published in newspapers of the era by the author.

Paredes, Américo. *Folktales of Mexico*. Chicago, University of Chicago Press [1970].

Paredes collected and published this unique collection of stories whose origins lie in oral history and that make use of legend, dance, and ritual.

Paredes, Américo. *George Washington Gómez: A Mexicotexan Novel*. Houston: Arte Publico, 1990.

First published in the 1930s, this novel depicts the struggles of the Mexican Americans who fought against the corruption and racism of the Texas Rangers and Anglo immigrants to the Rio Grande Valley.

CAROLINA CASTILLO CRIMM

Paredes, Américo, ed. *Humanidad: Essays in Honor of George I. Sánchez.* Monograph 6. Los Angeles: Chicano Studies Center Publications, University of California, Los Angeles, 1977.

In this publication, Paredes suggested that his friend and colleague George Sánchez enjoyed being the "thorn in the side of those who favored the academic status quo" at the University of Texas at Austin.

Paredes, Américo. *A Texas-Mexican Cancionero: Folksongs of the Lower Border.* 1976; repr., Austin: University of Texas Press, 1995.

The folksongs of Texas's Mexican population tell of the lives of folk heroes, gringos, smugglers, generals, jailbirds, and beautiful women. In his cancionero, or songbook, Américo Paredes presents sixty-six of these songs in bilingual text—along with their music, notes on tempo and performance, and a discography.

Paredes, Américo. *"With His Pistol in His Hand": A Border Ballad and Its Hero.* 1958; repr., Austin: University of Texas Press, 1971.

First published in 1958, this landmark work documented the travails of Gregorio Cortez who was wrongly accused of stealing a horse during the nineteenth century. When first published, the book popularized Cortez among Mexican Americans but created resentment in Anglo communities and among supporters of the Texas Rangers. Paredes revitalized the folk hero and challenged prevailing myths about the superiority and motivations of the Texas Rangers.

Paredes, Américo, and Richard Bauman, eds. *Toward New Perspectives in Folklore.* Publications of the American Folklore Society, Bibliographical and Special Series, vol. 23. Austin: University of Texas Press [1972]; repr., Bloomington: Trickster Press, Indiana University, 2000.

First published by the American Folklore Society, these essays gained immediate recognition among enthusiasts and academics. Since their publication, the volumes have come to be seen by scholars as constituting a watershed study of this genre.

NOTES

1. Américo Paredes, *Cantos de adolescencia: Songs of Youth (1932–1937)*, translated by B. V. Olguín and Omar Vásquez Barbosa (Houston: Arte Publico, 2007), xxxvii.

2. Ibid., xli.

3. Ibid., xxxix.

4. Ibid., xxxvii.

5. Ibid., lix.

6. Víctor J. Guerra, ed., *In Memory of Américo Paredes, 1915–1999* (Austin: Center for Mexican American Studies, University of Texas at Austin, 1999), 65.

7. Américo Paredes to Amelia Nagamine, April 24, 1948, box 1, folder 2, Américo Paredes Papers, 1886–1999, Nettie Lee Benson Latin American Collection, University of Texas at Austin (hereafter BLAC).

8. J. W. Irvine to Américo Paredes, May 14, 1934, box 6, folder 1, BLAC.

9. Paredes to Nagamine, April 24, 1948, box 1, folder 2, BLAC.

10. Paredes, *Cantos de adolescencia*, xxiii.

11. Ibid., xii.

12. Emilio Zamora, "The Américo Paredes Papers," paper presented at "Pasó por Aquí, an Américo Paredes Symposium," May 3–5, 2001, University of Texas at Austin, p. 11, in "Old Notes," box 8, BLAC.

13. Américo Paredes to Amelia Nagamine, April 24, 1948, box 1, folder 2, BLAC.

14. Américo Paredes to Horst de la Croix, December 20, 1946, box 4, folder 3, BLAC.

15. Ibid.

16. Paredes to Nagamine, April 24, 1948.

17. Américo Paredes to Amelia Nagamine, December 2, 1947, box 1, folder 2, BLAC.

18. Nena to Américo Paredes, December 5, 1947, box 1, folder 2, BLAC.

19. Ibid.

20. Paredes to Nagamine, December 2, 1947.

21. Américo Paredes to Horst de la Croix, May 1948, box 4, folder 3, BLAC.

22. Horst de la Croix to Américo Paredes, August 21, 1950, box 4, folder 3, BLAC.

23. José R. Lopez Morín, *The Legacy of Américo Paredes* (College Station: Texas A&M University Press, 2006), 59.

24. Ibid., 21.

25. Walter P. Webb, *The Texas Rangers: A Century of Frontier Defense* (Boston: Houghton Mifflin, 1935), quoted in Américo Paredes, *"With His Pistol in His Hand": A Border Ballad and Its Hero* (1958; repr., Austin: University of Texas Press, 1971), 17.

26. Ibid.

27. Ibid., 32.

28. Ibid., 26.

29. Américo Paredes to Jerry Langford, December 10, 1956, box 3, folder 9, BLAC.

30. Ibid.

31. Ibid.

32. Américo Paredes to Horst de la Croix, April 9, 1958, box 4, folder 4, BLAC.

33. Ibid.

34. Américo Paredes, ed., *Humanidad: Essays in Honor of George I. Sánchez*, Monograph 6 (Los Angeles: Chicano Studies Center Publications, University of California, Los Angeles, 1977), 120.

35. Ibid., 123.

36. Américo Paredes to TDPS, August 17, 1959, box 3, folder 10, BLAC.

37. Américo Paredes to Horst, March 2, 1965, box 4, folder 4, BLAC.

38. Amelia and Américo to Fred and Mary, January 23, 1963, box 3, folder 10, BLAC.

39. Américo Paredes to Gusai (Amelia), November 19, 1962, box 1, folder 5, BLAC.

40. Américo Paredes to Gusai, November 22, 1962, box 1, folder 5, BLAC.

41. Paredes to Gusai, November 19, 1962.

42. Ibid.

43. Ibid.

44. Américo Paredes to Hideo Nagamine, April 21, 1964, box 3, folder 10, BLAC.

45. Américo Paredes to Gusai, February 22, 1967, box 1, folder 8, BLAC.

46. Paredes, ed., *Humanidad*, 66–67.

47. Edward Simmen, ed., *The Chicano: From Caricature to Self-Portrait* (New York, 1971), 15, quoted in Paredes, ed., *Humanidad*, 125.

48. Ibid., 126.

49. José E. Limón, "The Return of the Mexican Ballad: Américo Paredes and His Anthropological Text as Persuasive Political Performance" (Stanford, CA: Stanford Center for Chicano Research, September 1986), 14–17.

---

50. Américo Paredes, "The United States, Mexico, and Machismo," *Journal of the Folklore Institute* 8, no. 1 (June 1971): 17–37; translated by Marcy Steen from "Estados Unidos, México y el Machísmo," *Journal of Inter-American Studies* 9 (January 1967): 65–84; Paredes, ed., *Humanidad*, 124–125.

51. Lopez Morín, *Legacy*.

52. Américo Paredes, foreword to *Toward New Perspectives in Folklore*, edited by Paredes and Richard Bauman, Publications of the American Folklore Society, Bibliographical and Special Series, vol. 23 (Austin: University of Texas Press [1972]; repr., Bloomington: Trickster Press, Indiana University, 2000).

53. Richard Bauman, "Conference Papers," in *En Memoria de Américo Paredes, 1915–1999,"* edited by Victor J. Guerra (Austin: Center for Mexican American Studies, University of Texas at Austin, 1999), 9.

DAVID G. MCCOMB

JOE B. FRANTZ

JOE B. FRANTZ (*CENTER*) ON HONORS DAY, UNIVERSITY OF TEXAS AT AUSTIN, 1957

Joe Frantz began life as an orphan, rose to become the first holder of the Walter Prescott Webb Chair of History and Ideas at the University of Texas at Austin, and ended by being dependent on his fourth wife, Betsy Chadderdon Frantz. He was born in Dallas on January 16, 1917, but his parents shortly after died of influenza, and a helpless grandmother put the baby in a foundlings' home. A brief placement failed, and the Texas Children's Home and Aid Society of Fort Worth (later the Gladney Center) gave shelter to the young child. At sixteen months he was adopted and named Joe Bertram by Ezra and Mary Frantz of Weatherford. As he grew up, he developed a love of music and sports, particularly baseball, while his mother provided a stream of books for her precocious child.

Joe graduated from Weatherford High School, attended Weatherford College for two years, and transferred to the University of Texas to earn a degree in journalism. After graduation he briefly worked for his father and also as a reporter, but he was restless. "I never made up my mind what profession I wanted to pursue, once I made up my mind that I lacked the arm to play centerfield for the St. Louis Cardinals," he later commented.[1] He returned to the university to study history and to write a master's thesis, "The Newspapers of the Republic of Texas" (1940), directed by Eugene C. Barker and William C. Binkly.

World War II intruded, and Frantz worked as archivist and acting director at the San Jacinto Museum of History in Houston before joining the U.S. Navy in 1943. Working mainly for the British as a decoder of U.S. messages to prevent language misunderstandings, he served on three destroyers in the Pacific campaigns. While at Texas Frantz had taken a class from Walter P. Webb about the American frontier, and later he received a letter from Webb that advised him to return to the university and finish a Ph.D. in history after the war was over. The navy discharged Lieutenant (jg) Frantz late in 1945, and he returned to Austin to write a dissertation and begin an academic career.

Under Webb, who became his mentor, colleague, and friend, Frantz wrote a biography and business history of Gail Borden, an eccentric nineteenth-century Galveston real estate manager who invented a method of condensing milk. This dissertation became his first book, *Gail Borden: Dairyman to a Nation* (1951). The biography attracted favorable reviews, won a book award from the Texas Institute of Letters, and established him as a business historian. The volume has remained the standard account of Borden and his company; at Christmastime for years afterward the author received a carton of condensed milk from the company in gratitude. Frantz followed the advice of his mentor to publish also in the popular media in order to reach a greater audience. "By Land and Sea," thus, appeared in *True West*.[2] It was a short article denoting Borden's wacky and unsuccessful invention of a wagon with a sail that could travel on land or water. Frantz continued to publish in newspapers and popular magazines for the rest of his life. His academic tally amounted to seventeen books, sixty articles, eighteen chapters in books, eighteen introductions to books, and countless book reviews scattered in numerous journals.

The University of Texas hired Frantz as a temporary instructor of history in 1949 and shortly after as an assistant professor. He passed rapidly through the ranks—associate professor in 1953, full professor in 1959, and chair of the department from 1959 to 1965. He inherited the mantle of Texas history from Webb, who had received it from his teacher, Eugene C. Barker, and there flowed between the three men an intergenerational generosity toward students that passed as if from father to son. In the 1950s, in order to ensure diversity, the department adopted a policy that excluded tenure-track employment of its own graduates, and so the line was broken. Frantz became the last full-time faculty member in the department whose degrees all came from the University of Texas. He wryly noted in his 1958 presidential address to the American Historical Association, "I am an example of institutional inbreeding which frightens all universities save the two that practice it most, Harvard and Oxford."[3]

Frantz's office on the first floor of Garrison Hall was next door to Webb's office, and the men shared ideas, coffee, and attitudes. Frantz witnessed Webb's delightful late-in-life courtship of Terrell Maverick, and as a close friend at the hospital in 1963 he dutifully and painfully informed Terrell of her husband's death in the rollover car accident that had injured them both. Webb was a giant among the first generation of western historians. He was concerned about the western movement of the American population and the interplay of technology and land on the frontier. He was also concerned about contemporary problems of water and economic sectionalism. Frantz, his student and friend, absorbed much from his mentor and can be considered "Webbian" in his attitude.

Savoie Lottinville, an editor at the University of Oklahoma Press—which published *Gail Borden*—wrote to Frantz in 1954 to suggest a collaboration with Julian E. Choate Jr. Choate had sent the press a manuscript about the image and work of the American cowboy, and although accurate, the manuscript needed to be organized and enlivened. Frantz reworked the material, and it came out as *The American Cowboy: The Myth and the Reality* (1955). *Time* magazine mocked it, but the book gained an enduring place among bibliographies of the American cowboy.[4] The same sort of collaboration occurred with Cordia Sloan Duke, who had collected cowboy memoirs on the XIT Ranch. This came out as *6,000 Miles of Fence: Life on the XIT Ranch of Texas* (1961). Of all Frantz's books on which he is a major author, only this one remains in print. These books established Frantz as a western historian, and he helped to found the Western History Association in 1961.

For Frantz and this generation of western historians, scholars like Eugene Hollon, Ray A. Billington, Herbert E. Bolton, and Rodman W. Paul, the history of the West was basically a story of "settlement" by miners, ranchers, railroad builders, and farmers. They utilized a model of successive western Anglo migration outlined before the turn of the twentieth century by Fredrick Jackson Turner. In a book chapter titled "Taming the West," Frantz followed that model to portray an eventual triumph of Anglo Americans over adversity. "The West is awesome today," he wrote. "What must it have been more than a century ago when it was largely unpeopled, a great void on the nation's map." He did not emphasize, but did not overlook, motives of "greed, revenge, and restlessness." Nor did he ignore the dismal fate of Indians and buffalo, nor the senseless acts of violence, nor the foolishness of George Armstrong Custer, nor the disaster brought by overstocked ranges. The settlement of the West that concluded in 1890 with the fencing of the open range, he thought, had an accidental quality as opportunities for exploitation revealed themselves.[5]

In a 1969 banquet speech to the Western History Association, "Western Impact on the Nation," Frantz was more explicit. "With all of that space, something just has to happen periodically. The West holds a self-renewing lottery ticket. . . . Every time the nation feels that it has closed all its economic frontiers . . . the West throws in a rich lagniappe, so unexpected as to be almost totally intoxicating. . . . When oil is found, it gushes. When silver is mined, it is the Comstock."[6] The importance of the West, for Frantz, was that it reinforced the American dream and gave the nation a faith in unplanned progress. This, he thought, was a mixed blessing—a reliance upon blind hope rather than reason.

Frantz rejected, in addition, the vaunted image of the westerner as independent and self-reliant, a Turner and Webb concept. He commented in a 1963 Phi Alpha Theta luncheon speech, "The truth is that from start to finish he [the westerner] was subsidized from his brogans to his sombrero." That quip pointed to a truth of longstanding, national financial support for the West and was quoted in the *Washington Post*.[7] This brought attention to Frantz, and, consequently, in 1964 Secretary of Interior Stewart Udall appointed him to the advisory board of the national parks. This experience with the board involved Joe with one of the older governmental organizations dealing with conservation. In "The Making of Yellowstone," he reasoned that the creation of Yellowstone National Park, the first of its kind, began a movement to safeguard some of the land out west from exploitation. It represented an effort to cooperate with the environment instead of "demanding its unconditional surrender to our short-tempered and temporary needs and demands."[8] The modern dilemma for the park, he noted, was how to preserve its natural beauty yet still provide access to increasing numbers of tourists.

Frantz, therefore, saw in the history of the American West a vastness that inspired not only exploitation and sanguine expectations, but also human and ecological misery. The West produced wealth, aided by governmental policy, and was a land sought after and captured by American pioneers and investors. Frantz was able to accept the West for better or for worse, and to address modern problems of preservation. Thus, he was "Webbian" with a difference.

A younger set of western history scholars, a third generation, largely inspired by Howard Lamar of Yale University, began to reshape the historiography of the American West in the late 1980s. Led by Patricia N. Limerick, Donald Worster, Richard White, and William Cronon, the new western historians attacked both Turner and Webb as being blindly nationalistic, neglectful of minorities, focused upon a badly defined frontier, and driven by narrow environmental determinism. The new historians emphasized the history of women, Asians, Indians, Hispanics, ethnic Europeans, cities, water, multicultural interactions, and class differences. The frontier became an "f-word" that no one could delimit. The older historians, they thought, were overly optimistic and failed to see the damage caused by western settlement. The younger writers were generally pessimistic and denouncing. They emphasized the harm that had been inflicted upon land and people. Donald Worster referred to the new historians as "clear-eyed, demythologized, and critical" as they advanced their own ideas and attacked their predecessors.[9]

In a cranky introduction to a book on the movement, Gene M. Gressley, one of the older western historians, commented, "The New West historians have not moved on to the field of Agincourt with superior intellectual weapons, but they have demonstrated an impressive array of youthful enthusiasm and energy—some might even say fanaticism. And although the New West agenda is often neither new or original, the emphasis has been adopted by those who run from deconstruction but concede that the topics of the underside West, the environmental West, and the urban West bear examination."[10]

Where does this leave Joe B. Frantz as a historian of the American West? Frantz wrote and spoke about cowboys, ranches, cattle trails, national parks, and Texas. These topics, although not of special interest to the new historians, could be accepted so long as the emphasis was upon business development or environmental change. Frantz did stress the business part but generally looked past the environmental aspect. He also wrote Texas state history that today would probably be ignored or subsumed under the topic of regional political organization.[11] However, he was concerned about image and myth, an acceptable theme, and his worry about preserving wilderness in the parks might ring a resonant note today.[12] He wrote about Webb, but Joe's basic optimism, like that of Webb and Turner, would be rejected by the younger club of historians.[13] Frantz is rarely mentioned in the historiographical commentaries of the new historians. In a comprehensive bibliography, *The American West in the Twentieth Century* (1994), he is cited but seven times, including twice for *The American*

Cowboy. In the bibliographies and articles of *The Oxford History of the American West* (1994), his name is not mentioned. The revisionists successfully moved western American history in another direction.

His many speeches and contributions to professional organizations have also proven largely ephemeral. Perhaps that is the nature of such efforts. Unlike his shy mentor, Joe B. entered into the politics and organization of historical organizations with enthusiasm. At conventions he could often be found happily greeting his acquaintances in the lobby. He was president of the Southwestern Social Science Association (1963), director of the Texas State Historical Association (1966–1977), president of the Southern Historical Association (1977–1978), president of the Western History Association (1978–1979), a commissioner—appointed by the governor—for the American Revolution Bicentennial Commission of Texas (1975–1979), and a member of the advisory board of the National Park Service (1964–1984). All of this was done while he taught graduate and undergraduate courses and guided twenty-three doctorial students as a professor of history at the University of Texas at Austin.

The time people expend on academic committees is rarely honored. Perhaps efforts are mentioned at an annual meeting, but largely they are buried and forgotten in obscure committee minutes. As director of the Texas State Historical Association, Frantz, however, was able to make a noticeable difference as an administrator. He pushed to completion the supplementary Volume 3 of the encyclopedic *Handbook of Texas* (1976); began *Riding Line*, a membership newsletter; started a summer institute of Texas studies for teachers; raised money; and maintained the tenuous relationship with the host institution, the University of Texas at Austin. With his assistant director, L. Tuffly Ellis, Joe was able to enliven the staid *Southwestern Historical Quarterly* with full-color art on the cover and higher standards of scholarship. These were tangible accomplishments, but eventually a six-volume *New Handbook of Texas* (1996) replaced the three-volume work, and the association left Austin in 2008 for new quarters at the University of North Texas in Denton.

As a popular professor Frantz rarely passed on an opportunity to give a speech, and during the American Revolution Bicentennial he was presenting talks to various groups around Texas at a rate of one per week. With a nasal Texas accent and a puckish wit, he drew upon a large repertoire of entertaining anecdotes, sometimes rambled a bit, but usually left his audience with something to think about. His popular presentations gained him a reputation as a "folksy, down-home tale spinner."[14] Much of what he said was spontaneous and improvised. Asked in 1967 for a copy of his speech to the Texas Library Association, he had to confess that nothing was written down and that he was guided only by five, short cryptic words. But his more important addresses usually ended up as published articles that often reflected the humor of the delivery. Examples of his humor include the following:

> From the 1820s to 1861 Sam Houston was like a larger-than-life stinkbug in America's life. No matter how many times you plugged his hole and pressed him down, he always reappeared somewhere else, as tangible a factor as ever.[15]

> Texas is 12 million people who are bright and dumb, conservative and liberal, tall and short and slim and fat, courageous and cowardly—just like the people in Connecticut and Oregon.[16]

> Being a historian has certain similarities to running a house of prostitution—no matter how often you sell the product of the house, the product remains in as plentiful supply as when the first sale was made. History is self-replacing. There is always more to be done, and there are always new interpretations.[17]

Considering that last quotation, Frantz easily would have acknowledged the limits of his own career. Nothing lasts; nothing is definitive. After finishing his acclaimed biography of Borden, Frantz found 30,000 more pages of Borden correspondence in an old tack house in upstate New York and wrote a confessional article in the *Southwest Review* titled "On Being Definitive."[18] His comments provided a warning for all ambitious scholars: nothing is ever complete. New material turns up and change occurs. Speeches, moreover, are forgotten; students grow old; institutions shift their focus; new interpretations of history take over. That is all to be expected. There is one of his accomplishments, however, that endures—the Lyndon B. Johnson Oral History Project.

Oral history involves the preserving of eyewitness memories about significant historical events. It means not only recording a voice, but also making the information accessible to the public with typed, edited transcripts, repositories, and legal releases. It is not as easy as it seems to be. Interviewees have to be located, contacted, persuaded, and asked appropriate questions. The interviewer has to be knowledgeable and capable of creating rapport; transcribers need intelligence, good ears, and patience. There is the cost of personnel, supplies, equipment, and travel. It is estimated that behind every hour of oral history there are twenty-five hours of preparation and processing.

Yet, for historians, oral history provides a priceless return for the effort. In this work the interviewer creates a primary document, a firsthand account that future historians will use as research material. In other words, a present historian will ask the questions that future historians would want asked, thus providing a richer explanation about historical matters. The current historian, therefore, helps to write future history. Think of the wealth of information we would possess if there had been an oral history project concerning Abraham Lincoln, Thomas Jefferson, or Benjamin Franklin. The Columbia University oral history project of important persons in the New York area, started by historian Allen Nevins shortly after World War II, was widely known among academics. The Oral History Association began in 1967, and the *Oral History Review* came to life in 1974. It was in this formative era that Frantz became active in the field.

Friends of John F. Kennedy had left behind a disorganized scramble of taped memorials in 1963–1964; consequently, thoughts about a future Lyndon B. Johnson project lingered in the White House. Johnson, however, had been burned in print by Eric Goldman, an early historian in residence, so he was understandably wary of such intellectuals. On the other hand, trust between the president and Frantz was growing. Joe accompanied Mrs. Johnson and a contingent of National Park personnel in 1966 on a broadly publicized float trip down the Rio Grande in order to publicize the Big Bend National Park of Texas. His job was to tell stories around a campfire at night. Johnson appointed him to the National Historical Publications Commission in 1966 and to the Historical Advisory Committee of the National Aeronautics and Space administration in 1968.

In 1967, as time ebbed away for Johnson, Herman Kahn, the assistant archivist for presidential libraries, recommended to the administration that an oral history project was needed to record unique and perishable memories before they were lost. Johnson, who did much of his negotiating over the telephone, readily understood the logic and asked Frantz to put together a proposal. The oral history interviews could supplement the Johnson papers that would be housed in the new Lyndon Baines Johnson Presidential Library at the University of Texas at Austin. Frantz consulted with Douglas Cater, a senior advisor, in May 1968 and met with the president. Johnson never asked Frantz to do the work; he just began to introduce him by saying, "This is Joe Frantz. He's going to run my oral history project."[19]

With the approval of the university Frantz canceled his summer and fall classes, set up an advisory board that included Allen Nevins, and proceeded to hire a team of young Ph.D.'s and staff to begin work in the fall. Funds came from undisclosed private sources funneled through the university. The oral history staff—Joe B. Frantz, Colleen T. Kain, Ruth Mathews, Mary Dale Ellis, T. Harrison Baker, Paige Mulhollon, David McComb, Steve Goodell, and Dorothy Pierce—met with President and Mrs. Johnson in September, and the president charged the group to find out what had gone on with friends and enemies. Johnson promised to respect the confidentiality of the interviews.[20]

The initial oral history team worked for a year and then scattered to various academic jobs. Joe remained as director until 1974, by which time about 700 interviews had been conducted. At that point Michael Gillette of the LBJ Library took over the project. Currently, the project contains about 1,200 interviews, with 81 of them available online. It is impossible to calculate the historical significance of the collection except to note that anyone writing about Lyndon Johnson and his times reads the interviews. They are an essential source of information and are consulted about 2,000 times per year. Merle Miller, for example, ransacked the collection and put together *Lyndon: An Oral Biography* (1980), that briefly made it to the *New York Times* best-seller list. Robert Caro and Robert Dallek have used it extensively for their multivolume studies of Lyndon Johnson. Most authors utilize the material and credit the library, but few give recognition to Frantz or the interviewers who were part of the creative process. Yet Frantz, unlike most historians, was able to reach into the future to influence the writing of history.

"What I think I've achieved more than anything else is great anecdotal depth. And while most historians disdain anecdotes, some of them are quite revealing," Frantz said. "I think these tapes are important because they will emphasize the fact that the government is made up of people, with their foibles, strengths and weaknesses."[21] It was ideal work for the loquacious Joe B. Frantz. He had a satisfactory budget and staff and was able to talk to the most important people in American society. Frantz became the preeminent oral historian in the nation, and thereafter his speeches and publications often reflected his knowledge of the Johnson administration. His book *37 Years of Public Service* (1974) was a memorial that highlighted a significant moment in each year of Johnson's public life; "Opening a Curtain: The Metamorphosis of Lyndon B. Johnson" was his presidential address to the Southern Historical Association in 1978; and "Why Lyndon?" was his presidential address to the Western History Association in 1979.[22]

Frantz was at the apogee of his professional career at this point, and the University of Texas at Austin named him the first recipient of the Walter Prescott Webb Chair of History and Ideas in 1977. In a golden moment, 450 friends and Texas dignitaries gathered at Webb's Friday Mountain Ranch southwest of Austin in the fall to honor Joe's accomplishments and new status. He had traveled a long way from the orphanage in Fort Worth.

His life, however, began to unravel in the last years of the decade. Starting in his early sixties he went through three divorces involving multiple children, stepchildren, and grandchildren, each divorce creating personal and professional stress and ravaging his fortune. He died in debt to the Internal Revenue Service. Joe, nonetheless, continued to work, and his ebullient personality remained undiminished. In 1981 he resigned from the Webb chair, retired to half-time teaching at the university in 1984, and accepted a new teaching post at Corpus Christi State University in 1986. His ragged end at the University of Texas involved the publication of *The Forty-Acre Follies* (1983).

The school had assigned him earlier to write an official history of the university, but neither President Lorene Rogers nor her successor, President Peter T. Flawn, liked his manuscript and they dismissed him from the project. Frantz took his rejected book, expanded it, and sent it to Texas Monthly Press for publication. His irreverent, somewhat embittered comments were well received by regional reviewers, and he won the Southwestern Booksellers Association award for the best nonfiction Texas book of the year. With no index, no footnotes, and a poor chronology, *The Forty-Acre Follies* was more of a memoir than a history. He damned the administrators and praised the students: "A university should be a place where the shades are raised and the world beyond is revealed, with no attempt to control the view," he wrote. "For all its faults and interrupted rhythms, I still think college is the best place for any halfway intelligent person between the ages of eighteen and twenty-five to be."[23]

At Corpus Christi Joe easily slid into a comfortable association with his new colleagues and into the civic life of the city. He became involved with the local Quincentennial Committee and helped route the replica ships of Christopher Columbus to Corpus Christi. He continued to speak and write. He collaborated with journalist Mike Cox to write *Lure of the Land: Texas County Maps and the History of Settlement* (1988), which involved the reproduction of rare nineteenth-century maps with a retelling of the story of migration and settlement. An editor had to blend the different writing styles, but the expensive, specialized volume sold out and won the Fehrenbach Award of the Texas Historical Commission for the best Texas book of the year. This was Joe's last book.

In the early 1990s his health began to break, and his oncoming diabetes became uncontrollable. He retired from the university at Corpus Christi, delivered the commencement address, and moved to Houston with his wife, Betsy. He died on November 13, 1993. His legacy included books and articles about Texas and the West, a scattering of loyal doctoral students, administrative work for historical associations, and the oral history project at the LBJ Library. He was the last of a line of famous Texas historians at the University of Texas—Barker, Webb, and Frantz—that amounts to a history in itself.

SUGGESTED READING

Frantz, Joe B. *Aspects of the American West: Three Essays*. College Station: Texas A&M University Press, 1976.

These are a sample of Frantz's published speeches. "The American West: Child of Federal

Subsidy" brought him to the attention of President Lyndon Johnson, became a part of the Congressional Record in 1964, and led eventually to the Johnson Oral History Project.

Frantz, Joe B. *The Forty-Acre Follies: An Opinionated History of the University of Texas*. Austin: Texas Monthly Press, 1983.

The book is a rambling commentary about and criticism of life at the University of Texas written at a stormy point during Frantz's career when he was separating from the university. Faculty, staff, and students are well treated, but not the administration.

Frantz, Joe B. *Gail Borden: Dairyman to a Nation*. Norman: University of Oklahoma Press, 1951.

This book was Joe B. Frantz's revised dissertation that was directed by Walter Prescott Webb. It stands as the basic work on Gail Borden, and for years after publication, in gratitude, the Borden Company sent Frantz a crate of condensed milk every Christmas.

Frantz, Joe B. *Texas: A Bicentennial History*. New York: Norton, 1976.

For the bicentennial of the United States Norton published individual histories of all the states. This was Frantz's contribution, demonstrating his prominence as the leading Texas historian at that time.

Frantz, Joe B., and Cordia Sloan Duke. *6,000 Miles of Fence: Life on the XIT Ranch of Texas*. Austin: University of Texas Press, 1961.

Frantz put together Duke's notes about ranch life into a fine descriptive memoir.

Frantz, Joe B., and Julian E. Choate Jr. *The American Cowboy: The Myth and the Reality*. Norman: University of Oklahoma Press, 1955.

Frantz established a lasting place for himself in Western U.S. history with this volume that explained the equipment and work of the cowboy.

Frantz, Joe B., and Mike Cox. *Lure of the Land: Texas County Maps and the History of Settlement*. Edited by Roger A. Griffin. College Station: Texas A&M University Press, 1988.

Although in faltering health Frantz produced this prize-winning book as a final major effort.

Walter Prescott Webb, *An Honest Preface*, ed. and with an introduction by Joe B. Frantz. Boston: Houghton Mifflin Company, 1959.

This collection of essays by Walter Prescott Webb represents not only the best writing of Webb but also an introduction that is considered the best writing of Joe B. Frantz.

NOTES

1. Much of the biographical information is taken from my book, *Travels with Joe: The Life Story of a Historian from Texas, 1917–1993* (Austin: Texas State Historical Association, 2001). This quotation is on page 14. The Frantz papers are, as of this writing, partially processed, and are housed at the Dolph Briscoe Center for American History, University of Texas at Austin.

2. Joe B. Frantz, "By Land and Sea," *True West* 9 (May–June 1962): 39, 71.

---

3. Walter Prescott Webb, *An Honest Preface*, ed. and with an introduction by Joe B. Frantz (Boston: Houghton Mifflin Company, 1959), 196.

4. Untitled article, *Time*, November 6, 1955.

5. Joe B. Frantz, "Taming the West," in Ross Bennett, ed., *Visiting Our Past: America's Historylands* (Washington, DC: National Geographic Society, 1977), 319.

6. Joe B. Frantz, "Western Impact on the Nation," *Western Historical Quarterly* 1 (July 1970): 263.

7. Ibid.

8. Joe B. Frantz, "The Meaning of Yellowstone," *Montana: The Magazine of Western History* 22 (July 1972): 11.

9. This is a summary of comments from Patricia Nelson Limerick, Clyde A. Milner II, and Charles E. Rankin, eds., *Trails: Toward a New Western History* (Lawrence: University Press of Kansas, 1991). The quote is from Donald Worster's chapter, "Beyond the Agrarian Myth," 7.

10. Gene M. Gressley, ed., *Old West/New West* (Norman: Oklahoma, 1997), 20. In this same volume Gerald Thompson evaluates the new western historians in "The New Western History: A Critical Analysis," 49–71. See also Richard W. Etulain, "Prologue: The Twentieth-Century West," in *The Twentieth-Century West: Historical Interpretations*, edited by Gerald D. Nash and Richard W. Etulain (Albuquerque: University of New Mexico Press, 1989), 1–31; and Charles S. Peterson, "Speaking for the Past," in *The Oxford History of the American West*, edited by Clyde A. Milner II, Carol A. O'Connor, and Martha A. Sandweiss (New York: Oxford University Press, 1994), 743–769.

11. Joe B. Frantz, *Texas: A Bicentennial History* (New York: Norton, 1976). Also, with J. Roy White, *Limestone and Log: A Hill Country Sketchbook* (Austin: Encino, 1968); with Robert K. Holz, Mildred P. Mayhill, and Sam W. Newman, *Texas and Its History* (Dallas: Pepper Jones Martinez, 1972); and, with Mike Cox, *Lure of the Land: Texas County Maps and the History of Settlement* (College Station: Texas A&M, 1988). See also *The Driskill Hotel* (Austin: Encino Press, 1973); and *The Forty-Acre Follies: An Opinionated History of the University of Texas* (Austin: Texas Monthly Press, 1983).

12. Joe B. Frantz, *Aspects of the American West: Three Essays* (College Station: Texas A&M University Press, 1976); "Lone Star Mystique," *American West* 5 (May 1968): 6–9.

13. Joe B. Frantz, introduction to *An Honest Preface*. Frantz's commentary about Webb, 3–58, is considered to be his best piece of writing. See also Wilbur R. Jacobs, John W. Caughey, and Joe B. Frantz, *Turner, Bolton, and Webb: Three Historians of the American Frontier* (Seattle: University of Washington Press, 1965).

14. University of Texas news release, October 13, 1978.

15. Joe B. Frantz, "Sam Houston: Texas Giant of Contradictions," *American West*, vol. 17 (July–August 1980), 65.

16. Joe B. Frantz, "Why Lyndon?" *Western Historical Quarterly* 11 (January 1980): 14.

17. Joe B. Frantz, "Restocking History," speech to the Tri-State Humanities Conference, Rapid City, South Dakota, September 24, 1977.

18. Joe B. Frantz, "On Being Definitive," *Southwest Review* 44 (Winter 1959): 72–74.

19. Quoted in McComb, *Travels with Joe*, 57.

20. Ibid., 58.

21. Quoted in *The Daily Texan*, April 24, 1978.

22. Joe B. Frantz, *37 Years of Public Service: The Honorable Lyndon B. Johnson* (Austin: Shoal Creek Press, 1974); "Opening a Curtain: The Metamorphosis of Lyndon B. Johnson," *Journal of Southern History* 45 (February 1979): 3–36; "Why Lyndon?," 4–15.

23. Frantz, *Forty-Acre Follies*, xiii.

NANCY BAKER JONES

RUTHE WINEGARTEN

RUTHE WINEGARTEN

In her poem "Each One, Pull One," writer and civil rights activist Alice Walker invokes the dead to provoke the living into saving lives through remembrance:

> Look, I, temporarily on the rim
> of the grave,
> have grasped my mother's hand
> my father's leg.
> There is the hand of Robeson
> Langston's thigh
> Zora's arm and hair
> your grandfather's lifted chin
> the lynched woman's elbow
> what you've tried to forget
> of your grandmother's frown.
>
> *Each one, pull one back into the sun*[1]

In the last years of her life, Ruthe Winegarten began a project to document the story of her maternal and paternal grandparents, who had immigrated to the United States from Russia and Germany at the turn of the twentieth century. "I'm haunted by these pictures," she wrote, referring to the images of Jennie and Max Cohen and Lena and Ludwig Lewin. "They're no longer here to tell their own stories or talk about their goals and aspirations, their loneliness and losses, their strengths and successes, separations from their loved ones, . . . how they survived sailing to America, and struggled with a new language and culture. I feel impelled to tell my grandparents' story, which is a part of my story, part of the South Dallas story, and part of the story of Texas Jewry."[2]

This deeply felt motivation to write about her grandparents, while perhaps intensified by kinship, nevertheless underlay everything that Ruthe Winegarten wrote: her reason for being an historian was, like Walker's purpose, to save lives, to preserve for future generations the knowledge that lives had been lived. During the twenty-five years before taking up her family's history, Winegarten had persistently uncovered and spread the word about many other Texans: groups like Jews, African American and Native American women, Tejanas; "unknown" women like Annie Mae Hunt, Tiny Hawkins, and poet Bernice Love Wiggins; and women's experiences, like winning the vote and serving in the Texas Legislature. Between 1980 and 2003 she wrote, cowrote, or edited twenty books and videotapes for audiences of all ages.

In addition to publishing, Winegarten had a wide-ranging professional life working with nonprofit organizations on women's issues. She was the director of the Austin Women's Center, the research director or curator for three major history exhibits about Texas women, and a consultant in women's history to the staff of the *Handbook of Texas* revision project and the nascent Bob Bullock Texas State History Museum. She was research director for the Texas Jewish Historical Society and did significant research for Mary Beth Rogers's biography of Barbara Jordan. She coordinated two major conferences—one about women and public policy and the other about women's relation to food production; served on the Governor's Commission for Women among many other boards and commissions related to women, education, Jews, and African Americans; was a fellow of the Texas State Historical Association; and gave countless speeches about Texas women and women's history to book festivals, associations, clubs, conferences, churches, temples, and civic groups throughout the state. She and composer Naomi Carrier turned her oral history of Annie Mae Hunt into a popular musical, *I Am Annie Mae*. She also left behind an unpublished collection of poetry. She was married and divorced four times and raised three children.[3]

While well educated, Ruthe Winegarten was not an academically trained historian. In 1950 she earned a B.A. in anthropology from the University of Texas at Austin (where she completed course work about Native Americans with W. W. Newcomb) and an M.S. in social work from the University of Texas at Arlington in 1970. She spent 1976 to 1978 working, teaching, and pursuing a Ph.D. in the humanities at the University of Texas at Dallas, but decided she was too eager to start collecting women's oral histories to complete the program. Her faculty mentor, Harvey Graff, recalls that "Ruthe really wanted to sort of cut to the heart . . . of women's history and to become . . . a women's historian." Graff eventually urged her to "get far away from Ph.D. programs" because "the longer she would have stayed studying for the Ph.D., the less she would have prepared herself for what she wanted to do."[4] Winegarten did not regret the decision. "Probably if I had gotten a doctorate, I never would have done all these things, because I wouldn't have tackled them," she said in 2003. "I would only have focused on narrower periods of time or a narrower topic. But since I didn't know that that's what you were supposed to do, I did pretty much what I wanted to."[5]

The kind of history Winegarten wanted to do did not include finding a tenured university position in which she could produce journal articles, biographies, or monographs. Her interdisciplinary interests, indefatigable, free-spirited nature, and love of archival research turned her into Texas history's freelance intrepid explorer, determined to discover the unknown and to spur others to do the same. "She makes history the way they supposedly make the best hashish in India," journalist and colleague Frieda Werden said. "They run naked through the fields, and whatever sticks to them, they scrape that off and use it to make the hashish. That's the way Ruthe started making history."[6]

Ruthe Winegarten's determination to make her own way as a historian, and as a person, was forged early in her life. The first of two children of Charles and Celia Cohen Lewin, Ruthe Lee Lewin was born August 26, 1929, the ninth anniversary of the ratification of the Nineteenth Amendment, granting women the right to vote. The family lived with Celia Cohen's parents in a middle-income Jewish neighborhood in South Dallas, in a Park Row house where Yiddish was commonly spoken. Celia Lewin had reluctantly given up employment as a stenographer when she became pregnant; Charles Lewin supported the family as a salesman and bookkeeper. Surrounded by adults, and an only child for ten years, Ruthe was the center of attention. "I don't think my feet touched the ground until I was about six. I mean having all these grownups, I think that has a lot to do with my personality, that these people all put me on a pedestal. Maybe it helped me develop self-confidence. . . . [P]retty much I always did what I wanted to." Or did not do what she did not want to do: in elementary school she refused to sing Christmas carols.[7]

Ruthe spent her childhood reading "constantly," and by the time she attended Forest Avenue High School, where most of the other students were also Jewish, Ruthe had become an articulate, studious, and occasionally irreverent young woman who worried about the poor and dispossessed. By the time she graduated in the spring of 1946, she had registered the highest IQ in her class, become a member of the National Honor Society, and missed being valedictorian by one point.[8] Among the most important influences in her life at the time were the weekly after-school meetings of Habonim ("the builders"), a Labor Zionist youth group founded by Jacob Levin, the principal of the Hebrew School of Dallas. Levin also founded and directed Camp Bonim, a residential summer camp that was unique in the Southwest in offering Labor Zionist, Hebrew, and Jewish studies.[9] Levin was a Latvian immigrant who had arrived in Baltimore in 1923, joined Zeire Zion, the Labor Zionist party that advocated a Jewish home in Palestine, and formed a youth group. He moved to Dallas in 1929, the same year Ruthe was born. Habonim and Camp Bonim were, like Levin's Baltimore group, inspired by Aaron David Gordon, an agrarian Zionist who encouraged Jews to work at hard labor, particularly in Palestine, as a way toward spiritual fulfillment.[10]

At Habonim meetings, Ruthe experienced intellectual challenge through *sicha,* or conversations, about important ideas. Although frequently led by Levin, these talks were also conducted by members: "I led a sicha at the meeting last week on the Ideal State by giving more or less a book review of the *Republic,* interspersed with a few of my own crackpot opinions. The discussion that followed really was good," she wrote of her experience.[11] These meetings also challenged her to think about her future: "I have decided I wouldn't mind living in Palestine. . . . [I]t might not be bad at all to work outside 13 hours all day or wear non-stylish clothes or be dead tired at the end of the day. I'm very serious."[12]

More than this, however, Habonim and summer stays at Camp Bonim provided the crucible in which Ruthe Lewin's social conscience formed. Letters she wrote to her high school sweetheart, Stanley Schneider, who was by then a student at the University of Chicago, reveal the extent to which these two organizations provided the connective social fabric for Jewish students at Forest Avenue High School in general and for her own circle of friends in particular. While her high school classes educated her in traditional academic subjects, Habonim and Camp Bonim forged her ethnic identity and challenged her to create a vision for an ethical, purposeful life. Ginger Jacobs, one of Ruthe Lewin's best friends, wrote later that the organizations were "strongly activist" in supporting Zionist causes, and members attended leadership training seminars and national conventions. What Lewin learned from them in these formative years was far less about religion than it was about intellectual curiosity and discipline, Jewish heritage and culture, and how best to live according to her burgeoning belief system. "Although I am and always will be a Jew, I do not observe the customs nor teachings. I only digest the material for how it can make me a better person, while discarding all the old legends and laws. If I do not believe in God and consequently not in the Jewish religion, why am I in favor of a Jewish homeland?" she wrote to Schneider.[13]

Ruthe's letters to Schneider are personal *sicha* in which the two young people share and refine their ideas about a wide array of subjects ranging from the state of the world to whether Ruthe would go to the senior prom. They clearly describe her intellectual and emotional struggles. "I am still trying to figure out . . . whether I am better off being a member of Habonim and being made conscious of current world problems," she wrote. "Would I not have been happier, perhaps, going out and raising hell every night? I think I have benefited most by the people I have met while being associated with the movement. For that, I am thankful."[14] Repeatedly, she returns to the themes of tolerance and racial prejudice:

> People are very intolerant. I only now realize how very narrow-minded I used to be. The Negro question seems to come to my mind very often, and every time I can put in a word which will perhaps give them an extra push, I do it. Not only the Negroes, but everyone, should be treated tolerantly. . . . I already see that the only way I will have peace of mind in later life is to know that I am furthering the causes in which I believe—equality of man and his security, economically and socially.[15]

> [. . .]
> No, I certainly would not mind being examined by a Negro physician if I were pregnant. Color of the skin means absolutely nothing to me. If I didn't feel this way, I wouldn't consider myself worthy of your friendship. . . . If I would go around saying "That Nigger did that, etc." I should expect for someone to turn right around and call me a damn Jew.[16]

Gradually, through Schneider, she began to see communism as a possible solution for discrimination and inequality. Early in 1946 Schneider sent her some "circulars" and apparently admonished her not to display them, to which Ruthe agreed. Not long afterward she wrote him, "Some kids are organizing a Communist Party at [the University of] Texas to support [Homer P.] Rainey in the gubernatorial elections."[17] By the fall of 1946, Ruthe Lewin had become an undergraduate student at Southern Methodist University (SMU) in Dallas, living at home, and had joined the Dallas Progressive Youth League (DPYL) as a representative from Habonim. The DPYL, she said, "stands for the brotherhood of man and is open to all races, creed, and colors. . . . I am very happy that now at last I really have something concrete to do. It is wonderful to associate with negroes and know we all are fighting for the same thing." Whether the DPYL was affiliated with the Communist Party (CP) is unclear, but in 1947 or 1948 Ruthe Lewin did formally join the party.[18] She joked to Schneider that when visitors came into the local Rainey campaign headquarters, "We all stand up, raise our right hands in salute and say in a very deep voice, 'Greetings, Comrade!'"[19] But her letters about communism itself remain serious, in part because her parents were "very opposed not only to the type of literature which you send me, but the kind of ideas I have."[20]

Ruthe Lewin's interest in communism was based less on historical information or political ideology than on the hope that it was the best belief system available for achieving labor reform, racial integration, social justice, and peace. Apparently unaware of Joseph Stalin's atrocities, she asked Schneider, "During the transition period from Tzarism to Communism, is it true that millions of people died because of starvation or because they were not in agreement with the Communist party? My mother always confronts me with this argument."[21] By early 1947 she was still unsure how to label herself:

> If it means "working for the underdog," if it means trying to look at both sides of a question before judging, if it means combating fascism, if it means a better general standard of living for everyone, if it means co-operation and happiness, if it means work for all those fit to work (no unemployment), then yes, I am a socialist or a communist.[22]

By 1948 Ruthe Lewin was active enough in the CP that the Federal Bureau of Investigation was collecting information about her; it maintained files on her from at least March 1948, while she was still at SMU, until May 1964, when the Dallas office recommended that her files be closed. During those years, several unnamed informants kept the FBI apprised of her political and social activities, acquaintances, marriages, divorces, addresses, and name changes; they even knew when she was pregnant.[23]

A "reliable" informant referred to as T-1 first met Ruthe Lewin at a Dallas Valentine's Day party in 1948 and later reported her attendance at an open meeting of the Dallas Branch of the CP less than one month later. Over the course of about four months, T-1 reported that she was an officer of an SMU student group called "The Forum," which "intended to take sides on national issues and to actually influence legislation and the opinion of others along certain lines"; that she and other CP members distributed *The Worker* to residents of Roseland Homes and Frazer Courts ("negro housing projects in Dallas"); attended Wallace for President meetings in Austin, Dallas, and Houston; wrote a letter published in the *Dallas Morning News* supporting "clean, healthy housing" for Dallas blacks; and addressed envelopes to mail leaflets protesting the Nixon-Mundt Bill (also known as the "Subversive Activities Control Bill"), all while in the company of many "well known members of the Communist Party."[24]

About this time, Ruthe Lewin learned that Stan Schneider had fallen in love with another woman. She was shattered by the news. On the rebound, to escape Dallas, and "to show [Stan]," she transferred to the University of Texas at Austin (UT) and, in December 1948, married Wendell Addington, a World War II veteran and youth director of the state Communist Party.[25] Ruthe Winegarten later surmised that there were probably no more than fifty party members in Texas at the time, and ten of them were at UT, working to ban the atomic bomb, promote peace, support Henry Wallace's presidential campaign, and advocate racial integration. Heman Sweatt's suit against the UT School of Law, *Sweatt v. Painter*, was working its way through the legal system while they were students and certainly supplied one context for the petitions supporting integration that the party distributed. Ruthe recalled continuing at UT the kind of activities she had engaged in at SMU: circulating petitions against atomic weapons, selling *The Worker*, and being arrested for both. She also lost a number of part-time jobs she had taken to put herself through school and always believed, correctly as it turned out, that she was fired because employers had been told that she was a communist. "This was pretty big harassment, you know. So obviously somebody was keeping tabs on us. And we always assumed our phones were tapped." Not one to remain quiet, she wrote a letter published in a 1950 issue of *The Daily Texan* complaining that she had been denied an office clerk position on campus because her name was on an FBI list of CP members and urging the FBI to "explain its methods to the public."[26]

In 1949, the Texas Legislature passed a law requiring college students to sign a loyalty oath and compelling students and faculty to verify they were not members of the Communist Party. Ruthe Addington agreed to sign the oath because "we weren't advocating the overthrow of the government."[27]

After graduation, Ruthe and Wendell Addington moved to New Orleans and then Newark, New Jersey. He became an organizer for the Labor Youth League, which she described as "a Communist front organization."[28] While he traveled, she worked at a cotton mill, a shirt factory, and with electrical workers, attempting to organize laborers. "Why I thought I could do this, I don't know. But I tried rather unsuccessfully. I was not a great industrial worker. . . . I had sympathy for the workers, but I . . . was still pretty young. . . . I was clueless." At the shirt factory, her job was to monitor the seamstresses' production, placing a button in each woman's tally box for every completed shirt. Frustrated by their low wages, she would wait for the foreman to look away, then add extra buttons.[29] The Addington marriage lasted four years. Ruthe returned to Texas, with her first child and no child support, to live with her mother-in-law in Lubbock.[30] By then, disillusioned by what she had learned about life in the Soviet Union under communism, she had effectively lost interest in the Communist Party. Nevertheless, she kept an activist streak: while working as a mail clerk for the Santa Fe Railroad in Slaton, near Lubbock, she read and destroyed letters to the office listing names of union supporters who should not be hired. "That was illegal, to blacklist people, so I took all those letters and . . . threw them away. [M]y acts of sabotage were sort of modest."[31]

In Lubbock, Ruthe married for the second time. Thomas Sanders, a "left-winger," worked for a credit collection company. Fairly soon the marriage soured, and Ruthe, pregnant with her second child, moved in with her parents in Dallas. This marriage ended in 1955. Angry with Sanders's attempt to take their son away from her and with his refusing to make child support payments, she "wrote the government and told them they should, you know, sign him up [for the draft]. That wasn't very nice of me." In 1956 she married Alvin Winegarten, an aeronautical engineer. They lived in Dallas and had a child, her third and last, in 1957.[32]

During the 1960s, Ruthe Winegarten, by now in her thirties, the wife of a professional, and the mother of three young children, earned income with her own bookkeeping and income tax preparation service. She also became active in a variety of voluntary civic activities, including the Council of Jewish Women, the League of Women Voters, and the Democratic Party, and she helped organize the North Dallas Democratic Women's Club to support John F. Kennedy's presidential campaign. It was there that she met Ann Richards, then the club's president and the politically active wife of a Dallas attorney.[33] As a fund-raiser for liberal Democratic candidates, the North Dallas club instituted yearly musical skits, called "Political Paranoia," in which costumed women played the parts of well-known candidates and officeholders (mostly men), both liberal and conservative, satirizing them with irreverent lyrics put to familiar tunes. Winegarten, Richards, Betty McCool, and Carolyn Choate wrote the lyrics and scripts. "As we were writing and composing and putting stuff together, we could tell if we were good or not by whether Ruthe laughed," Richards said. In 1968 the *Dallas News* described the shows as "an entertainment staple for politicians and paranoiacs alike, not to mention ordinary voters in search of a laugh." The club's own flyers described one performance as "Poop and Patter from the Pedernales to the Potomac. Again featuring 100 gorgeous housewives (Bobby Baker Rejects) bubbling with Exotic Amateur Talent. The most talked about show from Euless to Balch Springs."[34]

The first Political Paranoia satire was produced in 1963, the same year Winegarten read Betty Friedan's groundbreaking feminist treatise, *The Feminine Mystique*. "Reading [it] changed my life. I became convinced there was more to it than housewives and kids," she said. "Looking back, I can see that those women [involved in the skits] were the people that [Friedan] was talking about. . . . [T]he happy housewives who did everything they were supposed to and it wasn't enough. . . . You know, Ann Richards was making curtains for the . . . kitchen and cooking all these elaborate meals." Determined to get a job, Winegarten became a secretary to the director of the Anti-Defamation League in Dallas about 1966. In time, she was frustrated. "He had a degree in Social Work," she said of the director. "I could see that I was running the office and I knew more than he did, so I should go get a degree in Social Work."[35]

She applied for a Woodrow Wilson National Fellowship as part of a pilot project to attract older, married women to graduate school and then to teaching:

> I was interviewed by five great big professors sitting on one side of what seemed like a 30 foot table and believe me, I did poorly. I had prepared myself to give profound answers to such questions as disadvantaged children, urban problems, etc. Instead they asked things like, "Where does your husband work? Where did he go to school? What grades did you make in Analytical Geometry and will you be able to pass the statistic course?'" . . . I doubt that I will get the fellowship.[36]

She did not. However, she was awarded two other scholarships and in 1968 became a member of the first graduate class of the School of Social Work at the newly opened University of Texas at Arlington (UTA), along with three other North Dallas women who were married and had children. "They called us the

Intense Ladies from North Dallas," she recalled. "Three of us were Jewish, and we'd all made really good grades in school and it never occurred to us it was okay to make a B." She focused on community organizing and social planning, commuting to Arlington twice a week, departing at 6:30 a.m. and "leaving the kids asleep with lunches in the refrigerator."[37] In 1969, under the headline, "For One Jewish Mother, Chicken Soup is a No, No," a *Dallas Times Herald* feature about Winegarten opened with a discussion of the guilt she felt for returning to school, then focused on the effect on her family and how she balanced dual responsibilities. "Mrs. Alvin Winegarten sometimes sneaks off to the grocery store when she should be in the library—or is it vice versa?" the cutline next to her picture read. Winegarten took her studies seriously, however, acquiring skills in quantitative research, interviewing and oral history, group dynamics, and community organizing. She graduated in 1970.[38]

Winegarten spent most of the 1970s in Dallas applying what she learned in a variety of social service organizations: she worked at the Julius Schepps Community Center, directed the Council on Aging and the Community Relations Council for the Jewish Welfare Federation of Dallas, and became the Southwest regional director for the Anti-Defamation League of B'nai B'rith (ADL). In all of these positions, she honed skills in fund-raising, writing, editing, publishing, researching, organizing people and resources, lobbying, public speaking, analyzing issues, and working with local, state, and federal agencies and media outlets.[39] At the Community Relations Council she ran a leadership project to train young Jewish professionals for work in Jewish nonprofits. At the ADL, her skills coalesced around addressing anti-Semitism, racism, and discrimination. Winegarten's focus was to keep tabs on right-wing groups in the region. At times, she attended their meetings as "sort of an undercover spy." At one point a woman who had become active with the Minute Men and the American Nazi Party offered her services to the ADL. "So we contacted the FBI and they bought her a little Minox camera and she ingratiated herself into the American Nazi Party chapter. . . . She photographed and copied [meetings and publications] and gave us their names, which we passed on to [the New York ADL office], which went to the FBI."[40] The irony of this work was not lost on Winegarten. "I know. . . . I'm sure they visited all those people and got them fired from their jobs and god knows what else. . . . I'm sure the civil liberties people would not approve of what we did. . . . I suppose we justify on the grounds we can see what happens when the bad guys get in office or get too powerful."[41]

At the same time, Winegarten was researching the lives of women. She wrote a weekly column called "Remarkable Jewish Women" for the *Texas Jewish Post*, wrote occasional articles with the theme "Women for Change" for the Dallas *Iconoclast*, and coproduced features called "Sketching American Women" for radio station KERA. In 1975 she was recruited by the School of General Studies at the University of Texas at Dallas (UTD) to help its new College IX (nicknamed "Maturity College") get off the ground. She took the job and, in addition to fund-raising and community outreach, taught a course in community organizing and community relations for the sociology department.[42]

Working at a university, surrounded by professionals with Ph.D.'s, Winegarten felt insecure about lacking one. As there was no doctoral program in history, much less women's history, at UTD, she submitted an application to the School of Arts and Humanities in 1976. For the "Ph.D. Casebook" requirement, she offered several potential projects: a historical drama about Belle Starr, "the Bandit Queen of Dallas"; a documentary film about working women in Dallas; a monograph titled "The Social, Political, and Economic History of Texas Women," which, together with a slide and cassette tape presentation, could be used in seventh-grade Texas history classes; and writing a history of women for the Dallas Social History Project.[43]

Because women's history was a relatively new field, there were few established resources to draw on. Winegarten eventually took interdisciplinary courses, topical seminars, and also worked through a reading list from faculty mentor Harvey Graff. At the request of Graff and Dean Carolyn Galerstein, she coordinated a conference on women and public issues, sponsored by UTD and the Texas Committee for the Humanities, at which the German women's historian Renate Bridenthal spoke. Graff remembers Winegarten "just sort of grabbing Renate and spiriting her away for a long time and sitting her down, finding out what she could learn, and I see Ruthe glowing in the situation as she listened, as her questions got sharper." She also attended the National Women's Conference in Houston in 1977, the first meeting of its kind since the Women's Rights Convention at Seneca Falls in 1848.[44]

Galerstein, who had hired Winegarten for College IX, now wanted her to establish a women's studies program for UTD. To support that goal, Winegarten toured women's studies programs, centers, and archives around the country, including those at Barnard and Smith Colleges and the University of California at Berkeley. As part of her degree program and in support of the formation of a women's studies program, Winegarten also taught what was probably UTD's first women's history course; it enrolled ninety students. Because she had not taught one before, Winegarten again looked for existing resources. Her son sent her the syllabus from a women's history class he was taking at UT, taught by a doctoral student in American Civilization named Melissa Hield. Together with Elizabeth Fernea and Betty Sue Flowers, Hield was also working to create a women's studies program at the Austin campus.[45]

Despite the enjoyment Winegarten experienced as a doctoral student, she remained uncomfortable with university culture and politics. She met significant resistance when she invited two lesbian guest speakers to her class and was dismayed by the dearth of "deep philosophical discussions" among faculty. "Basically, they were arguing about who was going to have access to the Xerox machine. I was really shocked that . . . I did not get . . . stimulating discussion."[46] In addition, after twenty years, she had become unhappy in her marriage. These factors, and Graff's encouragement to escape the structure of the Ph.D. program, motivated Winegarten to leave not only the program, but also her marriage and Dallas. She moved to Austin in 1978.[47]

Austin in the 1970s was an invigorating place for anyone interested in the women's movement. Consciousness-raising groups, university courses in women's history and literature, and a women's center, rape crisis center, and battered women's shelter appeared. Liz Carpenter, former press secretary to Lady Bird Johnson, had helped form the National Women's Political Caucus (NWPC), and Frances "Sissy" Farenthold, who from 1969 to 1973 had been the only female member of the Texas House, became the NWPC chair. Texas voters overwhelmingly approved a state Equal Legal Rights Amendment to the Texas Constitution in 1972. Also that year, Farenthold became the first woman to have her nomination for vice president voted on by a national political convention, and Barbara Jordan left the Texas Senate to become the first black woman from the South to serve in the U.S. House of Representatives. Sarah Weddington successfully argued *Roe v. Wade* before the Supreme Court in 1973 and served in the Texas House from 1973 to 1977, as did Kay Bailey (later Hutchison), Chris Miller, Senfronia Thompson, and Eddie Bernice Johnson. Along with Betty Andujar in the Senate, this was the largest cohort of women to have ever served there at once.[48]

By the time Winegarten arrived, there were fourteen women in the Texas Legislature and "women's issues" like child care funding, family planning services, maternity leave, and equal access to credit were being more commonly discussed there. Austin had its first female mayor in Carole McClellan, and Ann Richards was a Travis County commissioner and a member of President Jimmy Carter's Advisory Committee for Women. Perhaps most important, at least for Winegarten, was that Richards and Weddington, along with Jane Hickie, Cathy Bonner, Judith Guthrie, and Martha Smiley, had become founding board members of the newly named Texas Foundation for Women's Resources (TFWR), whose mission was to "improve the personal, economic, and professional status of women" and to empower women to enable future generations to make a lasting impact. Its first major project was educational—to document and publicize the contributions of women to Texas history.[49]

Winegarten was excited to be in "a fantastic place for women," a city with a progressive, activist culture, a major university, libraries and research centers, and "brilliant" collaborators. She reconnected with Richards by working as her secretary for a few months. Through Richards, Winegarten met Hickie, who needed someone to solve political and personnel problems at the Austin Women's Center, on whose board she served. Hickie hired Winegarten, who tackled the job for another six months. By then, Richards had approached Jack Maguire, director of the Institute of Texan Cultures in San Antonio, to urge him to add more women to the institute's exhibits. Richards, Hickie, and Mary Beth Rogers were raising funds for the Texas Women's History Project, headed by Rogers, the foundation's director. Rogers was eager to know Winegarten, not just because she was an old friend of Ann Richards's and someone with academic credentials who had taught women's history, but also because Winegarten had worked with Rogers's mother, Anita Coniglio, countering right-wing interest groups in Dallas. Rogers hired Winegarten to be the project's research director and curator.[50]

The Texas Women's History Project was the single most important, formative experience on Winegarten's way to becoming the state's foremost historian of women. Built on a foundation offered by historian Gerda Lerner—that women were history's forgotten community builders—and created because women "had been virtually ignored in the state's history, textbooks, museums, major collections, and folklore," the project had as its principal goal the creation of widespread public awareness about the experiences and contributions of Texas women to the history of the state.[51] Its scope, however, was breathtaking: to assemble a statewide advisory committee of influential notables; raise funds; survey over 4,000 Texas libraries, museums, historical organizations, universities, and individuals for existing data and materials; compile a comprehensive bibliography; hold a public forum; locate and collect artifacts from throughout the state; mount a major traveling exhibit and five smaller exhibits; highlight five individual women in separate publications; create a documentary for use in schools; compile an exhibit catalogue; and establish a permanent archive, all in three years.[52] It was comprehensive, it was massive, and it was probably crazy to undertake. It was right up Ruthe Winegarten's alley.

Winegarten began pulling other women onto the research team: Sherry Smith as art and photography curator, and Frieda Werden, Janelle Scott, Mary Sanger, Melissa Hield, and Nevin Davis as editors, researchers, and writers. "Mary Sanger and I went and read the card catalogue at the Barker [Texas History] Center one summer," Winegarten recalled. "All one hundred thousand entries, and out of that we did a bibliography. . . . I typed it all on my correcting Selectric—no computers, 300 pages." Werden, called upon to copyedit the 2,000-item bibliography, was "astounded" that she had constructed it "in record time."[53] In 1980 the TFWR published the *Texas Women's History Project Bibliography*, the basis for subsequent research that uncovered countless resources in Texas women's history. To collect artifacts for the exhibit, Winegarten took Werden and Smith on "field trips" to Hereford, Canyon, Lubbock, and other cities, where they found such things as a crazy quilt, a World War I nurse's uniform, and a crazy jug. She recalled:

> I asked to see [the jug] and the curator said, "what do you want with that piece of junk?" It turned out to be the most popular artifact in the exhibit. The one that was most frequently photographed. A woman had lost her child and so to keep the memory alive, she glued the child's toys onto an old water jug and [painted] it gold. . . . Maybe she did it to keep herself from going crazy.[54]

They found the Mixmaster in which Bette Graham had concocted Liquid Paper, Bonnie Parker's pistol, posters from Mollie Bailey's circus, and a harmonica. At the Texas Tech Ranching Heritage Center, "Ruthe turned up a story about 'Mrs. Boles' French Harp,'" Werden recalled, and "Ruthe wouldn't let the curator rest until he found it." It was in a case titled "Cowboy Music," with pictures of cowboys playing music and dancing, but no mention of Mrs. Boles. "She had brought her piano out [west] in the back of a covered wagon, the harmonica was hers, but they just wiped her out of the history. This is an absolutely classic example of a woman making a huge personal contribution and being written out of the history, the kind of wrong we were out to right."[55]

By early 1981 the TFWR and the project's advisory board had raised almost $264,000 from foundations, corporations, banks, and individuals. In all, Winegarten and her staff collected biographical information about nearly 600 women and compiled and catalogued more than 20,000 items—photographs, diaries, letters, newspaper clippings, unpublished theses, and legal documents as well as artifacts—that were eventually housed at the Texas Woman's University library. They discovered so much, in fact, that a dozen exhibitions could have been produced. As the opening approached, Winegarten wrote of her excitement: "All of this represents much hard work on the part of the most wonderful staff I have ever had the good fortune to work with—a marvelously talented group of women."[56]

The final, 500-running-foot, multicultural museum exhibit, "Texas Women: A Celebration of History," opened at the Institute of Texan Cultures, with film star, dancer, and Texan Ginger Rogers performing in person. With sections called "We Fly," "We Build," "We Work," "We Serve," "We Love Children," among others, the exhibit delivered the astonishing news that women had been involved in virtually every aspect of Texas history. True to Gerda Lerner's premise, it also confirmed that they were at the heart of community building: without women's efforts, the San Antonio River might have remained a drainage ditch, and the Alamo would likely have been demolished. Without women, there would be fewer schools, hospitals, libraries, symphonies, and museums. Without women, there might still be no child labor laws, food inspection, or maternal and infant health care programs, and women might still not be allowed to serve on juries. The exhibit toured the state for eighteen months in 1981 and 1982, and more than one million people saw it. The TFWR commissioned six smaller versions of it for display in such venues as classrooms, bank lobbies, shopping centers, and libraries. The exhibit catalogue, *Texas Women: A Celebration of History,* which Winegarten coauthored with Mary Beth Rogers and Sherry Smith, was published in 1981, and it was still in demand five years after the exhibit closed.[57]

Although producing the exhibit was, to say the least, demanding, Winegarten and the staff were passionate about it. "Everybody who came to work for the project, whether as a volunteer or as a paid professional, loved it," she remembered. "They went far above and beyond what just a hired hand would do. . . . We came in every day just full of enthusiasm, full of excitement."[58] Winegarten had found the perfect combination of intellectual stimulation, community service, women's history, hard work, female camaraderie, and adventure in the Texas Women's History Project. Even more, however, she had discovered the bone-deep pleasure of saving lives. Every time she pulled an unknown woman's name from a card catalogue, found an Apache child's mother-made doll, or handled the iron a slave woman had used to press her master's clothes, Winegarten was rescuing a real woman from obscurity, placing her in the light, and notifying anyone who would listen that there were generations of women from the past to whom the present owed a debt of gratitude. She never lost this passion; it motivated and informed everything she published afterward.

The title of a presentation Winegarten and Werden made to the Berkshires Conference of Women Historians at Vassar College just before the exhibit opened, "Creating a Texas Women's History Industry," captured the goal Winegarten established for herself once the exhibit closed.[59] She immediately began publishing. Much like the *Texas Women: A Celebration of History* exhibit catalogue, the large-format, "pictorial history" books Winegarten first published were filled with photographs and reproductions of documents, luring readers with visuals but also offering captions, explanatory text, lists, timelines, notes, and bibliographies. They were also written with a large audience in mind, like the range of people who might visit a museum exhibit: historians, certainly, but also students, teachers, parents, librarians—virtually anyone interested in Texas history. Arranged chronologically, they also cover remarkably large swaths of time. The first, *Texas Women: A Pictorial History from Indians to Astronauts* (1986), begins with Native Americans and ends in the present. Winegarten's way of bringing to light the women who did not make it into the exhibit, this book drew on research that she and her staff had done and is clearly indebted to those efforts.[60]

Winegarten never overcame her desire to discover and include as many women as possible in her work. As a reminder of this addiction, she kept a "motto" above her desk that read, "Just because I know something doesn't mean I have to put it in the book." When the realities of time, budget, and authorial endurance intervened, she simply saved culled information for use another day. This strategy produced not only *Texas Women: A Pictorial History,* but also *Deep in the Heart: The Lives & Legends of Texas Jews, a Photographic History* (1990), which offered information collected for but too plentiful to include in *The New Handbook of Texas; Black Texas Women: A Sourcebook* (1996), which presented documents, biographies, and a timeline too numerous or hefty to publish in *Black Texas Women: 150 Years of Trial and Triumph* (1995); and *Capitol Women: Texas Female Legislators, 1923–1999* (2000), which grew from the information she and I collected but could not include in our video history, *Getting Where We've Got to Be: The Story of Women in the Texas Legislature.*[61]

While she also never relinquished her preference for the generous use of visuals, Winegarten over time began to reverse the visual/text proportion, producing publications that were more text- than picture-rich, less pictorial than narrative histories. In 1985 she and Frieda Werden published a detailed, six-page chronological overview, "Women in Texas History," in a Texas Sesquicentennial edition of the *Texas Almanac 1986–1987.* They were "sickened," in Werden's word, to find that the article was deleted from the next and subsequent editions.[62]

In 1987 Ellen C. Temple published *Citizens at Last: The Woman Suffrage Movement in Texas,* a groundbreaking documentary history edited by Winegarten and Judith N. McArthur that reprinted historian A. Elizabeth Taylor's 1951 *Journal of Southern History* article about the suffrage movement in Texas, with thirty-eight key documents, bibliographies, photographs, and a foreword by historian Anne Firor Scott. A scholarly work with visual appeal, *Citizens at Last* was what would now be called a "crossover" publication, a small, focused, reference book whose audience included academics as well as the general public. The book was the basis for a traveling exhibit by Texas Woman's University.[63]

For the next several years, Winegarten turned her attention to creating a book about African American women in Texas and to producing a musical about one of those women. She had empathized with the difficult lives led by African Americans since she had been a teenager in Dallas searching for ways to promote tolerance and racial equality. While in graduate school at UTD, she had conducted research about black Dallas women and had collected the oral history of one woman, Annie Mae Hunt. For the exhibit *Texas Women: A Celebration of History,* despite the difficulty staff had in finding information about black women, she and Frieda Werden had pieced together a timeline for black women's history to parallel the timeline for white women that was emerging from their research. She eventually realized that they had created "the spine for a future publication on the history of black women in Texas."[64]

Texas Women: A Pictorial History had included some preliminary information, as had *They Showed the Way: An Exhibition of Black Texas Women, 1836–1986*, a traveling museum exhibit about 125 black women that Winegarten had curated for the Museum of African-American Life and Culture in Dallas to celebrate the Texas Sesquicentennial. With that finished, she was ready for the massive task of organizing what she had assembled and looking for what she lacked. She also searched for a black scholar to coauthor the book. Unable to find anyone, she moved ahead, collaborating with Werden and Janet G. Humphrey to produce her masterwork, *Black Texas Women: 150 Years of Trial and Triumph*. Published in 1995, it is a compendium of hundreds of women's achievements, from the antebellum period to the present, that historian Darlene Clark Hine said "enriches and complicates African American and women's history by connecting threads of race, gender, class, and region." To celebrate its publication, Winegarten worked with Ada Anderson and Luci Baines Johnson to produce "Women Who Did," a symposium held at the LBJ Library on the seventy-fifth anniversary of the Voting Rights Act to honor the seventy-five living women featured in the book. Lady Bird Johnson chaired the ceremony and Luci Johnson opened it, calling the honorees "powerful but not necessarily prominent women who had achieved a great deal under great adversity."[65]

Black Texas Women represented everything Winegarten had been uncovering about the subject for nearly twenty years. Even so, she said, it was still incomplete. She issued a challenge to readers to "locate those records still hiding in attics, dresser drawers, antique chests, and musty suitcases, to preserve records of churches, clubs, and institutions, and to deposit these materials in accessible libraries" to create "in-depth scholarship, as well as stories for children, biographies, curriculum units, plays, films, television and radio programs, and more."[66] The nearly limitless scope of that challenge to her readers—find everything you can, then create everything possible from it—was at bottom the need that Winegarten drove herself to fulfill. Not satisfied to create books for adult readers, she also contributed to a children's book, a musical, and three educational videos.[67]

While working on *Black Texas Women*, Winegarten cowrote, cast, and produced the musical *I Am Annie Mae*, adapted from the first book she published, with the same title, in 1983. The story of a black Dallas cleaning woman turned saleswoman and public personality, the book was based on a series of oral history interviews Winegarten began in 1977 to use for the Ph.D. dissertation she never wrote. It also likely evoked, and perhaps closed the circle on, an experience she had had in 1947, when she and another SMU student visited a black neighborhood in West Dallas for a social outreach project. There they found a run-down section without water lines or toilets, where typhoid was not uncommon. "I never realized in Dallas, there were people living under such conditions," she wrote just after the visit. "I suppose that opportunity for service lies close at hand."[68]

When she was introduced to Annie Mae Hunt, she found the story that exemplified what she had witnessed, and she believed she could make a difference by publicizing Hunt's life story. "It's a political decision," she said. "One way I could empower people was to try to write their history. Because when you deprive people of their history, you deprive them of their power."[69] The grandchild of slaves, Hunt had picked cotton in East Texas as a child "under near-slavery conditions," suffered a broken arm in a brutal attack by a white man on her mother, sister, and herself for an "impertinent" remark made by her stepfather, and experienced thirteen pregnancies in her lifetime. Having a limited education, she became a domestic worker, then started selling Avon products and earned enough income eventually to own her own house and retire to participate in Democratic Party politics, through which she attended President Jimmy Carter's inauguration.[70] Told entirely in Hunt's words and illustrated with family photographs and documents, the book represented what Winegarten thought was the "best promise of oral history—the ability to document the lives of ordinary working class people who are at the base of all political structures, but who are seldom included in the history books."[71]

Winegarten self-published the book, and she and Hunt marketed it through television and radio appearances, newspaper and magazine articles, and meetings, autograph parties, and interviews in Texas, Miami, Memphis, and New York City. The book sold out its first printing of 1,000 copies in three months. Excerpts were dramatized at the White Barn Theater in Westport, Connecticut, and Winegarten saw its theatrical potential. In 1984 she met Houston composer Naomi Carrier and described her vision, and for the next three years, the two women wrote the script and composed twenty gospel, jazz, blues, and rock 'n' roll songs. Winegarten promoted the first performance (directed by Boyd Vance and produced by Rita Starpattern, head of the Austin nonprofit Women and Their Work) through her by-now impressive network of women in various cultural communities across the state. It premiered in 1987 as an ensemble production to a sold-out audience at the Mary Moody Northen Theater at Austin's St. Edward's University and garnered a story and interview on National Public Radio. Annie Mae Hunt attended and joined in with the cast at the end to standing ovations. The show played in Houston and Dallas in 1989. Likely in response to the production's costs and to reviews suggesting it was too long, Winegarten and Carrier converted it into a one-woman show with seven songs and staged it nearly twenty times between 1988 and 1997 in Texas and at universities in Kansas, Arizona, and Missouri.[72]

Winegarten was involved in making three video histories. The first was a twenty-four-minute live-action production called *Guts, Gumption, and Go-*

Ahead: Annie Mae Hunt Remembers, which appeared in 1993 and was shown on Dallas's WFAA television station during Black History Month that year. The second was a thirty-minute historical overview for seventh-grade students; produced by the Foundation for Women's Resources and written by Ruthe, foundation director Candace O'Keefe, and me, it was called *From Gutsy Mavericks to Quiet Heroes: True Tales of Texas Women* (1997).[73] The third began in 1995 when she and I were invited by Linda Schott, director of the Center for the Study of Women and Gender at the University of Texas at San Antonio (UTSA), and state representative Sylvia Romo (D-San Antonio) to participate in producing a video history of women in the Texas Legislature to celebrate the centennial anniversary of the first woman to have been elected to a state legislature (Colorado's). Romo was planning an event for Texas to mark the anniversary, as we understood every other state also planned to do, and the video was to be shown at this event. As a member of the Texas House, Romo secured permission for us and three videographers to use Speaker of the House Pete Laney's private conference room. In the last days of May 1995, during the hectic finale of the seventy-fourth legislative session, the women of the House and Senate came in to tell us the stories of their lives as numerical minorities in what had been an exclusively male world from 1846 to 1923. Even by 1995 women constituted less than 20 percent of the legislature's population.[74]

In all, we interviewed twenty-eight current and former male and female members, including Sissy Farenthold, who ran for governor after two terms as the only woman in the House; Sarah Weddington, a state representative when she argued *Roe v. Wade* before the U.S. Supreme Court; U.S. senator Kay Bailey Hutchison, the first Republican woman elected to the Texas House; Senfronia Thompson and Eddie Bernice Johnson, the first two African American women elected to the House; Irma Rangel, the first Latina elected to the legislature; Judith Zaffirini, the first Latina elected to the Senate; and Barbara Jordan, in one of her last video interviews. We also interviewed Speaker Laney and former governor Ann Richards, who had once been a legislative aide to Weddington.

As the oral historian, Winegarten conducted many of the interviews. Through her relaxed and respectful approach, she elicited a number of remarkable moments. These included the description by Myra Banfield Dippel (D-Rosenberg, 1961 to 1965) of the cigarettes, liquor, and call girls given by lobbyists to male solons, as well as the dismay described by Farenthold, who said she had come to the legislature aware that blacks and Mexican Americans were not represented, but soon realized "that Texans weren't even represented."[75] A short version of the production premiered before a statewide audience of politicians and the politically active in October 1995 and received attention in statewide media. UTSA distributed the full-length, forty-five-minute version, *Getting Where We've Got to Be: The Story of Women in the Texas Legislature,* together with a teacher's guide, to schools and universities; the University of Texas Press later distributed it with our book, *Capitol Women: Texas Female Legislators, 1923–1999*, the first history of women in the Texas Legislature.

The last major project Winegarten undertook was *Las Tejanas: 300 Years of History*, with Teresa Palomo Acosta.[76] The first history of women of Mexican descent in Texas, this book was another groundbreaking volume, surveying women of Spanish-Mexican origin from 1700 to 2000. The book is particularly remarkable because Acosta and Winegarten had so few resources to build upon. Not until the 1970s, as the field of women's history began to flourish, was the first Chicana history published.[77] The first generation of professionally trained historians did not appear until the 1980s; Tejanas with doctorates did not appear until the 1990s, in part because so many found Texas such an inhospitable place to pursue their graduate degrees that they left the state to study elsewhere.[78] Winegarten had some knowledge of the field: in 1981, she had presented a paper at the National Women's Studies Association meeting about the early Mexican American feminist movement in Texas. She had also contributed article suggestions about Tejanas to the *Handbook of Texas* revision project, which provided a brief opportunity for original research and writing about Tejanas in the late 1980s and early 1990s. While these entries helped in the production of *Las Tejanas*, the continuing dearth of resources caused Winegarten later to call it "the hardest book I've ever done."[79]

Winegarten was determined to produce it, however, because no one else had. "I kept waiting for somebody else to do it," she told a reporter.[80] First she wanted to find a Tejana scholar with whom to collaborate. She searched for over a year, only to have one, already spread thin from the reality of being a rare find, drop out of the project to attend to other professional commitments. Acosta, an accomplished journalist, educator, historian, and poet, joined Winegarten in 2000. "I laughed at my audacity and perhaps my foolishness for agreeing to be coauthor," Acosta wrote. "After all, I had only learned about Ruthe's plan to work on a 300-year history on Tejanas a few weeks before. At the time, I had practically shivered with fear at the thought of anyone embarking on what had to be a very challenging endeavor."[81]

Winegarten asked Acosta to write most of the manuscript and to rework the chapters Winegarten had already written. She organized her own files, some of which she had been collecting for over twenty-five years, then gave them to Acosta; she also acquired illustrations and drafted the timeline, a "notable Tejanas" section, and the bibliography. The two read and discussed everything and eventually revised their 500-page manuscript three times before submitting it for publication.[82]

Perhaps most significant, however, was that Winegarten wanted the book to have a single, Tejana voice. As a result, she gave Acosta the final word about what would appear. This was not simply deference, but grew from a clear understanding of the context within which the two women were collaborating. As Acosta said, "We were attempting to forge a new path, one where a Tejana was an equal and, as an equal, could be the leader for a change."[83]

> Like many people born and reared in Texas, Ruthe's and my individual and group identities were shaped in a state whose history is littered with falsities or half-truths about Texas Mexicans. As a result, we were both educated in an environment where obstinate reluctance to allow Tejanas a voice in our state's history was a common thread running through the state's official cultural and historical institutions.
>
> . . . Thus, our adherence to my role as the "final word" in our project was perhaps the most genuine way to bring balance to a first-time-ever effort to place Tejanas' 300-year-old story of living in the land that became Texas on more intellectually honest ground.[84]

In 2003, with the collaboration a success and the book published, Winegarten and Acosta moved ahead to their next project, a symposium on *Las Tejanas* that was held at UT, giving scholars a forum for discussing new research.[85]

In addition to the considerable variety and number of tangible works that Ruthe Winegarten produced, one of her most important was the friendship, energy, and support she offered anyone who was also interested in saving the stories of Texas women. She gave of her time, research files, famously large Rolodex of friends and associates, advice, and her experience. She loved to teach and encourage, but she was also not above reminding, prodding, correcting, and suggesting revisions. Winegarten offered her home as a gathering place and furnished food to nourish discussion, invoking the potluck dinner to bring diverse people together to learn from each other. The informal Texas Women's History Network was the most organized and long-lasting of these efforts. Started in the early 1980s as a way to keep the women of the Texas Women's History Project in touch with each other, it grew in membership and changed over the years but was open to anyone interested in Texas women's history. There were no dues, officers, or bylaws. Winegarten's 1920s bungalow on Keasbey Street was frequently the site of the network's get-togethers, during which people planned and discussed research projects, sought and gave advice, shared resources, and celebrated professional achievements and life events. One of its typical activities was to mark the anniversary of the first time Travis County suffragists registered to vote. Imitating a 1918 photograph, the Austin network members had themselves photographed in 1987 on the steps of the Travis County Courthouse, wearing similar clothing and striking similar poses as their forebears had.[86]

Winegarten was the glue that held the network together. Older than most of its members, she became a role model to many of them because she had created a career in women's history for herself and because she seemed always busy with a project that sparked ideas in others. More than that, however, Winegarten was a maternal figure to many and came to be regarded as the mother of the Texas women's history movement.

Although she needed to earn a living and increasingly sold her research and writing services to individuals and organizations, Winegarten also continued to volunteer. In the early 1980s, when the Texas State Historical Association (TSHA) announced a massive, multiyear revision to its venerable encyclopedia, *The Handbook of Texas*, she and Ellen Temple, with whom she had worked on the Texas Women's History Project, met with TSHA director L. Tuffly Ellis to make what Temple called "an eloquent plea" for the inclusion of significant information about women. When Ellis mentioned his limited knowledge of Texas women's history, "we knew we were in the process for the long haul," Temple recalled. "After the meeting, Ruthe laughingly described the struggle we would have to undertake as . . . 'water torture, one drip at a time.'"[87]

With her sense of humor intact, Winegarten volunteered her services to the *Handbook* for the next ten years. As the director of research on the revision project in the late 1980s and early 1990s, I became her contact person. She was a natural resource, relentlessly submitting ideas for entries about women from across ethnic, racial, and social groups, sometimes fifty to one hundred at a time. She was also willing to write them herself or to find someone else who would. Sometimes, she also asked for advice, as when she requested a meeting with three of the women's history research staff to discuss her work in progress, which became *Black Texas Women*.[88]

In addition, she actively pursued the creation of a Texas women's history research center at TSHA or its affiliated research unit at UT, the Center for Studies in Texas History (CSTH). In 1990 participants in "Women & Texas History," the first statewide conference on Texas women's history, had voiced their support for such a center.[89] Winegarten was particularly interested because for her, and for Ellen Temple, this was the continuation of efforts they had begun after the Texas Women's History Project ended in 1982. At that time, Winegarten wrote, "we all naively assumed that textbook publishers, the Texas Education Agency, college history departments, etc., would integrate the information. We were wrong."[90] For the next several years, the two had lobbied various UT entities and held meetings at the homes of such influential supporters as Bun Mark, wife of UT chancellor Hans Mark; author and UT benefactor Jean Andrews; and feminist activist Liz Carpenter.[91]

Building on conference keynote speaker Elizabeth Fox-Genovese's contention that Texas was in "desperate need" of basic information about the history of women, Winegarten began less than a month after the conference ended to survey key participants about what such a center should be and do. By early 1991, with Temple having been appointed to the UT board of regents by Governor Ann Richards, Winegarten was optimistic. She lobbied Standish Meacham, dean of Liberal Arts at UT, to add a women's studies center to those already in existence for Texas, Latin American, Mexican American, African American, Middle Eastern, and Asian studies. Initially reluctant, Meacham apparently thought locating such a center within the CSTH would be plausible financially and pedagogically, but warned Winegarten that the university administration was not in the mood to consider adding a new center to its budget.[92]

She also lobbied Alwyn Barr, vice president of TSHA and a historian of African American history, who politely reminded her that there were many claimants hoping for attention after the *Handbook* revision project ended. Feeling somewhat "mired in bureaucratic swampland," Winegarten suggested that supporters of a center go right to Richards by signing a petition to the governor asking her to assign one of her staff to "investigate the best possible way of establishing a Center and come up with a workable plan and timetable."[93]

Within TSHA/CSTH, I proposed an incremental plan that would result in a fully formed center ready to launch by the time *The New Handbook* of Texas was published in 1996.[94] Ron Tyler, the TSHA/CSTH director, agreed to the plan's first steps: add a women's history luncheon to the annual meeting and publish a collection of essays from the "Women & Texas History" conference.[95] Next on the list were two endowments, one to fund a yearly $1,000 publication award for the best scholarly book in Texas women's history and another to provide an annual $1,000 research grant. Temple soon funded the book award (named for Liz Carpenter).[96] Raising funds for the research endowment could begin in 1992.

Winegarten, a member of the Governor's Commission for Women, wrote to commission chair Amalia Rodríguez-Mendoza with a proposal that the commission support the creation of a center at TSHA/CSTH and recommend to Governor Richards that center funding be included in the budget for the next biennium. Temple supported the proposal. "The State of Texas is the only major state with no Center for Research on Women," Winegarten wrote to Rodríguez-Mendoza. "The University of Texas at Austin is the only major university in the country with no such Center. . . . Let's try to get this Center institutionalized . . . so that it will live on as do the other centers at UT."[97]

Winegarten had good reason for her optimism that a decade of effort to institutionalize Texas women's history at UT would end in success: Ann Richards and her colleagues at the FWR had a track record for initiating and raising funds for significant Texas women's history projects and women's leadership initiatives; she had appointed Temple, another longtime women's history advocate, to the UT board of regents; one of Richards's earliest official acts as governor had been to gather a number of women's history supporters to witness her signing an official declaration supporting Women's History Month; supporters all over the state saw the need for a research center; and TSHA's first women's history luncheon, held at its March 1992 annual meeting, generated such interest that thirty people had to be turned away. Temple shared her excitement about the burgeoning state of Texas women's history with the Foundation for Women's Resources board of directors, reminding them that "making research possible . . . is still the biggest challenge that we face."[98]

This hopeful effervescence evaporated, however, when TSHA announced in early June 1992 that a $200,000 shortfall in the *Handbook*'s budget required a change in direction that included substantial reductions in research staff and in research-related work: remaining research would focus on what the managing editor termed "bedrock" entries about traditional Texas history topics (called "local history" internally) that had been the revision project's priority since its earliest days. The histories of women, Mexican Americans, and African Americans (called "thematic histories" internally) were now called a "luxury." The managing editor's list of new work priorities put local history at the top and thematic history near the bottom. Finally, staff cuts included not only four research assistants with expertise in thematic history, but also the only editor responsible for thematic entries.[99]

While TSHA presented these changes publically as logical transitions into the final editing phase, they came as a disheartening surprise to the research staff doing thematic entries, who felt that they had just begun to scratch the surface of thematic history for the revision. Their concerns were justified: although TSHA started the *Handbook* revision process in 1980 and secured funding for three full-time scholars in residence to do local history, documenting women's history did not begin in earnest until 1984, when the association raised enough funding for one half-time research assistant. In 1987 the managing editor attempted to eliminate entirely the research assistantships in women's and African American history, but research staff convinced Tyler not to take that advice. In 1988, again after staff urging, Tyler equalized the status, title, and pay scale of thematic and local history research positions through a grant from the National Endowment for the Humanities (NEH). By March 1990, the managing editor was planning to cut them back to half time; research staff persuaded him not to.[100]

This track record had put the completion of entries about Texas's women, African Americans, and Mexican Americans at a disadvantage: not only were there fewer research staff working on them over a shorter period of time than there were for local history entries, but—because these fields were relative newcomers to Texas history—there were also fewer secondary sources to consult to complete them. As a result, these entries took longer because so many of them required original research in primary sources. The changes announced in June 1992, then, made it clear that work on the histories of women, African Americans, and Tejanas/Tejanos, although started late, was already effectively over.

Ruthe Winegarten was stunned by the news, then angry. Likely reminded of the excision of her "Women in Texas History" article from the *Texas Almanac* the year after it appeared, she called Tyler for a discussion about alternatives. Not satisfied, she then wrote a letter, cosigned by Rodríguez-Mendoza and David Williams, president of the Black Texans Historical Society, to TSHA president Alwyn Barr and the association's Executive Council objecting to shifting priorities and layoffs and expressing concern over jeopardy to TSHA's NEH grants, which were requested to promote thematic subjects and were obtained, she said, "in large part because of your commitment to a multi-cultural approach [to the *Handbook* revision]" and for which she had supplied personal letters of endorsement. The letter also requested permission for the three signatories to attend the Executive Council meeting. She sent copies to thirteen people: Tyler; Governor Richards; Temple; U.S. representative J. J. "Jake" Pickle; the heads of the Texas NAACP, Texas Jewish Historical Association, Tejano-Tejana Historical Association, Texas Committee for the Humanities, Foundation for Women's Resources, and the Research Division at the NEH; the chair of the UT history department; the vice provost for research at UT; and Wilhelmina Delco, the first female speaker pro tem of the Texas House of Representatives.[101]

In July Winegarten held a meeting of the Texas Women's History Network to encourage a large turnout at the Executive Council meeting. The council, however, allowed only two outside observers and one speaker: Winegarten. She was given five minutes. In that time, she reminded the council that women and people of color made up the majority of the state's population, suggested that the members ask themselves what kind of *Handbook* they wanted to produce, and requested that the jettisoned staff positions be reinstated. In the end, all the planned reductions in staff and research-related work went ahead as scheduled.[102]

This episode seriously undermined the tentative trust that had slowly developed during the *Handbook* revision between TSHA/CSTH and "minority history" communities. Winegarten, along with groups whose histories had been largely omitted from or underrepresented in the original *Handbook* (1952) and its one-volume supplement (1976), clearly understood the opportunity they had, finally, to establish a presence in this, the most widely consulted reference work about Texas. To be included in the *Handbook* was to be freed from mythology and recognized by history. That opportunity, she felt, had been largely squandered by parochial views about the kinds of entries that were essential to the new *Handbook* and the kinds that could be done without. And, despite her longstanding desire to see a women's history research center at TSHA/CSTH, that idea no longer seemed wise. What the episode taught Winegarten was that advocates of women's, African American, and Tejana/Tejano history were on their own.[103]

But working on her own, at least on her own terms, was what Ruthe Winegarten had always been about. What is less known about Winegarten than her dedication to women's history is her love of the arts, and her talent for writing comedies, musicals, and poetry, often about women in history. In addition to the musical *I Am Annie Mae,* she outlined, with Frieda Werden, *The Sancties of Belton,* a musical comedy about a nineteenth-century Texas women's collective, the Belton Sanctificationists. She also hoped to write one about Belle Starr, and drafted ideas for turning *Capitol Women* into a play.[104] Of her poetry, one of her most amusing poems imagines how World War I could have been avoided:

> First I stand where Gavrilo Princip stood.
> Then I position myself on the bridge where the
> Archduke Franz Ferdinand and the Duchess of Hohenburg
> Sophie (who is omitted from many accounts in the event)
> Posed in their carriage
>
> Then I imagine myself to be the Duchess.
> And I look across the bridge
> And see Princip aiming his pistol at us.
> And I turn to my husband, the Duke, and say,
> "Franzy, you *pherd,* you *esel,* you *dumkopf*!
> If you had listened to me,
> We would be in Dubrovnik now
> Taking the waters."[105]

Written on a vacation to Sarajevo in 1984, this poem reveals both Winegarten's sense of humor and her ability to place herself in other people's positions. It also reveals the extent to which she saw the world through the eyes of a historian of women's history: she skewers those who have left the incident's lone female out of their accounts and, pulling Sophie up from obscurity, names her, places her center stage, gives her the final word, and then imagines her plan to prevent one of the world's worst conflagrations. If only a woman's presence had been acknowledged, if only her voice had been heard, Winegarten is saying, her idea could have changed the course of history.

While Winegarten easily imagined such a grand fantasy as having a woman prevent the first worldwide war, she expressed mixed feelings about the reality of life lived on her own in her poem, "Alone at Last":

I shun the acquisition
Of a plant or pussycat
Or anything which makes demands on me
Insists on nurture, love, or tender care.

It's freedom that I crave
Though lonely in the silence of the night
When others lie in loving beds
Softness tender
Legs entwined.
I cry sometimes.[106]

Remarkably, she sent this poem to Stanley Schneider, the lost love of her youth, in a 1981 letter. Despite the fact that he had married someone else, raised a family, and embarked on his own career in another state, Winegarten continued for decades to correspond with him and his wife, as "dear friends," revealing the tenacity with which she tried to keep Schneider, if only tangentially, in her life. After Goldie Schneider became seriously ill, Winegarten began to write just to him again, expressing her sadness for his situation, her fondness for Goldie and their children, and her interest in his work. She and Al Winegarten divorced in late 1981, she moved to New York City to be closer to Schneider, and they reconnected. "After years of being miserably married," she wrote a friend, "I feel that it's nice to know what a good relationship can be like." Ruthe Winegarten and Stanley Schneider married, at last, in 1986 and lived in Austin. For a while they were happy. But that relationship, too, ended in divorce. When a friend told her she was sorry to hear about it, Winegarten replied, "Don't be. I'm not. I have my life back."[107]

Following her heart, which told her that she had to save as many Texas women's lives as possible, Ruthe Winegarten used her head to make a career in that endeavor a reality. Although never employed full time by a college or university; and although her four marriages, even to the love of her life, did not last; and although she was sometimes lonely, Ruthe Winegarten nevertheless constructed her own community of scholars, students, family, and friends who felt, like her, that they were on a mission to write women into Texas history. In that sense, she was, indeed, a community organizer. In the words of Melissa Hield, Winegarten understood and promoted the activities "that create connections among women and men. . . . She creates ties that bind us together. Through her, we see that we are all part of one community."[108]

In 1999, Winegarten suffered a heart attack that worried her but did not prevent her from completing her work on *Capitol Women*, then embarking on *Las*

Tejanas. By the time the latter was published in 2003, however, she was tired. Coronary artery disease that required angioplasty and stents, serious health problems in her family, and the end of yet another important relationship left her increasingly anxious. She sought help for her mental as well as her physical health, and underwent electroconvulsive therapy. But her condition worsened, and she attempted to commit suicide through a drug overdose. Her family and friends surrounded her with care, singly and in groups, urging her to take part in once-joyful group dinners or bringing her food, news, books, and conversation. But their ministrations were not solutions. In May 2004, after being diagnosed with early vascular dementia, which involved damage to the frontal lobe of her brain, she moved into an assisted living facility in Austin. Seeing no bright end to her situation, she took a cab one day in June and bought a handgun. Three days later, on June 14, she ended her life with a single shot to her heart.[109]

Many who knew Ruthe have struggled to come to terms with her death. She knew that her mind and her body were failing. Ever practical, she also knew that her condition was draining her finances. "It's freedom that I crave," she had written, and she no longer had it. For those left behind, what fills our minds and breaks our hearts is that, after all she had done to save so many lives, we could not save hers. What Ruthe Winegarten left behind, however, is a path forward, because she blazed it. What historians of Texas women's history have is the opportunity to continue on that path, remembering that her task is also ours: each one, pull one.[110]

SUGGESTED READING

Winegarten, Ruthe. *Black Texas Women: A Sourcebook: Documents, Biographies, Timeline.* With Janet G. Humphrey and Frieda Werden, consulting eds. Austin: University of Texas Press, 1996.

This volume presents 266 source documents, 56 brief biographies, and a timeline to accompany the previously published *Black Texas Women: 150 Years of Trial and Triumph.*

Winegarten, Ruthe. *Black Texas Women: 150 Years of Trial and Triumph.* With Janet G. Humphrey and Frieda Werden, consulting eds. Austin: University of Texas Press, 1994.

The first attempt to survey the lives of black women in Texas, this book is the essential starting place for anyone interested in the subject. It won the Liz Carpenter Award from the Texas State Historical Association and the Myers Center Award for the Study of Human Rights in North America from the Gustavus Myers Center for the Study of Intolerance in the United States.

Winegarten, Ruthe, and Teresa Palomo Acosta. *Las Tejanas: 300 Years of History.* Austin: University of Texas Press, 2003.

The first survey history of women of Mexican descent in Texas, this book is, like *Black*

Texas Women, another essential volume for anyone interested in the subject. It won the T. R. Feherenbach Book Award from the Texas Historical Commission.

Winegarten, Ruthe, and Annie Mae Hunt. *I Am Annie Mae: An Extraordinary Black Texas Woman in Her Own Words*. Edited by Frieda Werden. Austin: University of Texas Press, 1996. (Originally published as *I Am Annie Mae: An Extraordinary Woman in Her Own Words—The Personal Story of a Black Texas Woman*. Austin: Rosegarden Press, 1983.)

This oral history is told only in the words of its subject and represents Winegarten's lifelong commitment to recording the histories of "ordinary" women.

Winegarten, Ruthe, and Nancy Baker Jones. *Capitol Women: Texas Female Legislators, 1923–1999*. Austin: University of Texas Press, 2000.

The first history of women in the Texas Legislature, this book includes an historical overview of women in politics, an analysis of gender dynamics at the Capitol, biographies, a timeline, and statistical summaries. It won the Liz Carpenter Award from the Texas State Historical Association.

Winegarten, Ruthe, and Nancy Baker Jones. *Getting Where We've Got to Be: Women in the Texas Legislature*. Video (VHS). San Antonio: Center for the Study of Women and Gender, University of Texas at San Antonio, 1996.

Suitable for classroom use, this video includes interviews with such legislators as Sissy Farenthold, Barbara Jordan, Irma Rangel, and Kay Bailey Hutchison. Viewable at www.womenintexashistory.org.

Winegarten, Ruthe, and Nancy Baker Jones. *From Gutsy Mavericks to Quiet Heroes: True Tales of Texas Women*. Austin: Foundation for Women's Resources, 1997.

Designed for use in classrooms, this video and teachers' guide is a survey of women in Texas history.

Winegarten, Ruthe, and Judith N. McArthur. *Citizens at Last: The Woman Suffrage Movement in Texas*. Austin: Ellen C. Temple, 1987.

A compilation of essential documents related to Texas women's fight for the vote, this book includes an overview essay by A. Elizabeth Taylor, thirty-eight documents, and two bibliographies.

Winegarten, Ruthe, and Cathy Schechter. *Deep in the Heart: The Lives and Legends of Texas Jews*. Austin: Eakin Press, 1990.

Representative of the pictorial histories Winegarten published, this volume offers essential information about the lives of Jews in the state's history.

NOTES

1. Alice Walker, "Each One, Pull One," *Horses Make a Landscape Look More Beautiful: Poems by Alice Walker* (New York: Harcourt Brace Jovanovich, 1984), 52.

2. Ruthe Winegarten, introduction to untitled manuscript in the possession of Debra Winegarten.

NANCY BAKER JONES

3. Ruthe Winegarten resumes, Resumes folder, box 2.325/C128, Ruthe Winegarten Papers, Dolph Briscoe Center for American History, University of Texas at Austin (hereafter RWP); Mary Beth Rogers Research folders, box 4Ad69, RWP. Rogers was writing what became *Barbara Jordan: American Hero* (New York: Bantam Books, 1998). Poems folder, box 2.325/W68, RWP. One poem was published in *Fifty Prizewinning Poems* (Eugene, OR: Aesthetics West, 1986). Two poems were published in Diane Fanning and Susie Flatau, eds., *Red Boots and Attitude: The Spirit of Texas Women Writers* (Austin: Eakin Press, 2002).

4. Harvey J. Graff, untitled reminiscence, in *Mum's the Word: A Tribute to Ruthe Winegarten*, edited by Debra L. Winegarten (Austin: Sunbelt Media, 2001), 173, 175. Martha Norkunas, "Oral History Transcript. Narrator: Ruthe Winegarten," 2003, 37–38, box 2.325/W68, RWP; Official Academic Record Transcripts for Ruthe Lee Lewin, Southern Methodist University, Ruthe Addington, University of Texas at Austin, Ruthe Winegarten, University of Texas at Arlington, and Ruthe L. Winegarten, University of Texas at Dallas, in the author's possession.

5. Norkunas, "Oral History Transcript," 76.

6. Frieda Werden, untitled reminiscence, in *Mum's the Word*, 131. I knew Ruthe Winegarten as a fellow historian, coauthor, collaborator, and friend, and my own, far less colorful metaphor for Ruthe's approach was that she was like a middle-buster plow, relentlessly unearthing root vegetables from a fertile field, strewing them left and right for followers to explain and signify. When the board of the Ruthe Winegarten Memorial Foundation for Texas Women's History was editing Winegarten's massive women's history timeline for inclusion on its Web site, it found so many names of unknown women that it separated them from the timeline into a section called "research fodder."

7. Norkunas, "Oral History Transcript," 6, 8–9, 15, 19–20, 26. Ruthe Winegarten, typed index card, "Bio Info" folder, box 4Ad69, RWP.

8. Norkunas, "Oral History Transcript," 20. Ruthe Lewin to Stanley Schneider, October 26, 1945, October–November 1945 folder, box 2.325/W68; Lewin to Schneider, November 25, 1945, November–December 1945 folder, box 2.325/W68; Lewin to Schneider, May 25, 1946, Mid-March–May 1946 folder, box 2.325/W68, RWP.

9. Ginger Jacobs, "Ezekiel Jacob Levin," *The New Handbook of Texas*, edited by Ron Tyler (Austin: Texas State Historical Association, 1996), 4:177 (hereafter *NHOT*); Ginger Jacobs, "Dallas, the 1930s: 'We Became the Outstanding Jewish Youth Group in the City,'" in *Builders and Dreamers: Habonim Labor Zionist Youth in North America*, edited by J. J. Goldberg and Elliot King (New York: Herzl Press, 1993), 66.

10. Jacobs, "Ezekiel Jacob Levin"; Goldberg and King, *Builders and Dreamers*, 34–35; Anne Glickman, "Assuming Radical Potential: Stories from the Early Life and Letters of Ruthe Winegarten, a Dallas-bred Progressive," typescript, 2004, in the author's possession.

11. Lewin to Schneider, March 5, 1946, untitled folder, box 2.325/W68, RWP.

12. Lewin to Schneider, February 23, 1946, ibid.

13. Jacobs, "Dallas, the 1930s"; Lewin to Schneider, November 15, 1945, November–December 1945 folder, box 2.325/W68, RWP.

14. Lewin to Schneider, March 19, 1945, untitled folder, box 2.325/W68, RWP.

15. Lewin to Schneider, October 17, 1945, ibid.

16. Lewin to Schneider, March 5, 1946.

17. Lewin to Schneider, January 22, 1946, untitled folder, box 2.325/W68, RWP; Lewin to Schneider, March 5, 1946; Homer Price Rainey was president of the University of Texas from 1939 to 1944, when the board of regents fired him after fractious disputes over academic freedom. Rainey ran for governor in 1946 supporting academic freedom, labor union rights, and

integration and was branded a radical by opponents. He was the first statewide candidate to win support from the emerging Texas coalition of progressives, minorities, and labor. Rainey was soundly defeated by Beauford H. Jester. See George N. Green, "Homer Price Rainey," *NHOT*, 5:416.

18. Lewin to Schneider, October 29, 1946, untitled folder, box 2.325/W68, RWP; Norkunas, "Oral History Transcript," 31. In 1962 Ruthe Winegarten told the Federal Bureau of Investigation in Dallas that she joined the Communist Party when she was eighteen. "Ruthe Lewin Winegarten," FBI report, September 20, 1962, FBI File 100-8140, U.S. Department of Justice, Washington D.C. (hereafter FBI File 100-8140), secured through Freedom of Information/Privacy Acts (FOIPA) request.

19. Lewin to Schneider, June 10, 1946, untitled folder, box 2.325/W68, RWP.

20. Lewin to Schneider, March 27, 1947, March–July 1947 folder, ibid.

21. Lewin to Schneider, November 16, 1946, June–November 1946 folder, ibid.

22. Lewin to Schneider, February 17, 1947, December [1946]–February 1947 folder, ibid.

23. FBI File 100-8140 is incomplete: it contains 423 pages of the "approximately 1,516 pages," which were "potentially responsive" to my FOIPA request. The remaining pages were withheld due to federal exemptions or because they "were not in their expected location and could not be located." David M. Hardy, Section Chief, Record/Information Dissemination Section, Records Management Division, FBI, to Nancy Baker Jones, May 11, 2010.

24. Luther V. Dunn, FBI report, Dallas, Texas, July 14, 1948, FBI File 100-8140. The Nixon-Mundt Bill would have required CP members to register with the U.S. attorney general, denied passports to them, and forbidden federal employees from either participating in the CP or hiring any of its members. It passed the U.S. House on May 21, 1948, but was defeated in the Senate.

25. Norkunas, "Oral History Transcript," 28, 32, 34, 39; Certified copy of marriage license, Ruthe Lewin and Wendell Addington, December 30, 1948, by Thomas M. Maes, Justice of the Peace, Harris County, Texas. Copy dated January 29, 1949, box 2.325/G228 (restricted; access with family permission), RWP; "Lone Star v. Red," *Time*, April 4, 1949, http:www.time.com/time/magazine/article/0,9171,800010,00.html; "Wendell G. Addington 1925–1994" in Wendell Addington Obit folder, box 2P18, RWP.

26. Norkunas, "Oral History Transcript," 33, 40–43; Ruthe Winegarten to Marc Sanders, October 1, 1998, Bio Info folder, box 4Ad69, RWP. FBI File 100-8140 reveals that Ruthe Addington was taken into custody at least twice by the Austin Police Department in 1950 for petitioning to outlaw the atomic bomb and distributing *The Worker*. She was reportedly released uncharged (SAC Dallas to FBI Director, March 25, 1953). It also confirms that she was fired from at least one position, with Southwestern Bell Telephone Company in Austin, because of her affiliations with Communists, particularly her husband (George W. H. Carlson, Special Agent, to SAC, San Antonio, March 6, 1950; C. E. Weeks, Special Agent, to the Commanding General, Fourth Army, Fort Sam Houston, San Antonio, March 8, 1950). The file also contains a copy of her letter printed in the February 8, 1950, issue of *The Daily Texan*. The U.S. Supreme Court decided *Sweatt v. Painter* in 1950, the year Ruthe graduated from the University of Texas.

27. Norkunas, "Oral History Transcript," 42; "Lone Star v. Red"; Don E. Carleton, *Red Scare! Right-Wing Hysteria, Fifties Fanaticism, and Their Legacy in Texas* (Austin: Texas Monthly Press, 1985), 96.

28. Norkunas, "Oral History Transcript," 46, 49.

29. Ibid., 46, 48, 49; Debra Winegarten to Nancy Baker Jones, June 21, 2009.

30. Norkunas, "Oral History Transcript," 50–53.

31. Ibid., 52. Winegarten told the FBI she quit the CP in 1954, but it continued to affect her. Tom Sanders told the FBI she was a member and sued her for custody of their child (her second) because she was "therefore unfit to have care and custody." She retained custody. Her third husband, Al Winegarten, lost his job at Chance-Vought, a Dallas aerospace firm with government contracts, shortly after they married in 1956. She was convinced the FBI was still observing her (it was) and had caused the firing. Winegarten told the FBI that, at a 1962 hearing of a legislative textbook committee about which she was reporting for *The Texas Observer*, she was confronted by former general Edwin A. Walker, recently defeated gubernatorial candidate and John Birch Society member, about her CP affiliation; she later received a telephone threat of exposure as a Communist if she did not cease her political and social activism. Norkunas, "Oral History Transcript," 59–60; undated typescript of a petition to change custody, box 2.325/G228 (restricted; access with family permission), RWP; SAC Dallas to FBI Director, November 15, 1960, FBI Report, September 20, 1962, and "Ruthe Lewin Winegarten," FBI File 100-8140.

32. Norkunas, "Oral History Transcript," 52–56, 60.

33. Ruthe Winegarten resume, Bio-Info Misc. folder, box 4Ad69, RWP; Norkunas, "Oral History Transcript," 61. To operate her bookkeeping and tax service, Winegarten had returned to SMU for classes in accounting and income tax preparation in 1955 and 1958; Official Academic Record Transcript, Ruthe Winegarten, Southern Methodist University, in the author's possession. The FBI was particularly interested in her Dallas associations with Americans for Democratic Action, the G.I. Forum, the NAACP, and the interracial Community Committee for Better Schools (Memo, SAC, Dallas, Texas, May 20, 1959; James P. Hosty Jr., FBI Report, November 15, 1960, FBI File 100-8140).

34. Norkunas, "Oral History Transcript," 61–62; Ann Richards, untitled reminiscence, in *Mum's the Word*, 22–29, 227, which includes photographs of these skits in performance. *Dallas News*, April 19, 1968, and flyer for 1964 performance, both in Political Paranoia folder, box 2P20, RWP; Mary Beth Rogers to Nancy Baker Jones, July 12, 2009. Bobby Baker was an aide to Senate majority leader Lyndon Johnson. In 1963 Baker was forced to resign in light of an insurance kickback scheme. Ann Richards later divorced, moved to Austin, and became, in succession, Travis County commissioner, state treasurer, and governor.

35. "Midlife Degree Turns Career into History," *Social Work News* (University of Texas at Arlington), Spring 1997–1998, 11, Resumes folder, box 2.325/C128, RWP; Norkunas, "Oral History Transcript," 66.

36. Ruthe Winegarten to Mr. and Mrs. Stanley Schneider, January 12, 1966, 1960s–1970s folder, box 2.325/W68, RWP.

37. Norkunas, "Oral History Transcript," 67–68. The scholarships were awarded by the Women's Council of Dallas County and the National Council of Jewish Federations and Welfare Funds.

38. *Dallas Times Herald*, August 17, 1979; "Midlife Degree."

39. Ruthe Winegarten resume, Bio-Info. Misc. folder, box 4Ad69, RWP; Norkunas, "Oral History Transcript," 68–69; see also untitled reminiscences by Walter J. Levy and Gertrude Miller, in *Mum's the Word*, 33, 35–36; "Mrs. Winegarten Begins Duties," *Dallas Federation News*, n.d., reproduced in *Mum's the Word*, 30; "Mrs. Ruthe Winegarten Named Director Dallas ADL Office," *Texas Jewish Post*, September 13, 1973, reproduced in *Mum's the Word*, 34.

40. Debra Winegarten to Nancy Baker Jones, June 21, 2009; Norkunas, "Oral History Transcript," 69.

41. Norkunas, "Oral History Transcript," 70–71.

42. Ruthe Winegarten resume, Bio-Info. Misc. folder, box 4Ad69, RWP; Norkunas, "Oral History Transcript," 75–76.

43. Ruthe Winegarten to Dr. Paul Monaco, Director of Graduate Studies, University of Texas at Dallas, November 3, 1976, UT-Dallas Ph.D. Program folder, box 4Ad69, RWP. See also "1976 Graduate Program Application—the University of Texas at Dallas; Line 25: Narrative Outlining Academic Interests and Objectives," June 25, 1976, ibid.

44. Norkunas, "Oral History Transcript," 77–79; Ruthe Winegarten, resume, Resumes folder, box 2.325/C128, RWP; Graff, untitled reminiscence, 173–174; Official Graduate Transcript, Ruthe Winegarten, University of Texas at Dallas, in the author's possession.

45. "Introducing: Ruthe Winegarten, Author," *Women's History Network News*, April 1996, 2, Resumes folder, box 2.325/C128, RWP; Norkunas, "Oral History Transcript," 77–79; the School of General Studies at UTD is now named for Galerstein, as is the university's women's center and a number of scholarships. See http://www.utdallas.edu/womenscenter/UTDWomensCenter-AboutUs.html. Melissa Hield to Nancy Baker Jones, May 31, 2009. Hield later founded People's History of Texas, a nonprofit group that produced the film *Talking Union*. Elizabeth (B. J.) Fernea was director of women's studies at UT from 1980 to 1983 and a professor of comparative literature and Middle Eastern studies for over twenty years; after a teaching and administrative career at UT, Betty Sue Flowers became the director of the LBJ Presidential Library and Museum.

46. Norkunas, "Oral History Transcript," 78.

47. Ibid.

48. Nancy Baker Jones and Ruthe Winegarten, *Capitol Women: Texas Female Legislators, 1923–1999* (Austin: University of Texas Press, 2000), 50–55; Ruthe Winegarten, *Governor Ann Richards and Other Texas Women: From Indians to Astronauts: A Pictorial History* (Austin: Eakin Press, 1993), 135–142.

49. Jones and Winegarten, *Capitol Women*; Winegarten, *Governor Ann Richards*; "History," Foundation for Women's Resources, http://www.womensresources.org/History.asp.

50. "Ruthe Winegarten," *Austin American-Statesman*, July 4, 2000, Resumes folder, box 2.325/C128, RWP; Norkunas, "Oral History Transcript," 84–86; Mary Beth Rogers, untitled reminiscence, in *Mum's the Word*, 61; Mary Beth Rogers, "Acknowledgements," *Texas Women: A Celebration of History* (Austin: Texas Foundation for Women's Resources, 1981; second edition, 1986), 4; Mary Beth Rogers to Nancy Baker Jones, July 12, 2009.

51. "Acknowledgements," *Texas Women*, 4; "The Project," ibid., 5; "Project Narrative," Application for a Public Discussion Grant, submitted to the Texas Committee for the Humanities, 1980, 9, WITH & TCH Grant Proposal to TCH folder, box 2.325/C95, RWP. Winegarten discusses the importance of Gerda Lerner's work to her own in Norkunas, "Oral History Transcript," 94.

52. Mary Beth Rogers to Advisory Committee Members, April 1, 1979, Foundation for Women's Resources folder, box 2.325/C128, RWP; "Project Narrative," 9–10. These activities were accomplished through grants from the TCH and the NEH.

53. Norkunas, "Oral History Transcript," 86–87; Werden, untitled reminiscence, 131; Mary Beth Rogers, foreword to *Texas Women: A Pictorial History from Indians to Astronauts*, by Ruthe Winegarten (Austin: Eakin Press, 1986), vi.

54. Norkunas, "Oral History Transcript," 86; Ruthe Winegarten, ed., *Texas Women's History Project Bibliography* (Austin: Texas Foundation for Women's Resources, 1980). The bibliography was published with grant assistance from the Texas Committee for the Humanities (now Humanities Texas), the Texas affiliate of the National Endowment for the Humanities.

55. Werden, untitled reminiscence, 131; see also Sherry Smith, untitled reminiscence, in *Mum's the Word,* 139–140.

56. "Texas Women in History Project, Contributions, January 14, 1981," in FWR Donors, 1981 folder, box 2.325/C128, RWP; "The Project and Its Accomplishments," *Texas Women* (1986 edition), 5; Winegarten to Schneider, April 17, 1981, 1981 folder, box 2.325/W68, RWP.

57. Norkunas, "Oral History Transcript," 87; Rogers, foreword to *Texas Women*; Ruthe Winegarten, *Black Texas Women: 150 Years of Trial and Triumph* (Austin: University of Texas Press, 1995), ix. *Texas Women: A Celebration of History* describes the various exhibit sections and details contributions by Texas women. A picture of Ginger Rogers at the exhibit opening is in Winegarten, *Governor Ann Richards,* 162. The TFWR (renamed the Foundation for Women's Resources in 1986) continued its commitment to "the full inclusion of women in the published history of Texas and incorporation of information about women in every aspect of public life" in a number of ways: in 1983 it published, through the efforts of board member Ellen Temple, a book for young readers called *We Can Fly—Stories of Katherine Stinson and Other Gutsy Texas Women,* by Mary Beth Rogers, Janelle Scott, and Sherry Smith. In 1984 it underwrote a staff position in women's history for the *Handbook of Texas* revision project. In 1986 it reprinted the exhibit catalogue. See "The Project and Its Accomplishments."

58. Norkunas, "Oral History Transcript," 86.

59. Winegarten to Schneider, April 17, 1981.

60. Ruthe Winegarten, *Texas Women: A Pictorial History from Indians to Astronauts* (Austin: Eakin Press, 1986).

61. Winegarten's collaborator, Janet G. Humphrey, composed "Ruthe's New Motto" and taped it above her desk. A photograph of Winegarten with the sign appears in *Mum's the Word,* 200. Ruthe Winegarten and Cathy Schechter (with Rabbi Jimmy Kessler, consulting editor), *Deep in the Heart: The Lives and Legends of Texas Jews, a Photographic History* (Austin: Eakin Press, 1990); Ruthe Winegarten (with Janet G. Humphrey and Frieda Werden, consulting editors), *Black Texas Women: A Sourcebook: Documents, Biographies, Timeline* (Austin: University of Texas Press, 1996); Jones and Winegarten, *Capitol Women*; Nancy Baker Jones and Ruthe Winegarten, *Getting Where We've Got to Be: The Story of Women in the Texas Legislature,* Molly Dinkins, Dick DeJong, and Jim Cullers, videographers (Austin: Multimedia Associates, 1996), video (VHS).

62. Ruthe Winegarten and Frieda Werden, "Women in Texas History," *Texas Almanac and State Industrial Guide 1986–1987* (Dallas: A. H. Belo, 1985), 229–234; Frieda Werden to Nancy Baker Jones, July 4, 2009.

63. Ruthe Winegarten and Judith N. McArthur, eds., *Citizens at Last: The Woman Suffrage Movement in Texas* (Austin: Ellen C. Temple, 1987). The *Citizens at Last* traveling exhibit is, as of this writing, distributed by Humanities Texas.

64. Winegarten, *Black Texas Women,* x.

65. Darlene Clark Hine is quoted on the back cover of *Black Texas Women*; Norkunas, "Oral History Transcript," 89; catalogue draft in "They Showed the Way" folder, box 2.325/J13, RWP; Luci Baines Johnson, untitled reminiscence, in *Mum's the Word,* 117; Lady Bird Johnson to Ruthe Winegarten, February 10, 1995, and Luci Baines Johnson to Ada Anderson, February 28, 1995, Lady Bird and Luci Johnson folder, box 2.325/W68, RWP. Winegarten claimed to have "stolen" the subtitle for the book from an exhibit on the history of Austin women that she curated with Janet G. Humphrey in 1986, *Austin Women: 150 Years of Trial and Triumph.* Winegarten's inability to find an African American scholar with whom to collaborate was a function of the miniscule number of them who were working in Texas women's history. Frieda Werden believes this is the reason Winegarten persuaded the University of

Texas Press to publish *Black Texas Women: A Sourcebook* in 1996, so that black scholars could one day write a history from their own perspectives (Werden to Jones, July 4, 2009).

66. Winegarten, *Black Texas Women*, x–xi.

67. Ruthe Winegarten and Sharon Kahn wrote *Brave Black Women: From Slavery to the Space Shuttle* (Austin: University of Texas Press, 1997) for young readers.

68. Ruthe Winegarten, ed., *I Am Annie Mae: An Extraordinary Woman in Her Own Words: The Personal Story of a Black Texas Woman* (Austin: Rosegarden Press, 1983), ix. The TFWR distributed copies of it to schools and libraries around Texas in 1983 (see Stan—TFWR folder, box 2.325/G10, RWP). It was reprinted in 1996 by the University of Texas Press. Norkunas, "Oral History Transcript," 80; Winegarten to Schneider, April 27, 1947, March–July 1947 folder, box 2.325/W68, RWP.

69. Norkunas, "Oral History Transcript," 92.

70. Winegarten, ed., *I Am Annie Mae*, xii, 3–5, 49–52, 59, 101–106.

71. Ibid., xii.

72. Ibid., ix; Naomi Carrier Grundy, untitled reminiscence, in *Mum's the Word*, 45–46; Norkunas, "Oral History Transcript," 82–84; production history included in Script folder, box 2.325/A156a, RWP; Women & Their Work announcement of premiere, Letter to Groups folder, ibid.; Women & Their Work news release, Press Kit Info folder, ibid.; review, *Austin American-Statesman*, October 17, 1987, ibid.; Naomi Carrier to Leslie Lewis, March 18, 1997, 1997 Bookings folder, box 2.325/W69, RWP; program for one-woman version, "UT Austin, Nov. 3, 1997, I Am Annie Mae" folder, box 2.325/W71, RWP; Ruthe Winegarten to Debbie Cottrell March 30, 1994, Cottey College, Nevada, MO folder, ibid. Belinda Simmons starred in both versions. Janis Stinson starred in a number of the one-woman versions.

73. *Guts, Gumption, and Go-Ahead: Annie Mae Hunt Remembers* (Dallas: Media Projects, Inc., 1993). Winegarten worked with the producers, Cynthia and Allen Mondell, from 1987 to 1993 and later marketed the video to the Texas Education Agency as a seventh-grade teaching tool (see Winegarten-Mondell correspondence, Mondells–Media Projects, Inc. folder, box 2.325/J13, RWP; Ruthe Winegarten to Mary Lou Acres, February 26, 1993, "Guts, Gumption and Go-Ahead" folder, ibid.; *Dallas Morning News*, February 20, 1993, ibid.). *From Gutsy Mavericks to Quiet Heroes: True Tales of Texas Women*, video and study guide (Austin: Foundation for Women's Resources, 1997).

74. Much of the discussion about the third video history in this and the next paragraph was taken almost verbatim from Jones and Winegarten, *Capitol Women*, xi–xii.

75. Ruthe Winegarten, "Women in Red," *Capitol Women*, 3–6; Myra Banfield Dippel, videotape interview by Ruthe Winegarten, May 25, 1995; Frances T. Farenthold, videotape interview by Ruthe Winegarten, June 12, 1995, both in the author's possession.

76. Teresa Palomo Acosta and Ruthe Winegarten, *Las Tejanas: 300 Years of History* (Austin: University of Texas Press, 2003).

77. Martha Cotera, *Diosa y Hembra: The History and Heritage of Chicanas in the U.S.* (Austin: Information Systems Development, 1976).

78. Cynthia E. Orozco, foreword to *Las Tejanas*, ix–xi.

79. Winegarten to Schneider, April 17, 1981; Marina Pisano, "Preserving the Stories," *San Antonio Express-News*, August 26, 2001.

80. Pisano, "Preserving the Stories."

81. Teresa Palomo Acosta, "Women from Separate Corners of the Room: Forging a Collaborative Pathway to Tejana History," 5–6, typescript, in the author's possession.

82. Ibid., 7–9.

83. Ibid., 13–15.

84. Ibid., 15–16.

85. Teresa Palomo Acosta to Nancy Baker Jones, June 6, 2009.

86. Both photographs are reproduced in *Mum's the Word,* 80. The Polish Group was another way that Winegarten kept in touch with the women of the Texas Women's History Project. Based loosely on some of the members' experiences teaching in Poland, but primarily on their relationship to women's history, Winegarten, Mary Beth Rogers, Sherry Smith, Mary Sanger, Melissa Hield, Margaret Keys, Betty Sue Flowers, and Lavada Jackson Steed met periodically over dinner for almost a decade. "The Polish Group," in *Mum's the Word,* 136–142; Mary Beth Rogers to Nancy Baker Jones, July 12, 2009.

87. Ellen Temple, untitled reminiscence, in *Mum's the Word,* 65.

88. A sample of her assistance can be found in her July 29, 1991, letter to me listing thirty-seven African American women she recommended for inclusion and reasons for their worth ("Handbook of Texas" folder, box 2.325/J13, RWP). Ruthe Winegarten to Nancy Baker Jones, Sherilyn Brandenstein, and Debbie Cottrell, April 22, 1991, in the author's possession.

89. "Women & Texas History: A Conference," October 4–6, 1990, was sponsored by TSHA, the CSTH, the Barker Texas History Center, the Center for Mexican American Studies, the Foundation for Women's Resources, the LBJ Library and Museum, the RGK Foundation, the Texas Committee for the Humanities, the Texas Historical Commission, Texas Woman's University, the Women's Foundation of Texas, and the Women's Studies Program at UT. I was its coordinator.

90. Ruthe Winegarten to Amalia Rodríguez-Mendoza, April 13, 1992, in the author's possession.

91. Ibid.

92. Ruthe Winegarten to twelve recipients, October 31, 1990; Ruthe Winegarten to Ellen Temple and Nancy Baker Jones, February 18, 1991, both in the author's possession.

93. Ruthe Winegarten to Nancy Baker Jones and Ellen Temple, February 26, 1991, in the author's possession.

94. Nancy Baker Jones to Ron Tyler and Doug Barnett, March 1, 1991, in the author's possession.

95. Conference essays were published in *Women and Texas History: Selected Essays,* edited by Fane Downs and Nancy Baker Jones (Austin: Texas State Historical Association, 1993).

96. Nancy Baker Jones to Ron Tyler, August 8, 1991; Ellen Temple to Nancy Baker Jones, August 9, 1991; Jones to Tyler, September 1, 1991, all in the author's possession. The Liz Carpenter award is endowed through the Ellen Clarke Temple Excellence Fund for Research in Women's History at the University of Texas at Austin.

97. Ruthe Winegarten to Amalia Rodríguez-Mendoza, April 13, 1992, in the author's possession. Winegarten sent copies of the letter to Richards, Mary Beth Rogers, Temple, and Cynthia Galvan, then the director of the UT Women's Studies Program.

98. Ellen Temple to Foundation Board, March 4, 1992, in the author's possession.

99. Doug Barnett (managing editor) to Nancy Baker Jones, June 3, 1992; Doug Barnett to *Handbook* staff, June 3, 1992; Ron Tyler to Nancy Baker Jones, June 5, 1992; "1992–1993 Work Priorities," prepared by Barnett, undated but distributed to staff June 11, 1992; Doug Barnett to *Handbook* research staff, June 19, 1992, all in the author's possession. The terms "bedrock" and "luxury" were used verbally at a June 11, 1992, all-staff meeting. I was the editor whose position was eliminated.

100. The managing editor in 1987 was Tom Cutrer. "From the Managing Editor," *Hotline,* Summer 1992, 1–3; "Staff Changes," *Hotline,* Summer 1992, 3; Nancy Baker Jones to Alwyn Barr, June 17, 1992; Judith McArthur to Nancy Baker Jones, November 6, 1992; Nancy Baker

Jones to members of the TSHA Executive Council, August 31, 1992; María Cristina García to Nancy Baker Jones, May 3, 1990; Teresa Palomo Acosta to Nancy Baker Jones, April 9, 1990, all in the author's possession. The Texas Foundation for Women's Resources funded the women's history research assistantship. It later became the Katharine Sage Temple Fellowship for Women's History through grants from the T.L.L. Temple Foundation, Lufkin. Judith McArthur was the first women's history research assistant; I became the second, in 1986.

101. Ruthe Winegarten, Amalia Rodríguez-Mendoza, and David Williams to Alwyn Barr and the TSHA Executive Council, July 9, 1992, in the author's possession.

102. Nancy Baker Jones, personal log, July 23, 1992; Nancy Baker Jones to friends, October 29, 1992, in the author's possession. Observers at the TSHA Executive Council meeting were Sherilyn Brandenstein, a research assistant in women's history whose position had been cut, and David Williams, a signatory of Winegarten's letter.

103. For the next year, Winegarten and I continued trying to raise funds and find a home for what we started calling a think tank for women's history and public policy in Texas. In 1993, when the University of Texas at San Antonio opened its Center for the Study of Women and Gender through the efforts of Linda Schott and Linda Pritchard, we stopped our efforts and joined the CSWG community board of directors to help foster a Texas focus to the center's activities. UTSA president Ricardo Romo closed the CSWG in 2001 and reopened it as a women's studies institute and resource center.

104. Ruthe Winegarten and Frieda Werden, "The Sancties of Belton: A Musical Comedy in Two Acts and Six Scenes," unpublished draft, box 2.325/A119, RWP; "1976 Graduate Program Application—the University of Texas at Dallas"; Texas Female Legislators folder, box 2.325/G9, RWP.

105. Ruthe Winegarten, "While Standing on the Bridge in Sarajevo, February, 1984: June 14, 1914—How World War I Could Have Been Avoided," Poems folder, box 2.325/W68, RWP.

106. Ruthe Winegarten to Stanley Schneider, August 3, 1981, 1981 folder, box 2.325/W68, RWP.

107. Ruthe Winegarten correspondence to Stan and Goldie Schneider, 1948 folder, 1960s–1970s folder, and 1981 folder, box 2.325/W68, RWP; Ruthe Winegarten to Mira (last name unknown), July 30, 1982, Winegarten Correspondence 1982 folder, box 2.325/F53b, RWP; Wedding Album, Ruthe Winegarten and Stanley Schneider, 1986, box 2P21, RWP; Norkunas, "Oral History Transcript," 28.

108. Melissa Hield, untitled reminiscence, in *Mum's the Word*, 64.

109. Nancy Baker Jones to Frieda Werden, January 27, 2004; Ruthe Winegarten to Nancy Baker Jones, February 1, 2004; Debra Winegarten to Nancy Baker Jones et al., May 21, 2004; Debra Winegarten to Nancy Baker Jones, May 24, 2004; Ruthe Winegarten medical records, box 2.325/G228 (restricted; access with family permission), RWP.

110. In 2006 several of Ruthe Winegarten's friends and colleagues created a nonprofit organization in her memory, the Ruthe Winegarten Memorial Foundation for Texas Women's History. In 2009 the foundation launched an educational Web site, www.womenintexashistory.org.

JESÚS F. DE LA TEJA

DAVID J. WEBER

DAVID J. WEBER, 2004, ATOP EL MORRO (INSCRIPTION ROCK), NEW MEXICO

David J. Weber arrived at SMU in 1976; you could say, as the old trope has it, that he got to Texas as fast as he could. And although he made Dallas his base of operations for the next thirty-four years, even Texas was too small to contain him. An already published and rising young historian when he arrived in Dallas, no one, let alone David, could have imagined that he would become the most important exponent of borderlands studies of the last half century.

David has been gone too brief a time for a thoroughly objective appraisal of his life and work.[1] A special session at the fall 2010 Western History Association annual meeting, "Scholar of the Borderlands: The Many Contributions of David J. Weber,"[2] which was to have included David commenting on the observations of a panel composed of colleagues, turned into the first of numerous memorials and tributes. The Conference on Latin American History, which meets jointly with the American Historical Association, held a panel on David in January 2011 that was subsequently published in *Southern California Quarterly,* and the Texas State Historical Association also sponsored a special panel on David at its March 2011 meeting, "The Texas Borderlands and Beyond: A Roundtable on the Work of David J. Weber."[3] Writing about him is, therefore, still largely a matter of sifting through the very personal reminiscences and feelings of the large number of those whom he loved, taught, mentored, collaborated with, and influenced.[4]

The *New York Times* covered David's passing, noting how a once-aspiring high school musician from upstate New York whose ambition had been to be a high school teacher had gone on to receive Spain's Real Orden de Isabel la Católica and Mexico's Order of the Aztec Eagle for studying the legacies of Spain and Mexico in the Americas.[5] How he got from modest ambition to international honors is a remarkable story of taking the road less traveled, and of that choice making all the difference — for himself and for those whose lives he touched.

Born on December 20, 1940, to a German American father and a Polish American mother in Buffalo, New York, David was the eldest of three sons and a daughter. It is not surprising that David grew up thinking about a career somehow connected to music. His father, Theodore Carl, a sometime singer and onetime radio DJ, encouraged his children to pursue careers that would be both creative and lucrative, and discouraged careers in business. As the owner of a furniture and appliance store in downtown Buffalo who worked long hours and provided a good living for his family, David's father also provided a traditional role model of responsible adulthood. Although he managed his store personally from opening to closing, his father came home to the suburb of Cheektowaga every evening to a sit-down dinner with the whole family, expecting David's mother to have the children clean and neat and ready to go over the day's events. David's mother, Frances Jean, who had trained as a secretary, gave up her job and devoted herself to her new career as wife and mother. When the family went on vacation, they usually rented a cabin on Lake Erie, and David's father would commute daily back to Buffalo to run the store.[6]

David's middle-class suburban upbringing included a solid education and diverse extracurricular opportunities. Although Theodore Carl was not religious, Frances Jean brought up the children in the Catholic faith; David attended Catholic school for a few years before transferring to a new neighborhood public school. At Cheektowaga's public Maryvale High School, which he attended between 1954 and 1958, David was involved in the typical range of extracurricular activities. He was a member of the student government and the school band and lettered in track, basketball, and tennis. It was a time, as he later wrote, when "you could be a jock and a musician at the same time."[7] His athleticism and independence extended well beyond school. For a number of years his mother regularly dropped David off at the Zoar Valley wilderness area for weeklong camping trips by himself or in company with a friend or with one or both of his brothers, Don and Dan.[8] That appreciation for nature, roughing it, and risk-taking would follow him for the rest of his life and manifest itself especially in his love for the New Mexico countryside.

In the course of high school David came to see his future in music education. Although successful in high school sports, the anxiety of track competition proved so overwhelming to him that he rejected the offer of a track scholarship from Cornell University. On the other hand, the ex-marine who directed the school band and orchestra was a man to be admired, and David began to see a future for himself as a music teacher.[9] With hard work he excelled in clarinet competitions and in All-County Band performances, which probably convinced him that a degree in music education at nearby State University of New York at Fredonia was the right decision.[10]

Fredonia proved a life-altering experience in more than one way for David. As in the case of countless other high schoolers whose talents on the sports field, in the music hall, and on the stage fostered dreams of professional careers as athletes, musicians, and actors, competition at the college level proved a sobering experience for him. David soon came to the realization that his lack of perfect pitch would make a music career unlikely: "I knew that I didn't have any talent as a musician but still thought about becoming a high school teacher of something."[11] As Fredonia at the time was too small for a separate history department, he majored in social sciences and began thinking about going on for a master's degree in one of his two favorite fields, history and English.

In the end history won out because of the intervention of Fredonia's lone Latin Americanist, Marvin D. Bernstein. The young historian, who went on to a distinguished career at the University of Buffalo, pitched the radical idea that David consider not only pursuing an M.A. in history but also a doctorate in

Latin American history. The challenge to David's worldview was considerable. David was the first in his family to make it as far as college. His father had left school with an eighth-grade education, and his mother was a high school graduate. He had taken all of two years of high school Spanish and the single course on Latin American history offered at Fredonia.[12]

Even as he was deciding how to proceed on the education front, David was making another lifelong decision. He had not forgotten about the fellow clarinet player he had met during that All-County Band competition a couple of years earlier, and in the spring of his freshman year he sought her out and began dating her. He soon convinced her to attend Fredonia. As she recalled, "By the time I graduated from high school in 1959, David had convinced me to go to college at Fredonia with him and we had a wonderful three years there together."[13] We cannot be certain when David decided that Carol was the love of his life, but at about the same time he was deciding to head for the Southwest to continue his education, he proposed that she come with him as his wife.[14]

David credits Bernstein with his decision to go to the Southwest. "The University of New Mexico was not too big, Bernstein assured me, for someone from Fredonia. Larger places like Berkeley, Texas, or Florida that also specialized in Latin America might overwhelm me, but he thought I might do the M.A. at UNM and then move on."[15] And even with David's limited Spanish-language and history background, Bernstein was so confident in his student's abilities that he provided him with a letter of introduction to an old schoolmate, Edwin Lieuwen, the lead Latin Americanist at UNM. Armed with the letter and driving the 1957 Plymouth that his mother had given the newlyweds, David and Carol took eleven days to camp their way from Buffalo to Albuquerque.[16]

David described how he came to his interest in borderlands history as "serendipity."[17] Circumstances, in fact, made him take the road less traveled. Lieuwen, who had made a splash with his second book, *Arms and Politics in Latin America*, did not prove a good fit for David. At his passing in 1988, Lieuwen had trained thirty-five Ph.D.'s, and Michael C. Meyer would write about him that "Ed Lieuwen had a positive professional influence on many in the field and they will all regret his sudden and unanticipated passing. This is especially true for those of us who experienced that most remarkable metamorphosis, considering him first as a most inspiring teacher and then a warm, close friend."[18] David's experience was considerably different: "At age twenty-one, I found myself alienated by the impersonal treatment that I (and others) received from the "star" [Latin Americanist there], but was much taken with the warmth and enthusiasm exuded by the borderlands historian, Donald Cutter."[19]

What Cutter (a more mature scholar who was as new as David to the UNM campus in fall 1962) saw in the young New Yorker is hard to say.[20] Certainly David had a long way to go, and the borderlander, more than Lieuwen, may have been more willing to put in the time to nurture the twenty-one-year-old. David had substantial deficiencies to make up both in history and in Spanish.[21] Quickly, however, he proved himself to Cutter, who took him on as his doctoral student and recommended a suitable dissertation topic: "Cutter suggested that I write a thesis on early Anglo American fur traders who came into New Mexico. The book had never been done, he said, and the archives were right there. The thesis evolved into my dissertation and then into a book, *The Taos Trappers: The Fur Trade in the Far Southwest, 1540–1821*."[22]

David had also become "enchanted with the Land of Enchantment." The Weber family's time in New Mexico was typical of a young graduate school couple's experience. David played in a country club band to supplement his fellowships, which included being the first recipient of the JFK Scholarship, which Edward Kennedy came to UNM to present to him. The couple managed the apartment complex that they lived in on Sycamore Street to cover their monthly rent of seventy-five dollars. Carol's parents paid her senior-year tuition and sent the couple one hundred dollars a month while she finished her English degree. In fall 1963 Carol began teaching at Highland High School, but the job came to an end after one year when she became pregnant with the couple's first child, Scott, who was born in December 1964. In the early 1960s pregnancy was still a disqualifier for employment in the local schools, and Carol returned to UNM to obtain the M.A. in English literature and earn some money by serving as a teaching assistant. When the Webers completed their respective degrees in 1967, the newly minted Dr. David J. Weber, his wife Carol, and two-year-old Scott headed to San Diego, California. Before they left, they scraped together $500 to buy a small, ten-acre piece of New Mexico; it was tough to let go of the state.[23]

David described obtaining a job teaching Latin America and borderlands history at San Diego State College as "lucky," revealing what some of those close to him might recognize as his humility and hinting at what his wife describes as a certain sense of insecurity.[24] In fact, even before completing his doctorate, David had already proved his potential. Two edited works, *The Extranjeros: Selected Documents from the Mexican Side of the Trail, 1825–1828* and *Prose Sketches and Poems Written in the Western Country (with Additional Stories)*, by Albert Pike, were in press, as was his article "Spanish Fur Trade from New Mexico, 1540–1821," in *The Americas*. Two works had already appeared in the *New Mexico Historical Review*.[25]

San Diego was a place where both David's career and his family flourished. After renting for a year, they bought a home with large acreage in La Mesa. By then the family also included daughter Amy, who was born in October 1967. Although he was supportive of Carol's career ambitions, it was always clear to her that David's career would come first. As Carol recalls, "David was working for us more than he was working for himself," but that meant that, like most American men forty-five years ago, he expected her to take care of the home while he took care of business. "That's just the way it was in those days." Eventually, Carol taught freshman English at San Diego State before taking up environmental education for a local water district, at the same time managing a household that included a pony and chickens.[26]

For his part, despite having a course load of twelve hours per semester at the beginning, Weber threw himself with purpose and determination into the task of becoming a scholar. At first his work continued to focus on the mountain men who populated his dissertation work, culminating in publication of his first monograph, *The Taos Trappers: The Fur Trade in the Far Southwest, 1540–1846,* in 1971.[27] But he was already thinking about the Hispanic dimensions of the region's history. A project with a Chicano colleague on a two-volume documentary collection on Mexican Americans did not work out, but at Carol's suggestion David reworked his portion, documents from the late sixteenth through the early twentieth centuries, into *Foreigners in Their Native Land: Historical Roots of the Mexican Americans,* the first of a number of collaborations with the University of New Mexico Press.[28] In his foreword to the book the already well-established Latin Americanist Ramón Eduardo Ruiz, who had arrived at nearby UC San Diego in 1970, noted what would be a trademark of David's work in the decades to come: "Weber has chosen his documents with the insight of the professional historian, yet his choices reveal a refreshing sympathy for the Spaniards and Mexicans and their conquered descendants."[29]

Even before the appearance of *Foreigners,* David received ample validation of his efforts.[30] Nineteen-seventy not only brought promotion to associate professor at San Diego State, just three years into his academic career, but the award of a Fulbright-Hays Lectureship to the University of Costa Rica. In typical adventurous Weber fashion, David drove the family's 1967 Oldsmobile Vista Cruiser station wagon to and from Costa Rica, taking the opportunity of the long road trip to practice his Spanish by working through flashcards. He also sought his Costa Rican students' help in improving his conversational Spanish, which took the form of having a class member take down all his mistakes and present him with the notes at the end of class. By the end of his stay, Weber had cut the initial three pages of errors down to half a page. The Fulbright experience also reinforced his growing interest in and sympathy for the Spanish-speaking world. David found himself establishing contacts, making new friends, and expanding the sweep of his historical vision.[31]

David returned to California ready to reassess the work he had been doing from a much broader perspective. Comparing and contrasting New Mexico and California, he realized that the Spanish borderlands had gone their separate ways after 1821, their joint experience as Mexico's northern frontier becoming subsumed into the histories of the individual American states of which they were the nuclei. As bold as David had been in applying for and undertaking a Fulbright with the realization that he would have to improve his Spanish in the hard school of experience, he took an even bolder step in suggesting to the eminent western historian Ray Allen Billington that he add a volume on the borderlands during the Mexican national period to his Histories of the American Frontier series.[32] It was a bold move for at least two reasons. First, with only a few years under his belt as a scholar, David's scholarly output had been largely limited to New Mexico. He was at work on *Foreigners,* so he was learning about the region in general, but it would take a lot of work to gain enough command of the literature that he could produce anything of substance. Second, the scattered and uneven historiography of the period meant that Weber would have to identify and fill numerous gaps through fresh research. As he modestly recalled, "Ever gracious and supportive, Ray took a chance and gave me a contract."[33] Although the book would be a decade in the making, slowed down by his move to SMU and service as department chair there, when it did appear, *The Mexican Frontier, 1821–1846: The American Southwest under Mexico* proved to be a game changer in the field of the history of the Southwest.

Although David had visited Texas intellectually as he researched *Foreigners* and then *The Mexican Frontier,* it was not until 1976 that the opportunity arose to make the Lone Star State his home. San Diego State had provided him with a good first home, but despite promotion to full professor in 1973, the heavy teaching load and the public university's step-raise system had led him to start looking for other opportunities. Fortunately for him, for Southern Methodist University, and for Texas, that opportunity presented itself in the Dallas school's search for a new regional historian, one who had a bright career in his future and could help SMU's history department improve significantly. The department's chairman, Hal Williams, a master recruiter who had an "Eastern Yalee way,"[34] had consulted with Howard Lamar and worked hard to convince David that SMU was the right choice. So, too, did James Hopkins, a third-year faculty member who, as the department's British history expert, had been assigned to work on Carol because of her M.A. in British literature. When he noticed that Carol "was in no mood for tea and anglo-philism," Hopkins turned his attention to David: "I was convinced that I knew that he needed SMU and that SMU needed him. So, I somehow peeled him away from the senior members of the department, and we decamped for lunch at a burger place a block away from the campus. While I pounded the table, telling him all the reasons I thought he should come to SMU, he gravely listened to me, asked questions, and sent out the first tendrils of a friendship that was to be the most significant of my life."[35] Not much for standing on ceremony, with a way of getting straight to the point and an ability to see through phonies, David must have felt welcome at SMU, since a program that offered a lighter teaching load, smaller class sizes, greater opportunities for travel, and a merit-raise system that rewarded accomplishment and not simply longevity was precisely what he had been seeking. He had good friends among the faculty at San Diego State, but he was ready for new challenges.[36]

If David was ready for the change, the move was tougher for Carol. Her work as an educator with the water district was extremely satisfying for her, so "it was a hard move for me to leave my job that I loved and for us to leave that beautiful house." It was also tough to leave the beautiful San Diego area. The move itself proved challenging, as the couple had five days to find a house before David had to be back in San Diego to finish his tenure there. For the first four days, department chairman Williams and the real estate agent took them north of the university, where they saw "giant houses on postage stamp lots." On the fifth day, when they explained that they wanted a house with character, "nooks and crannies," and space, the realtor mentioned a possibility in the Stemmons neighborhood east of the university. That house had already been claimed, but its owners mentioned one down the street that was for sale by its owner. Although the house seemed a bit ostentatious and formal to them, the Webers found that it possessed potential—plenty of space inside and a large yard to accommodate the needs of nine- and twelve-year-olds. Over the years David, always handy with tools, did much work on the house, which served as his Texas home until the end of his life.[37]

Fortunately for SMU, Weber was not in the "monk historian" mold. He felt the need to be a good campus and community citizen. In San Diego he had served on the faculty advisory board of *The New Scholar: A Journal of Graduate Studies,* had done extensive service for the San Diego Historical Society and its journal, and had participated in the Mayor's Science Resources Panel of San Diego's Quality of Life Board. Shortly before his departure for Dallas, David had joined the board of editors of the *Western Historical Quarterly,* and soon after his arrival at SMU he joined the board of the *New Mexico Historical Review*. His professional commitments increased considerably from there, and for the next thirty years he participated on multiple boards, editorial and otherwise, and on prize and scholarship committees, some at the international level. But David also made room serving the needs of a broader audience. Aside from innumerable speaking engagements, he was among other things cofounder and then sheriff of the Dallas Corral of Westerners International and a member of the board of what is now Humanities Texas. He even cofounded a Friends of Woodrow Wilson High School booster group at the school his children attended, serving as its president for the period 1983–1986.

Before launching himself into the professional and community world of

Texas, Weber was ready to lead the family on yet another adventure. Neither he nor Carol had ever been to Europe, but David had been fortunate enough to negotiate a semester in the university's Madrid program as part of his hiring agreement. Consequently, he spent the spring semester and the summer of his first year at SMU traveling around Spain with the family. While Amy attended fourth grade at a British school, Scott, who would have been in seventh grade back home, became part of the SMU program, taking classes and tests in Spanish language, literature, and history with the SMU students. David's family background in business surfaced from time to time throughout his career, and in Spain it raised its head when he bought a car with tourist plates for $800 and sold it a few months later for $700 after driving it all over Europe.[38]

Back in Dallas in fall 1977, Weber was ready to become a full member of the SMU community. The following year he accepted an invitation to join the board of trustees of the DeGolyer Foundation. The library had been one of the attractions of SMU, and he came to establish a close working relationship with it in the course of his career, helping to bring the Book Club of Texas to campus and cofounding, with David Farmer, the Library of Texas.[39] Whether Hal Williams had seen David as a potential replacement as department chairman, by the following fall Weber had taken up the post, which he held until 1986. He had been keen on following Donald Cutter's advice from UNM days—never to teach in the summer and to avoid administrative work—and David always reserved summers for his research and writing. Heading the history department was another matter, however. Weber did not see it as administrative work but rather as an obligation, part of being a good colleague and university citizen.[40]

Weber took a practical approach to his duties as chairman, much as he did as a regular member of the department. His directness and businesslike attitude toward the job of being university faculty sometimes chafed colleagues—"he sometimes could be very stern"—but they always knew where he stood on issues.[41] When the administration imposed new evaluation criteria, including a requirement that each faculty member develop an annual plan, there was much grumbling until Weber pointed out that no business operated without a business plan, so why should faculty be exempt from that type of accountability? That deeply held belief in total commitment and making the most of one's talents sometimes led him to be quite "brutal" even with close friends, as James Hopkins, his best friend in the department, could attest. On his return from a trip abroad in the early 1980s, Hopkins found himself cornered by Weber, who demanded, "What about this book?" His harsh tone and demands that Hopkins produce resulted in a falling-out that lasted a few months, but Hopkins eventually understood the episode to have been David's way of getting him to fulfill his potential. Weber also understood that good work required adequate funding, and, unlike many academics, he was not shy about development work. Perhaps because he was the son of a businessman, David was comfortable working with the business community and fostering a positive "town and gown" relationship.

The demands of heading the history department, of participating on multiple boards and committees, and of family life did not get in the way of Weber's productivity. In fact, he was as much a workman as he was an artist. According to Hopkins, "He would come in twice a week and stay till midnight doing chair's work and on the other days he would teach and do his own writing."[42] That writing rested on a foundation of solid research in which nothing went to waste. While he was working on *The Mexican Frontier,* he produced two edited volumes and a number of articles, the most important of which, "Mexico's Far Northern Frontier, 1821–1854: Historiography Askew," and "Mexico's Far Northern Frontier: A Critical Bibliography, 1821–1845," represented the foundation blocks of the book.[43]

Another article that became Chapter 4 of *The Mexican Frontier,* "The Failure of a Frontier Institution: The Secular Church in the Borderlands under Independent Mexico, 1821–1846," represented Weber's first venture into a critique of the Catholic Church that would extend through his subsequent major works.[44] Although a devout Catholic in his youth, David had become disillusioned with religion as he studied the role of the church in Latin America.[45] In "The Failure of a Frontier Institution," despite some statements of balance, he by and large took a critical approach, at one point summing up the situation on the frontier: "If the Church ministered poorly to Mexican frontiersmen, its efforts to convert and care for new immigrants trickling in from other countries were a fiasco."[46] A decade later, in *The Spanish Frontier,* he abandoned any serious effort to present himself as a Christian insider and adopted a position of full-blown theological neutrality, consistently referring to the Christian "god" or "deity" in anthropological terms. He set the tone early in the book in discussing Coronado's encounter with the Zunis: "The Spaniards read aloud a statement that summarized Spanish theology, explaining that Spain's monarchs had received temporal powers from a deity through one they called Pope."[47] Recognizing that this was not a simple disparagement of the institutional church and its clergy, the reviewer of *The Spanish Frontier* in *Catholic Southwest* commented that "Weber's overall presentation of the various 'Conquistadores of the Spirit' does appear to be an effort at a balanced, sympathetic assessment."[48]

The Mexican Frontier did not appear until 1982, but it proved to be the seminal study that confirmed Weber's status as the leading representative of a new kind of borderlands history. As he had in the document collection *Foreigners* and a subsequent collection of articles on borderlands topics, *New Spain's Far Northern Frontier: Essays on Spain in the American West, 1540–1821* (which had appeared in a Spanish edition three years earlier), David demonstrated a great sensitivity for presenting the peoples and institutions of the region on their own terms.[49] Abandoning the standard interpretation of lazy and superstitious Mexicans who stood in the way of progress, he presented a complex analysis of political, economic, and environmental circumstances that Mexican frontiersmen were eager to overcome.[50] Similarly, his explanation of Texas secession as part of a general dissatisfaction with national government policies and political instability among Mexican frontiersmen made connections that had not been made previously. Texas was no longer unique, although it alone was successful in achieving independence: "Isolated outbreaks against federal officials and rumors of revolt turned into outright rebellion as the northern provinces sought to break away from the rest of the nation in the mid-1830s: Texas in 1835; California in 1836; and New Mexico and Sonora in 1837."[51] In the Texas case, more than anyone before him, Weber integrated an interpretation of the Tejanos' motives and behaviors into story lines previously dominated almost exclusively by a struggle between Anglo American settlers and the Mexican national government.

Praise and acclaim for *The Mexican Frontier* were not long in coming. It won the 1983 Ray Allen Billington Award from the Organization of American Historians for the best book to appear on the American frontier, the Westerners International Co-Founders Book Award for the best nonfiction appearing in 1982, and the 1982 History Award of the Border Regional Library Association. Recognition also came from Texas, where *The Mexican Frontier* won the 1982 Texas Institute of Letters Friends of the Dallas Public Library Award and the Presidio La Bahía Award from the Sons of the Texas Republic. It went on to Spanish-language editions in Mexico and Spain and has remained in print ever since.[52]

His synthesis of the frontier during the Mexican national period made Weber what might be considered a "crossover" historian and placed him in the top ranks of the profession. Having proved himself a "maestro de las inmensidades,"[53] he was invited to become a coeditor of the Histories of the American Frontier Series with Howard R. Lamar, Martin Ridge, and William Cronon, the successors to Ray Allen Billington. Within a year of *The Mexican Frontier*'s appearance he was elected to membership in the Academia Mexicana de la Historia, an extremely rare honor for a non-Mexican. Important recognition also came from the Texas historical establishment, the Texas Institute of Letters electing him to membership in 1984 and the Texas State Historical Association making him a lifetime fellow in 1985.

Weber's success in juggling administrative duties and scholarship was well rewarded when he stepped down as department chairman in 1986. In 1981 SMU had obtained a sizeable gift from alumni Robert H. Dedman Sr. and his wife, Nancy, to endow the Dedman College of Humanities and Sciences. Dedman, who had made a fortune in the golf course and resort industry, made a further gift to establish the Robert H. and Nancy Dedman Chair in History, with an emphasis on Hispanic borderlands, and David became the first holder of the chair.[54] Taking up the new chair would have to wait, as at the time of the appointment David was already in California, having received funding from the Andrew W. Mellon Foundation to spend a year as a fellow of the Center for Advanced Study in the Behavioral Sciences at Stanford. "There, in that fortunate setting," he said, "I began work on the book that would become *The Spanish Frontier in North America*."[55]

The idea for *The Spanish Frontier* had come to Weber out of his experience teaching courses on the Spanish borderlands ever since graduate school days at UNM. More than just a textbook, however, David intended for this work to serve as a way of getting American historians to "take the borderlands more seriously." Such a project would be a considerably more ambitious work than *The Mexican Frontier* had been. Chronologically it would have to cover 300 years, and geographically it would have to extend from the Atlantic to the Pacific. As in the earlier synthesis, he would be plunging into new areas of study for himself: "Indeed, there were entire areas of the borderlands that I knew nothing about, namely the entire region from Louisiana to Florida." In time he realized that he had faced this challenge earlier and that his work for *The Mexican Frontier* had prepared him to take it on: "I talked myself into starting the book by remembering that I hadn't known anything about other subjects before I'd chosen to write about them, either, and that this was only a larger version of a problem that I'd faced before. Indeed, there's little question in my mind that without the research and writing techniques that I'd developed in working on smaller regions, I could not have completed *The Spanish Frontier* successfully—and certainly not in five years."[56] Weber had another advantage in taking on the new project: for the first time he had a research assistant when Jane Elder began working for him in June 1987.[57]

Just as in *The Mexican Frontier*, the process through which David conceptualized and developed his history of Spain's North American possessions can be perceived in the various articles and lectures that preceded its appearance. In "Turner, the Boltonians, and the Spanish Borderlands," he wrestled with the disconnect between Bolton's repeated references to Frederick Jackson Turner's famous thesis regarding the influence of the westering experience on the American character as a model for studying Spanish frontier expansion and his own work's seeming rejection of the model: "Bolton's published work suggests that he was far more interested in the impact of Spaniards on the frontier than in the influence of the frontier on Spaniards. . . . Bolton clearly saw the mission and the presidio as 'characteristically and designedly frontier institutions,' but he saw them as extending, holding, and 'civilizing' the frontier. How frontier conditions might have altered these institutions or their inhabitants seldom concerned him."[58]

In "John Francis Bannon and the Historiography of the Spanish Borderlands: Retrospect and Prospect," Weber explored what he saw as the end of the Bolton school of borderlands history. For him, Bannon, who in 1970 produced the only real synthesis of Spanish borderlands history in *The Spanish Borderlands Frontier, 1513–1821,* "perpetuated Bolton's approach to the Borderlands even as the field began to move away from Bolton's framework and to fragment—as so many areas of history have done since the 1950s. Bannon's *Spanish Borderlands Frontier* gave the field an outward appearance of unity, even as it broke into parts that began to lose connection with one another."[59] Among those parts were Chicano studies, to the practitioners of which "the Borderlands tradition, with its emphasis on institutions and on *Spanish* activity seemed elitist and irrelevant to a generation increasingly interested in the social history of the mixed-blood population that comprised the vast majority of Mexicans and Mexican Americans."[60]

When *The Spanish Frontier in North America* appeared in 1992 as part of Yale University Press's Western Americana series, David hoped that it would serve to reconnect Americans with a part of their history largely ignored or forgotten. On the one hand, he asserted, the book offered "a fresh overview that reflects the concerns of current scholarship as well as the sound conclusions of earlier generations. Simply put, I try to explain Spain's impact on the lives, institutions, and environments of native peoples of North America, and impact of North America on the lives and institutions of those Spaniards who explored and settled what has now become the United States."[61] On the other hand, "In telling the story of America's Spanish origins I try not to cast Spaniards as the villains so often portrayed by hispanophobic writers. At the same time, I do not put a gloss on Spanish behavior, as the pro-Spanish Bolton tradition tended to do." In his own well-argued and meticulously documented narrative, David presented a synthesis of the nation's Hispanic history that also rejected the objectified role assigned to native peoples: "Even books like mine, which attempts to illuminate the Spanish experience, must come to terms with Indians, whose societies and cultures Spaniards transformed and who, in turn, transformed the frontier societies and cultures of the Spaniards."[62]

As had happened with *The Mexican Frontier, The Spanish Frontier* received national and international recognition. Among the accolades was its selection as a New York Times "notable book" of 1992. The History Book Club both made it a selection and honored it with its Western Heritage Award. The Texas Institute of Letters again honored Weber with the Carr P. Collins Award for the best nonfiction book of 1992, and from Spain came the Premio España y América from the Spanish Ministry of Culture. A Spanish-language edition, *La frontera española en América del Norte,* appeared in 2000 from Mexico's Fondo de Cultura Económica, and three years later King Juan Carlos inducted him into the Real Orden de Isabel la Católica (Spain's version of knighthood).

As David's career flourished in Dallas, so did his family life. Busy and committed as he was to his work, he enjoyed a rich private life. According to SMU colleague and fellow Latin Americanist Peter Bakewell, "He liked to work on his houses—his elegant residence in Dallas, the nearby lake house, and the house in New Mexico (in whose design he played a large part). I remember being invited with my wife to the lake house one Sunday soon after our arrival in Dallas. David asked if I would help him repair the dock. I found myself deep in water with him, tightening bolts with a cordless drill. I had the sense, as we emerged, of having passed some sort of test."[63] He had done more than just played a role in designing the house outside Ramah, in the Zuni Mountains of New Mexico; he had helped build it. In the meantime, Carol, who in 1979 had taken the position of curator of education at Old City Park, moved on to law school at SMU in 1985. When David got the fellowship at the Center for Advanced Study in the Behavioral Sciences, Carol followed him and completed her second year of law at Stanford. When David went off to Madrid to direct SMU's program in Spain for the 1989–1990 school year, Carol went along. She went to work on a part-time basis for SMU's general counsel in 1991, determined to remain flexible so that when David took off again she could go with him and needing time to deal with her daughter Amy's impending marriage and the arrival of their first grandchild from Scott. It proved to be her last career move. Within a few months, recognizing the value of adding another lawyer to the Legal Affairs Office staff, he offered Carol a permanent position. When Carol retired from SMU's Office of General Counsel in 2007, it was to accompany David on his last academic visit, as Frederick W. and Carrie S. Beinecke Senior Fellow at Yale University's Lamar Center for the Study of Frontiers and Borders and Beinecke Library. As for his children, they both obtained undergraduate degrees in history, Scott at Columbia and Amy at the University of Texas at Austin. Scott went on to law school at SMU, where he was a second-year student in a class in which his mother was a third-year student.

With *The Spanish Frontier* behind him and *Bárbaros: Spaniards and Their Savages in the Age of Enlightenment* still in the offing,[64] Weber turned his attention to his other great professional legacy, the Clements Center for the Study of the Southwest. Just when he first thought of a Southwest Studies program at SMU, a regional studies center, and possibly a Ph.D. program to go along with it has been impossible to pin down. According to Jane Elder, who served first as his research assistant beginning in June 1987 and then as factotum until she resigned to accept a position in the university libraries in February 2001, the year at the Center for Advanced Studies in the Behavioral Sciences "had a major impact on his thinking."[65] By December 1991 he had called a meeting of fellow faculty from across campus to discuss setting up a minor in Southwest Studies and, almost as an afterthought, an accompanying center. "The idea of establishing a Center for the Study of Southwestern Cultures has also arisen," he wrote. "Time allowing, we should put that on the table, too."[66]

The project seemed to lose steam in the course of 1992, but Weber was not done. A 1993 NEH summer institute that he organized at SMU was, according to Elder, "an exceptionally fun, productive, and fruitful time with a great group of people. Rich ideas and theories and discussions just percolated throughout those weeks."[67] Following this, Weber was ready to try again. He brought up the idea of an interdisciplinary studies program with the university's provost, Anya Royce, an anthropologist who proved open to the idea of a major or minor in the field. In following up with her, he coyly broached the possibility of something more: "Did you have in mind anything more ambitious than that? By which I mean the establishment of a Center for the Study of the Southwest, which would serve as an umbrella for the various components that we have on campus, and bring students and faculty together by sponsoring lectures and symposia."[68] Her response was all that he could have hoped for — not only was she willing to see that faculty release time and secretarial help was forthcoming for the curricular program, but she was enthusiastic about the idea of a center: "I would like us to think as expansively as possible. A Center could well be a wonderful mechanism for fostering research and community involvement. I believe that we can get funding from a variety of sources for such a center and for the related program at Taos. Some dinner conversation last week with Stanley Marcos made me feel quite positive."[69]

In the end it would not be a retail fortune but an oil fortune that funded David's center; but in the meantime there was work to be done. By the middle of November 1993, David had formed an informal brain trust to help him scope out resources across campus that might be applied to both the curricular program and a "research oriented Southwest Studies Center." Although he found enthusiastic support across most of the campus, there was skepticism from at least one department, to which Weber responded in his usual direct manner that concerns about employability were "irrelevant." He punctuated his argument with "SMU has not historically been a trade school."[70] By the end of the spring semester 1994, the college's undergraduate council had approved a major-minor in Southwest Studies, and all that remained to make David's project a reality was the approval of the higher administration for the establishment of the center.[71]

It took a year for that final approval to materialize. First, Provost Royce left the university, slowing down the implementation of new initiatives such as the major-minor. Second, the funding of the center had to be worked out, and it became tied up in the college's efforts to secure an endowment for the department of history and the development of a history Ph.D. program, always a costly endeavor. As it turned out, Dean James F. Jones Jr., of SMU's Dedman College of Humanities and Sciences, was courting former governor Bill Clements for a major gift: "I used David Weber and his distinguished colleagues as the sole reason Bill should endow the history department at SMU. And when he did, I stood up a bit straighter, knowing that one of the best of all the University's departments, one that produced stunning research every year while never shirking their teaching responsibilities had been so honored."[72] Clements was a perfect fit for such an endowment, as he was a former head of the SMU board of trustees with a "deep and abiding love for the Southwest and its history."[73]

In fact, Clements and Weber had a bit of a history behind them. The governor, who owned a ranch not far from SMU's Fort Burgwin campus outside Taos, New Mexico, had attended a lecture that David had presented at Fort Burgwin and took exception to the idea that Travis's line in the sand might be pure myth. Weber stood his ground in the discussion and eventually came to feel that the encounter had created a foundation for mutual respect.[74] On David's side of things it may have been the governor's demonstrated grasp of the region's history that allowed the relationship to flourish. As Jane Elder recalls: "I always found his knowledge of the contents of his Southwest book collection significant. On the two occasions I ever heard him speak publicly about the Southwest, I felt that he had a really good grip on many historical trends and patterns."[75] Whether Clements recalled that encounter when he agreed to fund the department, the center, and the Ph.D. program, the fact of the matter was that Weber was grateful for the governor's support and made sure to include him in center activities. At least twice a year David and the department chair would visit with Clements, sometimes on campus and sometimes at the governor's home, to give him status reports and present him with the latest center publications. In return, Clements became quite the supporter of the center; for example, in 1997 he asked that in lieu of birthday presents donations be made to the center.[76]

With Clements's support and Weber's ability to promote and make accessible the work of the center to potential donors and foundations, the Clements Center for Southwest Studies grew quickly. The center opened in 1996 in Dallas Hall with one fellow; David then obtained foundation support for additional fellowships, and by 2001 enough gifts had come in that the center could offer the three fellowships without reliance on grants. In 2008 a major gift from the Summerlee Foundation allowed for the addition of a fourth permanent fellowship dedicated to Texas history. Through his extensive contacts and appearances at national and international meetings, Weber met and recruited scholars, most often young ones. The man who made sure that he kept his office at the other end of Dallas Hall so that he could keep as much of his privacy as possible for writing well understood the value of time: "Residential research fellowships have been the heart of the Center's program. More than anything else the Center does, fellowships advance scholarship on the American Southwest by providing scholars with the precious gift of uninterrupted time to focus on their research and writing."[77]

The consistency of the tributes, remembrances, and informal comments with regard to David's generosity make clear that the Clements Center was merely a vehicle through which he could channel his real life's work, fostering an appreciation for and expanding our knowledge of history, particularly of the Southwest. Among the numerous fellows who got the opportunity not only to work in peace but to meet and exchange ideas there with a broad range of people—from fellow scholars to students to the general public—there is one who stands out. Andrew Graybill, who became Weber's successor as director of the center, was a Clements Center fellow in 2004–2005 and worked on his first book, *Policing the Great Plains*.[78] He later worked with the center's associate director, Ben Johnson, on a symposium-book project, *Bridging National Borders in North America*.[79] These were exactly the kinds of projects that excited Weber, as they pushed the borders of scholarship beyond the safe confines of well-defined and easily recognized national boundaries. Although a Texan himself, Andy was somewhat concerned that he was not really a good fit for the directorship, as his affinity lay in the direction of the U.S.-Canadian borderlands; however, he was assured that it was precisely that broader global borderlands perspective that found favor with Weber.[80]

David's work as a mentor stretched well back into the early part of his career but found full expression not only in the center's fellows program but in the history Ph.D. program, which he was also instrumental in bringing to SMU. As friendly and easygoing as he could be in public settings and with broad audiences, that tough all-business streak that marked his relations with colleagues also applied to his mentees. Francis Galán, who joined the Ph.D. program in 1999, having been recommended to SMU by his M.A. thesis advisor at the University of Texas at San Antonio, Félix Almaráz, remembers his initial encounter with Weber as all business: "I'll never forget the first time I met him, he peered down into my eyes and said, 'Tell me something I don't already know.'" His final assessment is representative of the opinions expressed by David's other students and many of the fellows: "Weber truly became a great mentor to me, beyond the intimidation and brutal honesty, because I would not have become the historian that I am, and still wish to be, without him constantly challenging me."[81]

Weber's blend of tough, honest, professional interaction and collegial friendliness constantly made him new friends and gained the respect of adversaries. Josefina Zoraida Vázquez, a prominent Mexican historian of the early national period, and Weber had squared off numerous times over interpreting who was responsible for Mexico's loss of Texas. In the mid-1990s both served as advisors on a four-part documentary, *The U.S.-Mexican War (1846–1848)*, produced by Dallas public television station KERA and aired on PBS in 1998. The two had sparred over how much American aggression was to blame for what she insisted should be styled, following Mexican convention, the "American Intervention." Nevertheless, Josefina fondly remembered their last encounter at an event in Monterrey, Mexico: "Both of us were speakers and for the first time were in agreement during the discussion, so that during the celebration I commented to him, 'It's easy to see we're getting old; we're not fighting anymore.' We both had a good laugh. Now I remember him with fond affection, as he was a fearsome adversary but also honest."[82] Alfredo Jiménez of the University of Seville came to know David through a recommendation from Oscar Martínez to read *The Spanish Frontier* while on a visit to the University of Arizona in 1992. Soon Jiménez and Weber were in communication, and a decade later David invited Alfredo to visit the Clements Center to be a part of one of those symposium-book projects that became *Choice, Persuasion, and Coercion*.[83] Alfredo spent a week at SMU, working in the library, lunching with David, and spending the evenings at the Webers' home. It was one of those subtle, liberal actions by David that might go unnoticed but that Alfredo understood as the essence of his character: "His human quality; his generosity for all (students, colleagues . . .), his humanity; that is to say, his human virtues."[84]

According to Jane Elder,

> The Center took shape absolutely as David had envisioned it. Of course he often wished for a little building on campus that could serve as office and residential space for the fellows—something along the lines of one of the old fraternity houses—but despite the fact that we looked into it frequently, it never happened. Otherwise, the ideas were all his: the annual seminars, the brown bag lunches, the residential fellowships, the book/writing seminars in which three scholars in the field would fly in to sit around the table and critique a fellow's manuscript, etc.[85]

Unfortunately, all this work that David was generating took its toll on their relationship, for it was Elder who had the responsibility of executing the plans. In its early years the center ran on a shoestring budget and Jane was its single staff member. Responsible for everything from budgeting and correspondence to planning programs, receptions, and dinners to getting participants to and from the airport to writing and editing newsletters and critiquing and editing manuscripts, while also collaborating with David on *Trading in Santa Fe: John M. Kingsbury's Correspondence with James Josiah Webb, 1853–1861* and serving as his research assistant on the preliminaries of *Bárbaros*, Elder came to see the job as too stressful for the rewards. In part, she reflects that "he was always willing to devote every waking hour to achieve his goals, which is why he became so successful. It probably never occurred to him that other people might not be able to stand his pace."[86]

To replace Elder, the center turned to Andrea Boardman, a KERA producer whom David had come to know from his advisory work on the U.S.-Mexican War documentary a few years earlier. Out of the documentary experience she took an interest in history and with Weber's support entered the M.A. program at SMU. She then became a part-time research assistant for *Bárbaros* and then administrator of the center when Elder departed. According to Andrea, she understood what was expected: "He didn't want to waste time on anything because he always wanted to be doing his research and writing. . . . My role, and Jane's role before me, was to deal with whatever I could to minimize what time he would have to put into whatever it was that was being done."[87] Considering this attitude, it is all the more significant that he made a commitment to organizations such as the Western History Association and the Texas State Historical Association, serving on the TSHA membership, fellows, and *Handbook* committees and its board of directors at various times from the 1980s through 2002.

There was, however, a need on David's part for assistance in his final push to complete *Bárbaros*, and that help came from Ruth Ann Elmore, who had been hired by Andrea as a part-time staffer at the center in 2002. Within a month of her arrival David had asked her to also serve as his research assistant. Elmore proved particularly useful as an image researcher on *Bárbaros* because of her previous career in art design. She came to appreciate his commitment: "He worked all the time on everything."[88] It was Ruth Ann who helped David complete those final major projects before his death, the abridgement of *The Spanish Frontier* and *Fiasco: George Clinton Gardner's Correspondence from the U.S.-Mexico Boundary Survey, 1849–1854*, which he coedited with Jane Elder.[89]

As for *Bárbaros*, it was yet another journey down an unfamiliar road. Just as *The Mexican Frontier* had pushed Weber beyond New Mexico and *The Spanish Frontier* had pushed him beyond the Southwest, *Bárbaros* pushed him beyond North America to look at the interactions of Spaniards and native peoples in all their complexity across the hemisphere. Ever conscious of historical fashion, he recognized the trend to focus on Indian "agency": "Thus, although I write at a time when, as the historian J. H. Elliot lamented, 'the observed have been accorded a privileged status that has been denied their observers,' I unfashionably focus more on the record-keeping observers than on the observed."[90] The book soon appeared in a Spanish-language edition published by Editorial Crítica in Barcelona and received its share of honors and awards. Like *The Spanish Frontier*, it became a History Book Club selection and was named an Outstanding

Academic Title for 2006 by *Choice*, a publication of the American Library Association. It won the 2006 John E. Fagg Prize, given by the American Historical Association.

Following publication of *Bárbaros*, David began thinking about retirement. (His idea of slowing down consisted of working on edited volumes, numerous articles, and the center.) Few recognitions in his field had eluded him. Adding to his earlier accolades, in 2005 the Mexican government awarded him the Orden Mexicana del Águila Azteca (the Order of the Aztec Eagle), and in 2007 he was admitted to the American Academy of Arts and Sciences. He was sure that the Clements Center for Southwest Studies had grown bigger than him; it now had an associate director in fellow historian Sherry Smith and would soon add a second associate in Ben Johnson, as well as executive directors Andrea Boardman and Ruth Ann Elmore. And he still exercised a leadership role on campus; in early 2007, challenging the opinion of many members of his own department, he spoke out in favor of bringing the George W. Bush Presidential Library to campus, declaring, "It will help move our very good regional university closer to national prominence and it will contribute to the intellectual ferment that makes universities great."[91] He had, however, begun thinking of fun projects, such as a book on archeological and geological sites around the Southwest that went back to first contact with Europeans, a sort of smart man's travel book.[92] Thus, he probably went off to Yale's Beinecke Library in the fall of 2007 proud that this last fellowship, bestowed on a kid from upstate New York with a public school education, would allow him to retire at the very top of his game.

Instead, the trip to New Haven became a last journey down a very different road. He accepted the diagnosis of multiple myeloma and subsequent three-year battle with the disease as a test. Howard Lamar, who hosted David and Carol's stay at Yale, recollected that "my wife and I saw them almost daily for a year. We were awed by David's optimism that he could conquer the threat of cancer. He never stopped his daily run, or his editing of a remarkable diary or revising two of his earlier books for publication by the Yale University Press, or continuing to create a sense of community with all members of the Western History Association."[93] Even as he lost weight and the treatment took a toll on his stamina, he kept up his pace. There were writing projects to complete and lectures to give. Aside from the physical evidence of the disease, those who knew him best could notice only one change in David, one for which he apologized, of increased emotion.[94]

David set his affairs in order. Retirement was no longer something to be thought about but to be accomplished, as gracefully and matter-of-factly as he had done most everything else. David's retirement notice appeared in the spring 2010 newsletter, just months before his death on August 20 at a hospital in Gallup, New Mexico, where Carol and the family had taken him from his

Ramah home a few days earlier. The notice came at the end of remarks from the previous November's ceremony marking the opening of the Clements Center's new offices. It was a festive occasion, with the governor and his wife, the university president, and other VIPs in attendance. He concluded,

> With the completion of these offices, I've finished my work as the Center director. I'm going to retire at the end of May, but I'll do so with reluctance. I've been privileged to be part of a wonderful team that has revitalized scholarship on the American Southwest and put SMU at the center of this revitalization. All of us on that team have been privileged to have the economic resources to get the job done. Please join me in thanking Bill and Rita Clements and their friends, who have provided the lion's share of support.[95]

In 2009 David enjoyed a remission of the cancer. That year, during a family stay at his New Mexico home, David joined Jerry Don Thompson, a fellow student from his UNM days four decades earlier and a fellow addict of the Land of Enchantment, for a hike:

> On another occasion after David had had his first bout with cancer and had lost so much weight, he said we should climb 11,305-feet Mount Taylor, the highest mountain in the western part of the state and one of the four sacred mountains (Txoodzil) of the Dinetah or Navajo. From here David said he had read that on a clear day one could see four states (NM, Arizona, Utah, and Colorado). . . . David and I met at his place in Ramah early one morning and the two of us drove in his four-wheel vehicle as far up the mountain on a primitive forest road as possible and proceeded on by foot. . . . I was concerned about David's health and fearful but knew that he wanted to climb the mountain and having climbed decades earlier in the Himalayas, Andes, and in the Pyrenees, I was not one to say no. Reaching the trailhead, David headed off into a forest of fir and aspen at a breakneck speed. It was incredible that he had retained such stamina after what he had been through with his cancer treatments. For two hours we struggled up the mountain, David in the lead, often thirty yards in advance, as I struggled and puffed along behind. When we reached the summit, much of the Rio Grande Valley near Albuquerque, far to the east, was in clouds and only the tops of the Sandia and Manzano mountains were visible, as was some of the malpais country to the south. To the west the sun was bright and in the clear air one could see the Zuni Mountains, near where David and Carol spent their summers, outlined on the southwestern horizon as was the Mangas and Gallo mountains far beyond to the south. . . . On the way back to Ramah, David parked near an *acequia* in San Mateo and proceeded with a lecture on the history of the

village followed by a discussion of how the cottonwood trees that lined the nearby *acequia* had to be some of the largest in the Southwest.[96]

SUGGESTED READING

Weber, David J. *Bárbaros: Spaniards and Their Savages in the Age of Enlightenment.* New Haven: Yale University Press, 2005.

An intellectual tour de force covering interactions between Spaniards and native peoples from Alaska to Patagonia, and well beyond the eighteenth century.

Weber, David J. *Foreigners in their Native Land: Historical Roots of the Mexican Americans.* Albuquerque: University of New Mexico Press, 1973; rev. ed., 2004.

A collection of documents, the first of its kind, demonstrating Weber's practical and forward-thinking approach. Published at the dawn of the Mexican-American studies era as an instructional resource, it has remained in print because it is comprehensive in scope both chronologically and geographically.

Weber, David J. *The Mexican Frontier, 1821–1846: The American Southwest under Mexico.* Histories of the American Frontier. Albuquerque: University of New Mexico Press, 1982.

Part of Ray Allen Billington's Histories of the American Frontier series, it remains in print as the best introduction to the period because of its balance and readability.

Weber, David J. *The Spanish Frontier in North America.* Yale Western Americana. New Haven: Yale University Press, 1992.

Part of Yale's Western Americana series, this is an award-winning, sweeping synthesis of the last century's scholarship on Spain's role in North American history. In 2009 Yale put out an abbreviated edition as part of its Lamar Series in Western History.

NOTES

1. A preemptive apology is in order. I requested information from a great number of people, most of whom responded promptly and enthusiastically. In the final preparation of this chapter some of those responses by necessity wound up on the cutting room floor. Thanks to everyone who helped me gather the information; I hope the spirit of all your responses is reflected in this essay.

2. Western History Association, *Fiftieth Annual Conference Program: Many Wests,* October 13–16, 2010, program for Thursday, 10:30–noon, p. 37, http://issuu.com/westernhistory association/docs/wha_50th_annual_conference_program (accessed February 20, 2012).

3. "David Weber and the Borderlands: Past, Present, Future," *Southern California Quarterly* 93, no. 3 (2011): 313–345; Texas State Historical Association, *115th Annual Meeting,* March 3–5, 2011, program for Friday, March 4, p. 19, http://www.tshaonline.org/sites/default/files/doc/annualmeeting/pdf/program_2011.pdf (accessed February 20, 2012).

4. In the interest of full disclosure, this observation includes the author of the present essay, who, like David, is a transplanted Yankee. Although I knew of his work beforehand, I first met David at the VIII Conference of Mexican and North American Historians in San

Diego, California, in 1990. After that we regularly visited at professional meetings and served together on the board of directors of the Texas State Historical Association in 1999–2002. He invited me to be on the board of the Library of Texas and to serve on a dissertation committee for one of his students. When he was asked to serve as special editor for an issue of the OAH *Magazine of History* on the borderlands, he asked me to contribute an article on urban life as represented in San Antonio. We also collaborated on a symposium-book project, and he supported my work in other ways during the twenty years that we knew each other.

5. "David Weber, Southwest Expert, Dies at 69," *New York Times*, August 27, 2010, http://www.nytimes.com/2010/08/27/arts/27weber.html?ref=obituaries& (accessed December 1, 2011).

6. Author interview with Carol Weber, February 23, 2012, Dallas; Daniel Weber to Carol Weber, e-mail communication forwarded by Carol Weber to author, March 24, 2012.

7. "David Weber and the Borderlands," 319.

8. Weber interview.

9. "David Weber and the Borderlands," 319.

10. Carol Weber to author, February 6, 2012.

11. "David Weber and the Borderlands," 319.

12. Ibid.; Weber to author; Weber interview.

13. Weber to author.

14. Ibid.; Weber interview.

15. "David Weber and the Borderlands," 321.

16. Weber to author.

17. "David Weber and the Borderlands," 319.

18. Michael C. Meyer, "Edwin Lieuwen (1923–1988)," *Hispanic American Historical Review* 69 (February 1989): 122.

19. "David Weber and the Borderlands," 319.

20. Donald Cutter, a nonagenarian, was in poor health and unavailable for an interview. His son Charles, himself a borderlands historian at Purdue University, commented that his father was proud of David's accomplishments but never took credit for any of them other than helping him get through the program at UNM. Charles Cutter to author, February 7, 2012. See also "Donald C. Cutter (1922–)," www.westernhistoryassociation.org/wp-content/uploads/Cutter.pdf (accessed March 5, 2012).

21. Weber interview.

22. "David Weber and the Borderlands," 321.

23. Ibid.; Weber to author; Weber interview.

24. Author interview with James Hopkins, February 23, 2012, Dallas; Weber interview.

25. David J. Weber, ed. and trans., *The Extranjeros: Selected Documents from the Mexican Side of the Santa Fe Trail, 1825–1828* (Santa Fe: Stagecoach Press, 1967); Weber, ed., *Prose Sketches and Poems Written in the Western Country, with Additional Stories*, by Albert Pike (Albuquerque: Calvin Horn, 1967); Weber, "Spanish Fur Trade from New Mexico, 1540–1821," *The Americas* 24 (October 1967): 122–136; Weber, "William Workman: A Letter from Taos, 1826," *New Mexico Historical Review* 41 (April 1966): 155–161; Weber, "The Municipal Archives of Ciudad Juarez," *New Mexico Historical Review* 42 (January 1967):26.

26. Weber interview.

27. Weber contributed a number of entries for volumes 3–8 (1966–1971) of *The Mountain Men and the Fur Trade of the Far West*, edited by Leroy R. Hafen (Glendale: Arthur H. Clark, 1965–1972); Weber, "Samuel Ellison on the Election of 1857," *New Mexico Historical Review*

44 (July 1969): 215–221; Weber, "Mexico and the Mountain Men, 1821–1828," *Journal of the West* 8 (July 1969): 369–378; Weber, *The Taos Trappers: The Fur Trade in the Far Southwest, 1540–1846* (Norman: University of Oklahoma Press, 1971).

28. "David Weber and the Borderlands," 322; David J. Weber, ed., *Foreigners in Their Native Land: Historical Roots of the Mexican Americans* (Albuquerque: University of New Mexico Press, 1973). Weber was particularly proud of *Foreigners,* which has never been out of print and in 2003 appeared in a thirtieth anniversary edition with a new afterword and a new introduction by Arnoldo De León.

29. Weber, *Foreigners,* viii.

30. References throughout the essay to Weber's many accolades, accomplishments, and awards come from the curriculum vitae available at http://faculty.smu.edu/dweber/CV.htm; accessed March 15, 2012.

31. Weber interview.

32. "David Weber and the Borderlands," 322.

33. Ibid.

34. Hopkins interview.

35. James Hopkins memorial remarks, SMU, October 4, 2010, copy furnished to author.

36. Weber interview; Hopkins interview; Hopkins memorial remarks; "David Weber and the Borderlands," 322.

37. Weber interview.

38. Ibid.

39. Author interview with Russell Martin, February 23, 2012, Dallas.

40. Weber interview; Hopkins interview.

41. Hopkins interview.

42. Ibid.

43. David J. Weber, "Mexico's Far Northern Frontier, 1821–1854: Historiography Askew," *Western Historical Quarterly* 7 (July 1976): 279–293; Weber, "Mexico's Far Northern Frontier: A Critical Bibliography, 1821–1845," *Arizona and the West* 19 (Autumn 1977): 225–266.

44. David J. Weber, "The Failure of a Frontier Institution: The Secular Church in the Borderlands under Independent Mexico, 1821–1846," *Western Historical Quarterly* 12 (April 1981): 125–143.

45. Weber interview.

46. Weber, "Failure of a Frontier Institution," 140.

47. David J. Weber, *The Spanish Frontier in North America,* Yale Western Americana (New Haven: Yale University Press, 1992), 15.

48. *Journal of Texas Catholic History and Culture* 5 (1994): 113.

49. Weber, *The Mexican Frontier, 1821–1846: The American Southwest under Mexico,* Histories of the American Frontier (Albuquerque: University of New Mexico Press, 1982); Weber, ed., *El México perdido. Ensayos escogidos sobre el antiguo norte de México, 1540–1821* (Mexico City: Secretaría de Educación Pública, SEP SETENTA), 1976; Weber, ed., *New Spain's Far Northern Frontier: Essays on Spain in the American West, 1540–1821* (Albuquerque: University of New Mexico Press, 1979).

50. Weber, *Mexican Frontier,* 140.

51. Ibid., 243.

52. Weber, *La frontera norte de México, 1821–1846. El sudoeste norteamericano en su época mexicana* (Mexico City: Fondo de Cultura Económica, 1988; Madrid: Editorial Mapfre, 1992).

53. "Master of the immensities," attributed to Spanish borderlands historian Salvador Bernabeu by William B. Taylor, "David Weber and the Borderlands," 324.

54. SMU Office of Public Affairs, "Dedman Family Legacy at SMU," news release, n.d., http://smu.edu/newsinfo/releases/01123d.html (accessed March 15, 2012); *Dallas Business Journal*, August 20, 2002, http://www.bizjournals.com/dallas/stories/2002/08/19/daily16.html (accessed March 15, 2012).

55. "David Weber and the Borderlands," 323.

56. Ibid.

57. Jane Elder to author, February 13, 2012.

58. Originally published in *American Historical Review* 91 (February 1986): 66–81, the article was reprinted as chapter 3 in *Myth and the History of the Hispanic Southwest: Essays by David J. Weber* (Albuquerque: University of New Mexico Press, 1988), in which the quoted text appears on pp. 36–37.

59. Originally published in *Journal of the Southwest* 29 (Winter 1987): 331–363, the article was reprinted as chapter 4 of *Myth and the History of the Hispanic Southwest*, in which the quoted text appears on p. 63.

60. *Myth and the History of the Hispanic Southwest*, 70.

61. Weber, *Spanish Frontier*, 8.

62. Ibid., 13.

63. Peter Bakewell, "David J. Weber," *Hispanic American Historical Review* 91 (2011): 532–533.

64. David J. Weber, *Bárbaros: Spaniards and Their Savages in the Age of Enlightenment* (New Haven: Yale University Press, 2005).

65. Jane Elder to author, February 24; Elder to author, February 13, 2012.

66. Weber to various (memo), December 10, 1991, box 1, folder 9, Clements Center Records, DeGolyer Library, SMU (hereafter CCR).

67. Elder to author, February 13, 2012.

68. Weber to Royce, October 7, 1993, box 1, folder 9, CCR.

69. Royce to Weber, October 20, 1993, ibid.

70. Weber to various, November 15, 1993, Fomby to Weber, February 15, 1994; Weber to Fomby, February 23, 1994, ibid.

71. Undergraduate Council Minutes, Dedman College, April 19, 1994, box 1, folder 9, CCR.

72. James Jones to author, February 10, 2012.

73. Elder to author, February 13, 2012. In fact, Clements was president of the board of governors in the mid-1980s, when the SMU football scandal erupted, leading the NCAA to impose for the only time ever a "death penalty" that prevented the school from playing in the 1987 and 1988 seasons. For a narrative of the entire story, see David Whitford, *A Payroll to Meet: A Story of Greed, Corruption, and Football at SMU* (New York: Collier Books, 1989).

74. Weber interview.

75. Elder to author, February 13, 2012.

76. Weber interview; Elder to author, February 13, 2012, Dallas; Weber to Clements, December 5, 1997, box 2, folder 11, CCR.

77. David J. Weber, "From the Director," *Newsletter* (Clements Center for Southwest Studies) 7, no. 2 (Spring 2006): 1. The center's newsletter, which began publication in 1999 and appears twice a year, contains a comprehensive account of center activities. A PDF version of all numbers can be accessed at http://smu.edu/swcenter/Archives.htm. Weber to William Babcock, September 14, 1995, box 2, folder 7, CCR.

78. Andrew R. Graybill, *Policing the Great Plains: Rangers, Mounties, and the North American Frontier, 1875–1910* (Lincoln: University of Nebraska Press, 2007).

79. Benjamin H. Johnson and Andrew R. Graybill, eds., *Bridging National Borders in North America: Transnational and Comparative Histories,* American Encounters/Global Interactions (Durham, NC: Duke University Press, 2010).

80. Author interview with Andrew Graybill, February 23, 2012, Dallas.

81. Francis X. Galán to author, February 25, 2012.

82. Josefina Zoraida Vázquez y Vera to author, February 6, 2012.

83. Jesús F. de la Teja and Ross Frank, eds., *Choice, Persuasion, and Coercion: Social Control on Spain's North American Frontiers* (Albuquerque: University of New Mexico Press, 2005).

84. Alfredo Jiménez to author, February 6, 2012.

85. Elder to author, February 13, 2012.

86. Jane Lenz Elder and David J. Weber, eds., *Trading in Santa Fe: John M. Kingsbury's Correspondence with James Josiah Webb, 1853–1861,* DeGolyer Library Series, no. 5 (Dallas: SMU University Press, 1996); Elder to author, February 24, 2012.

87. Author interview with Andrea Boardman, February 13, 2012, Dallas.

88. Author interview with Ruth Ann Elmore, February 13, 2012, Dallas.

89. David J. Weber and Jane Lenz Elder, eds., *Fiasco: George Clinton Gardner's Correspondence from the U.S.-Mexico Boundary Survey, 1849–1854,* DeGolyer Library Series, no. 6 (Dallas: SMU University Press for the DeGolyer Library and Clements Center for Southwest Studies, 2010).

90. Weber, *Bárbaros,* 17.

91. David J. Weber, "Faculty Should Welcome Debate with Conservatives," *Daily Campus* (SMU), January 24, 2007, http://www.smudailycampus.com/opinion/faculty-should-welcome-debate-with-conservatives-1.965315#.T2joVdmiaWE (accessed March 20, 2012).

92. Weber interview; Elmore interview.

93. Howard R. Lamar, "Remembering David J. Weber," office files, Center for Southwest Studies.

94. Elmore interview; Hopkins interview.

95. Newsletter (Clements Center for Southwest Studies) 11, no. 2 (Spring 2010): 2.

96. Jerry Don Thompson to author, March 19, 2012.

CONTRIBUTORS

Light Townsend Cummins is the Guy M. Bryan Jr. Professor of History at Austin College, where he has taught Texas history for thirty years. He holds a Ph.D. from Tulane University. A native of San Antonio, he is the author or editor of seven books dealing with various aspects of Texas, the Gulf Coast, and southwestern history along with several dozen scholarly articles. He has served on the board of directors of both the Texas State Historical Association and Humanities Texas, in addition to having been named a Minnie Stevens Piper Professor.

Patrick L. Cox is a professional historian and award-winning author. He is a member of Who's Who in America and the Philosophical Society of Texas, a Fellow of the Texas State Historical Association, and a member of the advisory board of the Austin College Center for Southwestern and Mexican Studies. He is also a member of the Allies of the Alamo and the Texas State Society. In 2010 he was presented with a Distinguished Alumni Achievement Award from Texas State University's College of Liberal Arts. He recently retired from the University of Texas at Austin after serving as associate director of the Dolph Briscoe Center for American History. He earned his B.A. and Ph.D. in history from the University of Texas and his M.A. from Texas State University. He resides with his wife and extended family of dogs, birds, deer, armadillos, and the occasional porcupine overlooking Lone Man Creek in Wimberley, Texas.

Michael L. Collins, Hardin Distinguished Professor of History, Regents Professor, and Professor Emeritus, has served Midwestern State University in Wichita Falls, Texas, for twenty-seven years. A fellow of the Texas State Historical Association, he is a specialist in the American West and, more specifically, Texas and the Southwest. His publications as author or editor include *Texas Devils: Rangers and Regulars on the Lower Grande, 1846–1861* (2008); *That Damned Cowboy: Theodore Roosevelt and the American West, 1883–1898* (1988); *Profiles in Power: Twentieth-Century Texans in Washington* (2004), coedited with Kenneth E. Hendrickson Jr. and Patrick L. Cox; and *Tales of Texoma: Episodes in the History of the Red River Border* (2005). In 2008 he was honored by the Piper Foundation of San Antonio for a lifetime of commitment to teaching excellence.

Dan Utley holds history degrees from the University of Texas and Sam Houston State. A former public school teacher, he joined the Texas Historical Commission in 1979 and became director of research. He later worked as a freelance public historian and served as a staff historian with the Texas Archeological Research Laboratory at the University of Texas and the Baylor University Institute for Oral History. He subsequently rejoined the Texas Historical Commission, where he served as chief historian until his retirement in 2007. He now serves as an adjunct professor and as chief historian of the Center for Texas Public History at Texas State University. He is the author of numerous publications, including *History Ahead: Stories beyond the Texas Roadside Markers* (2010), coauthored with Cynthia J. Beeman, and *Faded Glory: A Century of Forgotten Military Sites in Texas* (forthcoming), coauthored with Thomas E. Alexander. He is past president of the East Texas Historical Association and the Texas Oral History Association, a fellow of the Texas State Historical Association, and a recipient of the Thomas L. Charlton Award for Lifetime Achievement in Oral History.

Kenneth E. Hendrickson Jr. completed his Ph.D. in 1962 at the University of Oklahoma, where he studied under Gilbert Fite and Gene Hollon. He had come to Norman from the University of South Dakota, where he completed his M.A. in 1959. There he studied under Dr. Herbert Schell, who had also mentored Gilbert Fite. He came to Midwestern State University as chair of the history department in 1970 and served in that capacity for thirty-six years. He specializes in recent American history as well as the history of the South and Texas. He is the author of a dozen books and well over a hundred articles, essays, and reviews. He is best known for *The Chief Executives of Texas: From Stephen F. Austin to John B. Connally, Jr.* (1995); *The Waters of the Brazos: A History of the Brazos River Authority, 1929–1979* (1981); *Profiles in Power: Twentieth-Century Texans in Washington* (2004), coedited with Michael L. Collins and Patrick L. Cox; and *The Life and Presidency of Franklin Delano Roosevelt: An Annotated Bibliography* (2005). He has served as a member of the Board of Directors of the Texas State Historical Association, as president of the Texas Oral History Association, as president of the East Texas Historical Association, and as president of Phi Alpha Theta, the national history honorary society. At Midwestern State University he holds the titles of Regents' and Hardin Distinguished Professor of American History, emeritus. Although officially retired, he continues to teach and write.

Don Graham, a native Texan, graduated from North Texas State University with a B.A. with High Honors in 1962 and an M.A. in 1964. He took his doctorate in 1971 at the University of Texas at Austin, where, since 1987, he has held the J. Frank Dobie Regents Professorship of American and English Literature. His publications include scores of articles and essays dealing with Texas culture. Among his works are *Cowboys and Cadillacs: How Hollywood Looks at Texas* (1983); *Texas: A Literary Portrait* (1985); *No Name on the Bullet: A Biography of Audie Murphy* (1989); *Giant Country: Essays on Texas* (1998), which won a Violet Crown Award from the Austin Writers' League; and *Kings of Texas: The 150-Year Saga of an American Ranching Empire* (2003), which won the Carr P. Collins Prize for Best Nonfiction Book of the Year, awarded in 2004 by the Texas Institute of Letters; *State Fare: An Irreverent Guide to Texas Movies* (2008); and *State of Minds: Texas Culture and Its Discontents* (2011). A past president of the Texas Institute of Letters, he received the Best General Criticism Award for 2005 from the City and Regional Magazine Association for literary criticism published in *Texas Monthly*, for which he has been a Writer-at-Large since the late 1990s.

B. Byron Price currently holds the Charles Marion Russell Memorial Chair, is director of the Charles M. Russell Center for the Study of Art of the American West at the University of Oklahoma, and is director of the University of Oklahoma Press. He is a 1970 graduate of the United States Military Academy at West Point and earned an M.A. in museum science at Texas Tech University in 1977. Before taking his current position, he spent nearly twenty-five years in the museum profession, serving as executive director of the Panhandle Plains Historical Museum in Canyon, Texas (1982–1986), the National Cowboy Hall of Fame and Western Heritage Center in Oklahoma City (1987–1996), and the Buffalo Bill Historical Center in Cody, Wyoming (1996–2001). He is the author of more than three dozen journal articles on western American history and art and has written several books, including *Fine Art of the West* (2004); *The Chuck Wagon Cook Book* (2004); *Erwin E. Smith: Cowboy Photographer* (1997); and *Cowboys of the American West* (1996). He also edited *Charles M. Russell: A Catalogue Raisonné* (2007), which won the 2007 Western Heritage Award for the best art book of the year from the National Cowboy and Western Heritage Museum, the 2008 Caughey-Western History Association Prize for best book of the year in western history, the 2008 High Plains Book Award for nonfiction, and the 2009 Joan Patterson Kerr Award from the Western History Association for the best illustrated book on the American West.

Archie P. McDonald earned his Ph.D. from Louisiana State University and has taught history for forty-eight years at Stephen F. Austin University, where he is Regents Professor. He served as director of the East Texas Historical Association and editor of the association's journal for thirty-seven years. He is a past president of the Texas State Historical Association, past vice chair of the Texas Historical Commission, and author or editor of more than twenty books. Among his publications are *Texas? What Do You Know about the Lone Star State?* (1993) and *Dare-Devils All: The Texan Mier Expedition, 1842–1844* (1998), with Joseph Milton Nance.

Félix D. Almaráz Jr. is a professor of history at the University of Texas at San Antonio. He received his B.A. and M.A. from St. Mary's University in San Antonio and a Ph.D. from the University of New Mexico. His teaching and research reflect an engagement with processes within Hispanic communities. His main teaching areas include the Spanish borderlands, Texas, colonial Latin America, and imperial and modern Spain. In recent publications, such as *Knight without Armor: Carlos Eduardo Castañeda, 1896–1958* (1999) and *Madero in Texas* (2001), he examines the lives and contributions of transnational historical figures. His most recent and significant grants include a 1994 President's Distinguished Achievement Award, an Excellence in Research Award in 1988, and a Senior Fulbright Lectureship in the Republic of Argentina.

Mary L. Scheer is an associate professor and chair of the history department at Lamar University in Beaumont, Texas. She is also a former Fulbright Scholar to Germany. She received her Ph.D. from Texas Christian University in 2000. Dr. Scheer has authored *The Foundations of Texan Philanthropy* (2004) and coedited with John W. Storey *Twentieth-Century Texas: A Social and Cultural History (2008)*. Her research interests include Texas, women, and twentieth-century social history. She is a board member of the Texas State Historical Association and past board member of the East Texas Historical Association.

Carolina Castillo Crimm is a retired professor of history from Sam Houston State University. She was born and brought up in Mexico City and came to the United States in 1963, finishing her B.A. at the University of Miami and her M.A. at Texas Tech University before earning her Ph.D. from the University of Texas at Austin with Dr. Nettie Lee Benson in Latin American history. She taught on the high school level before starting at Sam Houston State University in 1992, where she won both local and statewide teaching awards, including the prestigious Piper Award, as one of the best teachers in Texas. She has published *De León: A Tejano Family History* (2003); *Turn-of-the-Century Photographs from San Diego, Texas* (2003), with Sara R. Massey; and, as editor, *Cabin Fever: The Roberts-Farris Cabin, a Campus, a Cabin, a Community* (2002). She has also published numerous introductions and chapters on Texas women, African Americans, and Hispanics. As a retiree, she is working on historical fiction that deals with Spanish and Mexican Texas during the eighteenth and nineteenth centuries.

David G. McComb is an emeritus professor of history at Colorado State University in Fort Collins. He grew up in Houston, Texas, and went to college in Texas and California. After a year as a member of an oral history team that gathered interviews concerning President Lyndon Johnson, he became a teacher at Colorado State, where he taught courses in urban history, technology history, American history, sports history, and world history, and sailed twice around the world as a teacher with Semester at Sea. He served a five-year term as chairman (1975–1980) and has won numerous awards: two Mortar Board teaching awards and two service awards from the university, the Tullis Prize of the Texas State Historical Association (1969), an Award of Merit from the American Association of State and Local History (1980), and a book award from the Texas Historical Commission (1987). He was elected a fellow of the Texas State Historical Association in 1988 and a member of Sigma Xi, the science honor society, in 2001. He has written fourteen books, including *Travels with Joe: The Life Story of a Historian from Texas, 1917–1993* (2001), a biography of Joe B. Frantz. Currently he is working on a survey of Texas urbanization.

Nancy Baker Jones is an independent scholar with professional experience in nonprofit, corporate, and academic settings. She earned a Ph.D. in American civilization from the University of Texas at Austin, an M.A. in English from Indiana State University, and an M.A. in American history from Texas Christian University. Long interested in equity issues, she has taught cross-cultural studies, writing, and women's history at the college level, assisted public schools with mediation, curriculum integration, desegregation, and Title IX implementation, and published essays, poetry, and video histories. She was the Katherine Sage Temple Foundation for Women's Resources Fellow for Women's History and director of research for the *Handbook of Texas* revision project. She also coordinated the first statewide academic conference about women and Texas history. She is coeditor (with Fane Downs) of *Women and Texas History: Selected Essays* (1993) and coauthor (with Ruthe Winegarten) of *Capitol Women: Texas Female Legislators, 1923–1999* (2000), which won the Liz Carpenter Award from the Texas State Historical Association. She is an alumnus of Leadership Texas, a founder and president of the Ruthe Winegarten Memorial Foundation for Texas Women's History, and a mentor for graduate students.

Jesús F. de la Teja is Regents' and University Distinguished Professor of History and holds a Ph.D. in Latin American history from the University of Texas at Austin. His research interests focus on the northeastern frontier of Spanish colonial Mexico and Texas through the Republic era. He is the author of *San Antonio de Béxar: A Community on New Spain's Northern Frontier* (1995) and coauthor of *Texas: Crossroads of North America* (2004), a college-level survey of the state's history, and his most recent work is the edited volume *Tejano Leadership in Mexican and Revolutionary Texas* (2010). He has published in *Americas, Historia Mexicana, Journal of the Early Republic,* and *Southwestern Historical Quarterly,* among other journals. In addition to his research activities he has served as a consultant on development of the Texas State History Museum and serves as book review editor of the *Southwestern Historical Quarterly*.

PHOTO CREDITS

1 Prints and Photographs, di_04311, Dolph Briscoe Center for American History, the University of Texas at Austin (hereafter DBCAH).
23 Photo by Bob Bailey, Bailey (Bob) Studios Photographic Archive, e_bb_4999, DBCAH.
43 Photo by Ray Covey, Webb (Walter Prescott) Papers, di_06846, DBCAH.
67 Prints and Photographs Collection, Winkler, E. W., di_04427, DBCAH.
85 Photo by Bill Malone, Prints and Photographs Collection, di_07915, DBCAH.
99 Photo by Russell Lee, Lee (Russell) Photograph Collection, di_07901, DBCAH.
115 Prints and Photographs, di_02307, DBCAH.
135 Photo by Robinson's Studio, Prints and Photographs Collection, di_07916, DBCAH.
147 Photo by Studer Photo, Prints and Photographs Collection, di_07900, DBCAH.
169 Prints and Photographs Collection, e_enr_128, DBCAH.
185 Photo by John Avant, UTTSP, Prints and Photographs Collection, di_07293, DBCAH.
211 Prints and Photographs Collection, di_07898, DBCAH.
223 Winegarten (Ruthe) Papers, di_07899, DBCAH.
261 Courtesy of the Weber family.

INDEX

Italic numbers indicate photographs.